Jeff Kurtz
Jerry Kurtz

D1307817

SAMS
Teach Yourself
Visual C++® 6
Online
in Web Time

SAMS

A Division of Macmillan Computer Publishing
201 West 103rd St., Indianapolis, Indiana, 46290 USA

Sams Teach Yourself Visual C++® 6 Online in Web Time

Copyright © 1999 by Sams Publishing

International Standard Book Number: 0-672-31666-8

Library of Congress Catalog Card Number: 99-64549

Printed in the United States of America

First Printing: August 1999

02   01   00   99   4   3   2   1

Trademarks

All terms mentioned in this book that are known to be trademarks or service marks have been appropriately capitalized. Sams Publishing cannot attest to the accuracy of this information. Use of a term in this book should not be regarded as affecting the validity of any trademark or service mark.

Visual C++ 6 is a registered trademark of Microsoft Corporation.

Warning and Disclaimer

Every effort has been made to make this book as complete and as accurate as possible, but no warranty or fitness is implied. The information provided is on an "as is" basis. The authors and the publisher shall have neither liability nor responsibility to any person or entity with respect to any loss or damages arising from the information contained in this book or from the use of the CD or programs accompanying it.

EXECUTIVE EDITOR
Charles Drucker

ACQUISITIONS EDITORS
Charles Drucker
Stephanie Wall

MANAGING EDITOR
Jodi Jensen

PROJECT EDITOR
Dana Rhodes Lesh

COPY EDITORS
Hugh Vandivier
Molly Schaller

INDEXER
Eric Schroeder

PROOFREADER
Megan Wade

LAYOUT TECHNICIAN
Lisa England

TECHNICAL EDITOR
Richard S. Wright, Jr.

MEDIA DEVELOPER
Craig Atkins

TEAM COORDINATOR
Karen Opal

INTERIOR DESIGNER
Gary Adair

COVER DESIGNER
Aren Howell

COPY WRITER
Eric Borgert

Sams Teach Yourself Online in Web Time Guided Tour

The best-selling computer tutorial series just got even better.

The *Sams Teach Yourself* series now has its own Web site. When you buy a book in the *Sams Teach Yourself Online in Web Time* series, you open the door to a new world of online learning. These books give you a full year of access to http://www.samsteachyourself.com, a virtual classroom and online educational community that offers in-depth, online courses to help you master the book's material more thoroughly and more rapidly.

When you take a *Sams Teach Yourself Online in Web Time* course, you can

- Assess your progress with interactive tests.
- Improve your skills and understanding with online exercises.
- Discuss technology topics online with other students and subject matter experts.
- Expand your knowledge with a complete searchable reference work.

Because these courses are offered in Web Time, you can take them at any hour of the day or night—at your convenience and at your own pace. When you enroll in a *Web Time* course, you're not alone; you join an online community of students and computer professionals who can help you work through the more difficult material.

What's on the Web Site

Sams Teach Yourself Online in Web Time courses follow the chapter-and-lesson organization of the *Sams Teach Yourself Online in Web Time* books, with an online section for each chapter. Online quizzes for every lesson help you gauge your progress. The quizzes are scored automatically, and your grades are stored in a database, so you can always review your work.

Each chapter in the Web course also contains a set of online exercises. Specially designed to enhance your understanding of the accompanying chapter in your *Sams Teach Yourself* book, these exercises give you hands-on practice with real-life problems. Sample solutions for the exercises are also provided online, along with hints on alternative solutions and tips on where to go for more information.

There's also a threaded discussion list overseen by a technical expert in the field, so if one of the exercises has you stumped or if an online solution doesn't appear to be the only way to work the problem, just post a message. One of the other students is likely to have passed this way before.

What You'll Need

The *Sams Teach Yourself Online in Web Time* course site is easy to access and use. First, though, you need to purchase one of the *Sams Teach Yourself Online in Web Time* books. The CD-ROM envelope in the back of this book contains a card with an authorization number that you'll need to register for your online course, so be sure that the seal on the envelope is intact.

After you've purchased a book, all you need is Internet access and browser software. The online course system works with most browsers that support frames, but is best viewed with recent versions of Netscape Navigator (4 or higher) or Microsoft Internet Explorer 5. You'll also need to configure your browser to accept JavaScript and cookies because the online course engine requires both of these features.

Finding the *Sams Teach Yourself Online* Site

To access the *Sams Teach Yourself Online* site, launch your browser and go to http://www.samsteachyourself.com. This is the gateway for all *Sams Teach Yourself Online* courses. When you're at the site, you'll find instructions on how to register as a student and how to access the *Sams Teach Yourself Visual C++ 6 Online* course. There's also a Guest area where you can sample the courses that accompany the other *Sams Teach Yourself Online in Web Time* titles.

Logging In

After you've registered and chosen your username and password, you'll be able to log in to the *Sams Teach Yourself Visual C++ 6 Online* class (see Figure 1).

FIGURE 1

The Login page.

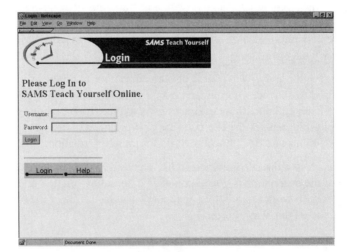

Be sure to set your browser to accept cookies because this is how the system keeps track of your status as a student.

The Student Home Page

After you've registered and logged in to the *Sams Teach Yourself Visual C++ Online* course, you'll be taken to the Student Home page (see Figure 2). From this point, you can view course materials, review your work on earlier chapters, check class announcements, go to the course discussion area, or search through the online reference materials for this course.

FIGURE 2

The Student Home page.

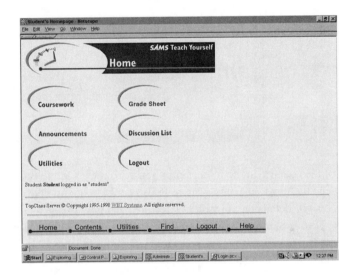

When you reach the Home page, you might see New tags on the Announcements and Discussion List banners. It's always a good idea to check the Announcements folder first for messages about your course or the *Sams Teach Yourself Online* site.

Click the Announcements banner to open the Announcements folder. Then click the highlighted Announcements link to view the folder's messages.

Wherever you are in the *Sams Teach Yourself Visual C++ 6 Online in Web Time* course, you can always return to the Home page by clicking the Home button at the bottom of the page.

The Student Home page also gives you access to a threaded discussion list. Only students who have registered for the *Sams Teach Yourself Visual C++ 6 Online* course can read and post messages. The discussion is overseen by a professional subject matter expert to steer the discussion threads, provide guidance, and come up with answers to the more difficult questions that are posed. Click the Discussion List banner to use this online community feature.

Online Course Materials

Click the Coursework banner on the Home page to access your course materials (see Figure 3).

FIGURE 3

The Coursework page.

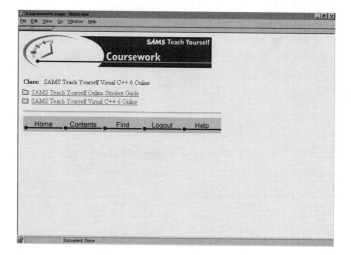

One of the courses, in the folder Sams Teach Yourself Online Student Guide, is designed to teach you how to use this system. It also contains a complete reference section that provides full details on the system's features and how to use them. Even if you've taken online classes before, it's a good idea to step through the Sams Teach Yourself Online Student Guide course to familiarize yourself with the messaging system and the navigation tools.

Click the Sams Teach Yourself Visual C++ 6 Online folder to see the main coursework for your class. Each chapter in the textbook has a corresponding folder of online material (see Figure 4). (The blue *U* means that a folder contains unread material; a red *N* means that a folder contains new material.) You'll also see a midterm and final exam, as well as a complete, searchable reference work.

If you open one of the chapter folders, you'll see that it contains a number of self-scoring quizzes—one for each lesson in the chapter—as well as a set of programming exercises (see Figure 5). Sample solutions for these exercises are also available online. Check the discussion board for any threads relating to exercises you're working on—or start a thread of your own, if there is something you want to talk about or don't fully understand.

FIGURE 4

The chapter folders.

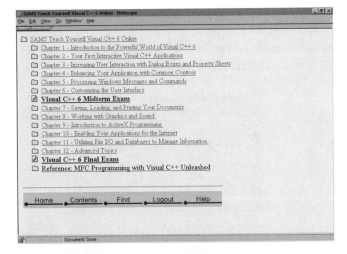

FIGURE 5

Each chapter folder contains quizzes and exercises, as well as sample solutions for the exercises.

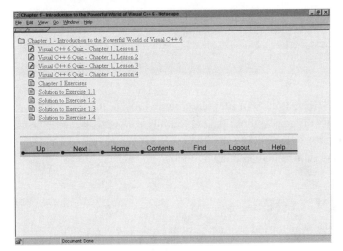

Searchable Reference Material

As a further benefit for *Sams Teach Yourself Online in Web Time* students, the full text of *MFC Programming with Visual C++ 6 Unleashed* has been made part of your course materials. This 1344-page book by MFC expert David White is one of the most extensive reference works available on the subject. It's a $49.99 value, and it's available free to registered students in the *Sams Teach Yourself Visual C++ 6 Online in Web Time* course.

You can use this reference work in two different ways. First, you can open the course folder containing the text and browse the material by chapter and section. Or you can use the simple but powerful text search engine that's part of the *Sams Teach Yourself Online* system. Just click the Find button at the bottom of any page and enter the words or phrases that interest you into the text box (see Figure 6). You can do a quick search by titles or a more complete search by titles and text.

FIGURE 6

An example of a search.

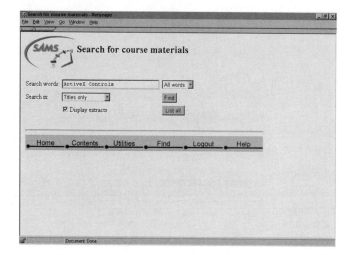

The search engine will supply you with links to the pages where the text was found. When you jump to those pages, you might want to use your browser's Find function to locate the specific line containing the text you searched for (by pressing Ctrl+F or opening the Edit menu and clicking Find).

Be Our Guest

The best way to find out more about *Sams Teach Yourself Online* courses is to go to the Guest area of the site, which you'll find at http://www.samsteachyourself.com. There you'll find the course material for the first chapter of each of the *Sams Teach Yourself Online in Web Time* books, as well as a portion of the reference material.

Overview

Table of Contents

About the Authors

JEFF KURTZ has a bachelor of science in computer information systems from DeVry Institute of Technology in Columbus, Ohio. He is employed by Macola, Inc., where he is currently designing and implementing custom internal applications. He lives in Delaware, Ohio, with his wife, Justine, his daughter, Kirsten, and their two cats, Snowball and Queen. In Jeff's spare time (when he can find it), he codevelops a set of freeware DirectX components for Delphi, known as Delphi Games Creator (DGC).

JERRY KURTZ graduated from DeVry Institute of Technology in Columbus, Ohio, with a bachelor of science. He is employed by Macola, Inc., and is responsible for writing custom applications for Macola's Web site (`http://www.macola.com`). He also designs and implements internal applications and database procedures. He lives in Delaware, Ohio, with his wife, Maria, and two children, Shannon and Stephen.

Dedication

This book is dedicated to my wife, Justine, and my daughter, Kirsten. Without their love, support, and encouragement, I would have never completed this book.

—Jeff Kurtz

This book is dedicated to my family: my wife, Maria, my daughter, Shannon, and my son, Stephen. Having their love, support, understanding, and encouragement while writing this book has made the process enjoyable—especially the question, "Working on the book, Daddy?" which I was asked too many times to count.

—Jerry Kurtz

Acknowledgments

The following goes without saying, but if we don't mention them, we will never hear the end of it. So to start off, we would like to thank our family for all its wonderful support and encouragement. Without this support, we would never have taken on such a challenge. Our special thanks go to Jack, Betty, Patty, Rita, Terry, Belle, Jim, Chad, Susan, Kevin, Ryan, Lori, and Chris.

We would like to thank all the wonderful people who we work with at Macola, Inc., for their encouragement, especially the following people that have to put up with us day in and day out. They are, in no specific order, Tim King, Doug Hawk, Gary Voorhies, Dave Reisch, Jeff Legan, Andy Smith, Mike Studer, Dave Woodard, John Rozmer, Gary Tait, Tom Glenn, and last but not least, the guys that sign our paychecks, Dale Haddad and Bruce Hollinger.

We would also like to thank the following people who we worked with throughout this project: Charles Drucker, Kurt Stephan, Russ Jacobs, Richard S. Wright Jr., Dan Scherf, Andrea Rosenberg, Susan Walton, and Stephanie Wall. We would also like to thank the rest of the Sams Publishing staff who we didn't get to work with directly.

We would also like to thank all our friends who always told us we could do it (to name a few…Kurt, Lisa, Bill, Bobbie, Lisa Kopp, Angie, Pete Bishop, Rick Cooper, Gary and Dave Mockus, Jason Woolard, Tom Pierce, Paul Fincato, Chuck Brand, Don Hone, Alfred Micus, Petra Gibbs, Todd Powers, and Stacy Howard)! And finally, a salute to the funny guy from Cleveland, Drew C.

Tell Us What You Think!

As the reader of this book, *you* are our most important critic and commentator. We value your opinion and want to know what we're doing right, what we could do better, what areas you'd like to see us publish in, and any other words of wisdom you're willing to pass our way.

As an executive editor for Sams Publishing, I welcome your comments. You can fax, email, or write me directly to let me know what you did or didn't like about this book— as well as what we can do to make our books stronger.

Please note that I cannot help you with technical problems related to the topic of this book, and that due to the high volume of mail I receive, I might not be able to reply to every message.

When you write, please be sure to include this book's title and author as well as your name and phone or fax number. I will carefully review your comments and share them with the authors and editors who worked on the book.

Fax: (317)581-4770

Email: blee@mcp.com

Mail: Benjamin Lee, Ph.D.
            Executive Editor
            Sams Publishing
            201 West 103rd Street
            Indianapolis, IN 46290 USA

Introduction

Microsoft Visual C++ 6 is the industry standard for professional C++ Windows programming. With the increasing complexity of the Windows operating system, common design elements must be used to assure platform compatibility in applications. The easiest way to achieve platform compatibility is to use a robust development tool that provides enough power for the seasoned vet, but is still easy enough for the beginner or casual programmer to use. Making the application development process easier for Windows is what Visual C++ is all about.

What This Book Is About

Sams Teach Yourself Visual C++ 6 Online in Web Time is the only interactive course available that will teach you, through a series of lessons and quizzes, how to use the preferred development tool used by professional developers, Microsoft Visual C++.

Written in an award-winning format, *Sams Teach Yourself Visual C++ 6 Online in Web Time* provides more than 50 comprehensible lessons that cover a wide range of Windows development topics. These topics include using common controls, designing user interfaces, working with documents and graphics, ActiveX, multitasking, database programming, Internet programming, and more.

Whom This Book Is For

Sams Teach Yourself Visual C++ 6 Online in Web Time is meant to be used by a C++ programmer who wants to learn how to use the industry standard development tool Visual C++. Therefore, a basic understanding of the Windows operating system, along with C++ knowledge, would be helpful, if not absolutely necessary.

This book gives you access to the online Web site, http://www.samsteachyourself.com/, which allows you to take online quizzes, ask questions of a mentor, find resources, complete exercises, and much more.

How This Book Is Organized

The book is divided into 12 chapters, with each chapter covering a different topic of programming with Visual C++ 6.

Chapter 1, "An Introduction to the Powerful World of Visual C++ 6"

This chapter discusses Visual C++ 6's intuitive interface for building Windows 95/98/NT applications. You will learn how to interact with the integrated development environment by using the built-in application wizards, property editors, views, menus, and toolbars.

Chapter 2, "Your First Interactive Visual C++ Applications"

Chapter 2 introduces the basics of Visual C++ 6 to get you started and on your way. You will learn how to use the MFC AppWizard to jump-start your development process by letting it create the necessary code framework. You will discover how to make Single Document Interface (SDI) applications as well as Multiple Document Applications (MDI). You will also learn how to make dialog-based applications.

Chapter 3, "Increasing User Interaction with Dialog Boxes and Property Sheets"

In this chapter, you will learn how to create, customize, and gather information from dialog boxes. You will also find out how to create and use property sheets for multiple pages of user options or data input.

Chapter 4, "Enhancing Your Application with Common Controls"

Chapter 4 shows you how to program the more basic Windows controls. You will use these controls throughout your application to either present information to a user or gather information from them. You will learn the properties, functions, and events necessary to make these controls work for you.

Chapter 5, "Processing Windows Messages and Commands"

In Chapter 5, you will learn what makes your Windows programs tick. You will discover how messages and commands are processed, how to capture these messages and commands, and how to act on them when an event arises. You will also learn how to create your own messages.

Chapter 6, "Customizing the User Interface"

In this chapter, you will learn how to make your application's user interface more user-friendly. You will start by building menus and then learn how to react to a menu choice. After you finish with the menus, you will learn how to create toolbars that will allow the user rapid access to common options in your application. You will also find out how to add a status bar to keep the user informed of what is going on in your application.

Chapter 7, "Saving, Loading, and Printing Your Documents"

Chapter 7 teaches you how to load and save document data. You will then learn how to preview, scale, and print your documents to the printer device.

Chapter 8, "Working with Graphics and Sound"

In this chapter, you will learn how the Windows GDI manages the graphics in your application through the device context. You will also learn other skills such as displaying bitmaps and shapes along with changing pens, brushes, and fonts on the same document. Finally, you will also learn how to play standard sound files in your applications.

Chapter 9, "An Introduction to ActiveX Programming"

Chapter 9 introduces you to ActiveX controls. First, you will learn how to contain ActiveX controls in your application. Then you will discover how to build a custom ActiveX control. You will also build ActiveX container and server applications.

Chapter 10, "Enabling Your Applications for the Internet"

This chapter teaches you about the basics of Internet programming. It begins with basic Winsock socket functionality and then progresses to the popular HTTP and FTP protocols for Web and file transfers. You will also learn about customizing Web applications through server extensions.

Chapter 11, "Using File I/O and Databases to Manage Information"

In Chapter 11, you will learn the fundamentals of standard file input and output to store your application's data. After that, you will learn about using VC++ to write applications that use databases to store and retrieve data.

Chapter 12, "Advanced Topics"

Chapter 12 introduces you to higher-level VC++ techniques. You will learn about some of the more advanced programming topics. You will discover and learn about multitasking with threads, thread synchronization, and programming the system Registry.

Appendix A, "Quiz Answers"

Appendix A contains the answers to the quizzes at the end of each lesson.

About the CD-ROM

The CD-ROM that accompanies *Sams Teach Yourself Visual C++ 6 Online in Web Time* includes all the source code developed in the book and a special book edition of Microsoft's Visual C++ 6 Introductory Edition Application. The source code is organized by chapter. See the "CD-ROM Installation Instructions" page at the back of the book for details on installing the CD-ROM.

Conventions Used in This Book

This book uses different typefaces to differentiate between code and regular English and to help you identify important concepts.

Text that you type and text that should appear on your screen is presented in a monospaced type:

```
It will look like this to mimic the way text looks on your screen.
```

Placeholders for variables and expressions appear in *monospace italic*. You should replace the placeholder with the specific value it represents.

The arrow ➥ at the beginning of a line of code means that a single line of code is too long to fit on the printed page. Continue typing all characters after the ➥ as though they were part of the preceding line.

CHAPTER 1

An Introduction to the Powerful World of Visual C++ 6

Welcome to the interactive world of Visual C++ 6. One of the key elements of that preceding sentence was *interactive*. VC++ 6, for practical purposes, is just another Windows application, the main function of which just happens to be creating Windows applications. As with any Windows application, the better you understand how to use it, the better you will be able to use it. You accomplish this through a high level of interaction, hence, the word *interactive*.

Knowing how to navigate your way through the Visual Studio interface isn't really that tough, but you must know how to do it if you want to be successful when you develop your applications.

This chapter will introduce to you the main elements of the Integrated Development Environment (IDE), which consists of many parts, views, areas, files, and so on. By the end of this chapter, you should understand the basics of moving around in these different parts and have the confidence to complete the tasks in the upcoming chapters without getting lost in the IDE.

This chapter does not explain every menu item and every toolbar button. Instead, the core functionality will be discussed, and as you progress through the chapters, menu items not discussed here will be discussed when appropriate.

LESSON 1

Exploring the Visual C++ Development Environment

Learning what each section of the Integrated Development Environment (IDE) does is an essential part to the successful development of projects you will be working on. If you are already familiar with how Visual Studio's user interface operates, then you are well on your way to successful navigation of VC++ 6 in IDE.

Looking at Figure 1.1, you will see that the screen is divided into five distinct areas: menus, toolbars, workspace, Code/Editor, and output.

FIGURE 1.1

VC++ 6's default screen.

Menus

Toolbars

Workspace

Code/Editor pane

Output pane

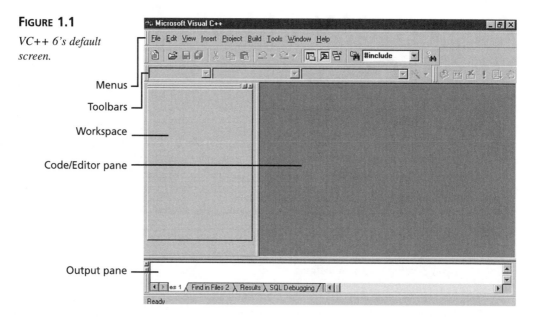

Menus

The menu bar sits across the top of the screen and contains many of the usual options that you would find in any Windows application, as well as options that are specific to VC++ 6. At times, some menu items will be disabled or not even visible.

Looking again at Figure 1.1, you'll notice that you can choose from nine available menus. As you progress throughout this book, you will be introduced to most of the menu items and their functionalities.

VC++ 6 uses a second type of menu, called a *context menu,* extensively. You can usually activate these menus by clicking your right mouse button on the element for which you wish to see the context menu. Figure 1.2 shows the context menu for the visible elements in the IDE.

FIGURE 1.2

Context menu for IDE areas and toolbars.

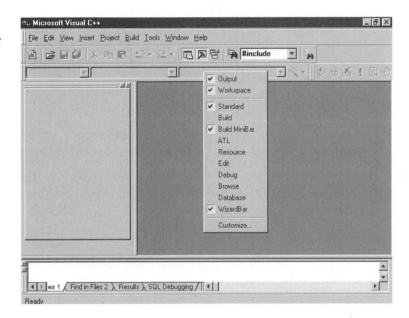

Toolbars

The toolbars have the same functionality as menus but are represented by strips of iconic buttons that, when clicked, perform a specific action. These actions are usually tied directly to a menu item in code. Most of the toolbars will reside just below the menus, whereas some of them are considered *floating toolbars*, meaning that you can move them around the screen by dragging them.

Different toolbars are available at certain times depending upon what you are currently working. Three are displayed by default: Standard, Build MiniBar, and WizardBar. Figure 1.2 shows a context menu that lists common toolbars starting with "Standard" and ending with "WizardBar." At other times, this list will be longer. The currently visible toolbars are indicated by a check mark to the left of the item. To toggle the visibility of a toolbar, you simply select it in the list. If it is not currently visible, it will be turned on, and if it is already visible, it will then be hidden.

Project Workspace

The workspace organizes your project's many elements. As shown in Figure 1.1 and 1.2, the workspace has nothing in it because a Project Workspace is not currently open.

The workspace is divided into three separate views: Class, Resource, and File view. Each view has its specific role in VC++ 6 and helps organize certain elements of your project. Lessons 3 and 4 of this chapter will discuss the workspace and each of the views in more detail.

Code/Editor

The Code/Editor area of the IDE is where the majority of your project's code and other resources, such as toolbars and menus, will be developed. This area is commonly referred to as the "editor," because this is where most of the actual editing is completed.

The editor area is rather versatile: It lets you have many items open at once so that you can switch back and forth between code and other resources with ease. This is what gives VC++ 6 the "Visual" boost.

Output

The IDE places results of certain tasks it performs in the output section so that you can track what happens. This area is divided into six panes: Build, Debug, Find in Files 1, Find in Files 2, Results, and SQL Debugging. SQL Debugging is only enabled if you have installed the Enterprise edition.

The task you have VC++ 6 perform determines into which pane the results will be dumped. For example, when you tell VC++ 6 to compile or build your project, the results are dumped into the Build pane.

Lesson Summary

This lesson introduced you to the five key areas of the Integrated Development Environment (IDE) and what each area's main functionality is. Knowing where to accomplish a certain task plays an important role in developing a project and therefore being able to navigate the areas without stumbling. The upcoming lessons in this chapter discuss the individual areas in greater detail.

Quiz 1

1. What do the letters *IDE* stand for in VC++ 6?

    a. Integrated Debugging Editor

    b. Integrated Development Environment

    c. Intuitive Developer Editor

    d. Integrated Development Editor

2. How do you toggle the display of a toolbar?

    a. Click the View menu and select the toolbar.

    b. Double-click the toolbar area and select it from a list of available toolbars.

    c. Click the Window menu and select it from the list of windows.

    d. Right-click the toolbar area and select from the context menu.

3. What area acts as the organizer of your project elements?

    a. The output area

    b. The Project Workspace area

    c. The editor area

    d. None of the above

4. What is the significance of the output area?

    a. It controls where your program's output will be displayed.

    b. The output area has no real significance.

    c. It is where VC++ 6 sends results from certain functions.

    d. You can control the operation of your program in this area.

Exercise 1

Complexity: Easy

1. Hide the three standard toolbars and display the Edit toolbar.

Complexity: Moderate

2. List all the icons in the Standard toolbar and their equivalent menu functions.

LESSON 2

Visual C++ 6's File and Edit Menus

In the previous lesson, you learned what each of the areas in the IDE are. Now, you will learn to perform some tasks in the IDE by using the menus and toolbars.

You should already be familiar with how menus operate within Windows and the basic tasks of clicking toolbar buttons to perform a task. In this lesson, you need to work on what these menus and toolbars actually do.

Chapter 2, "Your First Interactive Visual C++ Applications," will discuss how to create different kinds of applications, but for the purpose of this lesson and the remaining lessons in this chapter, we will create a test application that we can use for performing tasks. This application won't have any real functionality to it, but it will give you a head start when you move into Chapter 2.

The File Menu

The File menu is organized so that functions related to loading, saving, and printing files are under this menu. The File menu has a shortcut key of Alt+F.

First, you need to create a project. Just follow these steps:

1. Click the File, New menu item to display the New dialog box (shown in Figure 1.3).

FIGURE 1.3

The New dialog box.

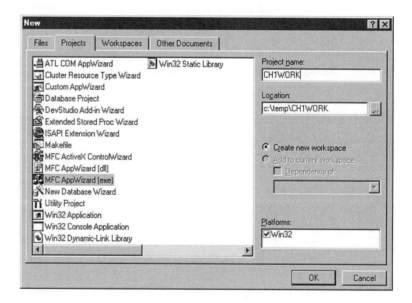

2. Click MFC AppWizard (exe) in the list of available project types and type **CH1WORK** into the edit box just beneath the Project Name label.

3. Click the OK button, and you should see the MFC AppWizard-Step 1 dialog box as displayed in Figure 1.4.

FIGURE 1.4

The MFC AppWizard-Step 1 dialog box.

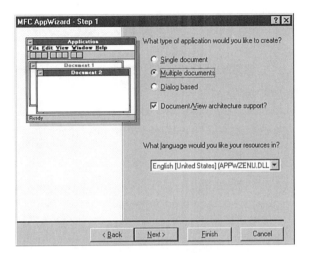

4. Because you are just creating a sample application, you will not need to change any of the settings; just use all the defaults. Go ahead and click the Finish button to bring up the New Project Information dialog box as displayed in Figure 1.5.

FIGURE 1.5

The New Project Information dialog box.

5. Click the OK button to have VC++ 6 create your project.

The IDE's changes reflect your creation of a project. If you look at the workspace in Figure 1.6, you will notice three tabs across the bottom.

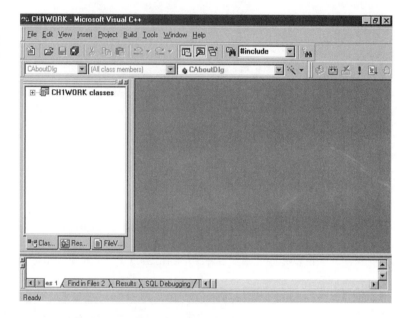

The three tabs that the workspace organizes are the following:

- Class view—Lists the classes your project uses.
- Resource view—Contains elements such as menus and dialog boxes.
- File view—Lists the files your project uses.

You will learn about the different views in later lessons in this chapter.

If you were to build and execute this project at this point, it would run as any normal Windows application. It just doesn't do much. In order to move on, you need to create a file in your project that you can perform given tasks against that won't harm anything else. To do this, you need to add a simple text file to the project. Follow these steps to add the text file:

1. Click File, New to bring up the New dialog box.
2. Select Text File at the bottom of the list of available file types.
3. Click the Add to project checkbox and type **LEARNING** into the edit box for the file name. Figure 1.7 shows the New dialog box filled out.

FIGURE 1.7

The New dialog box for a Text File.

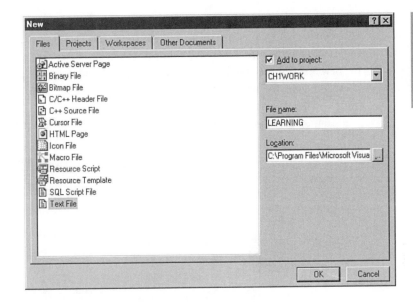

4. Click the OK button to finish adding the file to your project. Figure 1.8 shows the IDE after you have added the text file.

FIGURE 1.8

The IDE after adding a text file.

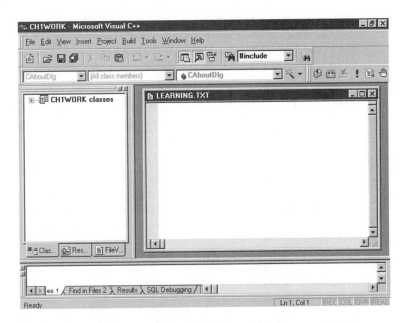

Even though that was pretty easy, that was the hard way to create a text file. On the Standard toolbar, you'll see a button named New Text File that will create a text file for you in one step. If you are not sure which button is the New Text File button, you can hover your mouse over each of the buttons to get the ToolTip text that gives you the name. In this instance, it's the first one on the left. The only difference with this method is that the new text file does not have a good name. If you create a text file in this manner, you should save the file with a name by using the File, Save As menu item. Selecting this item brings up the Save As dialog box, which is displayed in Figure 1.9. Simply type the name you want in the edit box next to File name and click the Save button.

FIGURE 1.9

The Save As dialog box.

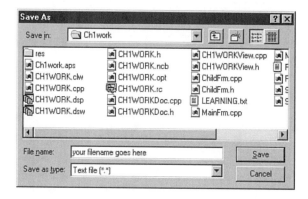

Depending on how you created the text file, the Save button on the Standard toolbar acts as either the Save or Save As menu items. If the file already has a name, it will be saved under that name. If the file doesn't have a name (created with the New button on the Standard toolbar), you will be prompted to name the file.

You will be using this text file to familiarize yourself with the menus and toolbars. You could actually change some of the code or other resources in the project, but because we haven't discussed the Workspace views yet, it would be safer to modify a text file that actually has no relevance to the project.

Now that you have the workspace open, it would be a good time to close it. When closing items in your workspace, keep a couple of things in mind. You can close individual windows in your editor or close the entire workspace at once. Closing a window by itself does not remove it from the project or the workspace. If you made any changes to the window, you will be asked to save them. To close the file that currently has focus in the IDE, click the File, Close menu item.

Closing the entire workspace—which is performed by selecting the File, Close Workspace menu item—will ask you to confirm your choice. If you have some outstanding changes, you will be asked to save them as well.

It would be good practice if you would close your project now by selecting the File, Close Workspace menu item. Go ahead and save your changes, if you made any.

Note   In projects that have only one application, the terms *project* and *workspace* are used synonymously.

1

With no project open in the workspace, you can now learn how to open a project. You can open projects in five common ways. Essentially, they all do the same thing:

- Select the File, Open menu item.
- Press the Ctrl+O shortcut key combination.
- Click the Open speed button in the Standard toolbar.
- Select the File, Open Workspace menu command.
- Use the File, Recent Workspaces to open one of the last four workspaces you've been working on.

The first three items actually do the same thing; you are just accomplishing the same task in different ways. At this point, you are probably sure of the method with which you are most comfortable. When you perform one of these tasks, you will see the Open dialog box, as shown in Figure 1.10.

FIGURE 1.10

The Open dialog box.

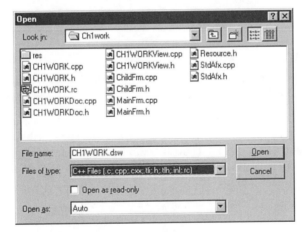

Using the Open dialog box is like using most other Windows open dialog boxes with a couple of exceptions. This one has two items that separate it from a normal Open dialog box. The first is an option to open the file you select as read only by placing a check mark in the box next to the "Open as read-only" label, and an option to open the file forcibly as a specific type of file. Usually, you won't need to change this option from Auto as it normally works.

To select a workspace, you need to select the Workspaces option from the drop-down list of file types. Once you do this, you will see only the files that match the file pattern that was listed at the end of the Workspaces option. In this case, the file extensions are .dsw and .mdp. Figure 1.11 shows the Open dialog box with just the Workspace file types listed.

FIGURE 1.11

The Open dialog box listing Workspace file types.

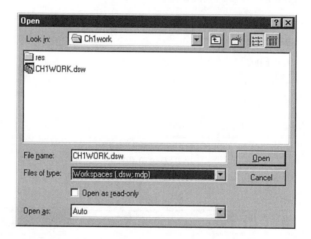

Once you have found the workspace you want to open, click on the file name and press the Open button to load it into your workspace. If all goes well, your workspace and project will be loaded, and you will be returned to the point where you closed the project.

The last two methods for opening a project are essentially the same as the first three, except that they immediately look for a workspace. The fourth method brings up an Open Workspace dialog box, which operates similarly to the Open dialog box; the fifth method opens one of the last four workspaces on which you've been working.

Now that you have your workspace and project opened back to the text file you created, type in the following lines (as shown in Figure 1.12), so you'll have some text to manipulate:

```
// Welcome to Visual C++ 6
// We are making changes to a text file.
```

Considering that you should be a little bit familiar with the C++ language, what you've typed in looks like a comment statement. Because this file isn't an actual .cpp file, it's not really a C++ comment.

FIGURE 1.12

Entering a sentence in the text file.

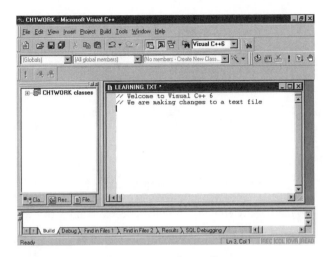

The Edit Menu

The Edit menu contains functions that control the editing of the current file selected in the IDE. Specific menu items are enabled and disabled, depending upon what kind of file is currently selected in the IDE. The Edit menu has a shortcut key of Alt+E.

The normal Cut, Copy, Paste, and Delete menu items work just like most other Windows applications; however, a couple of extra menu items make editing your files in VC++ 6 easier.

The two menu items right at the top of the list are Undo and Redo. If you make a change in one of your files that can be undone, that change is stored in a stack of changes and enables this menu item. When you select the Undo function, it reverts back one step in the stack and then adds the change to the Redo stack and enables that menu item.

Both items, Undo and Redo, have buttons on the Standard toolbar as well as shortcut keys (Ctrl+Z and Ctrl+Y, respectively) making them easy to access.

A few items on the Edit menu are quite useful when navigating through your code to find specific locations. Three of them use a search scenario to get you where you need to go, and one will let you give a name of a specific line and keep track of your specific names and locations throughout the project.

The three related items are Find, Find in Files, and Replace. Each of these menu items will display a dialog box specific to its function. The Find menu item finds the first and successive instances of your specified text in the currently selected file in the IDE. Figure 1.13 shows the Find dialog box.

FIGURE 1.13

The Find dialog box.

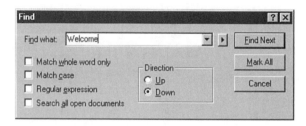

The Find dialog box enables you to enter items that will give you great control over what you want to find. If you notice in Figure 1.13 that the word *Welcome* is entered into the Find what edit box. This was automatically entered because that is where the cursor position was in the IDE. If you were to have selected a block of text, it would appear as well.

Let's change the text to find something we entered before. Type **C++** into the Find what edit box and then click the Find Next button. Figure 1.14 shows that the search found the text and selected it in the editor.

FIGURE 1.14

Search results from the Find dialog box.

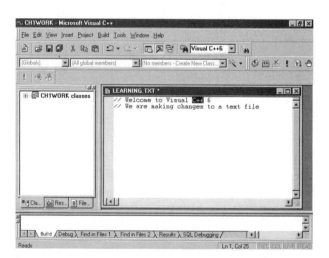

The Find in Files dialog box essentially achieves the same thing as the Find dialog box, but it has a lot more functionality. It will let you search folders on your hard drive to find text in a multitude of file types and generate a list of them in the output pane. Let's execute a sample of this by using Find in Files for the text *#INCLUDE*. We'll use this text since it's bound to give us a significant number of results. Figure 1.15 shows the Find in Files dialog box with the search criteria already entered.

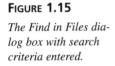

FIGURE **1.15**

The Find in Files dialog box with search criteria entered.

If you notice, the default file types are various types that exist in VC++ 6, and the In folder edit control already has the path for your current project. This dialog box includes several options that control how the search will be carried out. Because the defaults serve their purpose here, you should just click the Find button to execute your search.

After your hard drive cranks away for a few seconds, the output area's Find in Files 1 pane gives you some search results. This time, the search found 35 files that contain the search criteria. To see the list in more detail, you'll want to resize the output area to take up more of your screen. If you scroll through the list of results, you will notice that a file is listed each time your search criteria occur. In Figure 1.16, the file CH1WORK.CPP has been listed six times since the search criteria are in that file six times. A number in parenthesis appears at the end of each file name. This number tells you the line number where this result occurs. After the line number is the line of text as well.

To jump right to any of the occurrences, just double-click the line you want, and the IDE will display a window with your selection. Go ahead and double-click the first one in the list to see where it takes you. You may need to resize some of your areas and windows so you can see it easily. In Figure 1.17, you can see an indicator in the left gutter pointing to the line that you selected in the Find in Files 1 pane.

FIGURE 1.16

*The Find in Files
search results.*

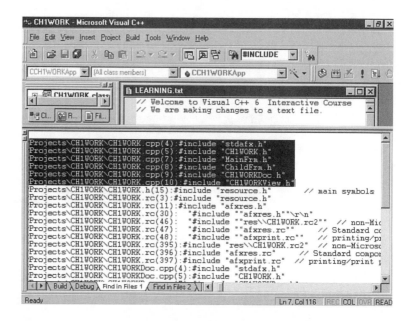

FIGURE 1.17

*One of the files found
by the search.*

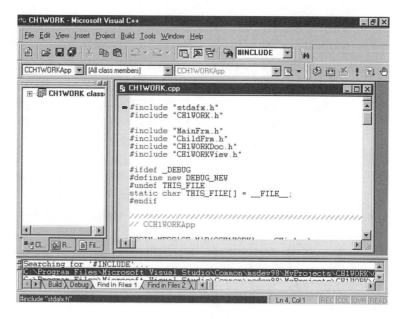

Because you don't need to edit this file, go ahead and close it so that you don't inadvertently make a change to the file. To clear the search results, right-click the Find in Files 1 pane to obtain a context menu and select the Clear menu item. You may have noticed a

1

Find in Files 2 pane as well. This is available so that you can have multiple search results available. To use this pane, select Output to pane 2 in the Find in Files dialog box before executing your search.

The Replace dialog box is similar to the Find dialog box in that you specify what text to find, but it allows you to go one step further and specify what to replace for the search results. Let's make a change in the text file using the Replace dialog box. To do this, select a small block of text on the "Visual C++6" text in the first line as shown in Figure 1.18.

FIGURE 1.18

Selecting text to use in the Replace dialog box.

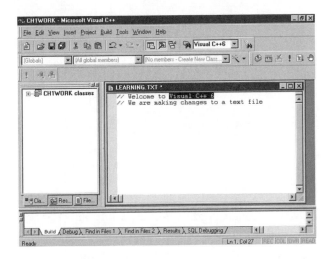

Once you have selected the text that you want to replace, select the Edit, Replace menu item. This will display the Replace dialog box with the text, "Visual C++6" already entered. Now type **VC++6** into the Replace with edit control as shown in Figure 1.19.

FIGURE 1.19

Replacing text in a file.

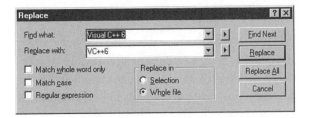

Next, you need to determine how many instances of what you are looking for need to be changed. You can step through each individual occurrence or automatically change them all in one step. For the purpose of this example, go ahead and click the Replace button to change the text.

When the search finds no more occurrences of the text you are looking for, click the Close button to exit from the Replace dialog box. Figure 1.20 shows what the new text looks like since executing the replace.

FIGURE 1.20

The file after executing the replace.

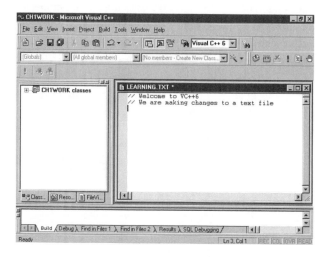

When using the Replace feature, you need to be careful not to change text that you don't intend to change. Changing text that occurs within other text, such as *active* in *Interactive*, could lead to undesirable results.

The last menu item that makes finding locations in files quick and painless is the Edit, Bookmarks menu item. This item associates a name with a specific spot in your project. These names are then kept in a list that allows you to call upon them throughout the entire project. You can easily maintain this list by using the Bookmark dialog box.

Select the Edit, Bookmarks menu item or press its shortcut key of Alt+F2 to display the Bookmark dialog box. Because no bookmarks exist yet, the Bookmark dialog box will be empty, as shown in Figure 1.21.

Using this dialog box is actually quite simple. To create an entry, make sure your cursor is on the line that has the location you want to remember, and activate the dialog box. Once activated, type in a name for the bookmark and click the Add button. You will immediately see the name added to the list of available bookmarks.

Let's add a bookmark for the first line of the file. To do so, place the cursor somewhere on the first line and activate the Bookmark dialog box. In the Name edit control, type **First line of file** and then click the Add button. Figure 1.22 depicts the result of these steps.

FIGURE 1.21

The empty Bookmark dialog box.

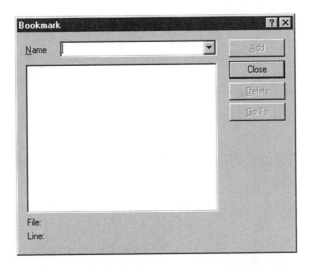

FIGURE 1.22

Adding a bookmark.

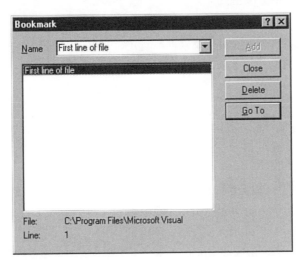

When you are done adding bookmarks, simply click the Close button to exit the Bookmark dialog box.

To jump to one of your bookmarks, just activate the Bookmark dialog box, select the bookmark you want from the available list, and click the Go To button.

Removing a bookmark from the list is just as simple. Activate the Bookmark dialog box, select the bookmark you want to remove, and click the Delete button.

Lesson Summary

In this lesson, you've learned how to use some of the most common functions in VC++ 6 when managing project files and using basic editing features. Knowing how to use basic features such as these to their fullest extent is an easy way to improve the quality of your projects and lessen the number of headaches you experience along the way.

Quiz 2

1. What menu item automatically opens the most recent workspace on which you've been working?

    a. The File, Open Last menu item

    b. The File, Recent Workspaces' first menu item

    c. The File, Open, Recent Workspace menu item

    d. None of the above

2. Why does the Output window have two panes for Find in Files?

    a. To allow dragging and dropping of files between the panes

    b. To allow multiple search result sets

    c. To keep a list of changed files

    d. None of the above

3. What menu item enables you to keep a named list of specific locations in your projects?

    a. The File, Locations menu item

    b. The Edit, Breakpoints menu item

    c. The File, Bookmarks menu item

    d. None of the above

4. When creating a new text file with the Standard toolbar's New button, what is an important step to remember?

    a. Make sure you set the border widths for the file.

    b. Drag the file to the Open Files folder.

    c. Save the file with a good file name.

    d. Turn on Spell and Syntax checking.

Exercise 2

Complexity: Easy

1. Create a new text file with the name EXER2.TXT.

Complexity: Moderate

2. Rename the previously created text file as EXERCISE.TXT.

LESSON 3

Visual C++ 6's View, Projects, Build, and Tools Menus

The View Menu

The View menu is organized to show special dialog boxes and controls the appearance of the IDE for certain aspects. The menu item Class Wizard is one of the most commonly used menu items and therefore has a shortcut key assigned to it of Ctrl+W. Activating this menu item will bring up the MFC ClassWizard dialog box, as displayed in Figure 1.23.

FIGURE 1.23

The MFC ClassWizard dialog box.

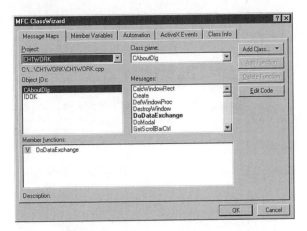

When working with resources, such as menus and controls, the Class Wizard connects them to actual code in your application. Because the Class Wizard is such a versatile tool, it will be discussed throughout the book where its relevance is apparent, starting with Chapter 4, "Enhancing Your Application with Common Controls." You should be aware that when you open the Class Wizard, it automatically saves any changes that you've made to your project.

The next menu item, Resource Symbols, will display the Resource Symbols dialog box. This dialog box primarily manages the IDs that your program uses and where they are used. In Figure 1.24, you can see that some IDs are already defined for the test project you've been working on. These IDs are what tie resources together with code.

FIGURE 1.24

The Resource Symbols dialog box.

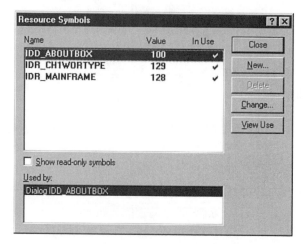

Selecting the Resource Includes menu item will display the Resource Includes dialog box, shown in Figure 1.25. This information is automatically generated as you continue to develop your program. Very rarely will you need to come into this dialog box for any reason, although instances may occur when you need to.

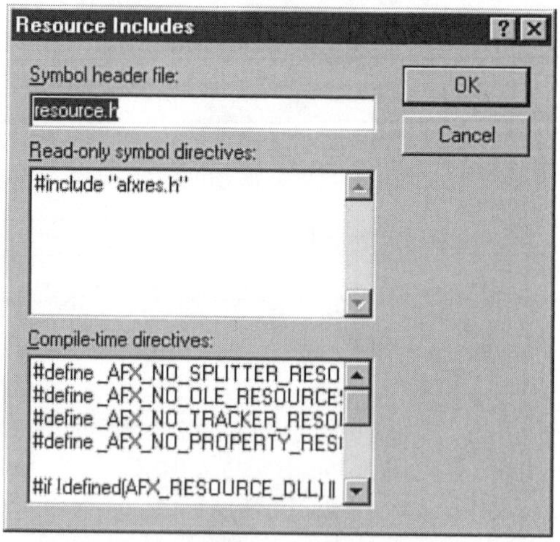

FIGURE 1.25

The Resource Includes dialog box.

The Full Screen menu item lets you hide all menus, toolbars, workspace, and output windows and gives you the full screen with which to work. One small window is left behind that will allow you to restore all of the items you just hid. To see how this operates, select this menu item, and you should see a screen similar to Figure 1.26.

Figure 1.26

Full Screen view.

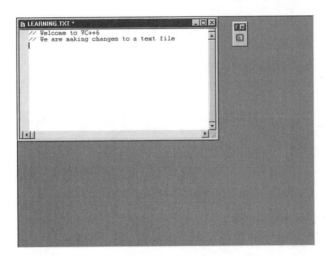

This gives you the entire screen to work with code and editors. If you right-click your mouse, you will see the context menu that displays what screen elements you can toggle on and off. When you are done with the full screen mode, simply click the little window with the little screen icon, and your desktop will be restored.

The Workspace or Output menu items are only useful when you've hidden the Project Workspace or the Output window. Selecting these menu items will make their respective window reappear. Buttons have been included on the Standard toolbar that will hide and display the Workspace and Output windows.

The Properties menu item brings up the Properties dialog box. This dialog box is another one that will be used quite frequently as you develop your project. This dialog box's appearance and options will change dependent upon which item currently has focus in the IDE. You will see more of this dialog box as you progress through the book where its options are relevant. You can press Alt+Enter to activate this menu item at any time and to bring up the Properties dialog box for the current IDE element.

The Project Menu

The Project menu houses the functions related to managing your projects. Until now, you've read about having only one project in the Project Workspace. The reality is, you can have more than one project in the workspace at a time. This is really useful when you are working on large projects.

To demonstrate how to manage multiple projects on one workspace, create another quick project as outlined in the following steps:

1. Click File, New to bring up the New dialog box.
2. Click the Projects tab in the New dialog box.
3. Type **CH1WORK2** for the Project Name. Figure 1.27 shows the dialog box with this step completed.

FIGURE 1.27

The New dialog box to add a new project.

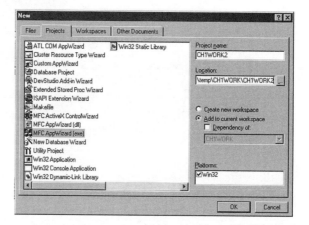

4. Notice that the option button Add to current workspace is selected. This allows us to add this project to our current workspace. Click the OK button to execute this dialog box.
5. The AppWizard is now displayed. Go ahead and click the Finish button.
6. The New Project Information dialog box appears. This is the last chance you have to go back or cancel the operation. Click the OK button to finish the process.

When you have completed the previous steps, you will have two distinct projects in your workspace. Now we can look at the Set Active Project menu item.

The Set Active Project menu has a submenu that currently contains our two projects, CH1WORK and CH1WORK2. To switch between projects, simply select one from this menu. Make sure you have CH1WORK as the current project. To do this, just select it in the list.

The Add to Project menu item also has a submenu where you can add resources, files, and other items to the current project.

1

Selecting the Dependencies menu item will display the Project Dependencies dialog box. This allows you to specify that when one project is changed, its dependent projects are rebuilt as well.

The Settings menu item will display the Project Settings dialog box, shown in Figure 1.28. As you can see, several tabs control many different settings. Some of the more common tabs are the following:

FIGURE 1.28

The Project Settings dialog box.

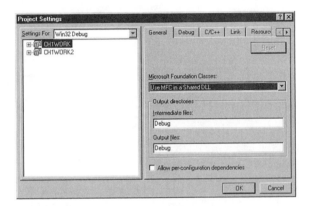

- General—Use this tab to specify in which directories certain files are kept, as well as how to incorporate the Microsoft Foundation Class (MFC) DLLs.
- C/C++—Use this to define compiler settings. You can control such things as how the compiler optimizes your program.
- Link—This tab will let you specify what name to give the actual executable program, as well as additional libraries that need to be included in your project for a successful build.

The Build Menu

The Build menu houses the functions related to compiling, debugging, and executing your application. VC++ 6 includes two toolbars for the compile and build processes, the Build toolbar and the Build MiniBar. The Build MiniBar is shown by default and includes a subset of what is found on the Build toolbar. What the Build menu has extra is the option to select which project to build and what kind of build to complete.

The first menu item, Compile, usually has the name of the file that is currently selected in the IDE added to it. Looking at Figure 1.29, the Compile menu item wants to compile the LEARNING.TXT file. If you were to select this menu item at this time, you would get an error message, because LEARNING.TXT isn't an actual code file.

FIGURE 1.29

The Build menu expanded.

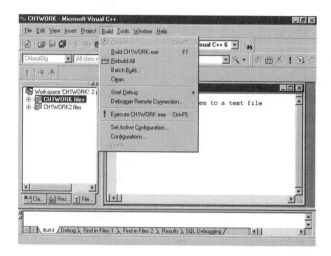

Assuming that you had a file that could be compiled, selecting this menu item would compile it and send the results of the file to the Build pane in the Output window.

The next menu item, Build, also adds something to itself, the name of the file to build. Selecting this menu item will create the actual .EXE for your program to run.

Because you haven't made any changes to the code portions of the project, it should be safe to build the project at this point. Go ahead and select the Build menu item. Your hard drive will start to crank away, and this could take a couple minutes. While this process is occurring, the Build menu item turns into Stop Build. Selecting it will cancel the build process. At this time, just let the project continue to build until it is complete. Stopping the build process, however, doesn't cause any errors.

When the build is complete, you will see a message in the Output window's Build pane. You should see a message stating that the build was complete with no errors, as shown in Figure 1.30.

If you look at the Build menu again, you will notice that the Stop Build menu item has returned to the Build menu item. The Build and Stop Build menu items both have buttons on the Build MiniBar toolbar.

Compile and Build accomplish essentially the same task: Both compile source code. Compile, however, only works with the current file in the IDE, whereas Build works with all files needed.

FIGURE 1.30

The Output window after the build is complete.

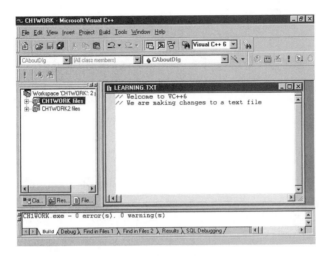

The next menu item, Rebuild All, is similar in function to the Build menu item except that it forces the build of all dependent projects. You can stop this process by clicking on the Stop Build toolbar button or selecting the Stop Build menu item.

The Batch Build menu item performs the same function as the Build menu item, except that it displays the dialog box shown in Figure 1.31, prompting you to select which projects to build and what types of build to perform.

FIGURE 1.31

The Batch Build dialog box.

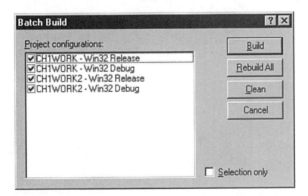

In this example, you'll notice two types of builds, Debug and Release. The Debug build contains information inside the program that will help you when you are tracking down problems in the program, whereas the Release build does not include this information. Having the Debug information in your program will increase its size in order to accommodate the information.

To batch build all the projects at once, just click the Rebuild All button. To build just the checked version, click the Build button.

The Clean button on this dialog box removes files created during the build process that the project doesn't need. The executable program that was built will also be removed. This will work just like the Build button on multiple projects if you have them selected.

The next menu item, Clean, is like the Clean button in the Batch Build dialog box, except that it defaults to the current project automatically. Output from the Batch Build and Clean operations is sent to the Output window's Build pane.

The next menu item, Execute, also adds the name of the executable program to the menu item itself. This is how you test your application to see if it performs the way you intend it to perform. If the project has not been built, you will be prompted to build it before running it. You can perform this same task with the Build MiniBar's Execute button.

At this time, select this menu item to build the project. If you see the dialog box telling you it's not already built, go ahead and build it. When the application runs, you should see the program as displayed in Figure 1.32. Although this program has no real functionality, it is a full-blown Windows application. The menus and toolbars work, and you can create and close multiple windows. This is what makes VC++ 6 an easy development tool to use.

FIGURE 1.32

The running program.

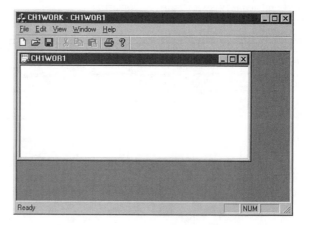

The last thing of importance to discuss on the Build menu is the Set Active Configuration menu item, shown in Figure 1.33. Selecting this item will display the Set Active Project Configuration dialog box, which sets the type of build you are working on. From an earlier discussion, you already learned the difference between a Debug build and a Release build. During your development process, you'll most likely want to stick with the Debug build in case you come across problems. Although, you'll want to create a Release build and execute it once in a while just to make sure it will operate properly. This is the build that you will distribute once your application is complete.

FIGURE 1.33

The Set Active Project Configuration dialog box.

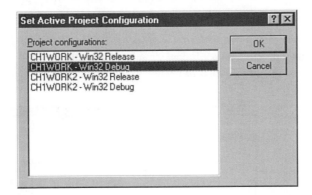

The Tools Menu

The Tools menu contains add-in applications that make working with VC++ 6 easier. This menu is also customizable; you may add your own items to it so that you can perform specific tasks right from the IDE.

The Source Browser is probably one of the most important tools on this menu. With it, you can quickly find a definition or reference for variables, IDs, or classes. Figure 1.34 shows the Browse dialog box with an ID specified. To display this dialog box, click the menu option or press the shortcut key of Alt+F12.

FIGURE 1.34

The Browse dialog box.

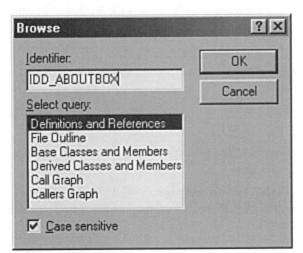

You may see a message stating that your project does not have browse information. If so, go ahead and tell it to rebuild the project with the browse info. You can manually select this option by going into Project, Settings and selecting the Browse Info tab. An entire toolbar is also devoted to Browse functions. To display this toolbar, right-click the toolbar area and select Browse from the list.

In the Browse dialog box, enter an identifier of **IDD_ABOUTBOX** and click the OK button. This will bring up a window showing the results of what it found. Figure 1.35 shows the results that the first project should have yielded.

FIGURE 1.35

Definitions and References from the Browse operation.

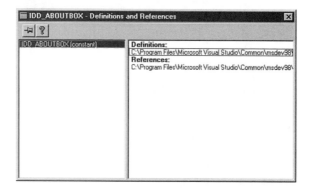

The next menu item, Close Source Browser File, will close the Browse window and return you to the IDE.

The Customize menu option will display the Customize dialog box, which manages the buttons appearing on toolbars, the toolbars that are visible, the external tools you have defined, keyboard shortcuts, and other add-ins that are tools which usually enhance the development environment.

The Standard toolbar doesn't come predefined with a button to print the current item in the IDE. Because this is standard in most applications, you can add it to the toolbar by following these steps:

1. Activate the Customize dialog box by selecting its menu item. Figure 1.36 shows the Customize dialog box.

2. Make sure you are on the Commands tab and that File is selected in the Category dropdown list.

3. Click the little printer image and drag it just to the right of the New button on the Standard toolbar. Figure 1.37 shows the new Standard toolbar with the print button added.

FIGURE 1.36

The Customize dialog box.

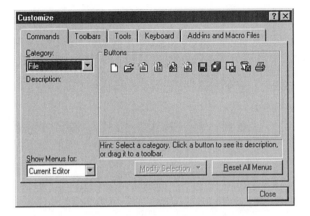

FIGURE 1.37

The Standard toolbar with the print button added.

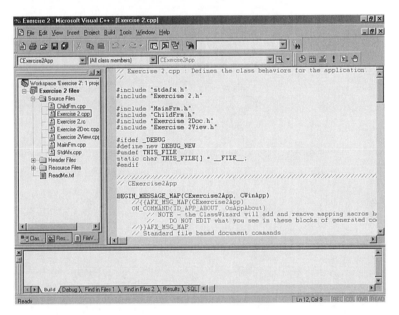

Look back to Figure 1.36. The Customize dialog box has five tab pages for different kinds of settings you can change:

- Commands—This page controls which buttons are on which toolbars.

- Toolbars—This page controls which toolbars are visible. Changing its state in the list immediately has the effect of showing or hiding the selected toolbar.

- Tools—This page lets you specify external applications and have them appear on the Tools menu.

- Keyboard—This page lets you change shortcut keys for specific VC++ 6 tasks.

- Add-ins and Macro Files—This page lets you manage add-ins and files that contain macros.

The Options menu item displays the Options dialog as shown in Figure 1.38. This is where you can really configure how VC++ 6 looks and behaves. Here are the sections for which you can change settings:

FIGURE 1.38

The Options dialog box.

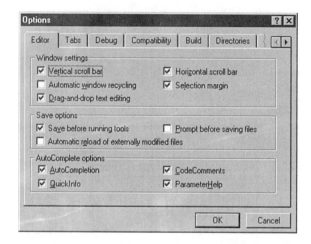

- Editor—Sets automatic saving, code completion, and window options.
- Tabs—Controls how the Tab key operates and how the auto-indenting features work.
- Debug—Controls what information is used for debugging.
- Compatibility—Controls how the editing functions of the IDE operate.
- Build—Sets general build options.
- Directories—Sets and displays directory and file locations.
- Workspace—Controls which items are displayed in the IDE.
- Macros—Tells Developer Studio how to handle changed macros.
- Help System—Specifies which help system and language to use.
- Data view—Controls settings when debugging SQL Server programs (Enterprise version only).
- Format—Controls the visual appearance of the IDE elements.

Lesson Summary

In this lesson, you learned quite a bit of information about managing projects, including how to add multiple projects to a workspace and how to switch between different projects. You also learned about compiling and building your projects, including information about two different kinds of builds, the Debug build and the Release Build.

This lesson also talked about customizing your environment and setting options that effect the way VC++ 6 handles certain functions, like including browse information.

Quiz 3

1. Which menu item sets the current project in a multiple project workspace?

    a. The Project, Set Project menu item

    b. The Project, Change Current Project menu item

    c. The View, Project Settings menu item

    d. The Project, Switch Project menu item

2. When adding a project to a workspace, which statement(s) is/are true?

    a. You can have only one project per workspace.

    b. Each project name must be different.

    c. The projects must be of the same type.

    d. You can have multiple projects.

3. Of the following, which statement(s) is/are true?

    a. The Debug build is smaller because it doesn't contain all the actual code.

    b. The Release build is used to debug your application.

    c. The Debug build is larger than a Release build.

    d. The Debug build contains extra information.

4. Which best describes project dependency?

    a. One project depends on certain system conditions for it to compile.

    b. A project must meet certain criteria in order to be considered Windows Logo compliant.

    c. Special lines of code are entered into source.

    d. One project depends on another project to be compiled.

Exercise 3

Complexity: Easy

1. Create a new workspace that has a single project named EXER3 in it. Name the workspace EXER3WRK.

Complexity: Moderate

2. Add a second project to the workspace created in the previous exercise.

LESSON 4

The Project Workspace Views

The Project Workspace in VC++ 6 is divided into three sections, or views: Class view, Resource view, and File view. These three views are used to organize your projects into manageable chunks.

The Resource View

Of the three views, the Resource view is the only one that manages items such as accelerators (shortcut keys), dialog boxes, menus, and toolbars. These items let your user interface with your application.

Resources are different from normal C++ code because they are actually not sections of code. Each resource is given an ID to represent it throughout your project. For example, a menu resource is essentially a list of items with a special ID assigned to it. It is this ID that ties a resource to actual C++ code.

Figure 1.39 shows the JDE with the Resource view selected in the Project Workspace window.

FIGURE 1.39

The Resource view.

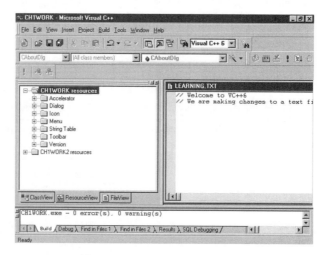

The current project has seven different resource categories:

- Accelerator—Associates an ID to a shortcut key, such as the one for Ctrl+C, which represents the Edit, Copy menu item.
- Dialog—Contains dialog boxes that your program uses, such as the About box that was automatically generated when you created the project.

- Icon—Holds all the icons your program uses. Usually, the program has an icon, and your program's documents have a separate one.
- Menu—Holds all menu resources for your project. The standard menu created in the text project is in here.
- String Table—Contains a table of strings used throughout your application. These are used for language translations.
- Toolbar—Contains the toolbar resources used in your application.
- Version—Holds the version information about your program.

Accelerator Resources

Accelerator resources are actually groups of key combinations associated to other resource IDs. They let you assign shortcut keys to resources, such as menu items.

To see a list of available accelerator groups, simply click the plus icon to the left of the Accelerator branch, or double-click on the branch itself. Once you do that, you will see the list of available accelerator groups.

Drilling down a little further by double-clicking one of the accelerators, IDR_MAINFRAME in this example, will open a window showing the contents of that group, as shown in Figure 1.40.

FIGURE 1.40

The accelerator collection.

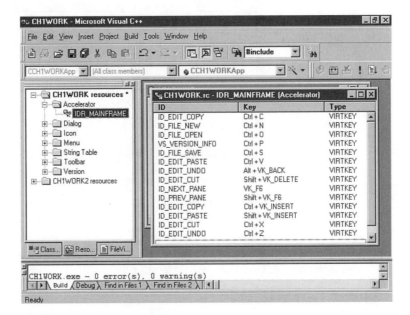

The window opened showing the accelerator collection is divided into three sections: ID, Key, and Type.

The ID column contains the resource IDs that have a shortcut key assigned to them. The Key column is a textual representation of the key assigned to each ID. The Type column tells whether each item is a virtual key (VIRTKEY) or an ASCII control character (ASCII).

Dialog Resources

Dialog resources are elements of your program that either convey or gather information from the user. With VC++ 6, dialog resources are easy to develop by using the built-in visual tools.

To see the list of dialog resources in a project, simply expand the Dialog branch of the Resource view. To display and edit a dialog box, just double-click the dialog resource you need, and a window will open containing the dialog box. Figure 1.41 shows the Dialog branch expanded with the IDD_ABOUTBOX dialog box opened for editing.

FIGURE 1.41

The Dialog resource branch expanded.

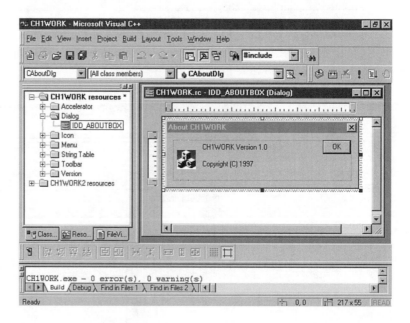

Because editing a dialog box is not covered in this chapter, go ahead and close the window that contains the About box dialog box.

Icon Resources

Icon resources are small graphics or images in the normal Windows icon format (32×32 or 16×16 pixels in 16-color format) that give graphical representation for program usage.

1

You can use an icon to represent a program in a Windows folder or desktop, in the title bar, in the taskbar, and (if the program is document-centric) for each document.

Double-click an icon's ID to bring up the icon resource editor. You will see the icon zoomed in, and you will be able to make changes to it. Figure 1.42 shows the Icon resource editor built into VC++ 6.

FIGURE 1.42

The Icon resource editor.

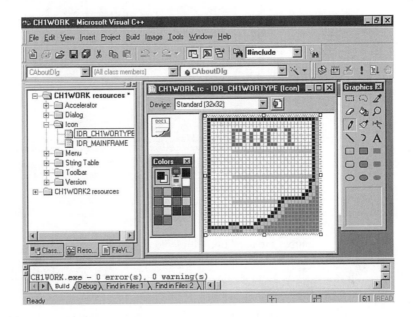

Menu Resources

Menu resources are one of the most important elements to any program because users generally look to the menus to perform tasks.

Remember that when you are developing your application, you should organize your menus into logical sections so that users can find the function they need without wasting a lot of time. To see a list of the menu resources in your project, expand the Menu branch in the Resource view.

At this point, double-click one of the menu resources to display the Menu resource editor, as shown in Figure 1.43. Chapter 6, "Customizing the User Interface," addresses the process of actually editing the menu resource. Go ahead and close the Menu resource editor window.

FIGURE 1.43

The Menu resource editor.

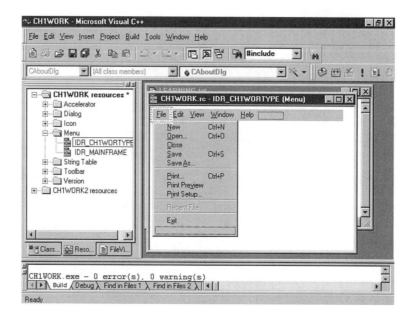

String Resources

String resources are used in multiple areas and are built in a table to make converting your application to another language simpler. They are also used to keep text that is displayed as fly-over hints and status bars common amongst items which share the same resource IDs.

To display the list of string tables in your project, expand the String Table resource. Go ahead and double-click the String Table resource to display a window that contains all the strings in your application. Figure 1.44 displays the String Table resource editor.

Typically, you won't need to use this editor to change a string's value; you'll normally do it in a property dialog box. For example, you would probably use the Menu resource editor when working on a menu, and if you needed to change the caption for the File, Print menu item, you would do it there. That change would then be reflected in this list, although you could change it here as well by double-clicking the string you wanted to change and entering a caption. Go ahead and close the String Table resource editor if you have it open.

FIGURE 1.44

The String Table resource editor.

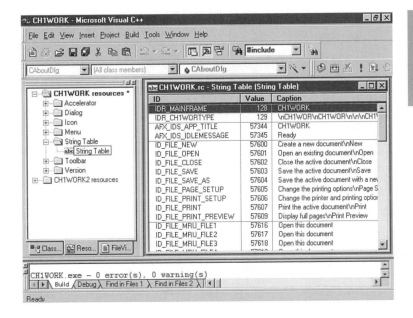

Toolbar Resources

Toolbar resources are collections of images, usually in 16×15 pixel bitmap format (the pixel size can be changed). These buttons, sometimes called *speed buttons*, usually have a direct relationship to a menu item.

To make the toolbar button link to a menu item, the same ID is given to the toolbar button as the menu item. This will let them share the same block of code and, hence, perform the same function.

To see a list of toolbars in your project, expand the Toolbar branch in the Resource view. To open a window containing the Toolbar resource editor, double-click the toolbar item you wish to edit. Figure 1.45 shows the Toolbar resource editor.

Chapter 6 discusses editing toolbars in more detail. If you have the Toolbar resource editor open, go ahead and close it now.

FIGURE **1.45**

The Toolbar resource editor.

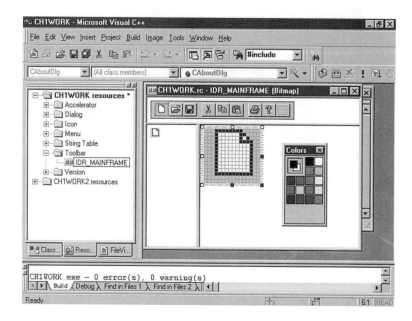

Version Resources

The Version resource holds internal information about your application to distinguish it from other applications and even an older or newer version of the same application. Installation programs typically use this type of information so that they won't accidentally overwrite a newer version of your program.

Even though version information isn't vital to make an application run, it's one of those things that help polish your application, and besides, if you're writing a Windows logo-compliant application, you'll need to have it in there.

To view the version information resource, expand the Version branch in the Resource view, and then double-click the VS_VERSION_INFO ID. Figure 1.46 shows the Version Info resource editor.

Before you make changes to the version information, make sure you know how your installation program handles it. Editing this information in your project is up to you, but for now, if you have the Version Info editor open, go ahead and close it.

FIGURE 1.46

The Version Info resource editor.

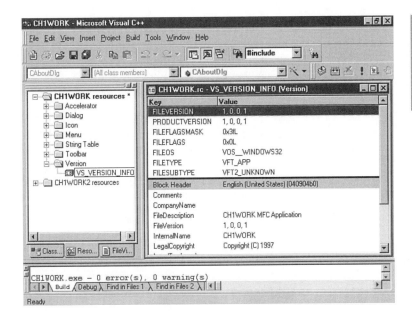

The Class View

The Class view displays your project's classes in one general location, enabling you to maneuver through your source code files with ease.

Looking at Figure 1.47, you'll notice that there is a branch for each project. This branch hierarchy works just like the one discussed in the Resource view. To expand a branch, click on the plus sign to the left of the project name or double-click on the project name itself.

FIGURE 1.47

The expanded Class view.

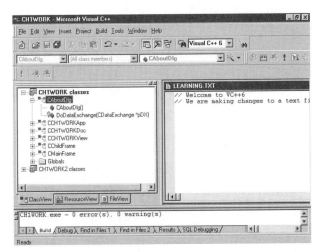

After you expand the branch for the project, you will see a list of classes that the project uses. Each of these classes can be expanded as well by clicking their respective plus signs. If you double-click this time, you will open a window containing the file that defines the class, and the cursor position will be placed at the beginning of the definition. If you haven't already done so, go ahead and double-click one of the classes in the list.

Once you expand the branch for a class, you will see a list of that class's functions. Double-clicking one of these will open a window where that function is defined, or, if the file is already opened, the cursor's position will be changed to the function definition.

This makes navigating through your source code easier and relieves the need to make bookmarks at the beginning of classes—sort of automatic bookmarks in a sense.

If you have any class files open, go ahead and close them at this time.

The File View

The File view organizes the physical files in your project. Because these are physical files on your hard drive, they are shown by their file names.

By default, three original folders are in the Project workspace that lists your files: Source Files, Header Files, and Resource Files. Please note that the folder names are not actual directories on your hard drive; they are just folders in the Project Workspace.

Looking at Figure 1.48, you will notice that the File view follows the same format as the Resource and Class views for organizing the files. To expand a folder, simply click the plus sign next to the folder or double-click the folder's name.

FIGURE 1.48

The expanded File view.

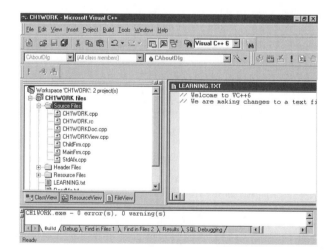

1

Go ahead and expand the Source Files folder to see a list of files that have been automatically organized in this folder. Now, double-click CH1WORK.cpp to open a window containing that file. At this point, you could actually start making code changes to the project. Because we're not actually changing code files yet, go ahead and close the window for this file.

One of the nice features of the File view is that it lets you create your own folders to manage files as well. As an example, let's create a new folder where we can put our stray .TXT files.

To do this, complete the following steps:

1. Right-click the CH1WORK project name to get a context menu.

2. Select New Folder from the context menu. This will display the New Folder dialog box, as displayed in Figure 1.49.

FIGURE 1.49

The New Folder dialog box.

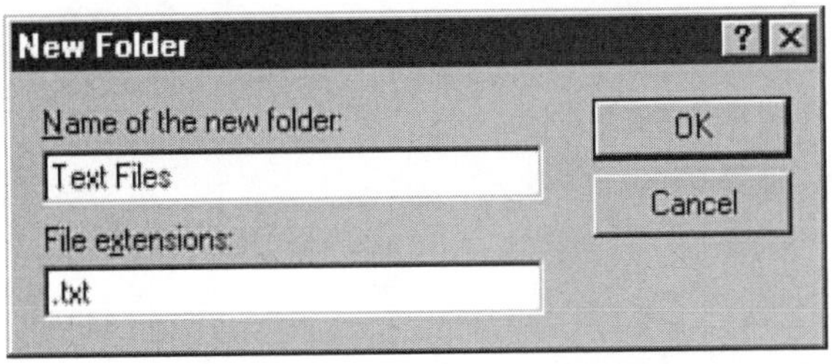

3. Give the folder a name. For this example, type **Text Files**.

4. If you want automatic filing for this folder when you create new files, enter a series of file extensions used to file with, each separated by a semicolon. For this example, use only one extension, .TXT.

5. Click the OK button to create the folder.

6. Now that the folder has been created, simply drag and drop the two text files from our sample project into the Text Files folder.

Being able to manage your files and having a lot of the hard work done for you is what makes working with a tool such as VC++ 6 easy and intuitive.

Lesson Summary

In this lesson, you've learned about the three different views in the Project Workspace: the Resource view, the Class view, and the File view. You've learned what each view is responsible for accomplishing and how to navigate your way through their entries.

Quiz 4

1. Which view will let you get to a dialog box so that you can make visual changes to it?

   a. The Dialog view

   b. The Resource view

   c. The Class view

   d. None of the above

2. In the Resource view, where would you find a list of shortcut keys?

   a. In the Menu resources

   b. In the Toolbar resources

   c. In the Accelerator resources

   d. In the Keyboard resources

3. What property of a resource links the resource to sections of code?

   a. The resource's group

   b. The resource's ID

   c. Resources are code themselves and don't need linked.

   d. None of the above

4. How does the Class view organize its elements?

   a. Its elements are organized first by project, then by class, then by class members.

   b. Its elements are organized first by physical file, then by class, then by class members.

   c. Classes are organized alphabetically throughout the project to make finding them faster.

   d. None of the above.

Exercise 4

Complexity: Easy

1. Create a new folder in the File view and tell it to contain files with the extension .OLD. Next, create two text files with the .OLD file extension with a couple of lines of text and make sure they are placed in the newly created folder.

1

Complexity: Moderate

2. Create a new project (or use the sample one) and edit the Version Information to show that the file is version 2.0. Once you've built the program, use Windows Explorer to see the properties for the generated .EXE file.

Chapter Summary

This chapter discussed where some of the most common menu and toolbar elements are in the Visual Studio Interface. You were also introduced to the various views that organize and manage your projects. The main concepts covered were the following:

- The File menu—The File menu is organized so that functions related to loading, saving, and printing files are under this menu.

- The Edit menu—The Edit menu contains functions that control the editing of the current file selected in the IDE.

- The View menu—The View menu shows special dialog boxes and controls the appearance of the IDE for certain aspects.

- The Project menu—The Project menu houses the functions that are related to managing your projects.

- The Resource view—The Resource view is responsible for managing the resources in your projects. Resources are items such as menus and toolbars.

- The Class view—The Class view is responsible for managing the list of classes used in your projects and the files that contain them.

- The File view—The File view manages the files in your projects.

CHAPTER 2

Your First Interactive Visual C++ Applications

Although you can create just about any type of application using Visual C++ 6, you will create three application types more often than others. These application types are SDI, MDI, and dialog applications.

SDI, short for *single document interface*, includes applications that allow you to work with only one document at a time. MDI, short for *multiple document interface*, includes applications that allow you to work with multiple documents concurrently. Dialog applications are generally applications that do not use documents. You will learn more about these different application types as you progress through the lessons in this chapter. You learn how to create each of these three application types, and you examine the differences among them. In the last lesson of this chapter, you learn about the other types of applications that you can create in Visual C++ 6 using the MFC AppWizard.

LESSON 1

Using the AppWizard to Create Your First Application

You can use the Visual C++ 6 AppWizard to create many different styles of applications. Using this AppWizard, you can create anything from a simple

.EXE application to a custom .DLL just by choosing a few options. To get you started, you will create a standard .EXE application.

Creating Your First Application

To create your first executable program, follow these steps:

1. Choose File, New from the VC++ 6 menu to create a new application.

2. Using Figure 2.1 as a guide, choose MFC AppWizard (exe) from the projects list, click in the Project name box, and enter **My First App**.

FIGURE 2.1

Creating a new application.

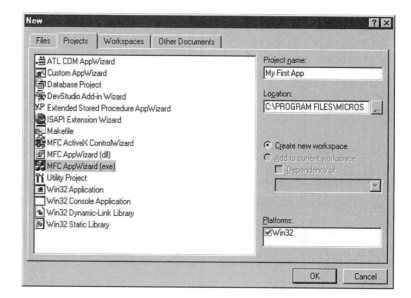

3. Click the OK button.

4. You will be presented with the MFC AppWizard - Step 1 dialog box, as shown in Figure 2.2.

   This dialog box determines what type of application you want to create:

   • Single Document—This option tells the MFC AppWizard to generate classes and code for an application. SDI applications can have only one document open at a time. An example of an SDI application would be WordPad, as shown in Figure 2.3. You will learn more about SDI applications in Lesson 2 of this chapter.

FIGURE 2.2

Choosing the application type.

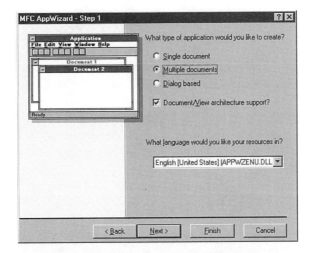

FIGURE 2.3

WordPad: an SDI application.

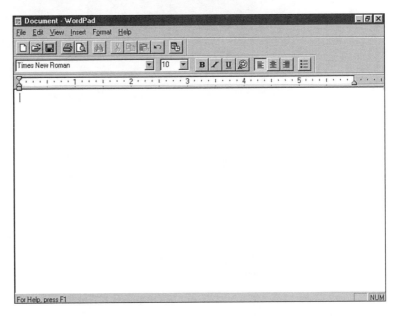

- Multiple Documents—This option tells the MFC AppWizard to generate classes and code for an MDI (Multiple Document Interface) application. Unlike an SDI application, MDI applications can have multiple documents open at one time. An example of an MDI application would be Microsoft Word, as shown in Figure 2.4. You will learn more about MDI applications in Lesson 3 of this chapter.

FIGURE 2.4

Microsoft Word: an MDI application.

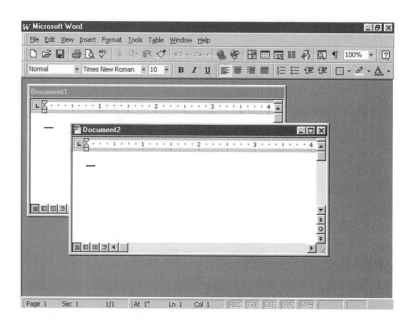

- Dialog Based—Dialog-based applications do not use the document and view classes that are used in SDI and MDI applications. An example of a dialog-based application would be Calculator, as shown in Figure 2.5. You will learn more about dialog applications in Lesson 4 of this chapter.

FIGURE 2.5

Calculator: a dialog-based application.

Go ahead and use the default options for the application type by clicking the Next button. You will learn more about SDI applications in Lesson 2, MDI applications in Lesson 3, and dialog-based applications in Lesson 4 of this chapter.

5. The MFC AppWizard - Step 2 of 6 dialog box, as shown in Figure 2.6, lets you determine the level of database support for your application:

FIGURE 2.6

Choosing the level of support for databases.

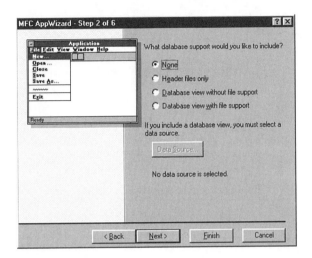

- None—Choose this option if you don't plan on using database support in your application. For this example, you will use this option, because it is the default option.
- Header Files Only—This option will give you access to a database, but you won't have a Record menu, and your view will not be derived from the CFormView.
- Database View Without File Support—This option will derive your view from the CFormView, and you will have a Record menu. Use this option if you don't need to serialize a document.
- Database View with File Support—This is the same as the previous option. Use this option if you need to serialize a document.

You do not need database support in this example, so go ahead and use the default options by clicking the Next button. You will learn more about database support in Chapter 11, "Using File I/O and Databases to Manage Information."

6. The MFC AppWizard - Step 3 of 6 dialog box, as shown in Figure 2.7, lets you determine the level of compound document support for your application. A *compound document* can contain data of different formats, such as a spreadsheet or a bitmap that was created by another application.

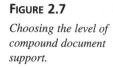

Figure 2.7

Choosing the level of compound document support.

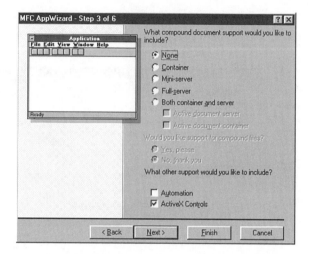

Here are your options:

- None—This option is used when you do not want to support ActiveX in your application. This is the default option, and it will be used for this example.
- Container—This option will allow you to contain ActiveX objects in your documents.
- Mini-Server—This option will allow your application to serve documents that do not need to run as standalone applications to other applications.
- Full-Server—This option lets your application run as a standalone application, and it also lets your application serve documents to other applications.
- Both Container and Server—This option lets your application serve documents to other applications as well as contain other application objects.

You do not need ActiveX support in this example, so go ahead and use the default options by clicking the Next button. You will learn more about ActiveX in Chapter 9, "An Introduction to ActiveX Programming."

7. The MFC AppWizard - Step 4 of 6 dialog box, as shown in Figure 2.8, lets you determine the user interface features for your application.

- Docking Toolbar—This option lets you include a toolbar in your application. Toolbars are a nice way to add quick access to features in your application. You will learn more about toolbars in Chapter 6, "Customizing the User Interface."

FIGURE 2.8

Choosing user interface features.

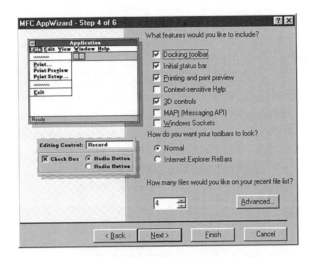

- Initial Status Bar—This option lets you include a status bar in your application. The status bar displays menu prompts and other messages that you want to present to the user. You will learn more about status bars in Chapter 6.

- Printing and Print Preview—With this option you can easily incorporate printing capabilities to your application. You will learn more about printing capabilities in Chapter 7, "Saving, Loading, and Printing Your Documents."

- Context-Sensitive Help—This option tells the MFC AppWizard to add the necessary code to implement Help. A couple of Help menu options will be added to your application when you choose this option.

- 3-D Controls—This option makes your application look like a typical Windows 95 application if you are developing applications for a Windows NT version earlier than 4.0. This option will make your .EXE file larger, so if you are developing for Windows 95 or Windows NT 4.0 or later, you may want to uncheck this option if you are trying to shrink the size of your executable file.

- MAPI (Messaging API)—This option enables your application to use features such as email and faxing. You will learn more about MAPI in Chapter 10, "Enabling Your Applications for the Internet."

- Windows Sockets—Enables your application to access the Internet directly using protocols such as http and ftp. You will learn more about sockets in Chapter 10.

- How Do You Want Your Toolbars to Look?—Here, you can determine how you want your toolbars to look.

- How Many Files Would You Like on Your Recent File List?—This option determines the number of files recently worked on that will be displayed at the end of the File menu.

- Advanced—This button displays the Advanced Options dialog box, as shown in Figure 2.9. In the first tab, Document Template Strings, you see the generated strings that will be used in your application. You can change these strings if you do not like the abbreviations created by the MFC AppWizard.

FIGURE 2.9

The Advanced Options dialog box.

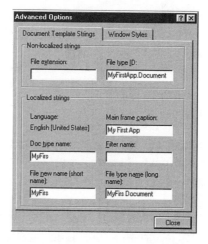

8. If you want to set an associated file type to your application for the options in the File menu, you can specify it in the File extension box. You can change the name displayed in your application's main window by changing the Main frame caption.

9. With the second tab of the Advanced Options dialog box, you can modify the window styles used for your application, as shown in Figure 2.10. When you are done looking at these options, click the Close button to go back to the MFC AppWizard. Because you want to use the default options presented for this example program, click the Next button to proceed.

10. The MFC AppWizard - Step 5 of 6 dialog box, as shown in Figure 2.11, enables you to specify the following options for your application:

FIGURE 2.10

The Window Styles tab of the Advanced Options dialog box.

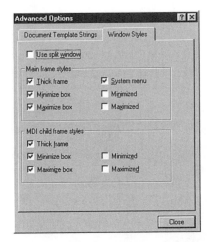

FIGURE 2.11

Choosing the application style.

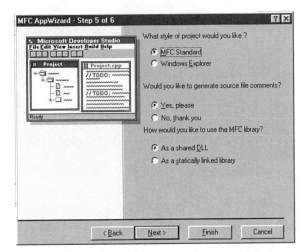

- What Style of Project Would You Like?—This option allows you to specify the appearance of the documents in your application. If you choose Windows Explorer, your child forms will have a splitter bar, just like Explorer.

- Would You Like to Generate Source File Comments?—This option will add comments to the code generated by the MFC AppWizard.

- How Would You Like to Use the MFC Library?—This option will either link to the DLL or use it externally. If you choose to use the linked option, your .EXE will be a little larger, but creating install programs and moving or copying the program will be a little easier. If you choose to use shared option, you will need to distribute the required .DLL files with your application.

11. For this example, you can use the default options, so go ahead and click the Next button to proceed.

12. The MFC AppWizard - Step 6 of 6 dialog box, as shown in Figure 2.12, displays a dialog box listing the classes that it will generate. If you want, you can change the base class used for the view class by changing the Base class option.

FIGURE 2.12

*Confirming the gener-
ated classes.*

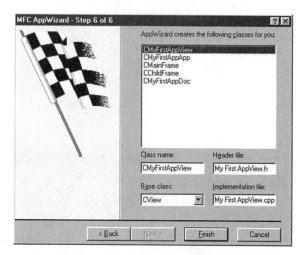

13. For this example, go ahead and use the generated classes. Click the Finish button to build the application framework. After you press the Finish button, you will be presented with a dialog box, such as the one shown in Figure 2.13. This dialog box outlines what the MFC AppWizard will generate.

FIGURE 2.13

*The New Project
Information dialog box.*

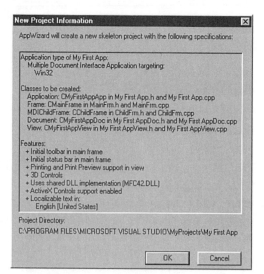

14. When you are ready, go ahead and click the OK button to start the code generation. Depending on your machine, this process can take several minutes to complete. A lot of code and resources are being created, so sit back and watch it go. If you wish to back out, you can always click the Cancel button.

Executing the Example Application

Now that the MFC AppWizard has generated the basic framework for this example application, you can compile and execute it to see what type of application was generated for you. To do this, simply choose Build, Execute My First App.exe from the main menu. A prompt will be displayed telling you that the .EXE doesn't exist. Click Yes to build the .EXE. As the application compiles, you can watch the progress of the compiler in the output area of the workspace. When the application executes, you should have a screen similar to Figure 2.14.

FIGURE 2.14

My First App executed.

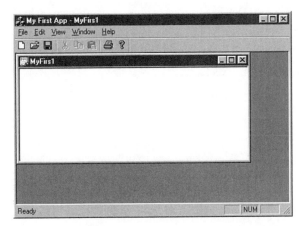

Go ahead and play around with the menu options to see what functionality the MFC AppWizard automatically created for you.

Lesson Summary

In this lesson, you learned how easy it is to create a standard .exe application. By using the MFC AppWizard, you learned that you are only a few mouse-clicks away from creating the necessary framework for your application. With this framework created for you, you can spend more time concentrating on the design of your application rather than worrying about how to implement the features discussed.

Quiz 1

1. Which of the following is an example of an SDI application?

   a. Microsoft Excel

   b. WordPad

   c. Calculator

   d. Microsoft Word

2. How do you include database access in your application while not deriving your view from CFormView and not including the Record menu?

   a. Choose None when selecting database support.

   b. Choose Database view without file support when selecting database support.

   c. Choose Header files only when selecting database support.

   d. Choose Database access with no Record menu when selecting database support.

3. Which of the following is an example of a dialog-based application?

   a. Microsoft Excel

   b. Microsoft Word

   c. Notepad

   d. Calculator

4. Using the MFC AppWizard, where or how can you change the window styles for your application?

   a. Under the Window, Style menu

   b. By choosing an MDI Application

   c. By right-clicking the Window and choosing Styles

   d. Under Advanced Options on Step 4 of 6

Exercise 1

Complexity: Easy

1. Create an MDI application with a project name "Exercise 1." Set up this application so that it does not have printing capabilities.

Complexity: Moderate

2. Create an MDI application with a project name "Exercise 2." Give this application's main caption the title "VC++ 6 MDI Example."

LESSON 2

Creating an SDI Application with the AppWizard

In Lesson 1, you learned how to use the MFC AppWizard to create the framework for your application. In this lesson, you will learn about the Single Document Interface (SDI) type of application. After creating the SDI application, you will examine some of the key elements of the code behind your SDI application.

The most distinguishing feature of an SDI application over an MDI application, which you will learn about in Lesson 3, is the fact that you can only have one document open at a time. In other words, when a user elects to open or create a new document, either the old one will be saved or the changes will be discarded. Therefore, if the type of application you want to create is an application that can only have one document open at a time, an SDI application is what you need.

Creating the SDI Example Application

In order to create an SDI application, you are going to follow some very easy steps. These steps are very similar to the steps in Lesson 1, but because you chose all the default values in Lesson 1, you created an MDI application. In order to create an SDI application, you will need to change one option when using the MFC AppWizard to create the desired application type. Follow these steps:

1. Choose File, New from the main menu to create a new project.
2. Choose MFC AppWizard (exe) from the Projects Type and then click in the Project name edit box and name the project **SDI Example**, as shown in Figure 2.15. Click the OK button when you are ready.

FIGURE 2.15

Naming the sample program.

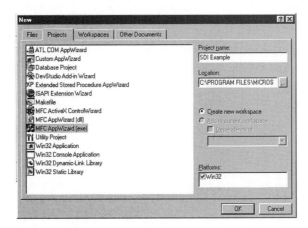

Note

You can name these examples whatever you want, but in order to follow along with the text of this interactive course, you should use the names given, because the project name determines the class names and other internal parts of the application.

3. This is where you determine what type of application you want to create. Because you want to create an SDI application, choose the option to create a Single document application, as shown in Figure 2.16.

FIGURE 2.16

Choosing a Single document application.

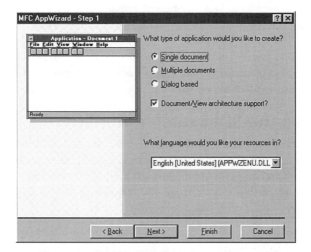

4. Now that you have selected to create a Single document application, (an SDI application), go ahead and click the Finish button, because you don't need to change any other options for this example. You will be prompted with the New Project Information dialog box; just click OK to continue.

After these simple steps, you will have generated an SDI application. If you want, you can build and execute the generated code to view the SDI application that was created for you. If you execute the example, your screen should look similar to Figure 2.17. After you are finished looking at the example application, close it and go back into VC++ 6.

FIGURE 2.17

Executing the SDI example application.

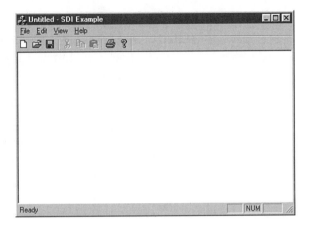

Examining the SDI Example

Using the MFC AppWizard, you have created an SDI application. To examine what was generated for you by this wizard, you start by looking at the generated classes. Inside the Workspace panel in the ClassView tab, you will see SDI Example classes. To see the name of the classes generated, click the plus icon to the left to expand the branch. Once you have done that, you will see the five generated classes:

- CaboutDlg—A dialog class
- CmainFrame—A frame window class
- CSDIExampleApp—An application class
- CSIDExampleDoc—A document class
- CSDIExampleView—A view class

The CAboutDlg Class

This class manages the About dialog box in your application. You will learn more about dialog boxes in Chapter 3, "Increasing User Interaction with Dialog Boxes and Property Sheets."

The CMainFrame Class

The CMainFrame class is derived from the CFrameWnd class, which provides the functionality of an SDI application, along with members for managing the window. The CFrameWnd class provides many functions for a typical Windows application, such as tracking the currently active view, delegating command messages and other frame-notification messages, managing the main menu bar, and managing the position control bars, views, and other child windows inside the frame window's client area.

The `CSDIExampleApp` Class

The `CSDIExampleApp` class is derived from the `CWinApp` class, which is the base class that you derive a Windows application object. Looking at Listing 2.1, you can see some function overrides that the MFC AppWizard has generated.

> **Note**   If you are looking at the source code from inside the Visual C++ 6 editor, you can double-click the `CSDIExampleApp` branch to bring up the SDI Example.h file into the editor area.

LISTING 2.1   The SDI Example.h File

```
// SDI Example.h : main header file for the SDI EXAMPLE application
//

#if !defined(AFX_SDIEXAMPLE_H__6F3D98C5_74B7_
➡11D1_9261_C80709C10000__INCLUDED_)
#define AFX_SDIEXAMPLE_H__6F3D98C5_74B7_
➡11D1_9261_C80709C10000__INCLUDED_

#if _MSC_VER > 1000
#pragma once
#endif // _MSC_VER > 1000

#ifndef __AFXWIN_H__
    #error include 'stdafx.h' before including this file for PCH
#endif

#include "resource.h"        // main symbols

/////////////////////////////////////////////////////////////////////
// CSDIExampleApp:
// See SDI Example.cpp for the implementation of this class
//

class CSDIExampleApp : public CWinApp
{
public:
    CSDIExampleApp();

// Overrides
    // ClassWizard generated virtual function overrides
    //{{AFX_VIRTUAL(CSDIExampleApp)
    public:
    virtual BOOL InitInstance();
    //}}AFX_VIRTUAL
```

```
// Implementation
                            •
    //{{AFX_MSG(CSDIExampleApp)
    afx_msg void OnAppAbout();
        // NOTE - the ClassWizard will add and remove
        // member functions here.
        //     DO NOT EDIT what you see in these blocks of
        //     generated code !
    //}}AFX_MSG
    DECLARE_MESSAGE_MAP()
};


//////////////////////////////////////////////////////////////////

//{{AFX_INSERT_LOCATION}}
// Microsoft Visual C++ will insert additional declarations
// immediately before the previous line.

#endif // !defined(AFX_SDIEXAMPLE_H__6F3D98C5_74B7_
        //   11D1_9261_C80709C10000__INCLUDED_)
```

You should be aware of three key elements that are defined in this header file. The first is the CSDIExampleApp class. This is where the CWinApp class is inherited.

```
class CSDIExampleApp : public CWinApp
```

The second key element of this header file is the overrides. The MFC AppWizard generates this area for virtual ;virtual function overridesfunction overrides.

The AppWizard already has one virtual function overridden: the InitInstance() function, which is used to do several things upon startup of your application, including

- Create the document template.
- Load standard file options from either the Registry or an .INI file.
- Register document templates.
- Process command-line options.

Go ahead and expand the CSDIExampleApp class to reveal the members of that class. Double-click the InitInstance member to bring up this block of code in the code editor. Listing 2.2 shows the actual code listing for the function.

LISTING 2.2 The InitInstance Function

```
/////////////////////////////////////////////////////////////////////
// CSDIExampleApp initialization

BOOL CSDIExampleApp::InitInstance()
{
    AfxEnableControlContainer();

    // Standard initialization
    // If you are not using these features and wish to reduce the
    // size of your final executable, you should remove from the
    // following the specific initialization routines you don't need.

#ifdef _AFXDLL
    Enable3dControls();          // Call this when using MFC
                                 // in a shared DLL
#else
    Enable3dControlsStatic();    // Call this when linking
                                 // to MFC statically
#endif

    // Change the registry key under which our settings are stored.
    // You should modify this string to be something appropriate
    // such as the name of your company or organization.
    SetRegistryKey(_T("Local AppWizard-Generated Applications"));

    LoadStdProfileSettings();  // Load standard INI
                               // file options (including MRU)

    // Register the application's document templates.  Document
    // templates serve as the connection between documents,
    // frame windows, and views.

    CSingleDocTemplate* pDocTemplate;
    pDocTemplate = new CSingleDocTemplate(
        IDR_MAINFRAME,
        RUNTIME_CLASS(CSDIExampleDoc),
        RUNTIME_CLASS(CMainFrame),        // main SDI frame window
        RUNTIME_CLASS(CSDIExampleView));
    AddDocTemplate(pDocTemplate);

    // Parse command line for standard shell commands, DDE, file open
    CCommandLineInfo cmdInfo;
    ParseCommandLine(cmdInfo);

    // Dispatch commands specified on the command line
    if (!ProcessShellCommand(cmdInfo))
        return FALSE;

    // The one and only window has been initialized,
```

```
        // so show and update it.
        m_pMainWnd->ShowWindow(SW_SHOW);
        m_pMainWnd->UpdateWindow();

        return TRUE;
}
```

The last key element that was generated by the AppWizard is the message map. Listing 2.3 shows you the message map generated by the MFC AppWizard. *Message maps* designate which functions will handle various messages for a particular class. You will learn more about this topic in Chapter 5, "Processing Windows Messages and Commands."

LISTING 2.3 The Message Map for the SDI Example Application

```
/////////////////////////////////////////////////////////////////////
// CSDIExampleApp

BEGIN_MESSAGE_MAP(CSDIExampleApp, CWinApp)
    //{{AFX_MSG_MAP(CSDIExampleApp)
    ON_COMMAND(ID_APP_ABOUT, OnAppAbout)
        // NOTE - the ClassWizard will add and remove mapping
        // macros here.
        //    DO NOT EDIT what you see in these blocks of
        //    generated code!
    //}}AFX_MSG_MAP
    // Standard file based document commands
    ON_COMMAND(ID_FILE_NEW, CWinApp::OnFileNew)
    ON_COMMAND(ID_FILE_OPEN, CWinApp::OnFileOpen)
    // Standard print setup command
    ON_COMMAND(ID_FILE_PRINT_SETUP, CWinApp::OnFilePrintSetup)
END_MESSAGE_MAP()
```

The `CSDIExampleDoc` Class

The `CSDIExampleDoc` Class is derived from the `CDocument` class, which provides the basic functionality for a user-defined document class. A document is usually described as the data that the user loads, saves, and prints from the File menu. You will learn more about working with documents in Chapter 7.

The `CSDIExampleView` Class

The `CSDIExampleView` Class is derived from the `CView` class, which provides the basic functionality for a user-defined view class. The view is responsible for rendering an image of the document on the screen or printer, while interpreting user input on the document. You will learn more about working with views in Chapter 7.

Lesson Summary

In this lesson, you learned how easy it is to create an SDI application, which is the basic functionality of an SDI application, and the core components of an SDI application—the classes.

Quiz 2

1. Which of the following is a generated class in the SDI Example application?

    a. `CMDIExampleApp`

    b. `CSDIDialogExampleClass`

    c. `CSDIExampleApp`

    d. `CAboutVC6Class`

2. By choosing the default options when building an SDI application, how many classes are generated for you?

    a. 4

    b. 3

    c. 6

    d. 5

3. Which class in the SDI Example application is derived from the `CDoc` class?

    a. `CSDIExampleApp`

    b. `CSDIExampleDoc`

    c. `CSDIExampleView`

    d. `CSDIExampleDocClass`

4. Which statement is true about the `CExampleApp` class?

    a. This class handles the presentation of the view.

    b. This class contains the `InitInstance` function.

    c. This class tracks the currently active application.

    d. This class is derived from the `CMainFrame` class.

Exercise 2

Complexity: Easy

1. Create an SDI application with a project name of "Exercise 1." Make this project style look like the style used in Explorer.

Complexity: Moderate

2. Create an SDI application with a project name of "Exercise 2." Derive the base class for this project from the CHtmlView class rather than the CView class.

2

LESSON 3

Creating an MDI Application with the AppWizard

In Lesson 2, you learned how to use the MFC AppWizard to create an SDI application. In this lesson, you will learn about the (MDI) type of application. An MDI application is very similar to an SDI application, with one major difference: Your application can have more than one document open at a time, whereas an SDI application can only have one document open at a time.

After creating an MDI application with the MFC AppWizard, you will examine some of the key elements of the code behind your MDI application, and you will notice that there really isn't much of a difference between an MDI application and an SDI application.

Creating the MDI Example Application

You've already created an MDI Application; you just didn't examine the actual program. In Lesson 1 of this chapter where you created your first Visual C++ 6 application, you followed a series of steps, selecting the default options along the way. By choosing the default options in the MFC AppWizard, you created an MDI Application.

In order to follow along with this lesson, you will need to create another MDI application, this time giving it an appropriate name. Do this by following these steps:

1. Choose File, New from the main menu to create a new project.

2. Choose MFC AppWizard (exe) from the Projects Type and then click in the Project name edit box and name the project **MDI Example**, as shown in Figure 2.18. Click the OK button when you are ready.

3. This is where you determine what type of application you want to create. Because you want to create an MDI application, you don't need to change any options here, as the default is Multiple Documents, as shown in Figure 2.19.

FIGURE 2.18

Naming the sample program.

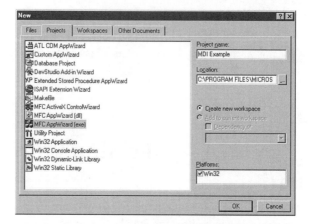

FIGURE 2.19

Choosing a multiple document application.

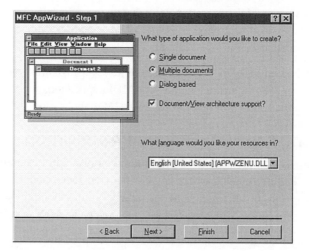

4. Now that you have elected to create an MDI application, go ahead and click the Finish button because you don't need to change any other options for this example. You will be prompted with the New Project Information dialog box; just click OK to continue.

After these simple steps, you will have generated an MDI application. If you want, you can build and execute the generated code to view the MDI application that was created for you. If you execute the example, your screen should look similar to Figure 2.20. After you are finished looking at the example application, close it and go back into VC++ 6.

FIGURE 2.20

Executing the MDI Example application.

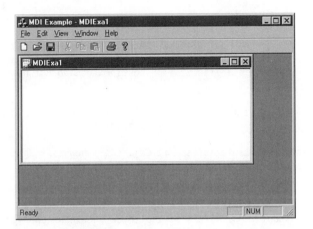

Examining the MDI Example

Once you have expanded the MDI Example classes branch of the MDI Example application, you will notice that the classes are named similarly to those of the SDI example, just preceded with MDI rather than SDI. For the most part, the classes are the same as those in the SDI example but with a couple of internal differences. One of the most notable differences is the addition of the CMDIChildFrame class, which is derived from the CMDIChildWnd class.

The CMDIChildWnd class provides the functionality of an MDI child window. An MDI child window appears inside an MDI frame window and looks like a normal window. The child window does not have its own menu—it shares the MDI application frame menu.

The other differences are not so noticeable. You will have to examine the generated code to see the difference. The most distinguishing differences are in the InitInstance() function of the CMDIExampleApp class. Listing 2.4 is the InitInstance() function from the SDI application and Listing 2.5 is the InitInstance() function from the MDI application. Can you spot the differences?

LISTING 2.4 The SDI's InitInstance() Function

```
/////////////////////////////////////////////////////////////////
// CSDIExampleApp initialization

BOOL CSDIExampleApp::InitInstance()
{
    AfxEnableControlContainer();

    // Standard initialization
```

continues

LISTING 2.4 continued

```
    // If you are not using these features and wish to reduce the size
    // of your final executable, you should remove from the following
    // the specific initialization routines you do not need.

#ifdef _AFXDLL
    Enable3dControls();        // Call this when using MFC
                               // in a shared DLL
#else
    Enable3dControlsStatic();  // Call this when linking to MFC
                               // statically
#endif

    // Change the registry key under which our settings are stored.
    // You should modify this string to be something appropriate
    // such as the name of your company or organization.
    SetRegistryKey(_T("Local AppWizard-Generated Applications"));

    LoadStdProfileSettings();  // Load standard INI file
                               // options (including MRU)

    // Register the application's document templates.  Document
    // templates serve as the connection between documents,
    // frame windows, and views.

    CSingleDocTemplate* pDocTemplate;
    pDocTemplate = new CSingleDocTemplate(
        IDR_MAINFRAME,
        RUNTIME_CLASS(CSDIExampleDoc),
        RUNTIME_CLASS(CMainFrame),        // main SDI frame window
        RUNTIME_CLASS(CSDIExampleView));
    AddDocTemplate(pDocTemplate);

    // Parse command line for standard shell commands, DDE, file open
    CCommandLineInfo cmdInfo;
    ParseCommandLine(cmdInfo);

    // Dispatch commands specified on the command line
    if (!ProcessShellCommand(cmdInfo))
        return FALSE;

    // The one and only window has been initialized,
    // so show and update it.
    m_pMainWnd->ShowWindow(SW_SHOW);
    m_pMainWnd->UpdateWindow();

    return TRUE;
}
```

LISTING 2.5 The MDI `InitInstance()` Function

```cpp
/////////////////////////////////////////////////////////////////////
// CMDIExampleApp initialization

BOOL CMDIExampleApp::InitInstance()
{
    AfxEnableControlContainer();

    // Standard initialization
    // If you are not using these features and wish to reduce the size
    //  of your final executable, you should remove from the following
    //  the specific initialization routines you do not need.

#ifdef _AFXDLL
    Enable3dControls();         // Call this when using MFC
                                // in a shared DLL
#else
    Enable3dControlsStatic();   // Call this when linking to MFC
                                // statically
#endif

    // Change the registry key under which our settings are stored.
    // You should modify this string to be something appropriate
    // such as the name of your company or organization.
    SetRegistryKey(_T("Local AppWizard-Generated Applications"));

    LoadStdProfileSettings();  // Load standard INI
                               // file options (including MRU)

    // Register the application's document templates.  Document
    // templates serve as the connection between documents,
    // frame windows, and views.

    CMultiDocTemplate* pDocTemplate;
    pDocTemplate = new CMultiDocTemplate(
        IDR_MDIEXATYPE,
        RUNTIME_CLASS(CMDIExampleDoc),
        RUNTIME_CLASS(CChildFrame), // custom MDI child frame
        RUNTIME_CLASS(CMDIExampleView));
    AddDocTemplate(pDocTemplate);

    // create main MDI Frame window
    CMainFrame* pMainFrame = new CMainFrame;
    if (!pMainFrame->LoadFrame(IDR_MAINFRAME))
        return FALSE;
    m_pMainWnd = pMainFrame;

    // Parse command line for standard shell commands, DDE, file open
    CCommandLineInfo cmdInfo;
```

continues

LISTING 2.5 continued

```
ParseCommandLine(cmdInfo);

// Dispatch commands specified on the command line
if (!ProcessShellCommand(cmdInfo))
    return FALSE;

// The main window has been initialized, so show and update it.
pMainFrame->ShowWindow(m_nCmdShow);
pMainFrame->UpdateWindow();

return TRUE;
}
```

In case you didn't spot the major differences right away, here is a list:

- CMultiDocTemplate is set up in the MDI application, and a CSingleDoc is set up in the SDI application. You will learn more about these in Chapter 7.

- The MDI application creates the main frame window and then displays it, whereas the SDI application does not. Here is that bit of code that is not included in the SDI application:

```
// create main MDI Frame window
    CMainFrame* pMainFrame = new CMainFrame;
    if (!pMainFrame->LoadFrame(IDR_MAINFRAME))
        return FALSE;
    m_pMainWnd = pMainFrame;
```

- The MDI application also includes the ChildFrm.h header file, whereas the SDI application does not.

Lesson Summary

In this lesson, you learned that there really isn't much of a difference in the setup in MDI application and an SDI application. A lot of the code differences are handled for you in the different classes, which makes working with documents and views a lot easier.

Quiz 3

1. Which class provides the functionality of an MDI child window?

   a. CDocumentView

   b. CMDIExampleWindow

   c. CMDIChildWnd

   d. CMDIChildWindow

2. Which header file is included in an MDI application that isn't included in an SDI application?

    a. MDIFrame.h

    b. StdFrame.h

    c. ChildWnd.h

    d. ChildFrm.h

3. Which statement is true about MDI applications?

    a. You are limited to one document open at a time.

    b. A CSingleDoc is set up in the InitInstance() function.

    c. You can work with multiple documents at once.

    d. The CAboutDlg class contains a special MDI About dialog box.

4. Which of the following is true when comparing an MDI application to an SDI application?

    a. The MDI application creates the main frame window and then displays it whereas the SDI application does not.

    b. Both an SDI and an MDI application have only five classes generated through the MFC AppWizard.

    c. The ChildFrm.h class is included in both an SDI and an MDI application by default.

    d. Both application types use the CMultiDocTemplate class.

Exercise 3

Complexity: Easy

1. Create an MDI application with a project name of "Exercise 1." Set up this application so that no docking toolbar is provided.

Complexity: Moderate

2. Create an MDI application with a project name of "Exercise 2." Set up this application so that it has preliminary database support. The application should not have a Record menu.

LESSON 4

Creating a Dialog Application with the AppWizard

Now that you have learned how to create applications that work with single and multiple documents, you will learn how to create an application that doesn't use documents or views. Therefore, dialog-based applications are much simpler than SDI or MDI applications.

Creating the Dialog Example Application

In order to learn about dialog-based applications, you will need to create a dialog-based application using the MFC AppWizard. To do this, you will need to follow a couple of steps that you have already become very familiar with:

1. Choose File, New from the main menu to create a new project.

2. Choose MFC AppWizard (exe) from the Projects Type and then click in the Project Name edit box and name the project **Dialog Example**, as shown in Figure 2.21. Click the OK button when you are ready.

FIGURE 2.21

Naming the dialog example program.

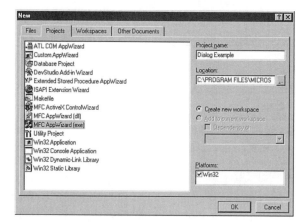

3. This is where you determine what type of application you want to create. Because you want to create a dialog-based application, you will need to select Dialog Based from the three choices, as shown in Figure 2.22.

FIGURE 2.22

Choosing a dialog-based application.

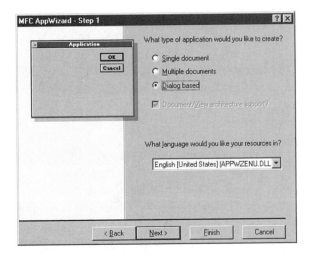

4. Now that you have elected to create a dialog-based application, go ahead and click the Finish button, because you don't need to change any other options for this example. You will be prompted with the New Project Information dialog box; just click OK to continue.

You have just created the framework for a dialog-based Windows application. After the project is built, you will be presented with the new project. When you are presented with the project, what looks like a normal dialog box will be presented in the editor area, as shown in Figure 2.23.

FIGURE 2.23

The project workspace while working with dialog boxes.

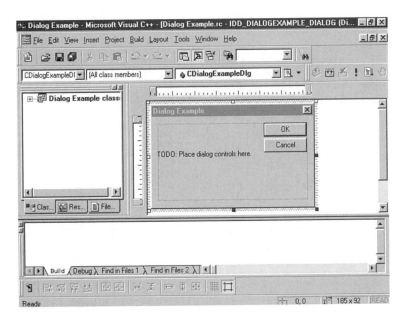

When you build and execute the Dialog Example application, all you will see is a normal dialog window in the center of the screen with a label and two buttons, as shown in Figure 2.24. You will notice that you can click the OK or the Cancel button to close the dialog box. The reason that the Dialog Example application closes is because you have not programmed any real functionality into the dialog box. When you press one of the default buttons, either the IDOK or IDCANCEL identifier will be returned, depending on which button you pressed.

FIGURE 2.24

Running the Dialog Example application.

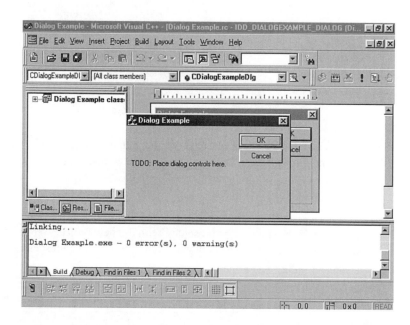

Examining the Dialog Example Application Code

To examine some of the code differences between an SDI or MDI application, you can click the ClassView tab of the Workspace panel and then expand the Dialog Example classes branch. You will notice that the MFC AppWizard generated only three classes:

- CAboutDlg
- CDialogExampleApp
- CDialogExampleDlg

You will learn more about dialog classes in Chapter 3. To show you the difference between the generated code for SDI and MDI applications against a dialog-based application, however, you will examine the InitInstance() function of the CDialogExampleApp class, as shown in Listing 2.6.

LISTING 2.6 The `InitInstance()` Function of a Dialog-Based Application

```
/////////////////////////////////////////////////////////////////
// CDialogExampleApp initialization

BOOL CDialogExampleApp::InitInstance()
{
    AfxEnableControlContainer();

    // Standard initialization
    // If you are not using these features and wish to reduce the size
    // of your final executable, you should remove from the following
    // the specific initialization routines you do not need.

#ifdef _AFXDLL
    Enable3dControls();         // Call this when using MFC
                                // in a shared DLL
#else
    Enable3dControlsStatic();   // Call this when linking to MFC
                                // statically
#endif

    CDialogExampleDlg dlg;
    m_pMainWnd = &dlg;
    int nResponse = dlg.DoModal();
    if (nResponse == IDOK)
    {
        // TODO: Place code here to handle when the dialog is
        //  dismissed with OK
    }
    else if (nResponse == IDCANCEL)
    {
        // TODO: Place code here to handle when the dialog is
        //  dismissed with Cancel
    }

    // Since the dialog has been closed, return FALSE so that we exit
    // the application rather than start the application's message pump
    return FALSE;
}
```

The `InitInstance()` function of a dialog-based application starts by enabling the 3-D controls. Next, an instance of the dialog box is declared and then shown to the user. If the user clicks the OK button from the dialog box, it returns IDOK, or if the user clicks the Cancel button, the dialog box will return IDCANCEL.

If you were to look back at Listing 2.4 and Listing 2.5 of the previous lesson, you will also notice that no documents or views were created, just the dialog box. Upon further examination, you will notice that the last line of code for the dialog-based application has a return value of False from the `InitIntance()` function. Dialog applications return False from this function to close the application, whereas an SDI or MDI application returns True telling the application that everything initialized properly.

You can edit the application dialog box just like you would any other dialog box. In order to do this, just click the Resource View tab of the Workspace panel and expand the Dialog branch of Dialog Example Resources. You can then double-click the `IDD_DIALOGEXAMPLE_DIALOG` to edit the dialog box.

When you created the Dialog Example application, the AppWizard generated three controls on the main dialog box. The first two controls are buttons that allow the user either to process options passed through the dialog box when the OK button was clicked or to dismiss any options when the Cancel button is clicked. The Dialog Example application has no real functionality, so either way the dialog application ends when either button is clicked. The third control is a static text control, which was placed on the dialog box to inform you, the developer, that you need to add some sort of functionality to the dialog box to make it a worthwhile application. You will learn more about dialog boxes in Chapter 3.

To examine the default controls that were generated, you will examine the static text control. Each control on the dialog box has associated properties. You can view the properties for a control by right-clicking the desired control and choosing Properties from the context menu. Go ahead and do this for the static text control. You should be presented with the Text Properties dialog box, as shown in Figure 2.25.

FIGURE 2.25

The properties dialog box of the text control.

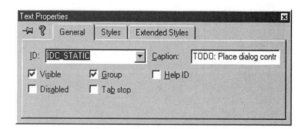

This property editor has three tabs, each of which will allow you to change certain aspects of the text control:

- General
- Styles
- Extended Styles

This first tab allows you to change the ID and the Caption properties, along with a couple other properties. The two major properties on this page are the ID and Caption properties. You can change the text displayed by changing the caption property. The last two tabs of the static text control will allow you to change the appearance of the text.

Lesson Summary

In this lesson, you learned how to use the MFC AppWizard to create a basic framework for a dialog-based application. You also examined the InitInstance() function to see what was different from an SDI and an MDI application, and you learned that each control on the dialog box has properties that determine the look and behavior of the control.

Quiz 4

1. Which statement is true about dialog-based applications?

    a. They can have only one document open at a time.

    b. They can have multiple documents open at a time.

    c. They don't use documents or views.

    d. They are derived from the CDialogView class.

2. In the Dialog Example application, what is the return value for the InitInstance() function?

    a. IDOK

    b. False

    c. True

    d. IDCancel

3. Which of the following methods can be used to view the properties of a control?

    a. Right-click the control and select Properties from the context menu.

    b. Click the control and press the F1 key.

    c. Click the control and choose Control, Properties from the File menu.

    d. Right-click the control and select Options from the context menu.

4. In the InitInstance() function of the Dialog Example application, what call is made to show the dialog box?

    a. int nResponse = dlg.ShowDialog();

    b. CDialogExampleDlg dlg.DoModal;

    c. m_pMainWnd = &dlg;

    d. int nResponse = dlg.DoModal();

Exercise 4

Complexity: Easy

1. Create a new dialog program named "Exercise 1." Once created, change the caption of the static text on the main dialog box to "Hello Interactive World."

Complexity: Moderate

2. Create a new dialog program named "Exercise 2." Once created, add a new button to the main dialog box. Give this button an ID of "IDC_ABOUTBUTTON" and a caption of "About."

LESSON 5

Other Applications You Can Create with the AppWizard

In the previous lessons, you learned about the three typical applications that you would create using the MFC AppWizard. Times exist, though, when you will need to create a different type of application that you can't create using those styles. This lesson will give you a brief description of the other types of applications that you can easily create using the MFC AppWizard.

To see what types of applications you can create with the MFC AppWizard, go ahead and close any workspaces that you may have open and then choose File, New. You will be presented with the New dialog box, as shown in Figure 2.26. This dialog box lets you select the type of project you want to create.

FIGURE 2.26

The different project types through AppWizard.

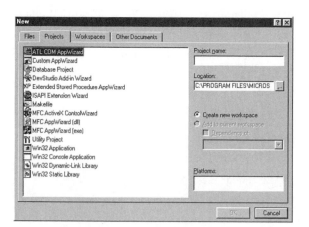

You can create 15 different project types with the MFC AppWizard:

- ATL COM AppWizard
- Custom AppWizard
- Database Project
- DevStudio Add-in Wizard
- Extended Stored Procedure Wizard
- ISAPI Extension Wizard
- Makefile
- MFC ActiveX ControlWizard
- MFC AppWizard (dll)
- MFC AppWizard (exe)
- Utility Project
- Win32 Application
- Win32 Console Application
- Win32 Dynamic-Link Library
- Win32 Static Library

ATL COM AppWizard

The Active Template Library (ATL) AppWizard creates ActiveX controls. You will learn more about creating ActiveX controls in Chapter 9.

Custom AppWizard

Although the MFC AppWizard can quickly create a basic framework for an application, there may be a time when you need to provide a wizard that allows you to create an application with your own custom features that the MFC AppWizard can't provide. If this is the case, you can create a custom AppWizard yourself.

Custom AppWizards are very useful when you need to create applications that use common functions. Just like the MFC AppWizard, you can present the user with choices that help generate the code, resources, and project files necessary for your basic application framework.

Database Project

You will learn about creating and managing databases in Chapter 11.

DevStudio Add-In Wizard

The DevStudio Add-In Wizard allows you to automate Developer Studio. With add-ins, you can automate routine tasks. For example, you could create an add-in that updates a project by opening the project, modifying some code, and then closing the project. By using OLE automation, the Visual C++ 6 environment and its components become objects that can be programmed.

Extended Stored Procedure AppWizard

The Extended Stored Procedure AppWizard will allow you to create an extended stored procedure. After the wizard obtains the project name, it will create a COM DLL with an exposed function named after the new extended stored procedure. Once this function is deployed and installed on an SQL server, it will return a rowset.

ISAPI Extension Wizard

The *ISAPI* (*Internet Server API*) server extension is a DLL that can be called by an HTTP server. You can use these extensions to add to the capabilities of an ISAPI-compliant server to your applications. You will learn more about ISAPI in Chapter 10.

Makefile

A Makefile project allows you to create a project that uses a different make utility than the one provided by Visual C++ 6. This type of project does not generate any code.

MFC ActiveX ControlWizard

You can use the MFC ActiveX ControlWizard to create ActiveX controls. You will learn more about creating ActiveX controls in Chapter 9.

MFC AppWizard (dll)

The MFC AppWizard (dll) will allow you to build a .DLL that contains a collection of functions that use MFC classes. This .DLL will act as a shared library of functions that can be used by multiple applications.

MFC AppWizard (exe)

You are already familiar with the MFC AppWizard. You can use this wizard to create a framework for SDI, MDI, or dialog-based applications.

Utility Project

A Utility Project does not add any files to your project nor does it create any type of pre-determined output, such as an .EXE, a .DLL, or a .LIB. A utility project can be used as a container for files that you can build without a link step.

Win32 Application

The Win32 Application wizard will generate the necessary framework for a Win32 application without using any MFC classes.

Win32 Console Application

The Win32 Console Application wizard will allow you to create a console application. A console application is an application that doesn't use mouse movement; rather, it uses the cursors. It looks very similar to a DOS application, and it uses a fixed font. You can also do normal input and output, such as `scanf()` and `printf()`.

Win32 Dynamic-Link Library

A Win32 DLL is a collection of functions that do not use MFC. If you need MFC or a framework, use the MFC AppWizard (dll) wizard.

Win32 Static Library

The difference between a Win32 DLL and a static library is that the DLL is linked into your executable file. If you want to distribute your application without having to distribute your functions in a separate DLL file, you should use a static library. Generally, executable files with DLL linked statically are larger in size. This is usually the case, because not all of the functionality of the DLL was used.

Lesson Summary

In this lesson, you learned briefly about the different types of projects that you can create with wizards. Although you will generally use the MFC AppWizard, at some time, you may need to create one of these other projects.

Quiz 5

1. Which wizard allows you to automate Developer Studio?
    a. DevStudio Macro Wizard
    b. DevStudio Add-in Wizard
    c. MFC Add-in Wizard
    d. DevStudio MFC AppWizard

2. Which of the following wizards will allow you to create an ActiveX control?
    a. MFC ActiveX ControlWizard
    b. ActiveX DLL ControlWizard
    c. ActiveX CtlWizard
    d. MFC AppWizard (ActiveX)

3. Which of the following wizards can you use to create a basic SDI application?
    a. MFC ActiveX ControlWizard
    b. Win32 Console Application

    c. DevStudio Add-in Wizard

    d. MFC AppWizard (exe)

4. Which wizard enables you to create a project that uses a different make utility?

    a. MFC AppWizard (dll)

    b. Makefile

    c. Database Project

    d. MFC ActiveX ControlWizard

Exercise 5

Complexity: Easy

1. Using the appropriate new project wizard, create a Win32 Application that is created like a typical Hello World application. Name this application "Exercise 1."

Complexity: Moderate

2. Modify the previous exercise so that the application displays "Hello Interactive World" rather than "Hello World." Name this application "Exercise 2."

Chapter Summary

This chapter was very important in learning about Visual C++ 6. In this chapter, you learned how to create the basic framework for three of the major application styles. You first started by creating a simple SDI application. You learned that these styles of applications will allow the user to work with only one document at a time.

After learning how to create an SDI application, you progressed, learning how to create an MDI application. You learned that an MDI application would allow a user to work with multiple applications at a time. You then examined dialog-based applications. You learned that dialog-based applications are very different from the SDI and MDI document style applications. While learning about these application types, you learned about their functional differences.

CHAPTER 3

Increasing User Interaction with Dialog Boxes and Property Sheets

Using dialog boxes and property sheets in your application is one of the most common ways of conveying and retrieving information from a user. This chapter will introduce to you the concepts of dialog boxes and property sheets and then demonstrate how to create and use them in your applications.

The key elements of this chapter will be using the dialog resource editor to build your resources and then using the ClassWizard to link your dialog resources to classes. Adding member variables and functions to these classes will be discussed as well.

LESSON 1

Creating Dialog Box Resources

When you create a dialog boxes resource, you are generally trying to accomplish one of two things: displaying information to users or asking them to provide information. Common uses are dialog boxes that display an error message, let the user set program options, or ask the user for specific input. Your dialog boxes resource should always have a specific purpose.

Visual C++ 6 has made creating dialog boxes resources very easy and intuitive. The steps involved with creating a dialog resource are minimal, but the code you add can be as simple or complex as you need.

Examining a Dialog Resource

Because you will be examining a dialog resource, you will need to create a new application. At this point, create a new SDI application with the name "Dialog Example." If you need help creating the SDI application, you can refer to Chapter 2, "Your First Interactive Visual C++ Applications." Go ahead and use all the default settings (making sure to select SDI).

Once you have created the application, click the Resource View tab in the Project Workspace. This will display the list of resources defined for this application. Expand the Dialog branch of the resource tree. Figure 3.1 shows the Resource view expanded, indicating that VC++ 6 has already created a dialog resource for you: IDD_ABOUTBOX. This is the dialog resource that you will be examining.

FIGURE 3.1

Resource view expanded to show dialog resources.

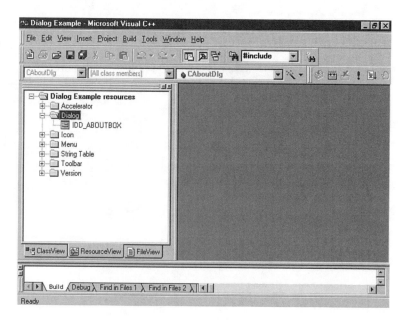

Let's examine the IDD_ABOUTBOX resource that was automatically created for you. To display the dialog editor for a resource, simply double-click the resource. Go ahead and double-click the IDD_ABOUTBOX resource. Figure 3.2 shows the dialog editor with the IDD_ABOUTBOX resource.

FIGURE 3.2

Dialog editor for IDD_ABOUTBOX.

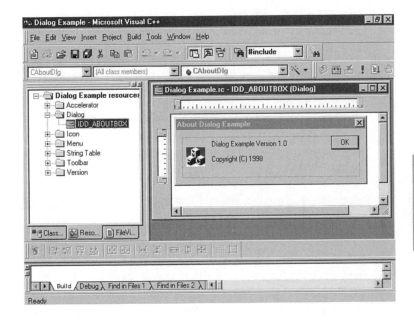

When looking at the dialog editor, you will notice that the purpose of IDD_ABOUTBOX is quite simple. It's an about box that by default shows the program's name, its version, and a copyright statement. This dialog box's sole purpose is to display some information to the user about the program.

Go ahead and click the different items in the dialog editor. You will notice that as you select an element such as the OK button, it receives focus. Selecting an element in this manner tells the dialog editor that the changes you are making are for this element.

Each of these elements are called *controls*. VC++ 6 has defined a palette of several controls that you can use to create dialog resources. Each control has its specific function and represents or collects data from the user in its own way. Some controls are even used in combination with other controls simply for visual effectiveness. Each of these controls will have properties and classes associated with it that will define and perform its functionality. These controls are usually referred to as *common controls*.

In the IDD_ABOUTBOX resource, a total of four different controls are being utilized, one of which is used twice. The small graphic that looks like an icon is a picture control. The two lines of text are text controls, and the OK button is a button control.

You can set a control's basic properties by right-clicking the control and selecting properties from the pop-up context menu.

When creating dialog boxes resources, VC++ 6 has two toolbars that aid in the development process, the Dialog and Controls toolbars.

The Dialog toolbar tests and controls the visual aspects of your dialog box, such as control alignment and spacing, whereas the Controls toolbar houses the collection of common controls that you can add to your dialog box.

To display these toolbars, right-click either a toolbar that already exists or an empty space in the editor area to bring up the pop-up context menu that displays available toolbars. In the list of available toolbars, look for Dialog or Controls. Toggle the checkmark on the left to display and hide the toolbars.

Adding Your Own Dialog Box Resources

You can create your own dialog box resources in several ways. You can right-click the Dialog branch in the Resource view to see the pop-up context menu and select Insert to bring up the Insert Resource dialog box. You will then be prompted for the kind of resource to add to your application. On the same context menu, you could select Insert Dialog, which would immediately add the default dialog resource to your application. Another method would be to select the Resource menu item from the Insert menu. This would bring up the Insert Resource dialog box as well. Figure 3.3 shows the Insert Resource dialog box.

FIGURE 3.3

The Insert Resource dialog box.

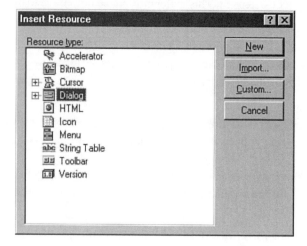

Go ahead and use one of the methods mentioned to add a dialog resource. If you use the Insert Resource dialog box, you will need to select Dialog from the tree and click the New button. Figure 3.4 shows the new dialog resource that was created for us.

FIGURE 3.4

*The newly created
Dialog resource.*

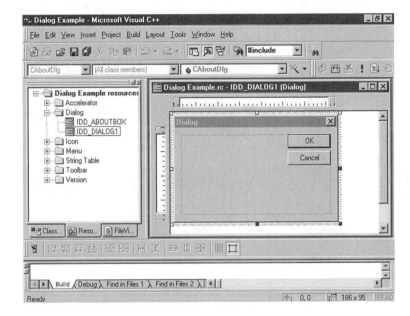

Looking at the dialog box, you'll notice that it is very basic. The only controls created for us were two buttons. Typically, most of your dialog boxes will have at least two buttons, one for OK and one for Cancel. The OK button indicates that the user accepts what the dialog box is displaying, and Cancel indicates that the user does not agree or that the changes made in the dialog box are not to be kept.

In order to examine the settings you can make for this dialog box, right-click an empty space in the dialog box and select properties from the pop-up context menu to display the Dialog Properties dialog box, shown in Figure 3.5. Click the push-pin in the top-left corner of the properties dialog box to force it to stay on top of the screen.

FIGURE 3.5

*The Dialog Properties
dialog box.*

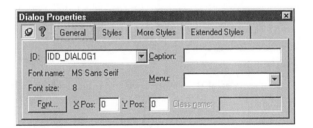

Looking at the Dialog Properties box, you will notice four tabs of properties that can be set: General, Styles, More Styles, and Extended Styles.

General

- ID—The resource ID that identifies this dialog box
- Font Name—The font that will be used in all of the controls for this dialog box
- Font Size—The point size for the font being used for controls in the dialog box
- X Pos—The x-coordinate for the dialog box
- Y Pos—The y-coordinate for the dialog box
- Caption—The text that is displayed in the title bar of the caption
- Menu—If a menu is being used for this dialog box, this is the resource ID of the menu resource
- Class Name—A C++ class name for this dialog box (this is disabled for MFC resources)

Styles

- Style—The type of window that will be created, a choice of overlapped, pop-up, or child
- Border—The type of border drawn on the dialog box, a choice of None, Thin, Resizing, or Dialog Frame
- Title Bar—Toggles display of the title bar
- System Menu—Toggles creation of the system menu for the dialog box
- Minimize Box—Toggles creation of the minimize button for the dialog box
- Maximize Box—Toggles creation of the maximize button for the dialog box
- Clip Siblings—Controls repainting of overlapped windows
- Clip Children—Excludes child window area when drawing the parent window
- Horizontal Scroll—Toggles a horizontal scroll bar on the dialog box
- Vertical Scroll—Toggles a vertical scroll bar on the dialog box

More Styles

- System Modal—When selected and the dialog box is visible, the user will not be able to switch to another window or program.
- Absolute Align—Toggles whether the dialog box is aligned from the top-left corner of the screen or of its parent window. When selected, the top-left corner of the screen is used.

- Visible—Toggles whether the dialog box is visible when it is first displayed
- Disabled—Toggles whether the dialog box is initially disabled when first displayed
- Context Help—Toggles the question mark in the title bar
- Set Foreground—Brings the dialog box to the foreground automatically
- 3D-look—Toggles default 3-D effects for the dialog box (a non-bold font and 3D borders on controls and the dialog box)
- No Fail Create—Toggles whether the dialog box should be created even if an error occurs
- No Idle Message—Toggles whether the WM_ENTERIDLE message is sent to a dialog box's parent when the dialog box's message queue contains no more messages
- Control—Toggles creation of a dialog box that works as a child of another dialog box
- Center—Toggles automatic centering of the dialog box in the workspace area of the desktop
- Center Mouse—Toggles automatic centering of the mouse in the dialog box
- Local Edit—Forces edit box controls for this dialog box to use memory in the application's data segment (normally memory outside the application's data segment is used)

Extended Styles

- Tool Window—Creates the dialog box as a window with a smaller title bar and font
- Client Edge—Creates a border with a sunken edge
- Static Edge—Creates a standard border around the dialog box
- Transparent—Allows windows below this dialog box to show through this dialog box
- Accept Files—Allows files to be dropped on the dialog box
- Control Parent—Allows navigation of child windows
- Context Help—Toggles the question mark in the title bar
- No Parent Notify—Turns off child windows sending a WM_PARENT_NOTIFY message
- Right-to-Left Reading Order—Displays text in right-to-left order (used for languages such as Hebrew)
- Right Aligned Text—Aligns text to the right
- Left Scroll Bar—Places the vertical scroll bar on the left (if present)

Depending upon the needs of your dialog box, you can change the look and feel of your dialog box by simply modifying the properties.

To make the dialog box show some sort of customization, go ahead and enter **Interactive Dialog Example** into the caption property for the dialog box. You will notice that as you type in the caption, the dialog box resource immediately reflects your entry.

Because you can quite possibly have numerous dialog boxes and other resources within your application, you should give your resources a good resource ID. Looking at the current resource ID, you will notice that its ID is IDD_DIALOG1. Even though this resource ID is functional, it's not really descriptive. As a convention, the first three characters, *IDD*, should not be changed. These letters will let you organize all of your dialog boxes so that when you look them up in an alphabetical list, they will be grouped together.

Use the ID IDD_DLGEXAMPLE for this resource. To change it, all you need to do is change the ID property and press Enter. Figure 3.6 shows the entered caption and descriptive resource ID.

FIGURE 3.6

The caption and ID properties for the dialog resource.

Also notice that in the Resource view, the dialog resource has been added to the list using its resource ID.

These are the only properties you will be changing for the dialog box itself. Go ahead and close the Dialog Properties dialog box.

Now that you have an actual dialog resource of your own, VC++ 6 has built in a mechanism for testing the controls to make sure they appear just how you want them. To test your dialog box, either select the Test menu item from the Layout menu or click the Test button on the Dialog toolbar (the one that looks like a light switch). Figure 3.7 shows what your dialog box should look like in test mode.

Before you start adding controls to the dialog box, you need to take a look at what controls are available on the Controls toolbar and what each one's primary function is. In the next lesson, you will actually add some controls to the dialog resource. If the Controls toolbar is not visible, select it from the toolbars context menu to display it. To see what each control is, hover your mouse above each control for a few seconds and a tool tip will tell you the name of the control. The controls are as follows:

FIGURE 3.7

Testing your dialog box.

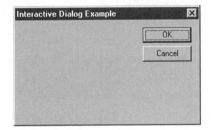

Controls Toolbar

- Picture—Displays a graphic image, such as the image in an about box
- Static Text—Displays a text message, such as the copyright message in an about box
- Edit Box—Obtains input from a user; can be any standard Windows character
- Group Box—Visually organizes controls in a section of a dialog box
- Button—Provides a mechanism for a user to initiate some kind of action, such as an OK button
- Check Box—Represents something that has an on/off or true/false state
- Option Button—Similar to a check box, but you can select only one of a group of buttons
- Combo Box—An edit box that has a drop-down list of selections available
- List Box—A control that shows a list of options
- Horizontal Scroll Bar—Enables scrolling from left to right
- Vertical Scroll Bar—This enables scrolling up and down
- Spin—Normally used in conjunction with an edit box to increase or decrease a value when clicked
- Progress—Shows how much a process has completed
- Slider—Selects a value from predefined limits
- Hot Key—Associates a shortcut key combination
- List Control—Displays a list of elements, such as files in Explorer
- Tree Control—Manages branches in an outline manner, such as the Resource view does in VC++ 6

- Tab Control—Visual control used to separate items into pages
- Animate—Displays AVI clips
- Rich Edit—Used to enter multiple lines of text
- Date Time Picker—Used to pick a date and time
- Month Calendar—Shows a calendar in which you can select months and days
- IP Address—An edit box that accepts input of an IP address in dotted decimal format (for example: 255.255.255.0)
- Custom Control—Allows you to add your own controls
- Extended Combo Box—A combo box that has been extended to add enhanced capabilities for the list options

Lesson Summary

In this lesson, you were introduced to dialog resources and some of their common uses. You briefly examined the dialog resource added automatically by VC++ 6 for an about box.

You also learned how to add a dialog resource to your application and what properties you could change that would affect the general appearance of the dialog box. Along with looking at the properties of a dialog box, you learned that VC++ 6 makes several common controls available that you can use in your dialog boxes to convey or retrieve information to and from a user of your application.

Most applications use dialog resources to set important program options that affect the way the application operates. When adding dialog resources to your applications, you may want to consider how a user could change the behavior of your application by giving them appropriate options to do so in your dialog boxes.

Quiz 1

1. Which control is used to play an AVI clip?
    a. `AVI Box` control
    b. `Animate` control
    c. `MoviePlayer` control
    d. `MediaPlayer` control
2. Which VC++ 6 menu item creates resources?
    a. Edit, Resource
    b. View, Insert
    c. Insert, Resource
    d. Control, Insert Resource

3. Which dialog property controls the text in the title bar?

    a. `Titlebar` property

    b. `Text` property

    c. `Comment` property

    d. `Caption` property

4. Which dialog property will force the dialog box to remain on top of all programs and windows until closed?

    a. `System modal` property

    b. `Stay on top` property

    c. `Force top` property

    d. `Top-most` property

Exercise 1

Complexity: Easy

1. Create a new SDI application named "Exercise 1" and add a dialog resource with the resource ID of `IDD_DLGEXER01`.

Complexity: Moderate

2. Create a new dialog-based application named "Exercise 2" and add a dialog resource with the resource ID of `IDD_DLGEXER02`. This dialog resource should be set up so that, when displayed, it must be closed before anything else can be done with the system.

LESSON 2

Custom Dialog Box Classes

When you create a dialog resource, a resource is all that is created. Even though you can test it or make your program display it, you can't really do anything with it. Once you create your dialog resource, you need to create a class for it. This class is what will allow you to set and read values for your controls inside the dialog box. Fortunately, VC++ 6 has made creating a class for your dialog box resources simple by using the ClassWizard.

Using ClassWizard to Create a Custom Class

Typically, you would complete the design of your resource before using ClassWizard to build a class for your new resource, but this is not necessary. You can create your basic resource, create the class, and then manage both of them as you continue to develop your application.

With that said, go ahead and create a class for this dialog box. You can accomplish this by right-clicking an empty spot in the dialog box and selecting ClassWizard from the pop-up context menu or by selecting ClassWizard from the View menu.

Once you make the menu selection, the ClassWizard will be displayed and automatically recognize that this is a new resource that does not yet have a class and will offer to make the class for you. Figure 3.8 shows the ClassWizard when it recognizes the new resource.

FIGURE 3.8

The ClassWizard and a new resource.

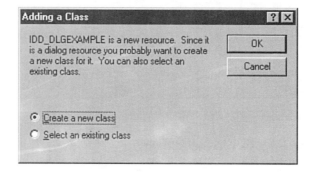

Make sure that the Create a new class item is selected and press the OK button. This will display the New Class dialog box, as shown in Figure 3.9.

FIGURE 3.9

The New Class dialog box.

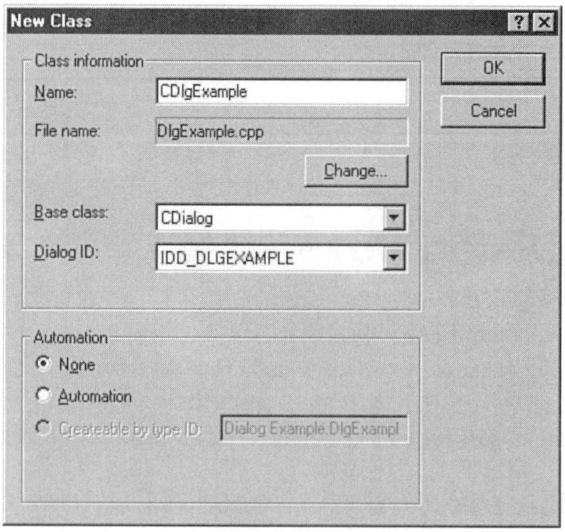

In order to create the class, you must give it a name. Go ahead and type in **CDlgExample** for the class name. Another convention to mention at this point is the letter *C* at the beginning of a class. This is used so that by simply looking at CDlgExample, you should immediately recognize it as a class. Once you make your entry, click the OK button to create the class. When you create this class, a new file is added to your project, DlgExample.cpp, which will contain the class' member functions and other code that makes the class complete.

Now that you have created a class for the dialog box, you should see it in the Class List drop-down in the ClassWizard. Figure 3.10 shows the ClassWizard with your newly created class.

FIGURE 3.10

ClassWizard with the newly created class.

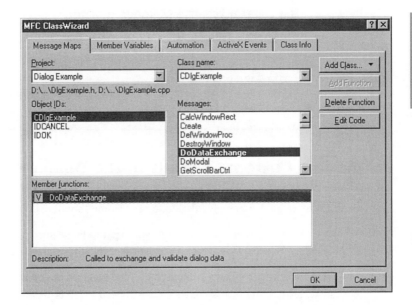

Looking at the ClassWizard in Figure 3.10, you should see your new class listed under Object IDs as well as IDs for the controls in your dialog box. Currently, there are only two controls, the Cancel button, listed as IDCANCEL, and the OK button, listed as IDOK.

Just to the right of the Object IDs is the Messages list. These are the messages to which the selected item can currently respond. If you see an item in bold, this means that a member function has been defined for that message.

Looking just below the Object IDs and Messages boxes, you'll see another box that lists the defined member functions. These member functions are how you actually add pieces of code to your project that respond to windows messages and user commands.

Go ahead and select CDlgExample in the list of Object IDs. Looking at the list of Messages, DoDataExchange is in bold. This means that a member function has been defined for this message. You can verify this by looking in the Member functions list box. Currently, DoDataExchange is the only one listed.

Looking at Listing 3.1, you can see that DoDataExchange is a member function of the CDlgExample class. This member function is called automatically for you when you click the OK button and is responsible for copying the values from the controls in your dialog box to their member functions. You will look at this listing again in just a while once you add some controls so that you can actually see what is happening behind the scenes.

LISTING 3.1   The DoDataExchange Member Function

```
void CDlgExample::DoDataExchange(CDataExchange* pDX)
{
    CDialog::DoDataExchange(pDX);
    //{{AFX_DATA_MAP(CDlgExample)
        // NOTE: the ClassWizard will add DDX and DDV calls here
    //}}AFX_DATA_MAP
}
```

Adding Custom Controls to the Dialog Resource

Now that you have a dialog resource with a class, it's time to add some controls to the dialog box so that we can give the dialog box some functionality.

However, before you can add a control, you need to make sure you can see the Controls toolbar. If it is not displayed, select it from the toolbar pop-up context menu.

You have three ways to manage the layout of the controls as you place them on the dialog box: none, grid, or rulers and guides. You will need to experiment with the different modes to determine which one you like best, or even if a mixture of them works well for you.

For the purpose of this lesson, you will need to use the grid method of layout control because Figure 3.11 shows the default grid points. To turn this option on, select the Guide settings menu item from the Layout menu to show the Guide Settings dialog box, select Grid, and click the OK button.

To place a control on the dialog resource, select the control you want to add by clicking it and click the dialog resource where you want to place the control. Once placed, you can make adjustments to its layout by clicking the control to give it focus. When the mouse hovers over the control, your mouse cursor will turn into crosshairs. Click and drag the control to your desired location.

FIGURE 3.11

*The dialog resource
with some controls
added.*

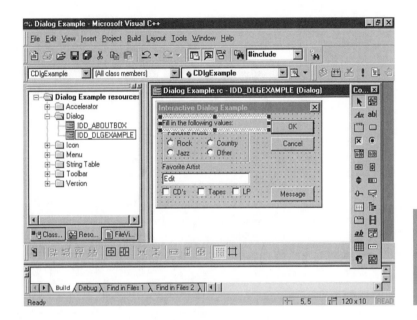

Depending upon which control you have placed on the dialog box, you can click the corners, sides, top, or bottom of the dialog box to change the size of the control.

Add the following controls, as shown in Figure 3.11, paying close attention to the order in which they are added and which properties to set:

- Static text with the caption "Fill in the following values."
- Group box with the caption "Favorite music."
- Option button inside of the group box with the caption "Rock," an ID of IDC_RBROCK, Group, and Tab Stop options selected.
- Option button inside of the group box with the caption "Jazz" and an ID of IDC_RBJAZZ.
- Option button inside of the group box with the caption "Country" and an ID of IDC_RBCOUNTRY.
- Option button inside of the group box with the caption "Other" and an ID of IDC_RBOTHER.
- Static text with the caption "Favorite artist" and Group option selected.
- Edit box with an ID of IDC_EBARTIST.
- Check box with the caption "CD's" and an ID of IDC_CBCD.
- Check box with the caption "Tapes" and an ID of IDC_CBTAPES.

- Check box with the caption "LP" and an ID of `IDC_CBLP`.
- Button with the caption "Message" and an ID of `IDC_BMESSAGE`.

You need to make sure that you added the controls in order. When you place controls on the dialog resource, the order in which you add them is their default tab order. If you need to change the tab order for the controls, select the Tab Order menu item from the Layout menu. This will put a number on top of each control. Simply click all the numbers in the order in which you want the tab order. For this example, the OK and Cancel buttons are 1 and 2, and the rest should be numbered sequentially in the order listed previously.

Now that you have added the controls, test the dialog resource to make sure the controls are behaving as expected. You should only be able to select one of the option buttons in the Favorite Music group. The check boxes should toggle a checkmark to indicate whether they are selected. You should also be able to type some text into the Favorite Artist edit box.

Just in case you didn't notice, the IDs for the controls began with the first three letters of IDC, and the dialog box began with IDD. Using IDC for the controls is another common convention when creating your application so that when you look at the ID, you immediately know it's for a control.

You may also have noticed that some IDs used meaningful names, and some were left to the automatically created ID. Usually, if you are expecting to use the control to display or accept some kind of value, you should give it a good name. Because the static text controls were only being used to show a small amount of text, the default IDs were fine, but, because you were using the edit box to collect data, a meaningful ID of `IDC_EBARTIST` was used.

You will want to come up with a way to generate the IDs that make sense to you. In this example, `IDC_EBARTIST` was built as follows:

- `IDC_`—Standard convention for controls.
- `EB`—One or two letter code to show the type of control, in this case, *EB* for the first letter or each word in edit box.
- `ARTIST`—A name that actually represents what kind of data is being collected. Because the edit box was asking for a favorite artist, *ARTIST* was used.

What happens when you click the Message button? Nothing. Buttons are usually used to initiate some kind of action. Because you have not yet defined what action the Message button will take, nothing should happen. In fact, in order for something to happen, you need to write a member function for the button and that function will only be called when the program is actually running, not when you are testing a dialog box.

Adding Code to Display the Dialog Box

Although you've created a resource and when you test it, it appears to work properly, you should actually execute the program to see if the dialog box operates as planned. The only problem at this point is that you have not programmed anything inside of your program that will activate the dialog box for the user.

Because you have not covered menus, you will make the dialog box automatically appear when the program executes. When AppWizard created the application, a class was created for the application, CDialogExampleApp. Looking at Figure 3.12, you will notice that this class is one that you can select from the list of available classes. Go ahead and select it from the list of classes.

FIGURE 3.12

ClassWizard with CDialogExampleApp *selected.*

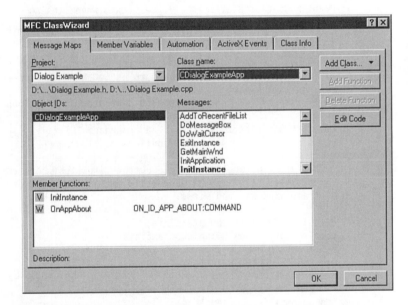

The only Object ID is the class itself. Select it and you will see that the InitInstance message is in bold. This means a member function has been defined for this message.

In the Member functions list, double-click the InitInstance entry. This will open up the Dialog Example.cpp file in your editor with the CDialogExampleApp::InitInstance member visible. Listing 3.2 shows what the generated function looks like.

LISTING 3.2   The `CDialogExampleApp::InitInstance()` function.

```
BOOL CDialogExampleApp::InitInstance()
{
    AfxEnableControlContainer();

    // Standard initialization
    // If you are not using these features and wish to reduce the size
    //  of your final executable, you should remove from the following
    //  the specific initialization routines you do not need.

#ifdef _AFXDLL
    Enable3dControls();          // Call this when using MFC
                                 // in a shared DLL
#else
    Enable3dControlsStatic();    // Call this when linking to MFC
                                 // statically
#endif

    // Change the registry key under which our settings are stored.
    // You should modify this string to be something appropriate
    // such as the name of your company or organization.
    SetRegistryKey(_T("Local AppWizard-Generated Applications"));

    LoadStdProfileSettings();  // Load standard INI file
                               // options (including MRU)

    // Register the application's document templates. Document
    // templates serve as the connection between documents,
    // frame windows, and views.

    CSingleDocTemplate* pDocTemplate;
    pDocTemplate = new CSingleDocTemplate(
        IDR_MAINFRAME,
        RUNTIME_CLASS(CDialogExampleDoc),
        RUNTIME_CLASS(CMainFrame),         // main SDI frame window
        RUNTIME_CLASS(CDialogExampleView));
    AddDocTemplate(pDocTemplate);

    // Parse command line for standard shell commands, DDE, file open
    CCommandLineInfo cmdInfo;
    ParseCommandLine(cmdInfo);

    // Dispatch commands specified on the command line
    if (!ProcessShellCommand(cmdInfo))
        return FALSE;

    // The one and only window has been initialized,
    // so show and update it.
    m_pMainWnd->ShowWindow(SW_SHOW);
```

```
    m_pMainWnd->UpdateWindow();

    return TRUE;
}
```

Looking through Listing 3.2, most of the lines of code initiate and register your documents and views with Windows. The last two lines before the return statement display the window. The first one displays the window by sending the SW_SHOW window message to your application, and the second forces the program to update the window to make sure it is drawn correctly. Once these are complete, the function returns showing that the process completed normally.

You will be adding some lines of code just before the return TRUE; program line. Because the dialog box is only a class and a resource, you will need to create a variable for the it.

Once you have created your variable, you can assign values to the member variables and then display the dialog box. Because you have not yet created any member variables, you will only be able to display the dialog box and tell which button was used to close it.

To create the variable and display the dialog box, add the following lines of code before the return TRUE; statement:

```
CDlgExample myDialog;
myDialog.DoModal();
```

Now that you have added the lines of code that will create a variable of your dialog type and called the DoModal() function, you can build and execute the program. Go ahead and build the project by selecting the Build Dialog Example.exe menu item from the Build menu, by selecting the Build button on the Build toolbar, or by simply pressing F7.

When you built the application, you should have seen the following errors:

- error C2065 'CDlgExample' : undeclared identifier
- error C2146 syntax error : missing ';' before identifier 'myDialog'
- error C2065 'myDialog' : undeclared identifier
- error C2228 left of '.DoModal' must have class/struct/union type

Why did these errors occur? All four happened because the compiler does not know where to find the CDlgExample class. In order to tell the compiler where to find your class, you need to add an include statement at the beginning of the Dialog Example.cpp file. Listing 3.3 shows what the default includes are.

LISTING 3.3   Code Segment That Lists the Default Includes

```
#include "stdafx.h"
#include "Dialog Example.h"

#include "MainFrm.h"
#include "Dialog ExampleDoc.h"
#include "Dialog ExampleView.h"
```

The `include` statements tell the compiler to add other files to the compile process. The AppWizard automatically generated the `include` statements in Listing 3.3, but because you have created your own class, you need to add an `include` statement that will include the file that defines the `CDlgExample` class. In this case, the `CDlgExample` class is defined in DlgExample.h. To add this, you need to add the following line somewhere in the list of includes. Go ahead and add it after the `#include "Dialog ExampleView.h"` line:

```
#include "DlgExample.h"
```

Now that the compiler will know where to find the definition for the `CDlgExample` class, you should be able to build and run your application. Go ahead and build your application. This time, you should not see any errors or warnings. If you do, you need to make sure you have added the lines to the program properly.

Once the compilation is complete with no errors, you can select the Execute Dialog Example.exe menu item from the Build menu to run the program. You can also run the program by pressing the Ctrl+F5 shortcut key or by selecting the Execute button on the build toolbar (the red exclamation mark).

Figure 3.13 shows the running application with the dialog box being displayed.

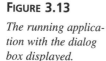

FIGURE 3.13

The running application with the dialog box displayed.

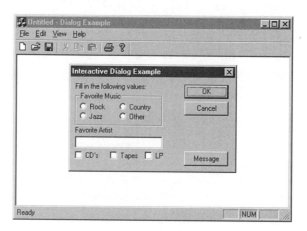

Go ahead and play around with the dialog box's controls to see how they operate. If you click the OK or Cancel buttons, the dialog box will close. If you still want to play with the dialog box, you will need to close the program and run it again.

Notice that if you click the Message button, it still doesn't do anything. This is because you still have not added code to the button to do anything when you click it. Unlike other controls, such as the check boxes, there is no automatic default, because you must code the event you want the button to accomplish.

With exception to the OK and Cancel buttons, all controls will perform their intended functions automatically, but you can still code a message handler for them to perform a specific action before they do their default process. If you haven't done so already, close the application.

Now that you have created a resource and defined your custom class, you are ready to start adding member variables and start using the resource to accomplish a task. The next lesson will cover these topics and give you a better understanding of how to use the dialog boxes.

Lesson Summary

In this lesson, you learned how to use the ClassWizard to link a class and your dialog resource together so that the resource could be used in your application. You were also introduced to placing controls on the dialog resource and creating meaningful IDs for the controls.

Next, you were introduced to the code that was actually needed to create and display the dialog box inside of the application. Because VC++ 6 does most of the work, you only needed to add three lines of code to make the application create and display your dialog resource: one to include the resource, one to create a variable of the dialog type, and one to display the dialog box.

During the process of learning how to display the dialog box in your application, you were introduced to one of the common mistakes that occur when adding resources. Letting you see compile errors before adding the `include` statement pointed out why you needed to add the `include` statement.

Quiz 2

1. Which VC++ 6 tool connects a dialog resource to a class?

    a. AppWizard

    b. Dialog Resource editor

        c. ClassCreator

        d. ClassWizard

2. Which three-letter prefix identifies controls?

        a. IDD

        b. DLG

        c. CTL

        d. IDC

3. Which member function displays a dialog box that must be closed before you can continue to use the application?

        a. `ShowModal()`

        b. `Display()`

        c. `DoModal()`

        d. `DlgModal()`

4. Which member function is responsible for transferring control values to member variables?

        a. `DoDataExchange()`

        b. `MemberVariableTransfer()`

        c. `AfxDataTransfer()`

        d. `DataExchange()`

Exercise 2

Complexity: Easy

1. Create a new SDI application named "Exercise 1" and add a dialog resource. Once you have the dialog resource created, use the ClassWizard to create a class for the dialog resource.

Complexity: Moderate

2. Create a new SDI application named "Exercise 2" and add a dialog resource. When displayed, this dialog resource should stay on top of all windows until closed.

   Once you have the dialog resource created, add the necessary lines of code that will display the dialog box.

LESSON 3

Using Your Custom Dialog Box

Now that you know how to create a dialog resource and how to create the custom class for the dialog box, it's time to do more with the resource so that you can put the dialog box to good use. You will build upon the application you have been working on in Lessons 1 and 2.

In this lesson, you will be adding member variables to the class, setting default values before displaying the dialog box, determining which button the user selected, adding a member function to handle a message, and showing what values were selected in the dialog box.

Adding Member Variables

The purpose of adding member variables to the class is to establish a link between the control's value and the application. How your program handles the member variable's value is up to you.

The ClassWizard adds member variables to your dialog box's class. In this lesson, you will add member variables for the controls you added to the dialog resource in Lesson 2.

At this time, right-click an empty spot in the dialog resource and select ClassWizard from the pop-up context menu. Figure 3.14 shows the ClassWizard.

FIGURE 3.14

The ClassWizard with the new resource IDs.

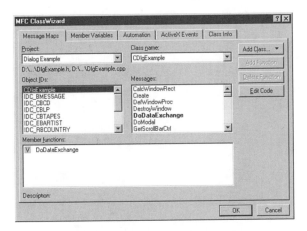

Notice that the ClassWizard now has several entries in the Object IDs list. These IDs are from the controls you added to the dialog resource. If you recall, before you added the controls, there were only three Object IDs. There are 12 of them now.

The Message Maps page defines member functions. You need to click the Member Variables tab of the ClassWizard to display the defined member variables. Figure 3.15 shows the ClassWizard on the Member Variables tab.

FIGURE 3.15

The Member Variables page of ClassWizard.

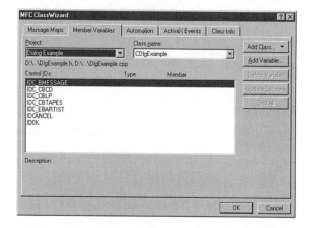

Looking at Figure 3.15, this page has one main section that lists the resource IDs in this class that can have a member variable associated with them. Looking through this list, you will notice that not all of the controls on the resource are in this list. One such example is the static text controls. The reason these don't appear in this list is that they don't return a value when their resource ID is set to IDC_STATIC. If you change its resource ID, however, it will show up in the ClassWizard as one of the resource IDs to which you can assign a member variable.

To add a member variable, you need to select a control ID from the list and either double-click it or click the Add Variable button. Go ahead and select the IDC_CBCD control ID and click Add Variable. Doing this will display the Add Member Variables dialog box, as displayed in Figure 3.16.

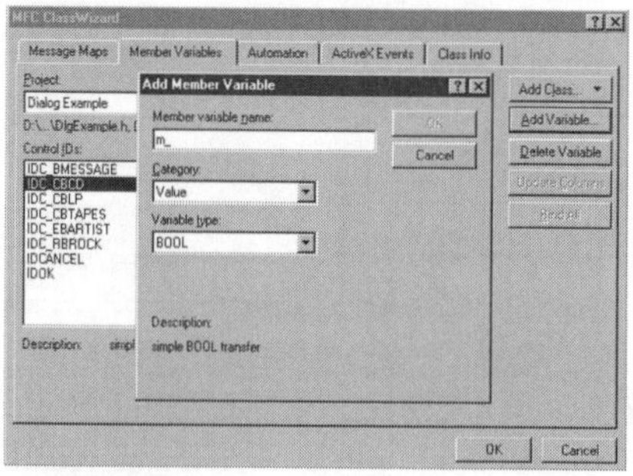

FIGURE 3.16

The Add Member Variable dialog box.

Looking at Figure 3.16, you need to enter text into the Member Variable Name edit box. The convention for a member variable is to begin with m_ and use something that is descriptive about the variable. The member variable name is set to m_cd_value.

Depending upon the type of control being represented, the Category drop-down list will specify whether you can select Value or Control. Value will return the value of the control as the user has specified in the member variable, whereas Control will give you access to the control itself. For this variable, select Value.

After you have selected the category for the variable, you can specify what the variable type will be. Because this variable is for a check box, the default variable type is BOOL. If you selected Control in the Category drop-down list, the variable type would be the class type for the control. Go ahead and leave the variable type as BOOL.

Now that you have specified the items needed to complete the member variable, click the OK button to add the member variable. Go ahead and repeat this process for IDC_CBLP and IDC_CBTAPES using the variable names m_lp_value and m_tapes_value, respectively. Figure 3.17 shows the ClassWizard with the newly defined member variables.

FIGURE 3.17

Newly defined member variables.

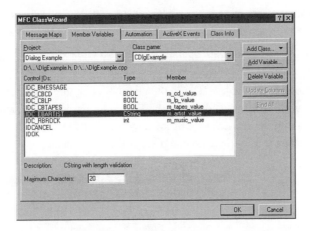

Before you define a member variable for IDC_EBARTIST, you should know that, because it is an edit box, it has more functionality than the check boxes for which you just defined variables. For this lesson, its variable type has been set to CString. If you look at the available variable types, you will see a list of several types. If, for example, you were expecting the user to enter a number, you could set the variable type to int, long, or another numeric type.

The other variable defined in Figure 3.17, IDC_RBROCK, has some special considerations as well. If you think back to Lesson 2 where you added four option buttons, this option button was the only one of the four for which you selected the group property. The group property, combined with the tab order of the controls, is what defines the beginning and end of groups of controls. Selecting the group property for the static text control immediately following the option buttons completed the group of option buttons.

Because the option buttons are a group, they only need to be represented by a single value. This is why only the first option button is listed. If you are either missing the IDC_RBROCK control ID or have more than one of your option buttons listed, you need to verify that only the first option button and the static control for favorite artist have the group property selected.

If you haven't already done so, go ahead and create the member variables for IDC_EBARTIST and IDC_RBROCK, as shown in Figure 3.17. Another benefit of the edit box control when using CString is limiting the number of characters the user can enter. For this lesson, enter a value of 20 by selecting the IDC_EBARTIST in the list of member variables and entering **20** in the edit box toward the bottom of the ClassWizard.

Setting Default Values

With the appropriate member variables added to the CDlgExample class, you can now add code to the program that will give some of the dialog controls a default value.

Using Figure 3.18 as a guide, display the ClassWizard and select the CDialogExampleApp class from the list of class names. Next, click the CDialogExampleApp Object ID and then double-click the InitInstance member function. This will display the editor for the Dialog Example.cpp file and put the cursor right at the CDialogExampleApp::InitInstance member function. This is the same function used in the last lesson to create and display the dialog box.

FIGURE 3.18

ClassWizard with
CDialogExampleApp_::
InitInstance *selected.*

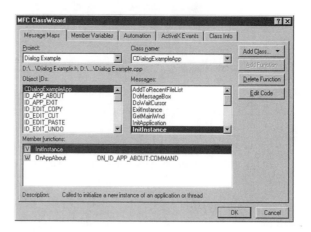

Listing 3.4 shows the listing of this member function.

LISTING 3.4   The `CDialogExampleApp::InitInstance()` Function

```
BOOL CDialogExampleApp::InitInstance()
{
    AfxEnableControlContainer();

    // Standard initialization
    // If you are not using these features and wish to reduce the size
    // of your final executable, you should remove from the following
    // the specific initialization routines you do not need.

#ifdef _AFXDLL
    Enable3dControls();        // Call this when using MFC
                               // in a shared DLL
#else
    Enable3dControlsStatic();  // Call this when linking to MFC
                               // statically
#endif

    // Change the registry key under which our settings are stored.
    // You should modify this string to be something appropriate
    // such as the name of your company or organization.
    SetRegistryKey(_T("Local AppWizard-Generated Applications"));

    LoadStdProfileSettings();  // Load standard INI file
                               // options (including MRU)

    // Register the application's document templates. Document
    // templates serve as the connection between documents,
    // frame windows, and views.

    CSingleDocTemplate* pDocTemplate;
    pDocTemplate = new CSingleDocTemplate_         (IDR_MAINFRAME,
        RUNTIME_CLASS(CDialogExampleDoc),
        RUNTIME_CLASS(CMainFrame),       // main SDI frame window
        RUNTIME_CLASS(CDialogExampleView));
    AddDocTemplate(pDocTemplate);

    // Parse command line for standard shell commands, DDE, file open
    CCommandLineInfo cmdInfo;
    ParseCommandLine(cmdInfo);

    // Dispatch commands specified on the command line
    if (!ProcessShellCommand(cmdInfo))
        return FALSE;

    // The one and only window has been initialized,
    // so show and update it.
```

continues

LISTING 3.4   continued

```
    m_pMainWnd->ShowWindow(SW_SHOW);
    m_pMainWnd->UpdateWindow();

    CDlgExample myDialog;
    myDialog.DoModal();

    return TRUE;
}
```

In Lesson 2, you added the following two lines of code to this function:

```
CDlgExample myDialog;
myDialog.DoModal();
```

The first line was responsible for creating a variable for the dialog resource, and the second displayed the dialog box.

When setting default values for the dialog box, you need to add lines of code after the variable has been created but before you display the dialog box. This means that you will be adding lines of code between these two lines.

Considering that this dialog box doesn't really have too many controls on it, you won't have to set too many values. For this lesson, you need to tell the dialog box to set the default value for the option buttons to Other and to have the check box for CDs preselected. You can accomplished this by assigning values to the member variables that you created earlier in this lesson.

To set the value for the option buttons, you need to give m_music_value a value, and to preselect the CD's check box, you need to set m_cd_value's value.

Because m_music_value has a data type of int, you will need to set its value to an integer. In order to figure out what value to give it, you need to know how many option buttons are in the group. In this lesson, there are four. The values for the option buttons begin with 0 and end at 3: 0 for Rock, 1 for Jazz, 2 for Country, and 3 for Other. This sequence is defined by the tab order of the controls in the option button group. Thus, to set the default favorite music type to Other, you need to assign the m_music_value member variable to 3. If you wanted to make none of the option buttons selected by default, you would assign the value -1.

Because m_cd_value has a data type of bool, its value can be set to either TRUE or FALSE. In this case, because you want it to be selected by default, you need to set its value to TRUE.

To set these default values, you need to add the following two lines of code between the two lines of code you entered earlier:

```
myDialog.m_music_value = 3;
myDialog.m_cd_value = TRUE;
```

Once you have entered these two lines of code, the section of code affected should look like the following:

```
CDlgExample myDialog;

myDialog.m_music_value = 3;
myDialog.m_cd_value = TRUE;

myDialog.DoModal();
```

To verify that the two lines of code work, build and run the application. This time, when the dialog box appears, the Other favorite music option button and the CD's check box should both be selected as shown in Figure 3.19.

FIGURE 3.19

Running application with the default dialog options.

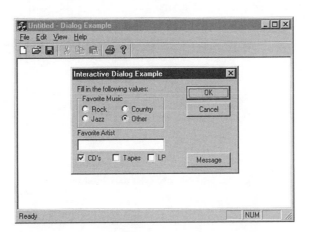

If you clicked the Message button while the application was running, you would have noticed that it still does nothing, but you are just about to change that. Now, you will be adding a member function that responds to a message. In this case, it's the BN_CLICKED message for the IDC_BMESSAGE button.

To create the stub for this message handler, use the ClassWizard's Message Maps page and select the IDC_BMESSAGE Object ID. Once you have selected it, the Messages list displays the two default messages for this control type, in this case, a button. Select BN_CLICKED from the list and click the Add Function button. This will display the Add Member Function dialog box as shown in Figure 3.20.

FIGURE 3.20

The Add Member Function dialog box.

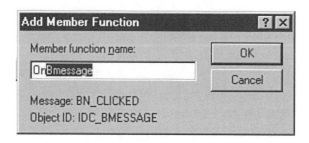

The only thing to do in this dialog box is give the member function a name. Generally, VC++ 6 generates an appropriate name for the member function. In this case, it defaults to OnBmessage. Typically, when you are writing a message handler for an event, it begins with the letters *On* to show action, followed by a name that represents the control causing the event. Go ahead and click the OK button as this member name is perfectly fine.

Looking at Figure 3.21, you will notice that ClassWizard has added a new entry in the list of member functions and it set the BN_CLICKED message to bold in the Messages list.

FIGURE 3.21

ClassWizard with the new member function selected.

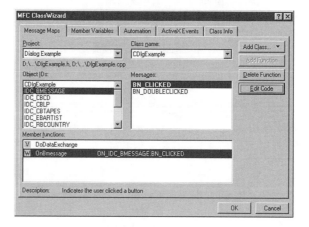

Looking a little closer at the list of member functions, you will notice that the new function has an icon on the left that has the letter *W* in it, whereas the previous one has the letter *V*.

The *V* means that this member function is a virtual function, and the *W* means this is a Windows message. Also notice that the new member function has a message mapping listed with it as well. This mapping indicates which control and which message accompany this function.

When the ClassWizard created this function, it created a small block of code in the DlgExample.cpp file, where you create code that will use the functions within the

CDlgExample class. Don't confuse this file with the Dialog Example.cpp file where you have already made changes. Listing 3.5 shows the DlgExample.cpp file in its current state.

LISTING 3.5   The DlgExample.cpp File

```cpp
// DlgExample.cpp : implementation file
//

#include "stdafx.h"
#include "Dialog Example.h"
#include "DlgExample.h"

#ifdef _DEBUG
#define new DEBUG_NEW
#undef THIS_FILE
static char THIS_FILE[] = __FILE__;
#endif

/////////////////////////////////////////////////////////////////////
// CDlgExample dialog

CDlgExample::CDlgExample(CWnd* pParent /*=NULL*/)
    : CDialog(CDlgExample::IDD, pParent)
{
    //{{AFX_DATA_INIT(CDlgExample)
    m_cd_value = FALSE;
    m_lp_value = FALSE;
    m_tapes_value = FALSE;
    m_artist_value = _T("");
    m_music_value = -1;
    //}}AFX_DATA_INIT
}

void CDlgExample::DoDataExchange(CDataExchange* pDX)
{
    CDialog::DoDataExchange(pDX);
    //{{AFX_DATA_MAP(CDlgExample)
    DDX_Check(pDX, IDC_CBCD, m_cd_value);
    DDX_Check(pDX, IDC_CBLP, m_lp_value);
    DDX_Check(pDX, IDC_CBTAPES, m_tapes_value);
    DDX_Text(pDX, IDC_EBARTIST, m_artist_value);
    DDV_MaxChars(pDX, m_artist_value, 20);
    DDX_Radio(pDX, IDC_RBROCK, m_music_value);
    //}}AFX_DATA_MAP
}

BEGIN_MESSAGE_MAP(CDlgExample, CDialog)
    //{{AFX_MSG_MAP(CDlgExample)
```

continues

LISTING 3.5   continued

```
      ON_BN_CLICKED(IDC_BMESSAGE, OnBmessage)
      //}}AFX_MSG_MAP
END_MESSAGE_MAP()

/////////////////////////////////////////////////////////////////////////
// CDlgExample message handlers

void CDlgExample::OnBmessage()
{
      // TODO: Add your control notification handler code here
}
```

Considering the importance of this file to the class, a small discussion is warranted. The first lines to look closely at are the following:

```
//{{AFX_DATA_INIT(CDlgExample)
m_cd_value = FALSE;
m_lp_value = FALSE;
m_tapes_value = FALSE;
m_artist_value = _T("");
m_music_value = -1;
//}}AFX_DATA_INIT
```

These lines of code are actually what set the default values for the controls in the dialog box. You could have changed the default values here instead of doing it in code, but, if you created another variable of this dialog box's type, the values you changed these to would have been the defaults for the new variable as well. Also notice that setting m_music_value to a -1, as done by default, will deselect all of the option buttons in the group.

The next member function, DoDataExchange, is actually responsible for managing the link between the member variables and the controls.

Which DDX_ function is used depends upon the type of the control. The first parameter is a pointer to a DataExchange structure. The second parameter is the resource ID for the control, and the third parameter is the member variable. Which DDX_ function is used depends upon the type of the control. For example, the check boxes use the DDX_Check function. Typically, you won't need to change any of these.

The next block of code is responsible for setting up the message map that makes events happen when messages are processed in the dialog box's message queue:

```
BEGIN_MESSAGE_MAP(CDlgExample, CDialog)
      //{{AFX_MSG_MAP(CDlgExample)
      ON_BN_CLICKED(IDC_BMESSAGE, OnBmessage)
      //}}AFX_MSG_MAP
END_MESSAGE_MAP()
```

After the message maps, you'll see the member functions that carry out the needed tasks. In this class, you have defined one member function for the dialog class at this point, OnBmessage().

When the Message button is clicked, a message is added to the dialog box's message queue. That message is then mapped to a member function. In this case, when the BN_CLICKED message is processed for the Message button, the CDlgExample::OnBmessage() function is called.

To make the Message button accomplish its task, you add your code in this function. Go ahead and enter the following line of code to the CDlgExample::OnBmessage() function:

```
AfxMessageBox("Hello interactive World!");
```

After you make the change, you will need to rebuild your application to see what happens when you click the Message button. Go ahead and do this now. Figure 3.22 shows the running application after you click the Message button.

FIGURE 3.22

The message displayed when the Message button is clicked.

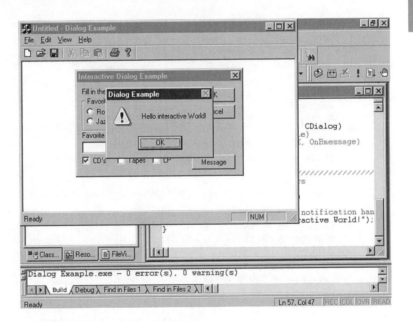

Determining Dialog Control Values

After a dialog box is displayed, most controls will have a value associated with them. The exception to the rule occurs when the user closes the window without clicking the OK button.

When the user clicks the OK button, the DoDataExchange function copies the control values to the member variables as defined. If the user clicks the Cancel button, the values are not copied to the member variables, meaning that the member variables will have the same value after the dialog box is closed as they had when the dialog box was displayed.

To react to the values of the controls, you need to add code after the dialog box has been closed. In this case, it will be in the CDialogExampleApp::InitInstance() function just after the code you've already entered.

Add the following lines of code just after you display the dialog box with the DoModal() call:

```
CString out_message;

out_message = "Favorite Music :";

switch (myDialog.m_music_value)
{
case 0 :
    out_message += "Rock\r\n";
    break;
case 1 :
    out_message += "Jazz\r\n";
    break;
case 2 :
    out_message += "Country\r\n";
    break;
case 3 :
    out_message += "Other\r\n";
    break;

}

out_message += "Favorite Artist :";
out_message += myDialog.m_artist_value;
out_message += "\r\n";

if (myDialog.m_cd_value == TRUE)
 out_message += "CD's : Yes\r\n";
else
 out_message += "CD's : No\r\n";

if (myDialog.m_tapes_value == TRUE)
 out_message += "Tapes : Yes\r\n";
else
 out_message += "Tapes : No\r\n";

if (myDialog.m_lp_value == TRUE)
 out_message += "LP : Yes\r\n";
```

```
else
 out_message += "LP : No\r\n";

AfxMessageBox(out_message);
```

This block of code builds a string containing the results of the member variables after the dialog box has been closed. Go ahead and build and run the application. When the dialog box appears, make your selections and click the OK button to see the displayed message.

Lesson Summary

In this lesson, you learned how to use ClassWizard to create member variables that link to the controls in a dialog resource. This included special considerations for control types such as option buttons that only have one variable that represents the whole group.

You also learned how to access the member variables to set and retrieve values for the controls. In this process, you also learned more about the classes behind the dialog box that make linking the member variables with the controls possible.

Using the ClassWizard to create member functions for messages was also covered. In this lesson, you added a function that responded when you clicked a button in your dialog resource.

Quiz 3

1. What value can be assigned to an option button group that will de-select all option buttons in the group?

   a. 0xFF

   b. -1

   c. 0

   d. None of the above

2. Which type of value does a check box control return?

   a. int

   b. CString

   c. long

   d. bool

3. Which statement best describes when to set default values?

   a. Right before you create the variable of the dialog box's type

   b. The default values can't be changed

   c. Right before showing the dialog box

   d. Right after showing the dialog box but before the user changes anything

4. Which message is mapped when responding to a button click?

   a. WM_BUTTONCLICK

   b. BN_CLICKED

   c. BN_CLICK

   d. OnButtonClick

Exercise 3

Complexity: Easy

1. Create a new SDI-based application named "Exercise 1" and add a dialog resource that has three option buttons. These option buttons should have the captions of "Yes," "No," and "Maybe."

   Once you have the dialog resource created, add the necessary lines of code that will display the dialog box.

Complexity: Moderate

2. Create a new SDI-based application named "Exercise 1" and add a dialog resource that has three option buttons. These option buttons should have the captions of "Yes," "No," and "Maybe."

   With the dialog resource created, add the necessary code that will display the dialog box and set the Yes option button as the default.

LESSON 4

Creating Property Sheets and Pages

You've already learned how to use the tools in VC++ 6 to create dialog boxes and classes. These tools are the same ones you will be using to create property pages and sheets. Before you start creating resources and classes, you need to understand what property sheets and property pages are and how they relate to each other.

About Property Sheets and Pages

If you've been using Windows 95 or Windows NT 4.0 for awhile, you probably have encountered property sheets. Most programs use them to organize program options and settings. How can you tell if you are using a property sheet? Typically, you will recognize a property sheet by its general appearance. Most have a series of dialog boxes organized by tabs across the top.

Figure 3.23 shows one of the common property sheets in Windows 95. To display this property sheet, right-click the My Computer icon on the desktop and select Properties from the pop-up context menu.

FIGURE 3.23

The property sheet for My Computer.

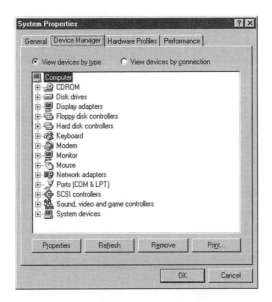

This property sheet shows information about your computer. This sheet has four tabs on it: General, Device Manager, Hardware Profiles, and Performance. Each tab in the property sheet represents a property page. This means that a property sheet is a collection of property pages.

Why use separate pages? Using property pages alleviates the problem of having a dialog box that appears too busy. Too many controls on a dialog box makes it difficult to comprehend exactly what is going on without careful study.

Using property pages will also allow you an easy mechanism for grouping common settings on a page by themselves. This aids in the organization of your program and, with thoughtful consideration, will help the user of your application utilize your program more effectively and efficiently. You need to be careful, though, not to overorganize the controls to the point that trying to find a setting or option becomes cumbersome.

Creating the Application Framework

Now that you have a basic understanding of what property sheets and pages are, it's time to start building the resources that will be used in this and the following lesson.

To start, you need to use MFC AppWizard to create a new project. This time, go ahead and create a dialog-based application and give it the name "PropertySheet Example." If you need help creating a dialog-based application, you can look back in Chapter 2.

Please note that you do not need to create a dialog-based application in order to use property sheets and pages. An SDI or MDI application would work just as well, but because this chapter is primarily about dialog resources, you are creating this type of application to build upon your knowledge of dialog resources.

Now that you have created the basic application framework, you will need to add some resources that will be used for the property pages. Considering that you will be using these new dialog resources for property pages, you will be introduced to a few more properties that play an important role in this process.

First, you need to make some changes to the main dialog box so it will contain controls that will house the functionality of this application. Look at the Resource view in the Project Workspace shown in Figure 3.24. You will notice that AppWizard has automatically created two dialog resources.

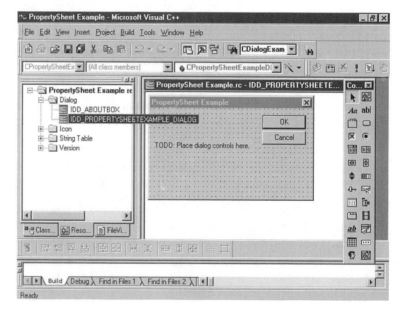

The first is the standard IDD_ABOUTBOX that was created by default. The second, IDD_PROPERTYSHEETEXAMPLE_DIALOG, is the resource for this application's main dialog box. This is the resource you will need to modify in this first step.

Make the following changes to the main dialog resource:

1. Select the static text control that begins with the text *TODO* and press the Delete key to remove it from the dialog box.

2. Add a static text control to the dialog box and set its caption property to *Property Settings:*.

3. Add a list box control to the dialog box and change its resource ID to IDC_LBPROPERTIES. Also deselect the Tab Stop property on the General page and deselect Sort on the Styles page.

4. Add a button control and change its resource ID property to IDC_BPROPERTIES. Also set its caption property to *Properties*.

Figure 3.25 shows what the modified dialog resource should look like after following these steps.

FIGURE 3.25

The modified main dialog resource.

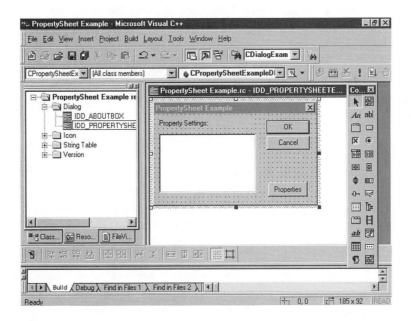

Because the AppWizard created this dialog box, the class has already been created for the dialog box as well. Your next step is to create the member functions needed for this dialog box.

Figure 3.26 shows the ClassWizard with the class selected for this dialog box. Go ahead and right-click an empty spot on the dialog box and select ClassWizard from the pop-up context menu.

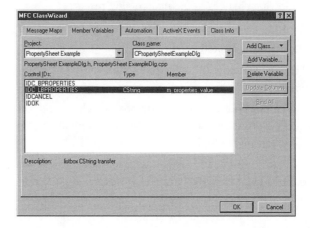

Notice that the CPropertySheetExampleDlg class has several member functions already defined for this dialog box. AppWizard created these as well.

Because you are adding member variables, click the Member Variables tab. Setting up the member variables for this application is a little different than what you learned in the previous lessons.

Select the IDC_LBPROPERTIES Control ID and click the Add Variable button. Give the member variable the name of m_properties_value with the category of Value and the variable type of CString. Click the OK button to add the member variable.

Next, select the IDC_LBPROPERTIES control ID again and click the Add Variable button. This time, give the member variable the name of m_properties_control. Set the category property to Control. The variable type will automatically default to CListBox. Click the OK button to add the member variable.

Look at Figure 3.27 to see if the member variables you created match those in the figure.

Even though you won't be using the m_properties_value member variable in the application, you created it to learn an important point. Doing this demonstrated that you could create two variables for a control—one for each category, value, and control type. Using the m_properties_control member variable will let you call the member functions of the control. You will use the m_properties_control member variable in the next lesson to add lines to the list box on the main dialog box.

FIGURE 3.27

The newly created member variables.

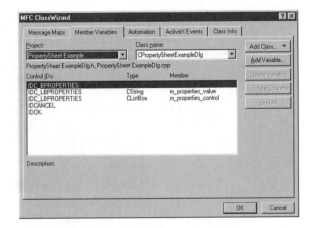

Adding Dialog Resources to Be Used as Property Pages

With the class created for the main dialog box, you are ready to create the dialog box resources needed for the property pages. For this lesson, you will be creating a set of three property pages, each of which will have its own dialog resource.

Add a dialog resource to the application by executing the following steps:

1. Create a new dialog resource by selecting the Resource menu item from the Insert menu. This will display the Insert Resource dialog box.

2. Once the Insert Resource dialog box has been displayed, click the Dialog resource and click the New button. This will add the resource to your application.

3. Delete the OK and Cancel buttons from the new resource by selecting them and pressing the Delete key.

4. Bring up the properties dialog box for the dialog resource by right-clicking the dialog box and selecting Properties from the pop-up context menu. Click the push-pin to set the properties dialog box to stay on top.

5. Change the resource ID for this control to IDD_DLGPLANES and press the Enter key.

6. Change the caption to "Planes."

7. On the Styles page of the properties dialog box, change the Style property to Child and the Border to Thin. Also make sure the System menu property is not selected.

The modified dialog box and property sheet should resemble Figure 3.28. You can look at the caption of the dialog box in Figure 3.28 to see that the caption was changed. The Resource view also reflects the change you made in step 5 to the resource ID.

FIGURE 3.28

The modified dialog resource and properties.

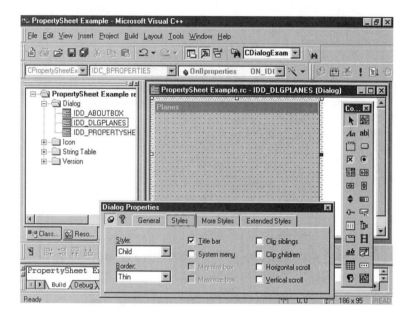

In step 7, you changed the style of the dialog box to Child. You did this so that this dialog box can be used as a property page for the property sheet that you will be creating later. The setting will let the property sheet be the parent of this property page.

Now that the dialog resource is ready to be a property page, you need to add controls on the page that will be used for options.

Execute the following steps and then make sure your IDD_DLGPLANES dialog resource resembles the dialog box in Figure 3.29:

1. Add a group box control and set its Caption property to "Engine." Set the Group property to selected.

2. Add an option button control inside of the Engine group and set its resource ID to IDC_RBENGINETYPE. Set the Caption property to "Single" and set its Tab stop and Group properties to selected.

3. Add an option button control below the Single option button and set its caption to "Double." Change the resource ID to IDC_RBDOUBLE.

4. Add an option button control to the right of the Single option button and set its caption to "Jet." Change the resource ID to IDC_RBJET.

5. Add an option button control below the "Jet" option button and set its caption to "Other." Change the resource ID to IDC_OTHER.

6. Add a second group box below the "Engine" group box and set its caption to Type. Set the Group property to selected.

7. Add an option button control inside of the Type group and set the caption to "Passenger." Change the resource ID to IDC_RBPLANETYPE. Also set the Tab stop and Group properties to selected.

8. Add an option button control to the right of the "Passenger" option button and set its caption to "Cargo." Change its resource ID to IDC_RBCARGO.

FIGURE 3.29

The Planes dialog resource.

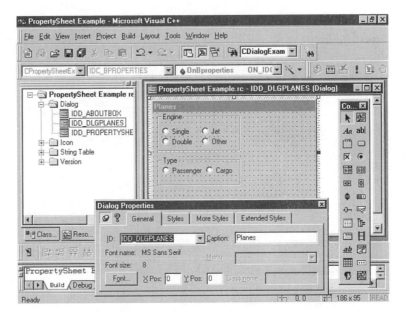

Now that the first dialog resource has been created, you need to create the next. Follow the seven-step process you used earlier when you created the IDD_DLGPLANES resource, but this time use the resource ID of IDD_DLGTRAINS and caption of "Trains."

Now that you have created the second dialog resource to be used as a property sheet, you need to add the controls that will give it some functionality. Execute the following steps and then make sure your dialog resembles the dialog box in Figure 3.30:

1. Add a static text control and set its caption to "Engine."

2. Add a combo box control just below the "Engine" static text control and set its resource ID to IDC_CMENGINE.

3. On the Data page of properties for the combo box, add the following three items each on a separate line: Steam, Electric, and Gas. To go to the next line as you type, press Ctrl+Enter.

4. Add a static text control below the combo box and set its caption to "Number of Cars."

5. Add an edit box just below the "Number of Cars" static text control and set its resource ID to IDC_EBCARS.

6. Add a check box control just below the edit box and set its caption to "Caboose attached." Set the resource ID to IDC_CBCABOOSE.

7. Add another check box control just below the previous one and set its caption to "Passenger only." Set the resource ID to IDC_CDPASSENGERONLY.

FIGURE 3.30

The Trains dialog resource.

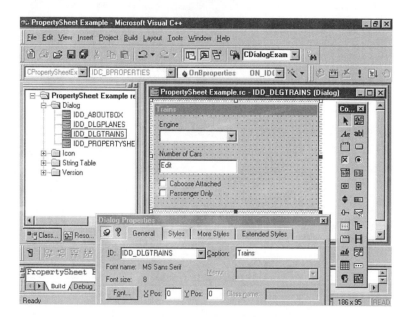

Now that you've created the second dialog resource, you need to create the next and final dialog resource. Follow the seven-step process used to create the previous two dialog resources, but this time use the resource ID of IDD_DLGCARS and the caption "Cars" for the new dialog resource.

Now that you have created the third and final dialog resource to be used as a property sheet, you need to add the controls that will give it some functionality. Execute the following steps and then make sure your dialog box resembles the IDD_DLGCARS dialog box in Figure 3.31.

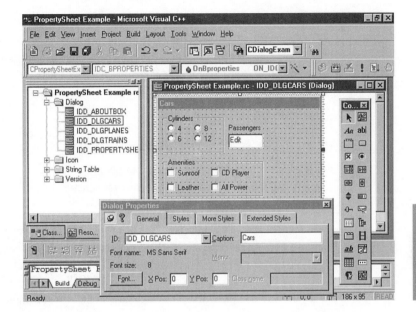

FIGURE 3.31

The Cars dialog resource.

1. Add a group box control and set its caption to "Cylinders." Also make sure the Group property is selected.

2. Inside of the "Cylinders" group box, add an option button control and set its caption property to "4." Set the resource ID to IDC_CYLINDERS. Also set the Tab stop and Group properties to selected.

3. Below the previous option button, add another option button control and set its caption to "6." Set the resource ID to IDC_RB6CYLINDERS.

4. Add a third option button to the right of the first option button control and set its caption to "8." Set the resource ID to IDC_RB8CYLINDERS.

5. Add a fourth option button control just below the one you just added and set its caption to "12." Set the resource ID to IDC_RB12CYLINDERS.

6. Add a static text control with the caption "Passengers" to the right of the group box.

7. Add an edit control just below the "Passengers" static text control and set its resource ID to IDC_EBPASSENGERS.

8. Add a second group box control below the "Cylinders" group box and set its caption to "Amenities."

9. Add a check box control inside the "Amenities" group and set its caption to "Sunroof." Set the resource ID to IDC_CBSUNROOF.

10. Add a check box control below the first check box and set its caption to "Leather." Set the resource ID to `IDC_CBLEATHER`.

11. Add a third check box control to the right of the first check box and set its caption to "CD Player." Set the resource ID to `IDC_CBCDPLAYER`.

12. Add a fourth check box control just below the third and set its caption to "All Power." Set the resource ID to `IDC_CBALLPOWER`.

Creating the Property Page Classes

Now that you have all of the dialog resources needed to create the three property pages, you are ready use the ClassWizard to generate the classes that will make these actual property pages.

If it is not already selected, select the first dialog resource you created, the `IDD_DLGPLANES` resource. Next, right-click an empty spot of the dialog resource and select ClassWizard from the pop-up context menu. Because no class has been associated with this dialog box, you will be prompted to create a class in the Adding a Class dialog box. Make sure Create a new class is selected and click the OK button. This will bring up the New Class Dialog box.

Even though you've already created a class for dialog resources earlier in this chapter, there are special considerations when creating a class for a property page. Figure 3.32 shows the New Class dialog box. The first thing you need to do is give the class a name. Because this class is for planes, use the class name `CDlgPlanes`.

FIGURE 3.32

New Class dialog box for `IDD_DLGPLANES` *dialog resource.*

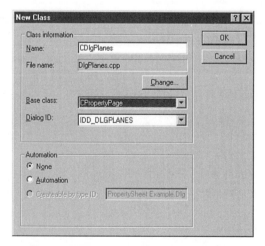

The next—and easily the most important—step is specifying which class to use as the base class. Select `CPropertyPage` from the drop-down list of available classes, making sure not to select the `CPropertySheet` class.

Once you have the class named and have specified the CPropertyPage base class, you can click the OK button to create the class.

After you have created the CDlgPlanes class, you need to add the member variables for the dialog box. Click the Member Variables page of the ClassWizard. You should have two Control IDs available that you can assign member variables to, IDC_RBENGINE and IDC_RBPLANETYPE. If either of these are not present or if you have more than these two Control IDs, you need to go back and make sure you have the properties set correctly for the option button controls.

Create a member variable for each dialog resource. Name the member variable m_engine_value for the IDC_RBENGINE resource with a category of Value and a variable type of int. Name the member variable m_plane_value for IDC_RBPLANETYPE resource with a category of Value and variable type of int.

Figure 3.33 shows the list of Control IDs and the member variables to which they've been assigned.

FIGURE 3.33

The CDlgPlanes *member variables.*

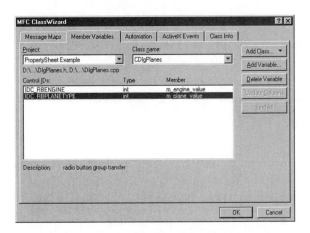

Once you have the member variables created, go ahead and close the ClassWizard by pressing the OK button.

Using Figure 3.34 as a guideline, select the IDC_DLGTRAINS resource by double-clicking its resource ID in the Resource view of the Project Workspace. Bring up the ClassWizard and click the OK button when you are asked to create a new class. This will bring up the New Class dialog box. Give this class the name of CDlgTrains and set its base class to CPropertyPage.

FIGURE 3.34

The CDlgTrains *class.*

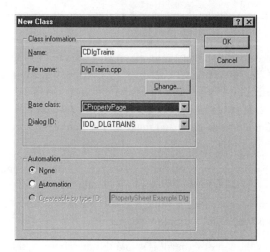

Once you have made these settings, click the OK button to create the class. This will take you the rest of the way into the ClassWizard.

Now that the class has been created for this resource, click the Member Variables page in ClassWizard, if not already selected, so that you can add the member variables for this class.

Create the following member variables for this class:

- m_caboose_value for IDC_CBCABOOSE with a category of Value and a variable type of BOOL
- m_passenger_value for IDC_CBPASSENGERONLY with a category of Value and a variable type of BOOL
- m_engine_value for IDC_CMENGINE with a category of Value and a variable type of CString
- m_cars_value for IDC_EBCARS with a category of Value and a variable type of int

Figure 3.35 displays the ClassWizard with the Control IDs assigned to member variables. Once you have set up the member variables properly, click the OK button to close the ClassWizard.

Using Figure 3.36 as a guideline, select the IDC_DLGCARS resource by double-clicking its resource ID in the Resource view of the Project Workspace. Bring up the ClassWizard and click the OK button when you are asked to create a new class. This will bring up the New Class dialog box. Give this class the name of CDlgCars and set its base class to CPropertyPage.

FIGURE 3.35

The CDlgTrains *member variables.*

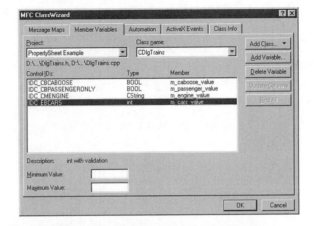

FIGURE 3.36

The CDlgCars *class.*

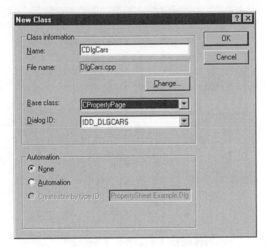

Once you have these settings, click the OK button to create the class. This will take you the rest of the way into the ClassWizard.

Now that the class has been created for this resource, click the Member Variables page in ClassWizard, if not already selected, so that you can add the member variables for this class.

Create the following member. variables for this class:

- m_allpower_value for IDC_CBALLPOWER with a category of Value and a variable type of BOOL
- m_cdplayer_value for IDC_CBCDPLAYER with a category of Value and a variable type of BOOL

- m_leather_value for IDC_CBLEATHER with a category of Value and a variable type of BOOL

- m_sunroof_value for IDC_CBSUNROOF with a category of Value and a variable type of BOOL

- m_passengers_value for IDC_EBPASSENGERS with a category of Value and a variable type of int

- m_cylinders_value for IDC_RBCYLINDERS with a category of Value and a variable of type int

Figure 3.37 displays the ClassWizard with the Control IDs assigned to member variables. Once you have the member variables set up properly, click the OK button to close the ClassWizard.

FIGURE 3.37

The CDlgCars *member variables.*

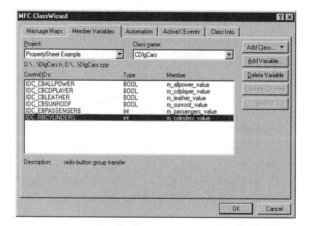

Creating the Property Sheet Class

Now that the process of creating the property page classes is complete, you need to create the property sheet class that will contain these property pages.

Unlike the classes you have built so far in this chapter, this class is not created based upon a resource such as a dialog box. Adding the needed property sheet class to your application is completed using the ClassWizard.

To create the class, select the ClassWizard menu item from the View menu. Once it appears, click the Add Class button and then, from the drop-down that appears, click New. This will display the New Class dialog box as shown in Figure 3.38.

FIGURE 3.38

The New Class dialog box for `CPropertySheet`.

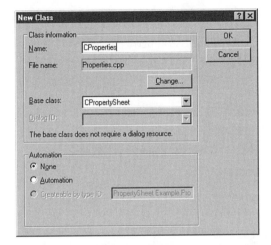

In the New Class dialog box, you need to specify a class name. Type in `CProperties` as the new class name. The next step is to specify the base class for this new class. From the drop-down list of base classes, select `CPropertySheet` class.

Notice that once you select this class, the Dialog ID drop-down list is disabled with a message just below it stating that a dialog resource is not required for this class.

Once you have the settings entered as shown in Figure 3.38, go ahead and click the OK button to add the class.

Even though you've added the property sheet class to the project, the class still doesn't know what dialog resources will be its children. Tying the property sheet class to the property page classes will be discussed in the next lesson.

Lesson Summary

In this lesson, you learned the basic concept of what property sheets and pages are, as well as the relationship they have to each other.

You also learned how to use ClassWizard to create property page classes that will be used with a property sheet class. During this process, you were introduced to the idea that the property pages are child windows of the property sheet.

You also used the ClassWizard again to create member variables for the new classes, reinforcing what you learned in the previous lessons.

Quiz 4

1. Which base class is used for property pages?

    a. `CProperties`

    b. `CPropertyPage`

    c. `CPropertySheet`

    d. `CDlgProperty`

2. Which base class is used for property sheets?

    a. `CPropertySheet`

    b. `CPropertyPage`

    c. `CDlgProperties`

    d. `CProperties`

3. What value is the Style property of a dialog box set to so it can be used as a property page?

    a. Parent

    b. SubClass

    c. Child

    d. Owner

4. Which statements are true about property sheets?

    a. Property sheets are collections of property pages.

    b. Property sheets are typically used to organize program options.

    c. Property sheets use dialog resources as child windows.

    d. The base class for a property sheet is `CPropertySheet`.

Exercise 4

Complexity: Easy

1. Create a new dialog-based application named "Exercise 1." Add two dialog resources to this application that will be used as property pages. Use ClassWizard to create the appropriate classes.

Complexity: Moderate

2. Create a new dialog-based application named "Exercise 2." Add two dialog resources to this application that will be used as property pages. Use ClassWizard to create the appropriate classes.

Add three option buttons to the first dialog page with the captions "One," "Two," and "Three." Remove the OK and Cancel buttons. Create a member variable to hold the value of the selection.

Add a check box to the second dialog resource, setting the caption to "Selected?" Remove the OK and Cancel buttons. Create a member variable to hold the value for the IDC_SELECTED resource ID.

Once you have created the property pages, create the appropriate class for the property sheet.

LESSON 5

Using Property Sheets and Pages

Now that the property page classes and the property sheet class have been created, your next step is to add the property pages to the property sheet class. Unfortunately, the ClassWizard does not handle this for you automatically.

Linking the Property Sheets and Pages

The first step in putting this all together is to let the CProperties class know that the property page classes exist. In order to do this, you need to add three include statements at the beginning of the Properties.h file, one for each of the classes created for the property pages. Enter the following three lines of code at the very beginning of the Properties.h file:

```
#include "DlgPlanes.h"
#include "DlgTrains.h"
#include "DlgCars.h"
```

After you have told the class where to find the new classes, you must manually create a member variable for each of the property pages you want in the property sheet. Because ClassWizard doesn't do this, you will need to do it manually by adding variables to the CProperties class declaration, which is also in the Properties.h file.

You need to add the following lines of code after the public statement in the //ATTRIBUTES section of the class declaration:

```
CDlgTrains m_trains;
CDlgPlanes m_planes;
CDlgCars   m_cars;
```

Once these lines are added, the class will have variables that represent each property page in the property sheet. Listing 3.6 shows what the Properties.h file should look like *after* you make the code changes.

LISTING 3.6   The Properties.h File After Code Changes

```
#include "DlgPlanes.h"
#include "DlgTrains.h"
#include "DlgCars.h"

#if !defined(AFX_PROPERTIES_H__20693A84_8A7C_
➥11D1_9B29_9AEAD2742A5E__INCLUDED_)
#define AFX_PROPERTIES_H__20693A84_8A7C_
➥11D1_9B29_9AEAD2742A5E__INCLUDED_

#if _MSC_VER > 1000
#pragma once
#endif // _MSC_VER > 1000
// Properties.h : header file
//


/////////////////////////////////////////////////////////////////////
// CProperties

class CProperties : public CPropertySheet
{
    DECLARE_DYNAMIC(CProperties)

// Construction
public:
    CProperties(UINT nIDCaption, CWnd* pParentWnd = NULL,
    ➥UINT iSelectPage = 0);
    CProperties(LPCTSTR pszCaption, CWnd* pParentWnd = NULL,
    ➥UINT iSelectPage = 0);

// Attributes
public:
    CDlgTrains m_trains;
    CDlgPlanes m_planes;
    CDlgCars   m_cars;

// Operations
public:

// Overrides
    // ClassWizard generated virtual function overrides
    //{{AFX_VIRTUAL(CProperties)
    //}}AFX_VIRTUAL

// Implementation
public:
    virtual ~CProperties();

    // Generated message map functions
```

```
protected:
    //{{AFX_MSG(CProperties)
        // NOTE - the ClassWizard will add and remove member
        // functions here.
    //}}AFX_MSG
    DECLARE_MESSAGE_MAP()
};

/////////////////////////////////////////////////////////////////////

//{{AFX_INSERT_LOCATION}}
// Microsoft Visual C++ will insert additional declarations
// immediately before the previous line.

#endif // !defined(AFX_PROPERTIES_H__20693A84_8A7C_
        //  11D1_9B29_9AEAD2742A5E__INCLUDED_)
```

These are all the code changes that you need to make to this file, but there is still another step in linking the property pages to the property sheet.

Now that the variables are created in the class for each property page, the pages must be added when the property sheet is being constructed. This involves editing yet another file, Properties.cpp.

The CPropertySheet base class has a function built in that will add the property pages to the property sheet, AddPage(). This function takes one parameter that specifies the variable for the property page and needs to be called for each page. The following three lines of code need to be added to both constructors in the Properties.cpp file:

```
AddPage(&m_planes);
AddPage(&m_trains);
AddPage(&m_cars);
```

If you are not sure what the constructors are, look ahead in Listing 3.7 and find the two locations where the above three lines have been added. Listing 3.7 shows what the Properties.cpp file looks like after you have made all the code changes necessary for this file.

LISTING 3.7 Properties.cpp After the Code Changes Are Complete

```
// Properties.cpp : implementation file
//

#include "stdafx.h"
#include "PropertySheet Example.h"
#include "Properties.h"
```

continues

LISTING 3.7   continued

```
#ifdef _DEBUG
#define new DEBUG_NEW
#undef THIS_FILE
static char THIS_FILE[] = __FILE__;
#endif


/////////////////////////////////////////////////////////////////////
// CProperties

IMPLEMENT_DYNAMIC(CProperties, CPropertySheet)

CProperties::CProperties(UINT nIDCaption, CWnd* pParentWnd,
➥UINT iSelectPage)
    :CPropertySheet(nIDCaption, pParentWnd, iSelectPage)
{
  AddPage(&m_planes);
  AddPage(&m_trains);
  AddPage(&m_cars);
}

CProperties::CProperties(LPCTSTR pszCaption, CWnd* pParentWnd,
➥UINT iSelectPage)
    :CPropertySheet(pszCaption, pParentWnd, iSelectPage)
{
  AddPage(&m_planes);
  AddPage(&m_trains);
  AddPage(&m_cars);
}

CProperties::~CProperties()
{
}

BEGIN_MESSAGE_MAP(CProperties, CPropertySheet)
    //{{AFX_MSG_MAP(CProperties)
        // NOTE - the ClassWizard will add and remove
        // mapping macros here.
    //}}AFX_MSG_MAP
END_MESSAGE_MAP()


/////////////////////////////////////////////////////////////////////
// CProperties message handlers
```

Displaying the Property Sheet

With the code changes from the previous section complete, the property pages are all
linked to the property sheet. Your next obstacle is to link the property sheet to the main
dialog box in your program so that when you click the Properties button, the properties
dialog box will be displayed.

In a previous lesson, you created a message handler event that would be executed when you clicked a button. You need to do the same type of process for this step. To start with, you need to display the ClassWizard and select CPropertySheetExampleDlg class from the list of classes in this application.

Once you have the class, notice that the resource ID IDC_BPROPERTIES is in the list of available Object IDs. Select this resource ID from the list and then select BN_CLICKED from the list of available messages by double-clicking it. This will bring up the Add Member Function dialog box. Remembering back to a discussion in an earlier lesson, go ahead and keep the default member function name OnBproperties by clicking the OK button. Figure 3.39 shows the ClassWizard with the new member function selected.

FIGURE 3.39

ClassWizard with the new member function selected.

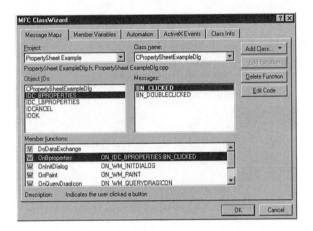

Once you have mapped the member function to the BN_CLICKED message, go ahead and click the Edit Code button to close the ClassWizard and jump right to the point in the PropertySheet ExampleDlg.cpp file, where you need to add code to create and display the property sheet.

You need to create a variable that will hold the property sheet and then call the DoModal() method to display it. In this case, add the following two lines of code to accomplish this task:

```
CProperties props("Properties", this, 0);
int result = props.DoModal();
```

The first line creates a variable named props of type CProperties. What's different about this statement is the presence of the three parameters after the variable name.

In order, these parameters are the property sheet's caption, a pointer to the property sheet's parent, and the first property sheet to display.

The second line is a little different than the one you used in previous lessons. This time, an integer variable named result is declared and holds the return value of the dialog box. This value will be the ID of the button that was used to close the dialog box.

You are missing only one more thing before you can build and test this application. The main dialog resource doesn't know where to find the declaration for the CProperties class. For the compilation to succeed, you need to include the Properties.h file. Adding the following line towards the beginning of the PropertySheet ExampleDlg.cpp file does this:

```
#include "Properties.h"
```

This should be added just after the other include statements at the top of the file.

Once you have this line added, go ahead and build and execute the application. Clicking the Properties button will display the property sheet as shown in Figure 3.40.

FIGURE 3.40

PropertySheet sample application executing.

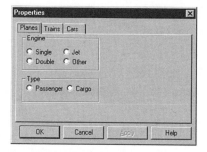

If you haven't done so already, go ahead and close the application.

Keeping the Property Sheet Values

Now that the application is displaying the property sheet properly, it would be nice to keep the values that are selected, and the values would be there when the properties are closed and redisplayed.

Because the values for the property pages are not kept each time the property sheet is displayed, you need to create variables inside your program that will hold the values. These values should be updated each time the property sheet is closed with the OK button.

One place to add variables to hold the property page values at all times is in the main dialog box's class. The CPropertyExampleDlg class is defined in the PropertySheet ExampleDlg.h file. Add the following lines of code in the public section of the class declaration just after the class constructor CPropertySheetExampleDlg(CWnd* pParent = NULL). If you are not sure where it goes, Listing 3.8 shows the entire listing of Property Sheet ExampleDlg.h after the code changes:

```
int     m_planes_engine;
int     m_planes_type;
CString m_trains_engine;
int     m_trains_cars;
bool    m_trains_caboose;
bool    m_trains_passengers;
int     m_cars_cylinders;
int     m_cars_passengers;
bool    m_cars_sunroof;
bool    m_cars_leather;
bool    m_cars_cdplayer;
bool    m_cars_allpower;
```

This will create the variables necessary for permanently holding the values as you go in and out of the property sheet. Listing 3.8 shows the entire file after the above lines of code have been added.

LISTING 3.8 PropertySheet ExampleDlg.h After the Code Changes

```
// PropertySheet ExampleDlg.h : header file
//

#if !defined_(AFX_PROPERTYSHEETEXAMPLEDLG_H__820D5A07_8A68_
➥11D1_9B29_9AEAD2742A5E__INCLUDED_)
#define AFX_PROPERTYSHEETEXAMPLEDLG_H__820D5A07_8A68_
➥11D1_9B29_9AEAD2742A5E__INCLUDED_

#if _MSC_VER > 1000
#pragma once
#endif // _MSC_VER > 1000

/////////////////////////////////////////////////////////////////
// CPropertySheetExampleDlg dialog box

class CPropertySheetExampleDlg : public CDialog
{
// Construction
public:
    CPropertySheetExampleDlg(CWnd* pParent = NULL); // standard
                                                    // constructor

    int     m_planes_engine;
    int     m_planes_type;
    CString m_trains_engine;
    int     m_trains_cars;
    bool    m_trains_caboose;
    bool    m_trains_passengers;
    int     m_cars_cylinders;
```

continues

LISTING 3.8   continued

```
        int      m_cars_passengers;
        bool     m_cars_sunroof;
        bool     m_cars_leather;
        bool     m_cars_cdplayer;
        bool     m_cars_allpower;


    // Dialog Data
        //{{AFX_DATA(CPropertySheetExampleDlg)
        enum { IDD = IDD_PROPERTYSHEETEXAMPLE_DIALOG };
        CListBox    m_properties_control;
        CString m_properties_value;
        //}}AFX_DATA

        // ClassWizard generated virtual function overrides
        //{{AFX_VIRTUAL(CPropertySheetExampleDlg)
        protected:
        virtual void DoDataExchange(CDataExchange* pDX);      // DDX/DDV
                                                             // support
        //}}AFX_VIRTUAL

    // Implementation
    protected:
        HICON m_hIcon;

        // Generated message map functions
        //{{AFX_MSG(CPropertySheetExampleDlg)
        virtual BOOL OnInitDialog();
        afx_msg void OnSysCommand(UINT nID, LPARAM lParam);
        afx_msg void OnPaint();
        afx_msg HCURSOR OnQueryDragIcon();
        afx_msg void OnBproperties();
        //}}AFX_MSG
        DECLARE_MESSAGE_MAP()
};

//{{AFX_INSERT_LOCATION}}
// Microsoft Visual C++ will insert additional declarations
// immediately before the previous line.

#endif // !defined(AFX_PROPERTYSHEETEXAMPLEDLG_H__820D5A07_8A68_
        // 11D1_9B29_9AEAD2742A5E___INCLUDED_)
```

Because these variables are new, you need to initialize them so that the first time the property sheet is displayed, bogus values are not represented in the property pages. To do this, the following lines of code need to be added to the PropertySheet ExampleDlg.cpp file in the `OnInitDialog()` method. Add them right after the `// TODO: Add extra initialization here` comment.

```
m_planes_engine     = -1;
m_planes_type       = -1;

m_trains_engine     = "";
m_trains_cars       = 0;
m_trains_caboose    = FALSE;
m_trains_passengers = FALSE;

m_cars_cylinders    = -1;
m_cars_passengers   = 0;
m_cars_sunroof      = FALSE;
m_cars_leather      = FALSE;
m_cars_cdplayer     = FALSE;
m_cars_allpower     = FALSE;
```

This section of code takes care of initializing the variables when the main dialog box is initialized. Now, the only step remaining is adding the code that assigns the default values before the property sheet is displayed and storing the values when the property sheet is closed.

To set the values for the property pages, add the following lines of code right after you create the prop variable and before you display the property sheet with DoModal(). These are in the OnBproperties method in the PropertySheet ExampleDlg.cpp file, which is the same file to which you just added the previous lines of code:

```
props.m_planes.m_engine_value    = m_planes_engine;
props.m_planes.m_plane_value     = m_planes_type;

props.m_trains.m_engine_value    = m_trains_engine;
props.m_trains.m_cars_value      = m_trains_cars;
props.m_trains.m_caboose_value   = m_trains_caboose;
props.m_trains.m_passenger_value = m_trains_passengers;

props.m_cars.m_cylinders_value   = m_cars_cylinders;
props.m_cars.m_passengers_value  = m_cars_passengers;
props.m_cars.m_sunroof_value     = m_cars_sunroof;
props.m_cars.m_leather_value     = m_cars_leather;
props.m_cars.m_cdplayer_value    = m_cars_cdplayer;
props.m_cars.m_allpower_value    = m_cars_allpower;
```

These lines of code set the initial values before the property sheet is displayed. Now, you need to check and see if the OK button was used to close the property sheet. If so, the values from the property pages need to be stored.

The following lines of code accomplish this task. They should be added just after the DoModal() line of code:

```
if (result == IDOK)
    {
```

```
m_planes_engine       = props.m_planes.m_engine_value;
m_planes_type         = props.m_planes.m_plane_value;

m_trains_engine       = props.m_trains.m_engine_value;
m_trains_cars         = props.m_trains.m_cars_value;
m_trains_caboose      = props.m_trains.m_caboose_value;
m_trains_passengers   = props.m_trains.m_passengers_value;

m_cars_cylinders      = props.m_cars.m_cylinders_value;
m_cars_passengers     = props.m_cars.m_passengers_value;
m_cars_sunroof        = props.m_cars.m_sunroof_value;
m_cars_leather        = props.m_cars.m_leather_value;
m_cars_cdplayer       = props.m_cars.m_cdplayer_value;
m_cars_allpower       = props.m_cars.m_allpower_value;

m_properties_control.AddString("Properties Stored");
}
else
{
    m_properties_control.AddString("Changes Ignored");
}
```

Examining these lines of code a little closer, you will notice that an if statement is used to check the value of the result variable. If the result was IDOK, the OK button was pressed to close the property sheet.

After all the values have been stored, a message is added to the list box on the main dialog box indicating that this was done. If the values were not stored, a message was added stating as much.

Your application is now complete. All you need to do is build and execute it. Go ahead and click the Properties button and set some values. Click OK on the property sheet to save the values or Cancel to ignore the changes.

Lesson Summary

In this lesson, you learned how to link the property pages with a property sheet and how to display the property sheet in your application.

You also learned how to store the values of property sheets in variables so that each time you display the property sheet, the values you selected will remain.

Quiz 5

1. Which CPropertySheet member function adds a property page to the class?

    a. AddPropertyPage()

    b. AddPage()

     c. `InsertPage()`

     d. `CreatePage()`

2. What must you do to the class declaration of your derived property sheet class?

     a. No changes are needed.

     b. You need to assign a value to the member variables.

     c. The member variables need to be changed to reflect the new property sheet.

     d. You need to add member variables for each property page.

3. What value will be returned from a dialog box if the user clicks the OK button?

     a. `IDC_OK`

     b. `OK_CLICKED`

     c. `BN_CLICKED`

     d. `IDOK`

4. What parameters are needed when declaring a variable type from a derived class of `CPropertySheet`?

     a. Caption, pointer to parent, index of beginning page

     b. Title and number of pages

     c. Title, number of pages, and beginning page index

     d. None of the above

Exercise 5

Complexity: Easy

1. Create a new dialog-based application named "Exercise 1." Add two dialog resources and set their properties so that it can be used as a property sheet.

    Add three option buttons to the first dialog page with the captions "One," "Two," and "Three." Remove the OK and Cancel Buttons and create a member variable to hold the group's value.

    Add a check box to the second dialog resource, setting the caption to "Selected?" Remove the OK and Cancel buttons and add a member variable to hold the check box's value.

    Add a button control to the main dialog resource with the caption "Properties." When this button is clicked, the property sheet should be displayed.

Complexity: Moderate

2. Create a new dialog-based application named "Exercise 2." Add two dialog resources and set their properties so that the application can be used as a property sheet.

   Add three option buttons to the first dialog page with the captions "One," "Two," and "Three." Remove the OK and Cancel Buttons and create a member variable to hold the group's value.

   Add a check box to the second dialog resource, setting the caption to "Selected?" Remove the OK and Cancel buttons and add a member variable to hold the check box's value.

   Add a button control to the main dialog resource with the caption "Properties." When this button is clicked, the property sheet should be displayed.

   The program should keep track of the values of the controls on the property pages so that each time the Properties button is clicked, the values are restored.

Chapter Summary

This chapter started off by introducing you to the concept of dialog boxes and their common uses. You then created a dialog box by building a dialog resource using common controls found on the Controls toolbar.

Once you built the resource dialog box, you learned how to use the ClassWizard to create a class that was associated with the dialog resource, and how to add member functions and variables that would allow your program to utilize the common controls.

After dialog resources, you learned about the concepts of property pages and property sheets and how these two items relate to each other. You also learned what the main purpose of a property sheet was.

Once the concepts of property sheets were covered, you learned how to build the dialog resources that are used for property pages and how to build a class with the ClassWizard. You also learned how to use the ClassWizard to build a class for a property sheet and what kind of code you had to write to link the two together. After which, you added code that would allow your program to remember the choices made in the property pages.

CHAPTER 4

Enhancing Your Application with Common Controls

Managing input from the user is an integral part of many applications. When you develop your application, you must present an interface that will enable the user to enter meaningful data easily for your application to process.

By using the custom controls supplied by the Windows 95 operating system, you can easily gather and manage the data provided by your users. If you have used any Windows application, then you are familiar with common controls. These common controls come in many different shapes and styles, such as edit boxes, buttons, and icons.

This chapter will cover some of the more advanced common controls. After you learn how to use these controls, you should have no problems applying the knowledge that you have gained to using other controls.

LESSON 1

Managing Ranges with Sliders and Spinners

When designing an application, one of the options that you might have to include is the capability to limit the user's input to selected values. This can be easily accomplished by using some of the Windows common controls. In this lesson, you learn how to limit a user's input range by using the slider control and the spin control.

The *slider control*, also known as a *trackbar*, is basically a small window that contains tick marks and a slider. When the slider moves along the track with either the mouse or keystrokes, the WM_HSCROLL notification message is sent to indicate that the slider position has changed. The functionality of the slider control is provided by the CSliderCtrl class.

The spin control, also known as an up-down control, is represented by two arrows that, when clicked on, will change the value of the control. This control is usually associated with another control on a dialog, known as a *buddy control*, which is used to represent the value of the spin control. The functionality of the spin control is provided by the CSpinButtonCtrl class.

Creating the Controls1 Example

To get started with this lesson, you will need to create a dialog-based application. Go ahead and create the dialog application, giving it the name "Controls1." If you are unsure how to do this, you should refer back to Chapter 2, "Your First Interactive Visual C++ Applications."

After you have created the necessary application, you should have a screen similar to Figure 4.1. If you don't have the control palette visible, you can easily turn it on by right-clicking the main menu bar and selecting "Controls" to toggle the control palette.

To make some space for the controls that you want to use in this example, you will need to move the static text control that was created automatically. Move this control up just a hair so that you can easily fit these other controls onto the dialog box. After you move the text control up, go ahead and add a slider control, an edit control, and a spin control to the dialog box. Use Figure 4.2 as a guide.

FIGURE 4.1

The default dialog-based application.

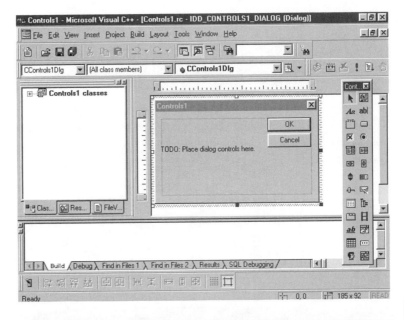

FIGURE 4.2

Adding controls to the dialog box.

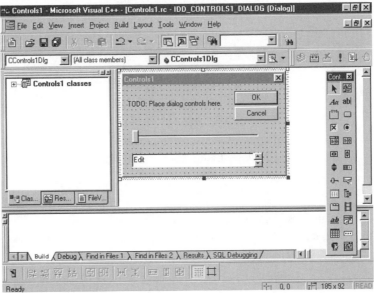

Note

To help align controls on a dialog box, you can choose Layout, Guide Settings from the menu to turn on the grid, or you can click the Toggle Grid icon on the dialog box toolbar.

After you place the necessary controls on the dialog box and align them so that they are visually the same as Figure 4.2, go ahead and compile and execute the application. You will be presented with a dialog box in the center of the screen, like the one in Figure 4.3. As you play with the controls on the dialog, you will notice that there is no real functionality to the application at this point.

FIGURE 4.3

Playing with the controls on the dialog box.

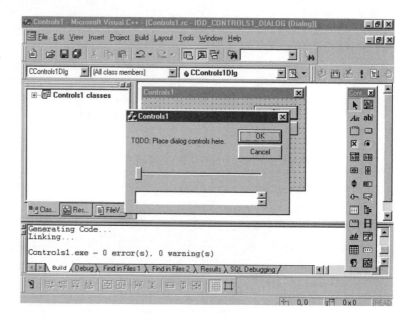

Setting Properties

One of the first things you need to do when you place a control on the dialog box is to set the properties to your liking. Each control has various properties that can change the look or behavior of the control.

To look at the properties for the slider control, simply right-click the control and select Properties from the context menu. You will be presented with a requester, as shown in Figure 4.4, that enables you to change some of the properties of the selected control, the slider in this case.

There are three tabs in this dialog box, separating the different properties into groups. Using these tabs, you can set the various properties for this control. While working with various controls, you will notice that many controls have some properties in common. Usually, these properties will be found in the General tab of the property editor.

FIGURE 4.4

The Slider Properties dialog box.

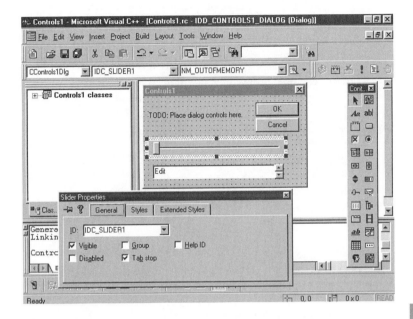

> **Note**
>
> You should already be familiar with the general properties from the previous chapters. From now on, when you are introduced to a new control, only the properties that are specific to that control will be discussed.

Here is a list of the properties of the slider control with a brief description of the functionality of each:

- Orientation—This property enables you to specify whether you want the control to be displayed horizontally or vertically in the dialog box. Horizontal is the default setting for this property.

- Point—This property determines where tick marks are placed. By default, tick marks will be drawn on both sides of the slider. You can specify that the tick marks be drawn on a specific side of the slider, depending on the orientation of the control.

- Tick Marks—This property works in conjunction with the Point property. By default, this property is set to False, which means that no tick marks are displayed. If you check this property, which sets it to true, the tick marks will be displayed according to the Point property.

- Auto Ticks—By default, this property is not set. By setting this property to True, a tick mark will be displayed for each increment on the slider.

- Enable Selection—This property will enable the user to select a range on the slider. By default, this property is set to False. When set to true, the user can use the slider control to select a range.

For this example program, you will need to set some of these properties. Using Table 4.1 as a guide, set the style properties for the slider control to the following settings.

TABLE 4.1   Properties for the Slider Control

Property	Value
Orientation	Horizontal
Point	Top/Left
Tick Marks	True (checked)
Auto Ticks	True (checked)
Border	False (unchecked)
Enable Selection	False (unchecked)

After you set the properties for the slider control, you may need to move the slider up just a hair on the dialog if part of the slider is cut off. If this is the case, simply move it up and adjust the size of the control so that the entire control is visible. When you are done setting the properties for the slider control, your dialog box should look similar to the one shown in Figure 4.5. You should see the tick marks at the top of the control, and the slider will be pointed at the top and flat on the bottom.

FIGURE 4.5

The new look of the slider control.

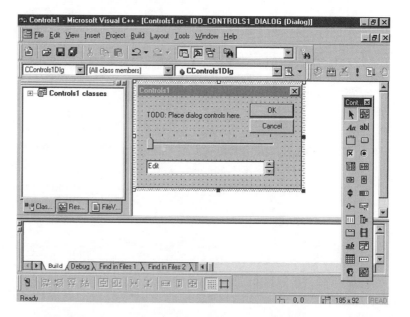

Now that the slider control properties are set, you need to set the properties of the edit box and the spin control. The edit box only has one property that you want to change for this lesson, so go ahead and bring up the property dialog box for the edit control. For this control, the property dialog has three tabs with the same names as the slider control, so go ahead and click the Styles tab since these are the properties that are unique to this control.

Here is a quick list of the properties for the edit box and a brief description of each property:

- Multiline—Enables the user to enter multiple lines into the edit box. The default for this property is False.

- Number—Enables only the user to enter numerical data. The default for this property is False.

- Horizontal Scroll—When this property is checked, it will add a scroll bar when the Multiline property is also set to True. By default, this property is False and disabled unless you check the Multiline property.

- Auto HScroll—This property tells the edit box to scroll the displayed text when the user passes the end of the edit box. By default, this property is set to True.

- Vertical Scroll—This property provides a vertical scroll bar when the Multiline property is checked. By default, this property is False and is disabled.

- Auto VScroll—If the Multiline property is set to True and this option is checked, the text will be automatically scrolled down when the user passes the bottom of the edit box. By default, this property is set to False and is disabled.

- Password—This property places an asterisk in the edit box as the user keys in data, just like a login prompt. By default, this property is False and will be disabled if you set the Multiline property to True.

- No Hide Selection—This option changes the way that the text is displayed in the edit box when it loses and regains focus. By default, this property is set to False. If this property is set to True and text is selected in the edit box, the text will stay selected when the control loses focus.

- OEM Convert—When this property is set to True, it will convert the text typed in from the Windows character set to the OEM character set, and then back to the Windows set. By default, this property is set to False.

- Want Return—When set to True, this property will enable the user to press enter key while typing in a multiline edit box. By default, this property is set to False.

- Border—This property draws a border around the edit box. This property is set to True by default.

4

- Uppercase—When this property is set to True, all text typed into the edit box will be converted to uppercase. By default, this property is set to False.
- Lowercase—When this property is set to True, all text typed into the edit box will be converted to lowercase. By default, this property is set to False.
- Read Only—When this property is set to True, the user will not be able to edit or type text into the edit box. By default, this property is set to False.

The only property that we are interested in for this example is the Number property. Go ahead and set this property to True by checking its box.

Now that you have the properties set for the edit box, you can go ahead and set the properties for the spin control. Go ahead and bring up the property dialog box for the spin control. As with the other two controls that you have worked on in this example, the spin control has the same three groups of properties. Go ahead and click the Styles tab.

Here is a list of the properties for the spin control along with a brief description of each property:

- Orientation—This property determines which way the spin control is drawn. By default, the property is set to Vertical, which draws the arrows pointing up and down. Setting this property to Horizontal will draw the arrows so that they point left and right.
- Alignment—This property positions the spin control next to a buddy control. By default, this property is set to Unattached, which means that it does not sit next to the buddy control. By setting this property to Left, the spin control will be placed on the left side of the buddy control. If set to Right, the spin control will sit at the right edge of the buddy control.
- Auto Buddy—By setting this property to True, the spin control will automatically set the buddy control by selecting the previous window control in the Z order. The buddy control is usually used to display the value of the spin control and is typically an edit box or a static text control. By default, this property is set to False.
- Set Buddy Integer—When this property is set to True, the spin control will set the text of the buddy control window when the spin position is changed. This is accomplished by the WM_SETTEXT message. By default, this property is set to False.
- No Thousands—When set to True, a thousands separator will not be inserted between every three decimal places. By default, this property is set to False.
- Wrap—When this property is set to True and the user passes the beginning or ending of the spin range, the value will automatically wrap around. By default, this property is set to False.
- Arrow Keys—This property will enable the user to press the up and down cursor keys to increment or decrement the value of the spin control. By default, this property is set to True.

By using Table 4.2 as a guide, go ahead and set the properties for the spin control.

TABLE 4.2   Properties for the Spin Control

Property	Value
Orientation	Vertical
Alignment	Unattached
Auto Buddy	True (checked)
Set Buddy Integer	True (checked)
No Thousands	True (checked)
Wrap	True (checked)
Arrow Keys	True (checked)

Creating the Member Variables

Now that you have the necessary properties assigned for the controls in this example, you need to create the member variables that enable you to access these controls on the dialog box from within the source code of your application. If you are unsure about this procedure, you should review Chapter 3, "Increasing User Interaction with Dialog Boxes and Property Sheets."

To create the member variables, go ahead and get into the Class Wizard and click the Member Variables tab. As well as the two normal control IDs for the OK and Cancel buttons, you will see that there are three new entries. There is one entry for each control that you placed on the dialog box, as shown in Figure 4.6.

FIGURE 4.6

The new member variables.

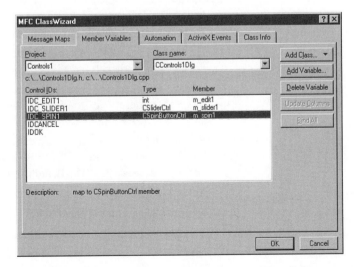

Using Table 4.3 as a guide, go ahead and create the member variables for the new control IDs. While looking at Table 4.3, you will notice that the IDC_EDIT1 ID has a type of int. Because you will be using the edit box to display the value from the slider and the spinner, it will make displaying the value much simpler when it's time to add code. You will see this in just a few minutes.

TABLE 4.3   Member Variables for the New Control IDs

ID	Type	Member Variable
IDC_EDIT1	int	m_edit1
IDC_SLIDER1	CSliderCtrl	m_slider1
IDC_SPIN1	CSpinButtonCtrl	m_spin1

Examining the Functions of the Slider and Spinner

By creating member variables for a control, you can access that control directly in your code. One function of the member variables is calling the member functions. Each control has unique member functions. The tasks that these functions perform vary from one control to another. You can use these functions to either retrieve information from a control or to change a control's characteristics.

The MFC CSliderCtrl class encapsulates the functionality of the Windows slider control. Table 4.4 outlines the common function members of this class.

TABLE 4.4   The Member Functions of the Slider Control

Function	Description
ClearSel	Clears the user's selection.
ClearTics	Removes all tick marks from the slider.
GetChannelRect	Returns the bounding rectangle for the slider control's channel (the area in which the slider moves).
GetPageSize	Returns the page size. The page size determines how much the slider moves for the TB_PAGEUP and TB_PAGEDOWN notification messages.
GetLineSize	Returns the line size. The line size determines how much the slider moves for the TB_LINEUP and TB_LINEDOWN notification messages. The default setting is 1.
GetNumTics	Returns the number of tick marks on the slider.
GetPos	Returns the position of the slider.
GetRange	Returns the minimum and maximum range values of the slider.

Function	Description
GetRangeMax	Returns the maximum range value.
GetRangeMin	Returns the minimum range value.
GetSelection	Returns the current range selection.
GetThumbRect	Returns the bounding rectangle for the slider.
GetTic	Returns the position of a tick mark.
GetTicArray	Returns the position of all tick marks.
GetTicPos	Returns the client coordinates of a tick mark.
SetPageSize	Sets the page size of the slider.
SetLineSize	Sets the line size of the slider.
SetPos	Sets the position of the slider.
SetRange	Sets the current range for the slider.
SetRangeMax	Sets the maximum range value.
SetRangeMin	Sets the minimum range value.
SetSelection	Sets the current selection range.
SetTic	Set the position of a tick mark.
SetTicFreq	Sets ticks at regular intervals.
VerifyPos	Determines if the current value is within the slider's minimum and maximum values.

The MFC CSpinButtonCtrl class encapsulates the functionality of the Windows spinner control. Table 4.5 outlines the common function members of this class.

TABLE 4.5 The Member Functions of the Spin Control

Function	Description
GetAccel	Returns the acceleration rate. The *acceleration rate* is the speed at which the spin control updates itself while holding down one of the arrows.
GetBase	Returns the numerical base. By default, the value is 10. A value of 16 represents HEX-based.
GetBuddy	Returns a pointer to the current buddy control.
GetPos	Returns the current position.
GetRange	Returns the minimum and maximum range values.
SetAccel	Sets the acceleration rate.

continues

TABLE 4.5   continued

Function	Description
SetBase	Sets the numerical base.
SetBuddy	Assign a buddy control.
SetPos	Sets the current position.
SetRange	Sets the minimum and maximum range.

Making the Controls Work Together

Before the user can use these controls to enter meaningful data, you must initialize the controls so that only meaningful data can be entered. By using the functions from Table 4.4 and Table 4.5, you can easily achieve this task.

When the MFC AppWizard generated the dialog box application for you, it created several classes and functions that make organizing and managing code easy. The place in which you want to insert the necessary code for the initialization of the controls is in the OnInitDialog() function of the CControls1Dlg class. Go ahead and expand the CControls1Dlg class and then double-click the OnInitDialog() function. This brings the OnInitDialog() function into the editor, as shown in Figure 4.7.

FIGURE 4.7

The OnInitDialog()
function.

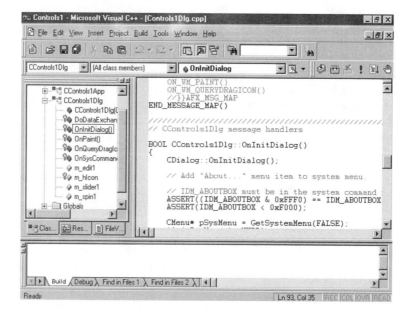

By looking at the OnInitDialog() function, as listed in Listing 4.1, you will notice that there is an area towards the bottom of the function designated for initialization code (after the TODO: comment). This is where you will add the initialization code for the controls.

LISTING 4.1 The `OnInitDialog()` Function

```
BOOL CControls1Dlg::OnInitDialog()
{
    CDialog::OnInitDialog();
    // Add "About..." menu item to system menu.
    // IDM_ABOUTBOX must be in the system command range.
    ASSERT((IDM_ABOUTBOX & 0xFFF0) == IDM_ABOUTBOX);
    ASSERT(IDM_ABOUTBOX < 0xF000);
    CMenu* pSysMenu = GetSystemMenu(FALSE); if (pSysMenu != NULL)
    {
        CString strAboutMenu;
        strAboutMenu.LoadString(IDS_ABOUTBOX);
        if (!strAboutMenu.IsEmpty())
        {
            pSysMenu->AppendMenu(MF_SEPARATOR);
            pSysMenu->AppendMenu(MF_STRING, IDM_ABOUTBOX, strAboutMenu);
        }
    }

    // Set the icon for this dialog.  The framework does this
    // automatically when the application's main window is not a dialog
    SetIcon(m_hIcon, TRUE);        // Set big icon
    SetIcon(m_hIcon, FALSE);       // Set small icon

    // TODO: Add extra initialization here
    return TRUE;  // return TRUE  unless you set the focus to a control
}
```

The objective of this example program is to enable the user to use the slider or the spinner to select a value between 0 and 10. So, one of the first things that you want to do is set the ranges for these controls. To do this, use the `CSliderCtrl::SetRange()` function for the slider control and the `CSpinButtonCtrl::SetRange()` function of the spinner control. Call these functions by using the member variables that you created for each control. The code to do this would look like the following:

```
// TODO: Add extra initialization here
    m_slider1.SetRange(0,10,TRUE);
    m_spin1.SetRange(0,10);
```

If you set the properties as discussed earlier, this should be all the initialization that these controls need to function properly. If you were to execute this application at this time, the spin control would update the edit box but the slider bar wouldn't. When you created the dialog, you placed a slider control on a form, then the edit box, then the spinner control (in that order). Then, when you set the Auto buddy property of the spin control, it automatically assigned it to the edit box. The slider doesn't have this functionality, so you must manually update the edit box when the user moves the slider.

When the user moves the slider control, a WM_HSCROLL message is generated. This message is handled by the dialog box, not the slider. To add the necessary code to handle this message, simply open the ClassWizard and on the Message Maps tab, click the

CControls1Dlg ID. When you do this, you will be presented with a list of messages to which this dialog can respond. Scroll the Messages list until you see the WM_HSCROLL message, as shown in Figure 4.8. Double-click this message to add this message to the member functions.

FIGURE **4.8**

Selecting the WM_HSCROLL message.

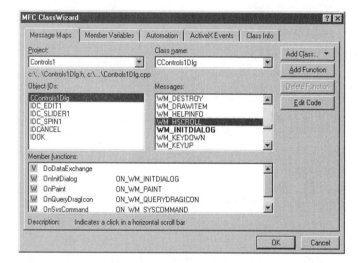

After the function is added to the member function list, double-click the OnHScroll() function to bring up the function in the code editor. You should have a screen similar to Figure 4.9.

FIGURE **4.9**

The OnHScroll() *function.*

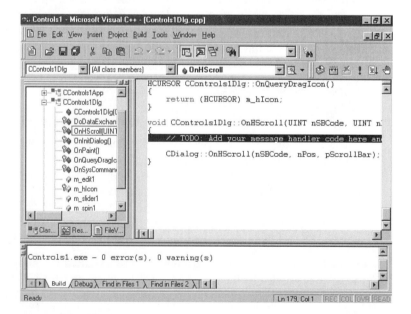

After the `OnHScroll()` function is in the editor, enter the following line of code after the TODO: comment:

```
m_spin1.SetPos(m_slider1.GetPos());
```

Because the `GetPos()` function of the slider returns an integer value, you can use the `SetPos()` function of the spinner to set its value from this return value, as done in the previous code.

If you were to execute the application at this point, you would notice that the slider control now updates the spin control, but the spin control doesn't do the same. This to can be easily handled by responding to a message. Because the spin control is using the edit box as a buddy control, you will use the EN_CHANGE message to update the slider.

Using the ClassWizard, select the IDC_EDIT1 ID from the list of Object IDs. In the Messages list, double-click EN_CHANGE to add a member function. You will be presented with a dialog box asking you what you want to name this member function, as shown in Figure 4.10. Go ahead and choose OK to accept the default naming. After the member function is created, double-click it to bring it into the code editor.

FIGURE 4.10

Naming the member function.

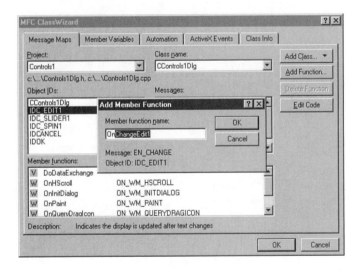

Just like every other function that you have worked with, you will see the infamous TODO: comment. Scroll down and add the following line of code:

```
m_slider1.SetPos(m_spin1.GetPos());
```

This line of code is pretty much the same as the one you used to set the spin control except that you are now using the spin control's `GetPos` return value to set the slider position.

After you have entered this line of code, go ahead and execute the application. This time, when you move the slider or the spin control, the other control will be updated.

Lesson Summary

In this lesson, you learned how to utilize the slider and spin controls to limit an input range. By using the combination of properties, the ClassWizard, and code, you learned how easy it is to use these controls, as well as tie them together.

Quiz 1

1. What class provides the functionality of the slider control?

    a. `CSliderClass`

    b. `CSliderObject`

    c. `CSliderCtrl`

    d. `CSliderControl`

2. What function of the `CSliderCtrl` class is used to set the range for a slider?

    a. `CSetRange`

    b. `SetRange`

    c. `SetSliderRange`

    d. `SetPos`

3. What class provides the functionality of the spin control?

    a. `CSpinButtonCtrl`

    b. `SpinnerClass`

    c. `SpinCtrlClass`

    d. `CSpinnerClass`

4. When the slider is moved, what notification message is sent to the dialog box?

    a. WM_SLIDERPOSCHANGED

    b. WM_HSCROLL

    c. WM_HZSCROLL

    d. WM_VSCROLL

Exercise 1

Complexity: Easy

1. Create a dialog-based application named "Exercise 1" that has a slider control on it. The range for the slider should be 0 to 20 and no tick marks should be showing.

Complexity: Moderate

2. Create a dialog-based application named "Exercise 2" that has a spin control and an edit box on it. The range for the spinner should be 0 to 1,000. The edit box is used to display the value of the spin control.

LESSON 2

Adding a Progress Bar to Your Application

When processing lengthy operations, you should display an indicator, which displays the current status of the operation. This is where the progress bar control comes into play.

The progress bar is a visual representation of an operation that shows the status as the operation progresses. The CProgressCtrl class provides the progress bar's functionality. In this lesson, you will learn how to add a progress bar to a dialog-based application.

Creating the Progress Example

The progress bar has a range and a position. The range represents the duration of the task and the position represents the percentage of the task that is complete.

To get started with this lesson, you will need to create another dialog-based application. Go ahead and create the dialog application, giving it the name "Progress." If you are unsure how to do this, refer back to Chapter 2.

Using Figure 4.11 as a guide, add a progress bar and a button to the dialog box. The button will be used to start the progress bar. While the progress bar is processing, the button will be disabled.

FIGURE 4.11

The Progress example dialog box.

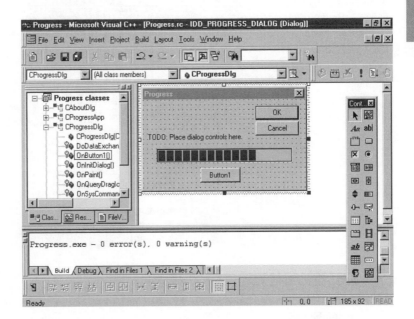

Setting Properties

Now that you have the necessary controls on the dialog box for this application, you need to set the properties for each control. The following is a quick description of the properties on the Styles tab:

- Border—Creates a border around the edge of the control. By default, this property is set to True.

- Vertical—By default, the progress bar operates horizontally. If you set this property to True, the progress bar will be drawn and filled vertically.

- Smooth—By default, the progress bar is filled with small blocks. Setting this property to True will fill the progress bar with a solid rectangle rather than the blocks.

Now that you know the properties of the progress bar, you can go ahead and close the property dialog box because you don't need to change any of them for this example application. However, to make the button look nice, go ahead and edit its properties to change the caption to "Start." When you are done with the properties for the controls, your dialog should look like the one in Figure 4.12. The only visible change will be the caption on the button.

FIGURE 4.12

The dialog controls with updated properties.

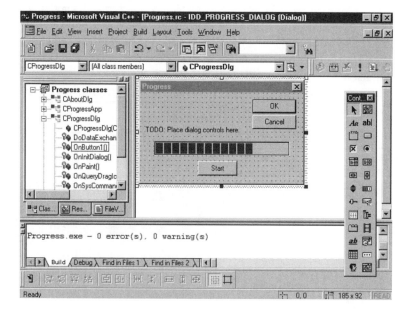

Creating the Member Variables

Now that you have all the necessary controls and properties set, you can go ahead and create the member variables for the progress bar and the button. Using Table 4.6 as a guide, create the member variables. After you are done, your screen should look like Figure 4.13.

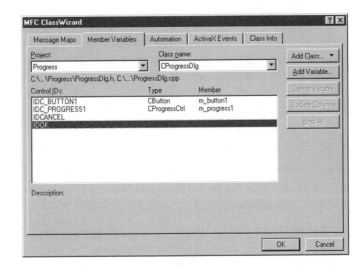

FIGURE 4.13

Creating the member variables.

TABLE 4.6   Member Variables for the New Control IDs

ID	Type	Member Variable
IDC_BUTTON1	CButton	m_button1
IDC_PROGRESS1	CProgressCtrl	m_progress1

Examining the Functions of the Progress Bar Control

The MFC CProgressCtrl class encapsulates the functionality of the Windows progress bar control. Table 4.7 outlines the common function members of this class.

TABLE 4.7   The Member Functions of the Progress Bar Control

Function	Description
GetPos	Returns the current position of the progress bar.
GetRange	Returns the low and high limits of the range.
OffsetPos	Advances the offset of the progress bar by the passed amount. After the advance, the control will be redrawn to reflect the change.
SetPos	Sets the position of the progress bar.
SetRange	Sets the low and high range amounts for the progress bar.
StepIt	Increases the position of the progress bar by the step value. The step value is set by the SetStep function.
SetStep	Sets the step increment used by the StepIt function.

4

Working with the Progress Bar Control

The first thing that you should do when you use any control is initialize it. As discussed in the previous lesson, there is a designated place for this. Go ahead and open up the `OnInitDialog()` function of the `CProgressDlg` class. After the function is in the code editor, scroll down to the line after the TODO: comment. Add the following code to the `OnInitialize()` function:

```
m_progress1.SetRange(0,5000);
m_progress1.SetStep(1);
```

The first line calls the `SetRange()` function of the `CProgressCtrl` class. The first value is the low value for the range and the second value is the high value for the range. The second line of code sets the step increment to 1 by calling the `SetStep()` function.

Other than the actual code to change the position of the progress bar, this is all the code necessary to set up the control. To make the progress bar do something visually, place a button on the dialog box. When you click the Start button, the progress bar will count from 0 through 5,000. However, before the counting is started, the button will be disabled until the counting is done and then re-enabled.

To add this code, you need to add a member function for the button to handle a message when the user clicks the button. To do this, go into the ClassWizard and on the Message Maps tab, and select the IDC_BUTTON1 ID. There will be two messages available for this button, as shown in Figure 4.14. Double-click BN_CLICKED to create the member function. You will be prompted for the member function name; accept the default name.

FIGURE 4.14

Selecting the BN_CLICKED message.

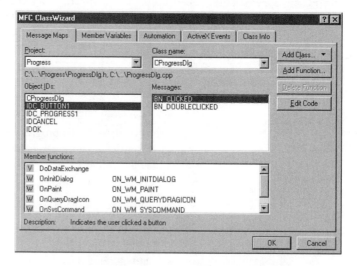

After the member function is created, double-click it to bring up the function into the code editor. Go ahead and edit this function so that it looks like Listing 4.2.

LISTING 4.2   The OnOnButton1 Function

```
void CProgressDlg::OnButton1()
{
    // TODO: Add your control notification handler code here
    m_button1.EnableWindow(FALSE);
    for (int d = 0; d < 5000; d++)
    {
        m_progress1.SetPos(d);
    }
    m_button1.EnableWindow(TRUE);
}
```

When you click the Start button, this function is executed. The code here is rather simple. The first line disables the button by calling the EnableWindow() member function of the CWnd class.

After the button is disabled, a small loop is used to count from 0 to 5,000. Inside this loop, the position of the progress bar is updated with the value of the counter by calling the SetPos function. When the loop has finished, the Start button is enabled.

After you have typed in the code, execute the Progress Example application. Although the progress bar will be moving after you press the Start button, your screen should look like Figure 4.15 when it is done counting.

FIGURE 4.15

The finished Progress example application.

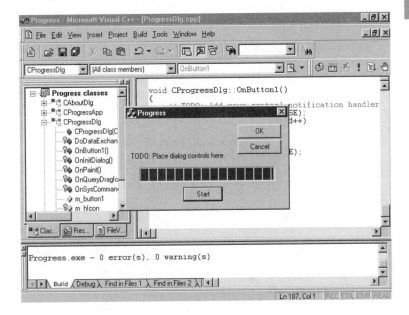

Lesson Summary

In this lesson, you learned how easy it is to use the progress bar. The progress bar has many uses. By using the properties and functions of this control, you can easily add an indicator to show the status of long processes in your applications.

Quiz 2

1. What class provides the functionality of the progress bar?

    a. `CProgressBar`

    b. `CProgCtrl`

    c. `CProgressCtrl`

    d. `CProgress`

2. What function returns the current position of the progress bar?

    a. `GetPos`

    b. `ReturnPos`

    c. `ProgressPos`

    d. `GetProgressPos`

3. What property would you set to tell the progress bar to fill with a single rectangle?

    a. Fill Box

    b. Smooth

    c. Single Box

    d. Small Box

4. What function sets the step increment used by the `StepIt` function?

    a. `SetPos`

    b. `StepSet`

    c. `SetStepInc`

    d. `SetStep`

Exercise 2

Complexity: Easy

1. Create a dialog-based application named "Exercise 1" that has a progress bar and a button on it. Initialize the progress bar with a range of 100 to 500. When the button is clicked, set the position of the progress bar to 300.

Complexity: Moderate

2. Create a dialog-based application named "Exercise 2" that has a progress bar and a track bar on it. Initialize both controls so that they have a range of 0 to 100. When the track bar is moved, the progress bar's position should be updated to match.

LESSON 3

Using a ListBox Control

One of the most common controls is the ListBox control. The ListBox control enables the user to easily view and select entries from a list of items. Depending on how the ListBox is set up, the user can select one item at a time, or a range of items.

When the user selects an item from the list box, that item is highlighted and a notification message is sent to the parent window. If there are too many items in the list box to be displayed at a single time, a scrollbar will automatically appear on the right side of the control to make it easier for the user to navigate through the list. The MFC CListBox class encapsulates the functionality of the Windows ListBox control.

Creating the ListBox Example

To get started with this lesson, you need to create another dialog-based application. Go ahead and create the dialog application, giving it the name "Listbox." If you are unsure how to do this, you should refer back to Chapter 2.

To make room on the dialog box for the ListBox control, delete the TODO: static text control. Using Figure 4.16 as a guide, add a list box, an edit box, and two buttons to the dialog box. The edit box will be used for data entry, and the two buttons will be used to add and delete entries from the list of items. In order to fit all of the controls on the dialog box, you may need to make the dialog box a little taller.

After all the controls are in place, you need to set their properties. Right-click the list box and select Properties from the context menu to view its properties, as shown in Figure 4.17. Select the styles tab. The following list briefly describes the properties on the Styles tab for the ListBox control.

FIGURE 4.16

The Listbox *example dialog box.*

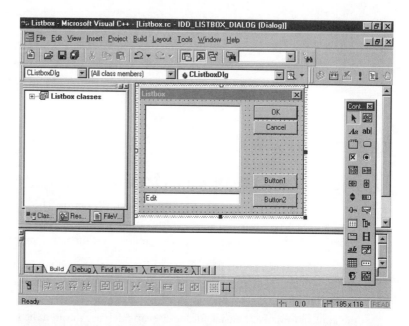

FIGURE 4.17

The ListBox *control Dialog Properties dialog box.*

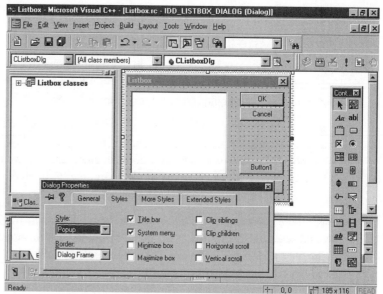

- Selection—This property determines how the items in the list box can be selected. By default, this property is set to Single, which will only enable the user to select one entry from the list. If this property is set to Multiple, the user can select multiple items from the list by holding the Shift or Ctrl key. If you want to enable the user to select an entire range by dragging, you can set this property to Extended. If the property is set to None, the user will not be allowed to select any item from the list.

- Owner Draw—By default, the list box will only display strings when this property is set to None. If you set this property to Fixed, you will be responsible for drawing the contents of the list box and each item in the list box should be the same height. If you need to use varying heights for the items in the list box, you can change this setting to Variable.

- Has Strings—This property indicates that an owner-draw list box contains string items. If the Owner draw property is set to No, this property is disabled because the list box contains strings. If the Owner draw property is set to Fixed or Variable, you can determine if you want the list box to maintain memory and pointers for strings. By default, this property is set to False.

- Border—Draws a border around the list box. By default, this property is set to True.

- Sort—By default, when items are added to the list box, they will be sorted alphabetically. Set this property to False if you do not want your list sorted.

- Notify—By default, this property tells the list box to notify the parent window when an item has been clicked on. You can turn this option off by setting this property to False.

- Multi-Column—By default, a list box has only one column. By changing this property to True, you can specify how many columns you want in your list box.

- Horizontal Scroll—To create a list box with a horizontal scroll bar, set this property to True. By default, this property is set to False.

- Vertical Scroll—By default, a list box has a vertical scroll bar that will be displayed when there are too many items in the list to fit in the box area. By setting this property to False, the scroll bar will not become visible when this occurs.

- No Redraw—By default, the list box will redraw itself when a change occurs. By setting this property to False, the list box will not redraw when a change occurs.

- Use Tabstops—When drawing the items in the list, tab spaces are not drawn. By setting this property to True, the list box will expand tab characters while drawing.

- Want Key Input—When this property is set to True, the owner of the list box will receive the WM_VKEYTOITEM or WM_CHARTOITEM messages when a key is pressed while the list box has input focus. If the Has strings property is used, the owner receives the WM_VKEYTOITEM message, otherwise, he receives the WM_CHARTOITEM message. By default, this property is set to False.

- Disable No Scroll—By default, the list box will display a vertical scroll bar when there are more items in the list than will fit in the box area. By setting this property to True, a vertical scroll bar will be visible at all times; however, it will be disabled if there are not enough items in the list to fill the box.

4

- No Integral Height—When Windows creates a list box, it will be sized so that no partial items will be drawn. By setting this property to True, the list box size will be exactly the same size as designed.

Go ahead and accept the default settings for the list box. By accepting the defaults, you have a generic list box that contains strings as items and will be sorted when an item is added to the list.

Using Table 4.8 as a reference, set the properties for the other controls on the dialog box.

TABLE 4.8   The Control Properties

Control	Property	Setting
IDOK	Default button	False (unchecked)
IDC_BUTTON1	Default button	True (checked)
	Caption	Add
IDC_BUTTON2	Caption	Delete

By setting the Default button property of the OK button to False and setting the Default button property of Button1 to True, when the user presses the Enter key after typing in the edit box, Button1's OnButton1 event will be triggered. If you were to leave the Default button property set to True on the OK button, the application would exit because dialog will assume the Enter keystroke was for the OK button. After you change the captions of the two buttons, your dialog box should look like the one shown in Figure 4.18.

FIGURE 4.18

The updated controls on the dialog box.

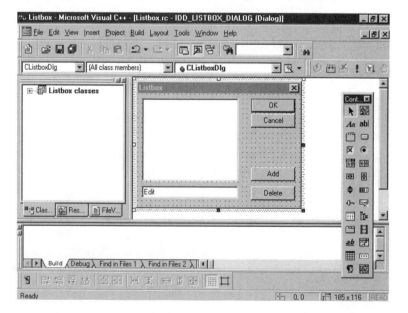

Creating the Member Variables

Now that you have all the necessary controls and properties set, you can create the member variables for the controls on the dialog. Using Table 4.9 as a guide, go ahead and create the member variables. After you are done, your screen should look like Figure 4.19.

FIGURE 4.19

Creating the member variables.

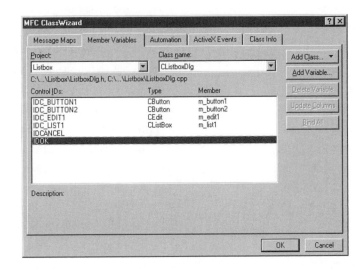

TABLE 4.9 Member Variables for the New Control IDs

ID	Type	Member Variable
IDC_BUTTON1	CButton	m_button1
IDC_BUTTON2	CButton	m_button2
IDC_EDIT1	CEdit	m_edit1
IDC_LIST1	CListBox	m_list1

Examining the Functions of the ListBox Control

Tables 4.10, 4.11, 4.12, and 4.13 outline the common function members of the CListBox class.

TABLE 4.10 The General Member Functions of the Progress Bar Control

Functions	Description
GetCount	Returns the number of string items in the list box.
GetHorizontalExtent	Returns the width, in pixels, that the list box can be scrolled horizontally.

continues

TABLE 4.10   continued

Functions	Description
GetItemData	Returns the value associated with an item.
GetItemDataPtr	Returns the pointer to an item's data.
GetItemHeight	Returns the height of the items in the list box.
GetItemRect	Returns the bounding rectangle of an item.
GetLocale	Returns the list box's locale identifier.
GetSel	Returns the selection state of an item.
GetText	Copies an item into a buffer.
GetTextLen	Returns the length of an item.
GetTopIndex	Returns the index of the top-most visible item.
ItemFromPoint	Returns the index closest to the given point.
SetColumnWidth	Sets the column width of a multicolumn list box.
SetHorizontalExtent	Sets the width, in pixels, that the list box can scroll horizontally.
SetItemData	Sets a value associated with an item.
SetItemDataPtr	Sets a pointer to the list box item.
SetItemHeight	Sets the item height for the list box.
SetLocale	Sets the locale identifier.
SetTabStops	Sets the tab stop positions.
SetTopIndex	Sets the index of the first visible string.

TABLE 4.11   Single-Selection Functions

Functions	Description
GetCurSel	Returns the index of the current item.
SetCurSel	Sets the current item.

TABLE 4.12   Multiselection Functions

Functions	Description
GetCaretIndex	Returns the index of an item.
GetAnchorIndex	Returns the index of the current anchor item.
GetSelCount	Returns the number of items selected.
GetSelItems	Returns the indices of the currently selected items.

Functions	Description
SelItemRange	Selects or deselects a range of items.
SetAnchorIndex	Sets the anchor index.
SetCaretIndex	Sets the focus rectangle to an item at a specified index.
SelSel	Selects or deselects an item.

TABLE 4.13 String Functions

Functions	Description
AddString	Adds a string to the list box.
DeleteString	Deletes the string at a given index.
Dir	Adds filenames from the current directory.
FindString	Searches for a string.
FindStringExact	Finds the first list box string that matches a specified string.
InsertString	Inserts a string at a given index.
ResetContent	Clears the strings from the list box.
SelectString	Searches and selects a specified string in the item list.

Working with the ListBox Control

After you place this list box on the dialog, you don't need to perform any special initialization code to set up the list box. However, just to have something in the list box when the application first starts up, you are going to add a line of code to the CListbox::OnInitDialog() function. By now, you should be familiar to the OnInitDialog() function, so go ahead and add the following line of code after the TODO: comment.

```
m_list1.AddString("Visual C++ 6");
```

This line of code is very simple. It calls the AddString() function of the CListBox class. Its only parameter is the string that you want to add. If you were to execute the application at this time, the list box would have "Visual C++ 6" as its first entry, as shown in Figure 4.20.

FIGURE 4.20

The first item in the Listbox.

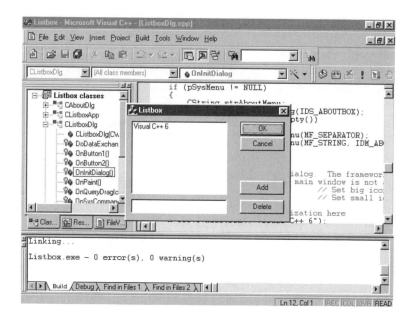

To make the buttons on the dialog add and delete items when the button is pressed, you must first set up the message handlers. By now, you should be getting familiar with this process. In case you need a small reminder, just follow the following steps to set up the message handlers for the buttons:

1. Open the ClassWizard.
2. Select the Message Maps tab.
3. Select the IDC_BUTTON1 Object ID.
4. Double-click the BN_CLICKED message.
5. Accept the default member function name.
6. Repeat steps 4 and 5 for the IDC_BUTTON2 ID.

After you have created the two message handlers, double-click the OnButton1() member function to bring up that function into the code editor. When the function is in the code editor, modify that function so that it looks like the code presented in Listing 4.3.

LISTING 4.3   The OnButton1() Function

```
void CListboxDlg::OnButton1()
{
    // TODO: Add your control notification handler code here
    CString text;
```

```
    m_edit1.GetWindowText(text);
    m_list1.AddString(text);
}
```

When the user clicks the Add button, this code will be executed. The code starts off by defining a variable named text as a CString. This variable will be used to hold the string passed back from the GetWindowText function of the edit box. This value is then passed into the AddString function of the list box, which in turn adds the string from the edit box to the list box.

To delete a string from the list box, you need to add some code to the OnButton2() function. Because you already have the code editor opened and the classes for CListbox are expanded, just double-click the function to bring it up into the editor. After you have the function in the editor, go ahead and modify the function so that it matches the code presented in Listing 4.4.

LISTING 4.4 The OnButton2() Function

```
void CListboxDlg::OnButton2()
{
    // TODO: Add your control notification handler code here
    if (m_list1.GetCurSel() != LB_ERR)
        m_list1.DeleteString(m_list1.GetCurSel());
}
```

When the user selects an item from the list box and then clicks the Delete button, the OnButton2() function is called. The first thing this function does is check to see which item was selected from the list box. If the GetCurSel() function returns the LB_ERR value, no item was selected and, therefore, nothing can be deleted. If the return value is anything other than LB_ERR, an index to a currently selected string was returned. If this is the case, the DeleteString() function is then called to delete the currently selected item.

To see this program in action, execute it. After the application is running, play around with adding and deleting items from the list box. Unless you happen to enter the very same things I enter, your screen should look something like Figure 4.21.

FIGURE 4.21

The Listbox application.

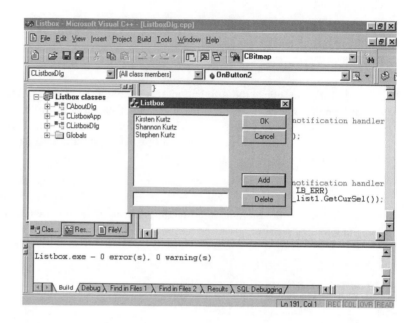

Lesson Summary

In this lesson, you learned how easy it is to manage a list of items using the ListBox control. By using the functions of this control, you learned how easy it is to add and remove items from a list. By examining the properties of the control, you learned about the different styles of list boxes, such as single-select and multiselect boxes.

Quiz 3

1. The list box is encapsulated in which MFC class?

    a. CListBoxClass

    b. CListView

    c. CListBox

    d. CLstBox

2. Which of the following statements about a list box is true?

    a. The contents of a list box can be sorted.

    b. The ListBox control can only hold 999 items.

    c. The ListBox control gets its functionality from the CListView class.

    d. The ListBox control sorts in descending order.

3. Which function will add the filenames from the current directory?

    a. `GetFiles`

    b. `ReadDir`

    c. `GetDir`

    d. `Dir`

4. Which property determines how the items in the list box can be selected?

    a. Sort

    b. Selection

    c. List Style

    d. Arrangement

Exercise 3

Complexity: Easy

1. Create a dialog-based application named "Exercise 1" that has a list box, an edit box, and a button named "Insert" on it. The edit box should only allow numerical entries and when the "Insert" button is clicked, add the contents of the edit box to the sorted list box.

Complexity: Moderate

2. Create a dialog-based application named "Exercise 2" that has a list box, an edit box, and two buttons on it. One button should be named "Add" and the other "Change." Whenever the "Add" button is pressed, the contents of the edit box should be added to the sorted list box. Whenever the "Change" button is clicked, the currently selected item in the list should be exchanged with the text from the edit box.

LESSON 4

Using the Tree Control and List Control

The `TreeView` and `ListView` controls provide an easy way for a user to navigate through information. As a Windows 95 user, you should be very familiar with these controls. A very good example of these controls is the Windows 95 Explorer, as shown in Figure 4.22. Looking at this figure, you will notice that Explorer has two main views. The view on the left shows the use of tree control and the view on the right shows the use of the list control.

FIGURE 4.22

The Windows 95 Explorer.

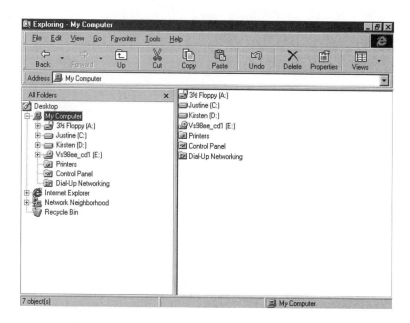

In this lesson, you will learn how to use these two controls. By building an example application, you will learn how to populate the items shown and how to tie these two controls together.

Creating the TreeList Example

To get started with this lesson, you will need to build a dialog-based application named "TreeList." After you have built the application, you need to add the tree control and the list control onto the dialog box. Using Figure 4.23 as a guide, place these controls on the dialog box. By looking at this figure, you will notice that the OK and Cancel buttons were moved to the bottom of the dialog box and that the TODO: comment text was removed. This was done to make room for the two controls on the dialog box. Also, if you need a little more room, you can make the dialog box a little bigger, as I've done for this example.

FIGURE 4.23

The TreeList dialog box.

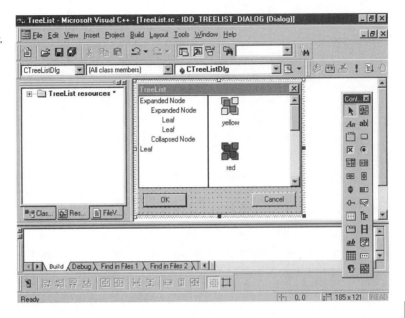

Setting Properties

Now that you have the tree and list controls on the dialog box, you need to set the properties of these controls so that they operate the way you want them to for this example. When you bring up the property window for these two controls, you will notice that they have an extra tab, as shown in Figure 4.24.

FIGURE 4.24

The List Control Properties dialog box with an extra tab.

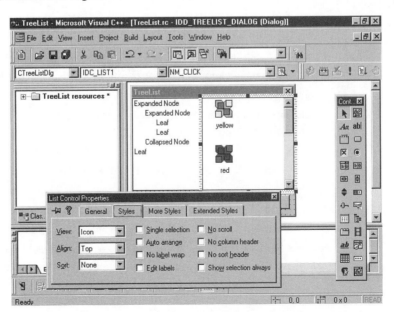

The following is a list of properties for the tree control. This list shows the Styles properties.

- Has Buttons—For the tree view to display the small plus (+) and minus (-) signs when navigating the list, this property must be set to True. By default, this property is set to False, which means it doesn't display these buttons.

- Has Lines—By setting this option to True, the items in the list will be displayed with lines showing the hierarchy of the items. By default, this property is set to False.

- Lines at Root—This property tells the tree control to display the lines starting at the root level of the list. By default, this property is set to False.

- Edit Labels—This property will enable the users to edit the item's text. By default, this property is set to False.

- Disable Drag Drop—When this property is set to True, it will prevent the tree control from sending TVN_BEGINDRAG notification messages. By default, this property is set to False.

- Border—By default, a box will be drawn around the tree control. Set this property to False if you do not want the box to be drawn.

- Show Selection Always—If you want the selected item to use the system highlight color when drawn, set this property to True. By default, this property is set to False.

The following is a list of the Styles properties for the tree control:

- Check Boxes—Enables check boxes as items in the control. By default, this property is set to False.

- Full Row Select—When this property is set to True, an entire item will be selected. By clicking anywhere in the row, that item will be selected. By default, this property is set to False.

- Info Tip—If you want the tree control to send the TVN_GETINFOTIP notification, set this property to True. You can use this option to supply your own descriptions rather than the default tips. By default, this property is set to False.

- Scroll—By default, both horizontal and vertical scrollbars are enabled in the control.

- Tool Tips—By default, the control will display a yellow pop-up tip that displays the full name of an item that doesn't fit in the display.

- Track Select—When this property is set to True, a visible outline will be displayed as the pointer passes over the control. By default, this property is set to False.

- Single Expand—If you want only one node to be expanded at a time, set this property. By default, this property is set to False, which will allow any node to be expanded while others are expanded.

The following is a list of the Styles properties for the list control:

- View—Determines how the items of the list control are displayed. By default, this value is set to Icon. Other settings include Small Icon, List, and Report.

- Align—Determines how the icons are aligned when displayed. By default, this property is set to Top. You can also elect to have the icons align to the left.

- Sort—Enables you to sort the icons so they appear in a certain order. By default, the icons are not sorted. You can choose to have them sorted in ascending or descending order.

- Single Selection—This option enables you to select multiple items from the list. By default, this property is set to False.

- Auto Arrange—This property will keep the icons auto-arranged in the Icon and Small Icon view types. By default, this property is set to False.

- No Label Wrap—By default, the item text may wrap lines when displayed in Icon view. By setting this property to True, the text will be displayed on a single line.

- Edit Labels—Allows the item text to be edited as long as the parent window processes the LVN_ENDLABELEDIT notification message. By default, this property is set to False.

- No Scroll—By default, this property is set to false. By setting this property to True, scrolling will be disabled.

- No Column Header—By default, columns in the Report view mode will have headers. Setting this property to True will not display these headers.

- No Sort Header—Specifies that column headers do not work like buttons. By default, this property is set to False.

- Show Selection Always—If you want the selected item to use the system highlight color when drawn, set this property to True. By default, this property is set to False.

Using Table 4.14, set the properties for the tree and list controls. After you finish setting the properties for both controls, your dialog box should look similar to Figure 4.25.

4

FIGURE 4.25

*The dialog box after
setting the properties
for the controls.*

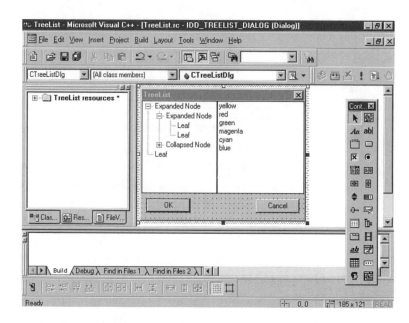

TABLE 4.14   The Control Properties

Control	Property	Setting
IDC_TREE1	Has Buttons	True
	Has Lines	True
	Lines at Root	True
IDC_LIST1	View	List
	Align	Left

Creating the Member Variables

Now that you have all the necessary controls and properties set, you can create the member variables for the controls on the dialog. Using Table 4.15 as a guide, create the member variables for the tree and list controls. When you are done, your screen should look like Figure 4.26.

FIGURE 4.26

Creating the member variables.

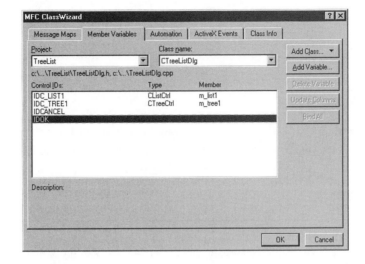

TABLE 4.15 Member Variables for the New Control IDs

ID	Type	Member Variable
IDC_LIST1	CListCtrl	m_list1
IDC_TREE1	CTreeCtrl	m_tree1

Examining the Functions of the `Tree` and `List` Controls

The `CTreeCtrl` class encapsulates the functionality of the Windows tree control. Table 4.16 outlines the common function members of this class. Because of the sheer number of functions in this control, only the most common are described.

TABLE 4.16 The General Member Functions of the Tree Control

Functions	Description
DeleteItem	Removes an item from the tree.
DeleteAllItems	Removes all items from the tree.
Expand	Expands or collapses a branch of the tree.
GetChildItem	Retrieves the child item of a specified item.
GetCount	Retrieves the number of items in the tree.
GetImageList	Retrieves the handle of an associated image list.
GetItem	Retrieves the attributes of an item.
GetItemText	Returns the text of an item.
GetNextSiblingItem	Retrieves the next sibling item of a specified item.

continues

TABLE 4.16 continued

Functions	Description
GetPrevSiblingItem	Retrieves the previous sibling item of a specified item.
GetRootItem	Retrieves the root of a specified item.
GetSelectedItem	Retrieves the currently selected item.
InsertItem	Adds an item to the tree.
ItemHasChildren	Determines if an item has children items.
SetItem	Sets the attributes of an item.
SetImageList	Associates images with an item.
SetItemText	Sets the text of an item.

The CListCtrl class encapsulates the functionality of the Windows list control. Table 4.17 outlines the common function members of this class. Because of the sheer number of functions in this control, only the most common are described.

TABLE 4.17 The General Member Functions of the List Control

Functions	Description
DeleteItem	Removes an item from the list.
DeleteAllItems	Removes all items from the list.
GetColumn	Retrieves the attributes of a column.
GetColumnWidth	Retrieves the width of a column.
GetImageList	Retrieves the handle of an image list used for drawing list view items.
GetItem	Retrieves the attributes for an item.
GetItemCount	Retrieves the number of items in the list.
GetItemData	Retrieves the value associated with an item.
GetItemText	Returns the text of an item.
GetSelectedCount	Retrieves the number of selected items.
InsertItem	Adds an item to the list.
SetColumn	Sets the attributes of a column.
SetColumnWidth	Sets the width of a column.
SetImageList	Assigns an image list.
SetItem	Sets the attributes of an item.
SetItemData	Sets the associate value of an item.
SetItemText	Sets the text of an item.

Working With the Tree and List Controls

For this example, the first thing that you are going to do is populate the tree view with some items. You will accomplish this by adding some code to the CTreeListDlg::OnInitDialog() function. Open this function and modify it so that it matches Listing 4.5.

LISTING 4.5 Modifying the OnInitialize Function to Add Items to the Tree Control

```
BOOL CTreeListDlg::OnInitDialog()
{
    CDialog::OnInitDialog();
    // Add "About..." menu item to system menu.
    // IDM_ABOUTBOX must be in the system command range.
    ASSERT((IDM_ABOUTBOX & 0xFFF0) == IDM_ABOUTBOX);
    ASSERT(IDM_ABOUTBOX < 0xF000);
    CMenu* pSysMenu = GetSystemMenu(FALSE); if (pSysMenu != NULL)
    {
        CString strAboutMenu;
        strAboutMenu.LoadString(IDS_ABOUTBOX);
        if (!strAboutMenu.IsEmpty())
        {
            pSysMenu->AppendMenu(MF_SEPARATOR);
            pSysMenu->AppendMenu(MF_STRING, IDM_ABOUTBOX, strAboutMenu);
        }
    }

    // Set the icon for this dialog.  The framework does this
    // automatically when the application's main window is not a dialog
    SetIcon(m_hIcon, TRUE);          // Set big icon
    SetIcon(m_hIcon, FALSE);         // Set small icon

    // TODO: Add extra initialization here
    //Item 1
    TV_ITEM item;
    item.mask = TVIF_TEXT;
    item.pszText = "Item 1";

    TV_INSERTSTRUCT insert;
    insert.hParent = TVI_ROOT;
    insert.hInsertAfter = TVI_FIRST;
    insert.item = item;
    HTREEITEM hItem1 = m_tree1.InsertItem(&insert);
    //Item 1 Sub 1
    item.pszText = "Item 1 Sub 1";
    insert.hParent = hItem1;
    insert.hInsertAfter = TVI_FIRST;
```

continues

4

LISTING 4.5   continued

```
            insert.item = item;
            HTREEITEM hItem1Sub1 = m_tree1.InsertItem(&insert);
            //Item 1 Sub 2
            item.pszText = "Item 1 Sub 2";
            insert.hParent = hItem1;
            insert.hInsertAfter = TVI_LAST;
            insert.item = item;
            HTREEITEM hItem1Sub2 = m_tree1.InsertItem(&insert);
            //Item 2
            item.pszText = "Item 2";
            insert.hParent = TVI_ROOT;
            insert.hInsertAfter = TVI_LAST;
            insert.item = item;
            HTREEITEM hItem2 = m_tree1.InsertItem(&insert);
            //Item 2 Sub 1
            item.pszText = "Item 2 Sub 1";
            insert.hParent = hItem2;
            insert.hInsertAfter = TVI_FIRST;
            insert.item = item;
            HTREEITEM hItem2Sub1 = m_tree1.InsertItem(&insert);
            //Item 2 Sub 2
            item.pszText = "Item 2 Sub 2";
            insert.hParent = hItem2;
            insert.hInsertAfter = TVI_LAST;
            insert.item = item;
            HTREEITEM hItem2Sub2 = m_tree1.InsertItem(&insert);
            return TRUE;  // return TRUE  unless you set the focus to a control
        }
```

As normal, the code that you needed to add starts after the TODO: comment. Looking at this code, it starts off by declaring a variable of type TV_ITEM. Listing 4.6 shows the declaration of this structure. Using this structure, the next two lines set up the text for the first item.

LISTING 4.6   The TV_ITEM Structure

```
typedef struct _TV_ITEM
{
    UINT            mask;
    HTREEITEM       hItem;
    UINT            state;
    UINT            stateMask;
    LPSTR           pszText;
    int             cchTextMax;
    int             iImage;
    int             iSelectedImage;
    int             cChildren;
    LPARAM          lParam;
} TV_ITEM;
```

The next bit of code declares a variable of type TV_INSERTSTRUCT. This structure is used to tell where to insert the item into the list. Listing 4.7 shows the declaration of this structure.

LISTING 4.7 The TV_INSERTSTRUCT Structure

```
typedef struct _TV_INSERTSTRUCT
{
    HTREEITEM hParent
    HTREEITEM hInsertAfter;
    TV_ITEM   item;
} TV_INSERTSTRUCT;
```

Because you want the first item to start at the root of the tree, hParent is set to TVI_ROOT and because you want this to be the first root item, hInsertAfter is set to TVI_FIRST. The item is set to the item created in the previous step.

After the item is set up and is ready to be inserted into the list, the InsertItem() function is called. This function returns a handle to a tree item, and as you can see in Listing 4.5, this handle is used to set the hParent member.

The rest of the code in Listing 4.5 uses the same technique to set up the other item and sub items. If you examine the code, you will see how easily this is done.

At this point, execute the application. After you run it, you will have a screen similar to Figure 4.27. You will be able to expand the levels in the tree view to reveal the sub items.

FIGURE 4.27

Revealing the sub items.

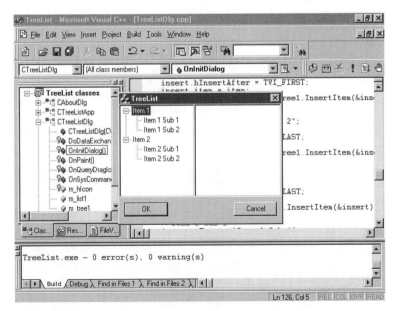

Now that you have the tree view functional, add the necessary code to change the list view when you click one of the items. To make the list view change when you click the tree view, you will need to add a message handler for the TVN_SELCHANGED message of the tree control. Create this handler using the ClassWizard. After you have the function created, bring it up in the code editor and modify it so that the code is the same as Listing 4.8.

LISTING 4.8 The `OnSelchangedTree1()` Function

```
void CTreeListDlg::OnSelchangedTree1(NMHDR* pNMHDR, LRESULT* pResult)
{
    NM_TREEVIEW* pNMTreeView = (NM_TREEVIEW*)pNMHDR;
    // TODO: Add your control notification handler code here
    HTREEITEM selected;
    HTREEITEM child;
    CString   text;
    int       item_no;

    m_list1.DeleteAllItems();

    selected = m_tree1.GetSelectedItem();
    if (m_tree1.ItemHasChildren(selected))
    {
        item_no = 0;
        child = m_tree1.GetChildItem(selected);
        text = m_tree1.GetItemText(child);
        m_list1.InsertItem(item_no, text);

        while (child != NULL)
        {
            item_no = item_no + 1;
            child = m_tree1.GetNextSiblingItem(child);
            if (child != NULL)
            {
                text = m_tree1.GetItemText(child);
                m_list1.InsertItem(item_no, text);
            }
        }
    }
    *pResult = 0;
}
```

After declaring the variables that will be used, the first instruction is to remove all of the items currently in the list view. This is accomplished by calling the `DeleteAllItems()` function. After all of the items are removed from the list view, the code captures the currently selected item in the tree view. After the selected item is captured, it is checked to see if there are any child items for the selected item. This is accomplished by using the `ItemHasChildren()` function.

If there are child items to the selected item, the next section of code is executed. This section of code will get the first child item and add the text of this item to the list view. After that, a loop is performed to gather all other sibling items of that level. If there are any siblings, they too will be added to the list. After there are no more siblings at the same level, the loop will exit.

If you were to execute the application at this point, you would have a screen similar to Figure 4.28. While playing with the example application, you will notice that when you click one of the root items of the tree view, the two sub items will be displayed in the list view.

FIGURE 4.28

Displaying sub items in the list view.

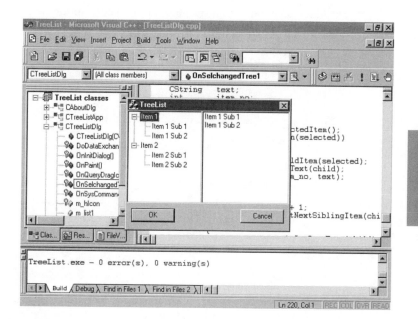

Lesson Summary

In this lesson, you learned how to manage a list of items using the tree and list controls. You learned about the various properties and functions of these controls. Along with learning about each control, you learned how to tie these two controls together to make a more functional application.

Quiz 4

1. The tree control is encapsulated in which MFC class?

    a. CTreeView

    b. CListCtrl

   c. `CTreeCtrl`

   d. `CTreeClass`

2. Which property of the tree control determines if the plus (+) and minus (-) buttons will be displayed?

   a. Show Buttons

   b. Show Signs

   c. Has Lines

   d. Has Buttons

3. Which function returns the attributes of a column for the list control?

   a. `GetColumn`

   b. `GetColumnAttr`

   c. `GetItemAttr`

   d. `GetColumnSettings`

4. Which control displays items in a hierarchy format?

   a. The view control

   b. The list control

   c. The tree-house control

   d. The tree control

Exercise 4

Complexity: Easy

1. Create a dialog-based application named "Exercise 1" that utilizes the tree and list controls. On initialization, add three root items, each with 3 sub items. You can name these items whatever you want. Also, when you click one of the root items, the sub items of the tree view should be listed in the list view.

Complexity: Moderate

2. Create a dialog-based application named "Exercise 2" that utilizes the tree and list controls. Along with these controls, add an edit box and a button. The caption on the button should read "Add" and when this button is clicked, a sub item should be added to the current item with the text from the edit box. To start with, create three root items when the dialog is initialized. You can name these items whatever you want.

LESSON 5

Using the `Animate` Control

You've spent the last few lessons learning about the normal controls that are used in everyday applications. In this lesson, you're going to learn about one of the fun controls. The animate control enables you to play a simple AVI file.

Often, the animate control is used to show that a process is underway, just as the progress bar does, just a little more appealing to the eye. An animation isn't just limited to this type of use. You can use the animate control wherever you need to animate a simple AVI clip. Another common place where developers are using this control is in their About boxes.

If you have ever copied a large file in Windows 95, you will have seen the small animation of a piece of paper moving between two folders. In this lesson, you will use the animate control to make a dialog that displays this animation. One thing to remember about the animate control is that it only plays AVI clips and that it does not play the audio stream if there is one in the AVI.

Creating the Animate Example

To get started with this lesson, you will need to build a dialog based application named "Animate." After you have built the application, add the animate control and two buttons to the dialog box. Using Figure 4.29 as a guide, place these controls on the dialog box. Looking at this figure, you will notice that the TODO: static text control was removed, just like before.

FIGURE 4.29

The Animate dialog box.

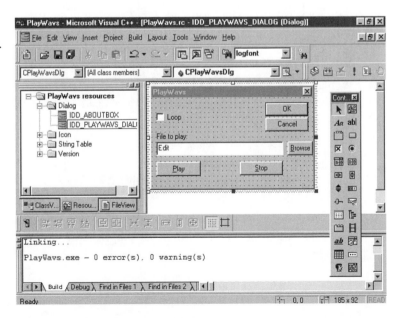

After you have all of the controls on the dialog box, you will need to add a resource to the dialog box that holds the AVI clip that the animate control will display.

When you installed Visual C++ 6 onto your machine, you had an option to install some graphics. If you elected not to install the graphics, then the AVI clip for this example was not installed on your machine. If this is the case, you can find the necessary graphics on your Visual C++ 6 CD.

The version of Visual C++ 6 and how the CD was packaged determine where the necessary AVI clip is located; however, it should be rather easy to find. The name of the AVI that you are looking for is "Filecopy.avi." Again, depending on your install or CD package, the directory structure will be something such as "D:\COMMON\GRAPHICS\AVIS\."

When you locate this AVI clip, create a resource for it. Follow these simple steps to add the necessary resource:

1. Click the Resource tab of the workspace panel.
2. Right-click "Animate Resources" root branch.
3. Choose Import from the context menu displayed.
4. Change the "File of type" edit box to "All Files (*.*)."
5. Move to the path where the AVI is located.
6. Choose the "Filecopy" file.
7. Click the Import button.
8. Type "AVI" into the "Resource type" edit box that is presented.
9. Click the OK button to import the AVI clip.

Setting Properties

With all of the necessary controls on the dialog box, it's time to review and set the necessary properties. The following is a list of the properties on the Styles tab of the animate control.

- Center—By default, when an animation is opened, it will resize the control to the size of the images in the AVI clip. If you set this property to True, the control size will stay the same as designed and the AVI clip will be centered within the control's display area.

- Transparent—By default, the AVI clip will be drawn with a background color specified within the AVI. By setting this property to True, the AVI clip will be draw transparently.

- Auto Play—By setting this property to True, the animation will automatically begin to play as soon as it is opened. It will also continue to loop. By default, this property is set to False.

- Border—By default, this options draws a box around the control. You can turn the border off by setting this property to False.

Using Table 4.18, set the properties of the controls for this example application. When you are done setting properties, your dialog box should look like the one in Figure 4.30.

FIGURE 4.30

The updated Animate dialog box.

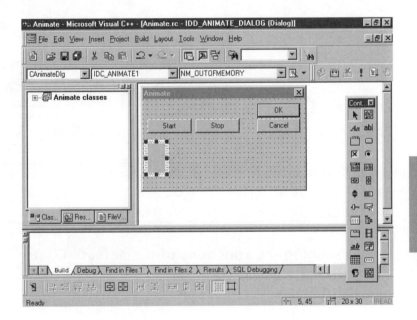

TABLE 4.18 The Control Properties

Control	Property	Setting
IDC_BUTTON1	Caption	Start
IDC_BUTTON2	Caption	Stop
IDC_ANIMATE1	Transparent	True
	Border	False

Creating the Member Variables

Now that you have all the necessary controls and properties set, you can create the member variables for the controls on the dialog box. Using Table 4.19 as a guide, create the member variables for the two buttons and the animate control. When you are done, your screen should look like Figure 4.31.

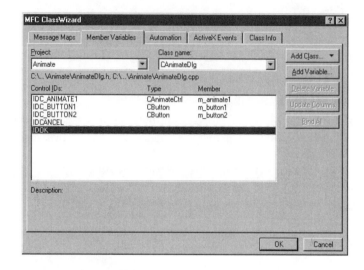

FIGURE 4.31

Creating the member variables.

TABLE 4.19   Member Variables for the New Control IDs

ID	Type	Member Variable
IDC_ANIMATE1	CAnimateCtrl	m_animate1
IDC_BUTTON1	CButton	m_button1
IDC_BUTTON2	CButton	m_button2

Examining the Functions of the `Animate` Control

The `CAnimateCtrl` class encapsulates the functionality of the Windows animate control. Table 4.20 outlines the common function members of this class.

TABLE 4.20   The Member Functions of the Animate Control

Function	Description
Close	Closes the AVI clip that was previously opened.
Open	Opens an AVI clip.
Play	Plays an AVI clip.
Seek	Displays a single frame of an AVI clip.
Stop	Stops an AVI clip.

Working With the `Animate` Control

The first thing you need to do for this example is open the AVI animation. This is easily done in the `CAnimateDlg::OnInitDialog()` function. Go ahead and add the following line of code after the TODO: comment line of this function.

```
m_animate1.Open(IDR_AVI1);
```

This line of code calls the Open() function with the resource ID of the AVI clip. When the AVI clip is opened, it displays the first frame of the animation in the animate control. If you execute the example application at this time, all you see is the first frame of the animation, as shown in Figure 4.32.

FIGURE 4.32

The first clip of the AVI animation.

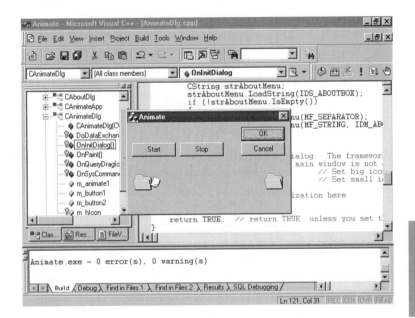

Use the Start and Stop buttons to start and stop the AVI clip. Set up the necessary message handlers to handle the BN_CLICKED messages for these buttons. After you have created them, go ahead and bring up the OnButton1() function into the code editor and modify it so that it looks like the code in Listing 4.9.

LISTING 4.9 The Function That Starts the AVI Animation

```
void CAnimateDlg::OnButton1()
{
    // TODO: Add your control notification handler code here
    m_animate1.Play(0,-1,-1);
}
```

Wow! It only takes one line of code to play an AVI file. To start the animation when you click the Start button, the Play() function is called. This function takes three parameters. The first parameter is the starting frame, the second parameter is the ending frame, and the last parameter is the number of times to repeat the AVI. A value of -1 for the stop frame indicates that the AVI should play all frames and a value of -1 for the third parameter makes the AVI play continuously.

To add the code to stop the AVI clip, bring up the OnButton2() function and modify the code so that it matches Listing 4.10.

LISTING 4.10 The Function That Stops the AVI Animation

```
void CAnimateDlg::OnButton2()
{
    // TODO: Add your control notification handler code here
    m_animate1.Stop();
}
```

This function simply calls the Stop() function, which stops the AVI. To restart the AVI, simply call the Play() function again.

Execute the example application. When the application starts, the first frame of the AVI will be displayed, as discussed earlier. Go ahead and click the Start button to watch the AVI animation flow.

Lesson Summary

In this lesson, you learned how to use the animate control to start and stop AVI animations. You learned about the various properties and functions of the animate control. By using this control, you can add simple animations to your application. You can use these animations for just about anything, from indicating that a process is busy to just adding a little visual appeal to your application.

Quiz 5

1. Which of the following is a characteristic of the animate control?

   a. It will play both the audio and video streams of an AVI clip.

   b. It can be used to play .mpeg files.

   c. It will not play the audio stream.

   d. It can play AVI clips backwards by setting the reverse property.

2. Which property is used to tell the animate control not to use the background color when drawing the AVI frames?

   a. Background color

   b. Transparent

   c. Border

   d. Background off

3. Which function will position an AVI clip to a certain frame?

    a. `Play`

    b. `Stop`

    c. `Open`

    d. `Seek`

4. In which MFC class is the animate class encapsulated?

    a. `CAviAnimation`

    b. `CAnimationCtrl`

    c. `CAnimateCtrl`

    d. `CAnimate`

Exercise 5

Complexity: Easy

1. Create a dialog-based application named "Exercise 1" that has an animate control on it. You will need to add an AVI resource as well. You can use the same AVI that was used in the example program for this lesson. When the application starts, the AVI animation should automatically open and play without using the `Play()` function.

Complexity: Moderate

2. Create a dialog-based application named "Exercise 2" that has two animate controls and two checkboxes. Each checkbox determines if one of the animations is running. If the first checkbox is checked, the animation will play. If it is unchecked, the animation will stop. The same goes for the second animation. You will need to have at least one AVI resource. You can use the AVI resource that was used in the example program for this lesson. Or, you can use two separate AVI clips.

Chapter Summary

You have learned a great deal about the Windows common controls in this chapter. Even though you only covered a selected number of controls, what you learned through this lesson can be applied to just about any control. The following list outlines the controls that you learned in this chapter:

- You learned how to use the slider and spin controls to limit the user's input to a certain range.

- You learned how to use the progress bar to show activity of a process.
- You learned how to add and remove entries from a list box.
- You learned how to organize information by using the tree and list controls.
- You learned how to play simple AVI clips, which will add a little bit of eye-candy to your application.

What you learned in this chapter is not limited to the controls presented. Just about every control you use in your programming endeavors will have associated properties and functions. You will use these properties and functions to manage the behavior of the controls.

CHAPTER 5

Processing Windows Messages and Commands

Improving how a user interacts with a program has always been at the forefront of progress. With that, technology is always improving on how users interact with programs. One such improvement was the use of the mouse. Even though this technology is simple to use now, it wasn't simple too many years ago. If you wanted to use a mouse, your program had to support it directly by polling for it.

That concept really hasn't changed; where the concept is implemented *has* changed. The Windows operating system now manages the mouse, making it available to all programs that run in Windows. Your program still needs to know how to use the mouse, but now, Windows communicates with your program, telling it that an event has happened. Deep within the MFC is the framework that makes this seem transparent to the user.

Expanding on this concept, the Windows operating system lets running applications know many things—not just that the mouse moved or was clicked—such as resources becoming available, a file being changed, file dragging and dropping, and a slew of other actions.

To communicate this effectively, Windows uses the message approach. When something happens, a message is generated. Applications can then either respond to the message or ignore it.

Messages come in all kinds of flavors. They can be system commands, user messages, or messages directed to a particular item, such as a control on a form. With this in mind, you can see what is happening "under the hood" in the operating system managed by messages.

LESSON 1

Message Loops, Maps, and Macros

Because Windows programs are essentially event oriented, they rely on a mechanism that will tell them when something happens. This can range from simple tasks, such as the user passing the mouse over a control, to actual user interaction with the program.

These mechanisms are called *messages*. Behind the scenes in Windows, messages are literally being sent back and forth between the system and your application. Each window (and each control is a window) has a message queue. These queues store these messages and are in turn processed in a FIFO (first-in first-out) manner. After the message is handled, it is removed from the queue.

Your application will determine how the messages are handled. They can be ignored, or they can be used to trigger a reaction within your application. You will see that a lot of messages are handled automatically. For example, a message telling an edit box to receive focus when the user clicks it is automatically handled by the MFC. Although, having a button do something when clicked usually requires that you create an event handler that is called when that message is processed.

Note The terms *event handler*, *event function*, *event procedure*, *control notification handler*, and *message handler* are used synonymously throughout this book.

Tools such as VC++ 6 have simplified the process of managing messages. Originally, a long and tedious block of code had to be written to process each message that flows through the application. These were referred to as message loops. Veteran Windows programmers can tell you that this was a nightmare to manage. The MFC has implemented message maps to replace this daunting task.

Message maps, simply put, are tables that match a message to a message handler. The MFC has special macros that are used to manage these message maps. To get a firsthand look at a message map and the macros involved, create a new project using the following steps:

1. Create a new dialog-based project named MssgMap.
2. Add a button to the main dialog resource with the resource ID of IDC_BMSG and a caption of "Message."
3. Add an event handler for the Message button by double-clicking it and accepting the default function name of OnBmsg.

Figure 5.1 shows how your dialog resource should look.

FIGURE 5.1

Dialog resource with Message button.

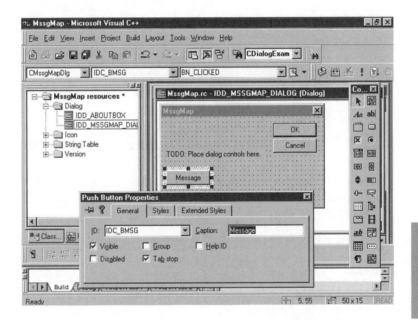

Now that you have created an event handler that is executed when you click the Message button, add the following line of code to the event handler:

```
AfxMessageBox("Hello Interactive World!");
```

The OnBmsg event handler should look like the following code segment after you add the above line of code:

```
void CMssgMapDlg::OnBmsg()
{
    // TODO: Add your control notification handler code here
    AfxMessageBox("Hello Interactive World!");
}
```

Build and execute the program to make sure you don't have any compilation errors and that the application runs. When it is running, click the Message button. When you click this button, you should see the message Hello Interactive World! displayed as your code is instructed to do in the OnBmsg event handler.

So how does the program know to execute that function when you click the button? It knows because the message map has mapped the button's click event to this function.

To see how this is implemented, look at Listing 5.1, which shows the message map defined in MssgMapDlg.cpp.

LISTING 5.1   Message Map in MssgMapDlg.cpp

```
BEGIN_MESSAGE_MAP(CMssgMapDlg, CDialog)
    //{{AFX_MSG_MAP(CMssgMapDlg)
    ON_WM_SYSCOMMAND()
    ON_WM_PAINT()
    ON_WM_QUERYDRAGICON()
    ON_BN_CLICKED(IDC_BMSG, OnBmsg)
    //}}AFX_MSG_MAP
END_MESSAGE_MAP()
```

The first thing of importance to note about this message map is its location. This message map belongs to the class of the main dialog and therefore, is defined in its source file, MssgMapDlg.cpp.

Next, there are two macros being used: BEGIN_MESSAGE_MAP and END_MESSAGE_MAP. These macros are used to define the start and end of a message map. The first comment line, //{{AFX_MSG_MAP, inside of the message map is used by VC++ 6 to parse the code and to define to which class the message map belongs. This is indicated by the class name within the parenthesis.

The rest of the lines remaining up until the //}}AFX_MSG_MAP comment are used to map commands to functions. Specifically, the ON_BN_CLICKED(IDC_BMSG, OnBmsg) line tells the program to execute the OnBmsg function when the IDC_BMSG control (the Message button) is clicked.

The ON_BN_CLICKED is just one of over 100 different macros defined that make the message mapping work. The other ON_ macros you see in the previous code segment are specific macros that handle a specific function. These macros are defined within the MFC and are expanded by the preprocessor when you compile and build your application. Table 5.1 lists some commonly seen macros.

TABLE 5.1   Some Common Macros

Macro	Description
DECLARE_MESSAGE_MAP	Signifies that a message map will be used. This is seen in an include file.
BEGIN_MESSAGE_MAP	Marks the beginning of a message map. This is seen in a source file.
END_MESSAGE_MAP	Marks the end of a message map. This is seen in a source file.
ON_COMMAND	Controls handling of a command to a member function.
ON_MESSAGE	Controls handling of a user-defined message to a member function of the class.

Note   To see a list of these macros, one good reference would be in one of VC++ 6's own header files, Afxmsg_.h. This file should be located in your Visual Studio directory under VC6\MFC\INCLUDE\Afxmsg_.h. Be careful NOT to edit any of it.

You've seen how your event is triggered via the message map, but you haven't seen how the message map finds your procedure. Because the event procedure you coded was a member of the dialog's class, it is declared in the class's declaration. Listing 5.2 shows the class declaration for the main dialog resource.

LISTING 5.2   MssgMapDlg Class Declaration in MssgMapDlg.h

```
/////////////////////////////////////////////////////////////////////
// CMssgMapDlg dialog

class CMssgMapDlg : public CDialog
{
// Construction
public:
    CMssgMapDlg(CWnd* pParent = NULL);     // standard constructor

// Dialog Data
    //{{AFX_DATA(CMssgMapDlg)
    enum { IDD = IDD_MSSGMAP_DIALOG };
        // NOTE: the ClassWizard will add data members here
    //}}AFX_DATA

    // ClassWizard generated virtual function overrides
    //{{AFX_VIRTUAL(CMssgMapDlg)
```

continues

5

LISTING 5.2   continued

```
    protected:
    virtual void DoDataExchange(CDataExchange* pDX);
        // DDX/DDV support
    //}}AFX_VIRTUAL

// Implementation
protected:
    HICON m_hIcon;

    // Generated message map functions
    //{{AFX_MSG(CMssgMapDlg)
    virtual BOOL OnInitDialog();
    afx_msg void OnSysCommand(UINT nID, LPARAM lParam);
    afx_msg void OnPaint();
    afx_msg HCURSOR OnQueryDragIcon();
    afx_msg void OnBmsg();
    //}}AFX_MSG
    DECLARE_MESSAGE_MAP()
};
```

Looking at the class declaration in Listing 5.2, you will notice that the protected section after the //Implementation comment declares the OnBmsg() function. This is the standard place to declare protected functions of a class following good object-oriented programming techniques. VC++ 6 declared this function here automatically.

The thing that you need to be looking at is the afx_msg at the beginning of the line. This tells the compiler that this function will have a mapping in the message map.

After the functions have been declared, another macro is used, DECLARE_MESSAGE_MAP. This macro tells the preprocessor that a message map will be used in the corresponding source file (MssgMapDlg.cpp).

To expand on what you've learned so far in this lesson, add an edit control to the main dialog resource with the resource ID of IDC_EBCAPTION. Compare your dialog to the one shown in Figure 5.2.

You will be adding a message handler that will change the main dialog's caption when you type something into the edit control. This type of scenario is good for when you need to set a flag when the user changes the text in the edit box. For this example though, you'll change the caption to show that the message was handled.

To do this, you need to add the message handler. An easy way to do this is to double-click the edit control. This is possible because the default message in MFC for an edit control is the EN_CHANGE message. This message indicates that there was a change in the edit box.

FIGURE 5.2

Dialog resource with an edit control added.

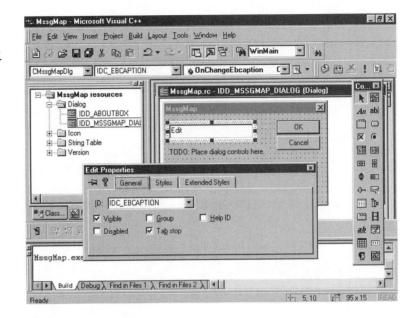

When you are prompted for the function name, click OK to use the default name of OnChangeEbcaption. After clicking OK, the code editor will be displayed. Add the following line of code after the //TODO comment:

```
SetWindowText("Hello Interactive World");
```

The following code segment shows what the complete function should look like after you have entered the above line of code:

```
void CMssgMapDlg::OnChangeEbcaption()
{
    // TODO: If this is a RICHEDIT control, the control will not
    // send this notification unless you override the
    // CDialog::OnInitialUpdate() function and call
    // CRichEditCrtl().SetEventMask() with the EN_CHANGE flag
    // ORed into the mask.

    // TODO: Add your control notification handler code here
    SetWindowText("Hello Interactive World!");
}
```

What you've done is manually added code to control what happens when the text is changed in the edit control. VC++ 6 has also done some work for you. It declared the function in the header file and added the necessary macro in the message map to call this function.

5

The following code segment is the class declaration for `CMssgMapDlg` with the newly added declaration for the `OnChangeEbcaption()` function:

```cpp
class CMssgMapDlg : public CDialog
{
// Construction
public:
    CMssgMapDlg(CWnd* pParent = NULL);     // standard constructor

// Dialog Data
    //{{AFX_DATA(CMssgMapDlg)
    enum { IDD = IDD_MSSGMAP_DIALOG };
    //}}AFX_DATA

    // ClassWizard generated virtual function overrides
    //{{AFX_VIRTUAL(CMssgMapDlg)
    protected:
    virtual void DoDataExchange(CDataExchange* pDX);     // DDX/DDV
                                                         // support

    //}}AFX_VIRTUAL

// Implementation
protected:
    HICON m_hIcon;

    // Generated message map functions
    //{{AFX_MSG(CMssgMapDlg)
    virtual BOOL OnInitDialog();
    afx_msg void OnSysCommand(UINT nID, LPARAM lParam);
    afx_msg void OnPaint();
    afx_msg HCURSOR OnQueryDragIcon();
    afx_msg void OnBmsg();
    afx_msg void OnChangeEbcaption();
    //}}AFX_MSG
    DECLARE_MESSAGE_MAP()
};
```

Looking at the newly added declaration for `OnChangeEbcaption()` function just above the `DECLARE_MESSAGE_MAP` macro, you will notice that it is defined just like the others in the list.

The following code segment is from the MssgMapDlg.cpp source file and has a macro defined for the new function to coincide with the one declared in the header file for this class:

```cpp
BEGIN_MESSAGE_MAP(CMssgMapDlg, CDialog)
    //{{AFX_MSG_MAP(CMssgMapDlg)
    ON_WM_SYSCOMMAND()
    ON_WM_PAINT()
    ON_WM_QUERYDRAGICON()
```

```
    ON_BN_CLICKED(IDC_BMSG, OnBmsg)
    ON_EN_CHANGE(IDC_EBCAPTION, OnChangeEbcaption)
    //}}AFX_MSG_MAP
END_MESSAGE_MAP()
```

Looking at the new macro, you'll notice that the macro name is different from the ones used so far. This macro's name is ON_EN_CHANGE. Its parameter list consists of the resource ID and the function that it is mapped to.

The message for the button click is BN_CLICKED and the message for the edit box's change event is EN_CHANGE. The prefix (letters up to the _) is used to organize the messages. After working with VC++ 6 for a while, you will get familiar with what these codes are and how they are divided. Table 5.2 outlines some of these prefixes and how they are used.

TABLE 5.2   Common Message Prefixes

Prefix	Window/Control type
ACM	Animation control message
ACN	Animation control notification
ABM	Appbar message
ABN	Appbar notification
BM	Button message
BN	Button notification
CB	Combo box message
CBN	Combo box notification
CDM	Common dialog message
CDN	Common dialog notification
DL	Drag list box message
DM	Dialog message
EM	Edit box message
EN	Edit box notification
HDM	Header control message
HDN	Header control notification
LB	List box message
LBN	List box notification
PBM	Progress bar message
PSM	Property sheet message

5

continues

TABLE 5.2   continued

Prefix	Window/Control type
PSN	Property sheet notification
SB	Status bar message
SBM	Scroll bar message
STM	Static control message
STN	Static control notification
TTM	Tool tip message
TTN	Tool tip notification
WM	Generic windows message

Looking at the table, you should have noticed that some items listed were messages, and some items were notifications. Both are messages. The notifications are messages from a window to a window that owns it, whereas messages (as listed in the table) are messages to the window. For example, EM is used when an edit control is sent a message, whereas EN is used when an edit control sends a message to its parent. In the example program, EN_CHANGE is telling its parent, the main dialog resource, that the contents of the control have been changed.

Lesson Summary

This lesson primarily focused on message maps and some of the macros that make them work. You were introduced to the concept of message loops and shown how the MFC has shielded you from programming such long and tedious structures.

Unlike legacy DOS applications that use a polling method to check for events, Windows programs use a message system. These messages can range from simple tasks such as a user clicking a button to a message from the system stating that a resource has been made available or disabled.

It's important to understand the basics of how messaging works in Windows to be successful at developing Windows applications.

Quiz 1

1. What types of loops were used to manage messages before the advent of VC++ and the MFC?

    a. WinMessage loops

    b. Message loops, usually coded with switch or if statements

   c. Message maps

   d. Macros

2. What macro is used to declare a message map?

   a. `BEGIN_MESSAGE_MAP`

   b. `END_MESSAGE_MAP`

   c. `DECLARE_MAP`

   d. `DECLARE_MESSAGE_MAP`

3. Which macro is used to define the beginning of a message map?

   a. `MESSAGE_MAP_BEGIN`

   b. `MESSAGE_MAP_START`

   c. `BEGIN_MESSAGE_MAP`

   d. `MESSAGE_MAP_ON`

4. What is (are) the prefix (es) for an edit control in a message map?

   a. `EBM, EBN`

   b. `EN, EM`

   c. `EMM, ENN`

   d. `WM, ON`

Exercise 1

Complexity: Easy

1. Create a new dialog-based application named "Exercise 1" that has two button controls on it. These buttons should have the captions "Hello" and "Good Bye."

   Add a function handler for each button that will display a message relative to the button clicked. After you have added the function handlers for the buttons, examine the code to see the message maps that were created.

LESSON 2

Messages and the ClassWizard

Considering the importance of messages in your application and how tightly they are wrapped up inside of the many classes that make up the MFC, it's no surprise that the ClassWizard can be used to manage some of the tasks of programming for messages in your application.

In this lesson, you will see how the ClassWizard can be used to add messages to your application, as well as another dialog which adds message handlers.

In Chapter 3, "Increasing User Interaction with Dialog Boxes and Property Sheets," you learned how to use the ClassWizard to add member functions, member variables, and link a message to a class function. As you progress through this chapter, you should see how what you learned earlier plays an important role in building an application.

You will be using the same application (MssgMap) you built in Lesson 1 to perform the tasks in this lesson. If it is not already loaded, do so now. The first thing you will do to this application is limit the number of characters that can be entered into the edit control and display a message if that limit has been exceeded.

Using the ClassWizard to Create Message Handlers

To show how the ClassWizard can manage the event procedures, display the ClassWizard and select the CMssgMapDlg class. Figure 5.3 shows the ClassWizard with the CMssgMapDlg class selected.

FIGURE 5.3

ClassWizard with CMssgMapDlg class selected.

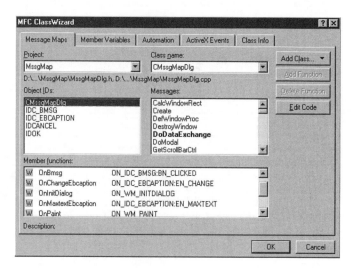

After you have selected the class, you need to select the IDC_EBCAPTION resource ID from the list of Object IDs. When you have selected it, you can see what messages are predefined by the MFC for this type of control. The EN_CHANGE message should be in bold, meaning that an event handler has been defined for this message.

Because we want to show a message when too many characters have been entered into the edit control, you need to add an event procedure for the EN_MAXTEXT message.

Double-click EN_MAXTEXT to bring up the dialog box that asks for the member function name. Click OK, as the default name of OnMaxtextEbcaption should be sufficient. Figure 5.4 shows the ClassWizard after you have added the message handler.

FIGURE 5.4

ClassWizard with the new message handler defined.

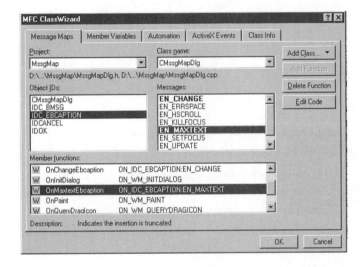

After the message handler has been defined, click the Edit Code button of the ClassWizard to edit the code for the newly created message handler. Add the following line of code:

```
AfxMessageBox("Too many characters");
```

The complete event procedure should look like this:

```
void CMssgMapDlg::OnMaxtextEbcaption()
{
    // TODO: Add your control notification handler code here
    AfxMessageBox("Too many characters");
}
```

Taking what you have learned from the previous lesson, you should be aware that the ClassWizard has added the necessary function declaration in the header file as well as the necessary macro in the message map. The following listing shows the modified message map:

```
BEGIN_MESSAGE_MAP(CMssgMapDlg, CDialog)
    //{{AFX_MSG_MAP(CMssgMapDlg)
    ON_WM_SYSCOMMAND()
    ON_WM_PAINT()
    ON_WM_QUERYDRAGICON()
    ON_BN_CLICKED(IDC_BMSG, OnBmsg)
```

5

```
        ON_EN_CHANGE(IDC_EBCAPTION, OnChangeEbcaption)
        ON_EN_MAXTEXT(IDC_EBCAPTION, OnMaxtextEbcaption)
        //}}AFX_MSG_MAP
END_MESSAGE_MAP()
```

Yet another of the many macro functions has been used. This time, the `ON_EN_MAXTEXT`
macro function has been used. Again, this one takes the resource ID and the function
name as its parameters.

If you were to build and run the application at this point, it would take quite a few keystrokes before the maximum length of the edit control was exceeded. For this reason, you
need to set the limit manually.

To set the limit, create a couple member variables for the edit control. This is accomplished via the following steps:

1. Use the ClassWizard to create a member variable named `m_ebcaption_value` on
   the `IDC_EBCAPTION` resource ID. The member variable should be defined with a
   Category of Value and a Variable type of `CString`.

2. After the `m_ebcaption_value` variable has been created, select it in the list of
   defined member variables and set its Maximum Characters to 25.

3. Add another member variable named `m_ebcaption_control` on the `IDC_EBCAPTION`
   resource ID. This member variable should be defined with a Category of Control
   and a Variable type of `CEdit`.

Figure 5.5 shows the newly created member variables with `m_ebcaption_value` selected
so you can see where to enter the maximum length of the edit control.

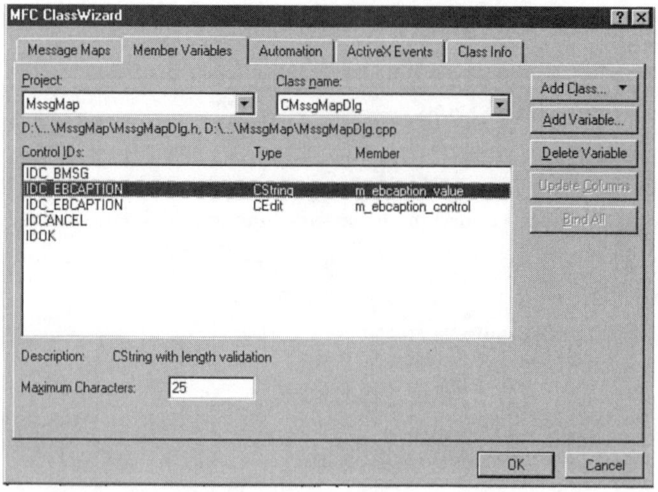

FIGURE 5.5

ClassWizard with the
new member variables.

Really, only the `m_ebcaption_value` member variable needed to be created in order to set the maximum number of characters. You created the other one so you could enhance the message handler for the `EN_CHANGE` message to reflect its execution in real time.

Locate the `OnChangeEbcaption()` function in the MssgMapDlg.cpp file and add the following lines of code before the `SetWindowText()` function call.

```
CString caption;
m_ebcaption_control.GetWindowText(caption);
SetWindowText(caption);
```

Comment out the `SetWindowText ("Hello Interactive World!")` line of code that you entered in the previous lesson. The complete function should look as follows:

```
void CMssgMapDlg::OnChangeEbcaption()
{
    // TODO: If this is a RICHEDIT control, the control will not
    // send this notification unless you override the
    // CDialog::OnInitialUpdate() function and call
    // CRichEditCrtl().SetEventMask() with the EN_CHANGE flag
    // ORed into the mask.

    // TODO: Add your control notification handler code here
    CString caption;
    m_ebcaption_control.GetWindowText(caption);
    SetWindowText(caption);
//   SetWindowText("Hello Interactive World!");
}
```

So, what was the purpose of the new lines of code? In order, these three lines of code accomplish the following:

1. Create a variable named "caption" of type `CString`.
2. Populate the caption variable with the current value of the edit control by calling one of the edit control's member functions.
3. Set the title of the dialog to the value of the caption variable.

Build and execute this program. While the program is running, enter `Hello Interactive World!!!` into the edit control. Figure 5.6 shows the application with the entered text.

If you entered the caption properly, you should have gotten the message that too many characters were entered as you tried to type the third exclamation mark (!), which was the 26th character—one more than was allowed. If you haven't already done so, close the application.

5

FIGURE 5.6

*The MssgMap applica-
tion running.*

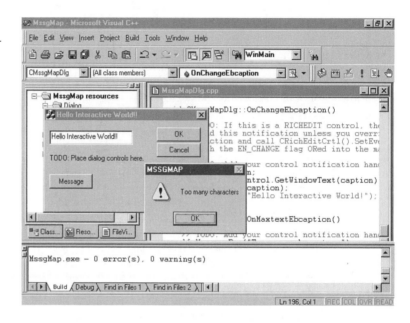

FIGURE 5.6

*The MssgMap applica-
tion running.*

Using the Events Dialog to Create Message Handlers

Although the ClassWizard is an effective tool for creating message handlers, there is another
dialog box that is simple to use that encompasses creating and editing message handlers.

To activate this dialog box, right-click a control and select Event from the pop-up context
menu. In this case, right-click the edit box on the main dialog resource and select the
Event menu item. Figure 5.7 shows this dialog box.

FIGURE 5.7

*The New Windows
Message and Event
Handlers for class*
`CMssgMapDlg` *dialog box.*

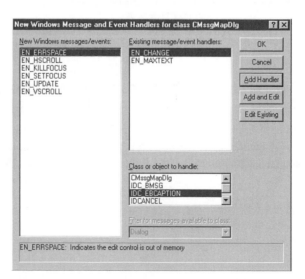

Looking at this dialog box, there are five areas of focus:

- New Windows Messages/Events—This section is used to show which messages are predefined in the MFC for the current class or object and that have not yet been assigned to a message handler.
- Existing Message/Event Handlers—This section shows which messages for this class or object have been defined.
- Class or Object to Handle—This drop-down lets you select the class or object for which you want to manage message handlers.
- Filter for Messages Available to Class—If you have a class selected in section 3, this drop-down will let you filter what messages are in section 1. This can be useful, because there are literally hundreds of messages.
- The unlabeled area at the bottom of the dialog box gives you a brief explanation of the selected message from section 1.

This dialog box is a convenient and useful tool for jumping from message handler to message handler as your project grows.

Using this dialog box, you are going to add two more message handlers. First, make sure that IDC_EBCAPTION is the selected object. Next, select EN_SETFOCUS and click the Add and Edit button. You will be asked to name the new function. Click the OK button, as OnSetfocusEbcaption is a good enough function name.

This will take you directly to the new message handler. Enter the following line of code just after the //TODO comment:

```
SetWindowText("Enter your Caption");
```

The complete event procedure should look as follows:

```
void CMssgMapDlg::OnSetfocusEbcaption()
{
    // TODO: Add your control notification handler code here
    SetWindowText("Enter your Caption");
}
```

This event procedure will be fired as soon as you click in the edit box to give it focus on the dialog box. Build and run the application. When the dialog box appears, click in the edit box, but don't type anything. You should notice that as you set focus to the edit box, the message Enter your Caption appears in the dialog box's title bar.

Now, type in Hello Interactive World!. You will notice that what you type is still being reflected in the edit control. This means that the message handler is called only once when the control receives focus, not repeatedly for each key press.

5

To take focus away from the edit box control, click somewhere outside of it. Click the Message button. This will cause its event procedure to be executed and to display the message from Lesson 1. Now, click back into the edit box. Because the EN_SETFOCUS message handler was called again, it overwrites the dialog box's title as instructed. When you change the text in the edit control, the EN_CHANGE message handler gets called again, changing the caption back to what you have entered in the edit box.

If you haven't done so, close the application.

To expand on what you've learned so far in this lesson, you are going to add yet another message handler for the edit box. Use the events dialog box to add a message handler for the EN_KILLFOCUS message for the IDC_EBCAPTION edit box. Do this by selecting the IDC_EBCAPTION object, then the EN_KILLFOCUS message, and finally, clicking the Add and Edit button. You will be prompted for the name of the function. The default name of OnKillfocusEbcaption is fine. Click OK.

This will take you to the code editor again, placing you in the newly created message handler. Add the following line of code:

```
SetWindowText("Edit lost Focus");
```

The complete message handler should look like the following:

```
void CMssgMapDlg::OnKillfocusEbcaption()
{
    // TODO: Add your control notification handler code here
    SetWindowText("Edit lost Focus");
}
```

Build and execute the program. This time, when it runs, click in the edit box. The message handler EN_SETFOCUS gets called and the dialog's caption is set to Enter your Caption. Next, type in Hello Interactive World!, and as you type, the EN_CHANGE message handler is called and the dialog box's caption gets updated as instructed.

Now, click the Message button. Its message handler, BN_CLICKED, gets called. Before it is called, the EN_KILLFOCUS for the edit control is called, because it's losing focus. Going from the EN_KILLFOCUS to the BN_CLICKED happens so fast that it seems almost instantaneous. Figure 5.8 shows the dialog box that is displayed when you click the Message button. Look carefully at the main dialog's caption. It says Edit lost Focus.

FIGURE 5.8

Application running with the Edit lost Focus dialog box caption.

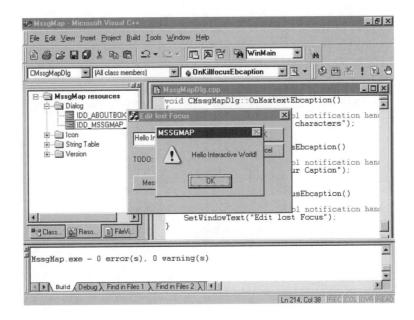

By now, you should understand the sequence of events discussed so far for the edit control. Figure 5.9 shows the three messages and the order in which they were executed.

FIGURE 5.9

The EN_SETFOCUS, EN_CHANGE, *and* EN_KILLFOCUS *sequence.*

Looking at the diagram, the EN_SETFOCUS message is fired when the control receives focus. Then, if changes are made, the EN_CHANGE message is fired. When focus leaves the edit control, the EN_KILLFOCUS message is fired. Although it's not shown in the diagram, if too many characters are entered in the edit box, the EN_MAXTEXT message handler is executed.

Reviewing the Message Map

Now that you have defined several message handlers, it would be a good time to look at the class declaration and source files again.

5

As you learned in Lesson 1, there are two parts to the message map. The function declarations in the header and the message map in the source file.

Listing 5.3 shows the class declaration after all changes that have been made so far.

LISTING 5.3   MssgMapDlg Class Declaration in MssgMapDlg.h

```
class CMssgMapDlg : public CDialog
{
// Construction
public:
    CMssgMapDlg(CWnd* pParent = NULL);     // standard constructor

// Dialog Data
    //{{AFX_DATA(CMssgMapDlg)
    enum { IDD = IDD_MSSGMAP_DIALOG };
    CEdit    m_ebcaption_control;
    CString    m_ebcaption_value;
    //}}AFX_DATA

    // ClassWizard generated virtual function overrides
    //{{AFX_VIRTUAL(CMssgMapDlg)
    protected:
    virtual void DoDataExchange(CDataExchange* pDX);     // DDX/DDV
                                                          // support
    //}}AFX_VIRTUAL

// Implementation
protected:
    HICON m_hIcon;

    // Generated message map functions
    //{{AFX_MSG(CMssgMapDlg)
    virtual BOOL OnInitDialog();
    afx_msg void OnSysCommand(UINT nID, LPARAM lParam);
    afx_msg void OnPaint();
    afx_msg HCURSOR OnQueryDragIcon();
    afx_msg void OnBmsg();
    afx_msg void OnChangeEbcaption();
    afx_msg void OnMaxtextEbcaption();
    afx_msg void OnSetfocusEbcaption();
    afx_msg void OnKillfocusEbcaption();
    //}}AFX_MSG
    DECLARE_MESSAGE_MAP()
};
```

Looking at the class declaration, you will notice that the functions have been declared and added to the list of generated message map functions, just above the DECLARE_MESSAGE_MAP macro.

Listing 5.4 shows the message map as defined in the source file, MssgMapDlg.cpp.

LISTING 5.4 `MssgMapDlg` Message Map in MssgMapDlg.cpp

```
BEGIN_MESSAGE_MAP(CMssgMapDlg, CDialog)
    //{{AFX_MSG_MAP(CMssgMapDlg)
    ON_WM_SYSCOMMAND()
    ON_WM_PAINT()
    ON_WM_QUERYDRAGICON()
    ON_BN_CLICKED(IDC_BMSG, OnBmsg)
    ON_EN_CHANGE(IDC_EBCAPTION, OnChangeEbcaption)
    ON_EN_MAXTEXT(IDC_EBCAPTION, OnMaxtextEbcaption)
    ON_EN_SETFOCUS(IDC_EBCAPTION, OnSetfocusEbcaption)
    ON_EN_KILLFOCUS(IDC_EBCAPTION, OnKillfocusEbcaption)
    //}}AFX_MSG_MAP
END_MESSAGE_MAP()
```

Looking at the message map in Listing 5.4, you should really start to notice the pattern for the ON macro functions. For example, the newly created message handler for EN_KILLFOCUS takes two parameters: a resource ID and the function.

You should also see the pattern on the macro function's name itself as well. EN_KILLFOCUS has a macro function named ON_EN_KILLFOCUS.

Lesson Summary

This lesson focused on using the MFC ClassWizard and the New Windows Message and Event Handlers dialog box to create message handlers. You learned more about the different macros used in the message maps to link resource IDs to functions.

Because messages are tied in well with the object-oriented approach of the MFC classes, VC++ 6's ClassWizard becomes an increasingly important tool when building your application. You saw that the MFC has quite a few messages defined for its numerous classes.

You also learned about some of the timing issues of messages when controls and windows receive and lose focus. This particular example used the edit control's EN_SETFOCUS, EN_CHANGE, and EN_KILLFOCUS messages to demonstrate this point.

Quiz 2

1. Which message map macro function is used for an edit control when the edit control's number of characters exceeds the allowed number?

    a. WM_MAXCHARS

    b. EN_MAXTEXT

    c. ON_EN_MAXTEXT

    d. ON_EM_MAXTEXT

2. Which statement(s) best describes a message map?

    a. Message maps are used to replace the task of writing long window procedures.

    b. Message maps are declared in the class' header file.

    c. Message maps are defined in the class' source file.

    d. You can have only one message map per application.

3. Assuming that you have set up a message handler for an edit box that should be executed when too many characters have been typed, what is needed from the following options to complete the process?

    a. A member variable for the control needs to be created so you can use the `GetTextLen` member function of the class to check its size.

    b. You need to specify the maximum number of characters in the Properties dialog box for the edit control.

    c. A third parameter for the message macro function is needed that tells the maximum number of characters for the edit box.

    d. A member variable for the edit control's value needs to be created and assigned a maximum number of characters.

4. Which messages are used to indicate that an edit control has received and lost focus?

    a. `WM_EDIT_SETFOCUS` and `WM_EDIT_LOOSEFOCUS`

    b. `EN_SETFOCUS` and `EN_LOOSEFOCUS`

    c. `EN_SETFOCUS` and `EN_KILLFOCUS`

    d. `EDM_SETFOCUS` and `EDM_KILLFOCUS`

Exercise 2

Complexity: Easy

1. Create a new dialog-based application named "Exercise 1." Place a button and an edit control on the dialog resource.

The purpose of the button is to clear the window's caption when clicked. The purpose of the edit control is to update the window's caption as you type in the edit box.

Complexity: Moderate

2. Create a new dialog-based application named "Exercise 2." Place a button and an edit control on the dialog resource.

The purpose of the button is to clear the window's caption when clicked. The purpose of the edit control is to update the window's caption as you type in the edit box.

As you enter and exit the edit control, change the window's caption with a message that states the relative operation.

LESSON 3

Processing Commands

At this point, you should have a basic understanding of how Windows uses messages to keep applications functioning. Messages are truly at the heart of every Windows program.

Really, commands are messages too. They are used to instruct the application to do something. For example, when you click the File, Exit menu item, a command gets processed that tells the program to exit. Typically, commands are issued by selecting a menu item, clicking a speed button, or using an accelerator key.

You will be using an SDI application in this lesson, because the AppWizard automatically creates a menu resource for you. Creating menus will be covered in Chapter 6, "Customizing the User Interface." To start exploring how commands are processed, you need to build a new application. Create a new workspace named "Commands." This time, choose an SDI style of application with the rest of the defaults.

With the application framework created, build and execute the project. While it is running, click the Help, About Commands menu item. This will display the default About box. Click the OK button to close the About box.

Exploring the menus, you should notice that some menu items are disabled, specifically the menu items under the Edit menu. Exploring a little further, if you click the File, Open, or File, Save menu items, they perform the function of displaying the proper system dialog boxes. Again, this is because the MFC implements these features, saving you the development time of doing so. Go ahead and close the application.

Looking at the Application's Message Map

So, what's happening when you click a menu item? The application is being told to perform a command. The menu items have a resource ID associated with them just as other controls. Typically, they follow a specific pattern. For example, ID_FILE_SAVE is used for the File, Save menu item. The more you develop with VC++ 6, the more commonplace these names will become.

Listing 5.5 shows the message map from the class definition source file for the Commands project, Commands.cpp.

5

LISTING 5.5 Message Map in Commands.cpp

```
BEGIN_MESSAGE_MAP(CCommandsApp, CWinApp)
    //{{AFX_MSG_MAP(CCommandsApp)
    ON_COMMAND(ID_APP_ABOUT, OnAppAbout)
        // NOTE - the ClassWizard will add and remove mapping macros
        // here.   DO NOT EDIT what you see in these blocks of
        // generated code!
    //}}AFX_MSG_MAP
    // Standard file based document commands
    ON_COMMAND(ID_FILE_NEW, CWinApp::OnFileNew)
    ON_COMMAND(ID_FILE_OPEN, CWinApp::OnFileOpen)
    // Standard print setup command
    ON_COMMAND(ID_FILE_PRINT_SETUP, CWinApp::OnFilePrintSetup)
END_MESSAGE_MAP()
```

Looking at this message map, you should immediately notice a new macro, ON_COMMAND. This macro is similar to the ones you've already seen in the sense that it takes a resource ID as the first parameter and a function name as the second.

The first time it is used is for the resource ID, ID_APP_ABOUT. It is linked to the OnAppAbout function. The resource ID ID_APP_ABOUT was created automatically by the AppWizard. This resource ID is assigned to the menu item Help, About Commands. Figure 5.10 shows the properties for the Help, About Commands menu item. Looking at this figure, you can see the properties window for a menu item. In it, the resource ID is assigned ID_APP_ABOUT.

FIGURE 5.10

Properties for the Help, About Commands menu item.

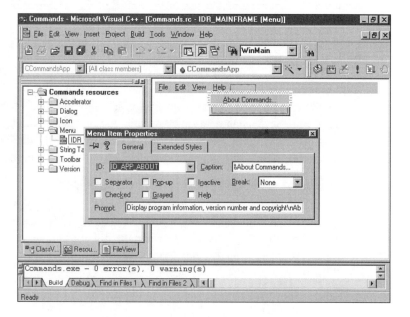

Commands from Other Classes

Examining Listing 5.5 again, you should notice that the next entry for an ON_COMMAND macro is for the ID_FILE_NEW resource ID. The difference here is the function that gets called CWinApp::OnFileOpen.

If you look through the Commands.cpp source file, you won't see it defined in that file. The reason is the CWinApp:: prefix. It is telling the message map to get this function from the CWinApp class, which is defined by MFC. Listing 5.6 shows the class declaration for the CCommandsApp class in the Commands.cpp source file.

LISTING 5.6 Class Declaration in Commands.cpp

```
class CCommandsApp : public CWinApp
{
public:
    CCommandsApp();

// Overrides
    // ClassWizard generated virtual function overrides
    //{{AFX_VIRTUAL(CCommandsApp)
    public:
    virtual BOOL InitInstance();
    //}}AFX_VIRTUAL

// Implementation

    //{{AFX_MSG(CCommandsApp)
    afx_msg void OnAppAbout();
        // NOTE - the ClassWizard will add and remove member functions
        // here.   DO NOT EDIT what you see in these blocks of
        // generated code !
    //}}AFX_MSG
    DECLARE_MESSAGE_MAP()
};
```

If you look at the first line of this listing, you can see that the CCommandsApp class was derived from MFC's CWinApp class.

Looking again at Listing 5.6, you can see that not all of the menu items were defined in the message map. This again is because the MFC hides a lot of the implementation details from you.

A Deeper Look into MFC

In order for the menu item to perform its command, it has to be defined. One of the menu items you were instructed to use was the File, Save menu item. Because it's not defined in the message map above, how is it processed?

5

The MFC has many files. In this case, we want to look at one of its core components, doccore.cpp.

 Note   Do not manually edit any of VC++ 6's include or source files.

Looking at Listing 5.7, you can see that the message map inside the doccore.cpp file contains the ON_COMMAND macro for the ID_FILE_SAVE resource ID, as well as a couple others.

LISTING 5.7   MFC's doccore.cpp Message Map

```
BEGIN_MESSAGE_MAP(CDocument, CCmdTarget)
    //{{AFX_MSG_MAP(CDocument)
    ON_COMMAND(ID_FILE_CLOSE, OnFileClose)
    ON_COMMAND(ID_FILE_SAVE, OnFileSave)
    ON_COMMAND(ID_FILE_SAVE_AS, OnFileSaveAs)
    //}}AFX_MSG_MAP
END_MESSAGE_MAP()
```

When the menu item File, Save is selected, a command is issued to save the file. The macro ON_COMMAND catches this command for the resource id ID_FILE_SAVE and calls the function OnFileSave, also defined in the doccore.cpp file. Listing 5.8 shows the OnFileSave function.

LISTING 5.8   MFC's doccore.cpp Message Map

```
void CDocument::OnFileSave()
{
    DoFileSave();
}
```

You should immediately notice that this function has only one line of code, DoFileSave(). You should also notice that this function is part of the CDocument class.

Because this application is an SDI application, it is based upon a document. The document for this application is derived from the CDocument class. It's this class that knows how to handle the File, Save menu item. But that's not all there is to it.

The OnFileSave function calls the DoFileSave function of the same class. This function in turn calls the DoSave function of the CDocument class. After this function performs a couple validations, it calls the OnSaveDocument function of the CDocument class.

OnSaveDocument does some finalizing for the archive it's about to create and then calls the Serialize() function. Finally, this function is found inside the CommandsDoc.cpp file of your application. This file houses the class implementation for this application's document. The `Serialize()` function from this file is as follows:

```
void CCommandsDoc::Serialize(CArchive& ar)
{
    if (ar.IsStoring())
    {
        // TODO: add storing code here
    }
    else
    {
        // TODO: add loading code here
    }
}
```

Looking at this function, the comments tell you to add your code that actually saves (or loads) the document.

The important point of this is not how to save a file, but to see how the MFC has gone to great lengths to provide a stable framework for your application and processes many commands behind the scenes for you automatically.

ClassWizard and Commands

It should be no surprise by now that you can use the ClassWizard to manage the processing of commands.

To see the ClassWizard in action, select the menu resource, IDR_MAINFRAME from the Menu section of the Resource View. Double-clicking the menu's resource ID will display the menu editor. Right-click somewhere on the menu editor and select ClassWizard from the pop-up context menu. Figure 5.11 shows the ClassWizard with the ID_APP_ABOUT resource ID selected.

FIGURE 5.11

ClassWizard with the ID_APP_ABOUT resource ID selected.

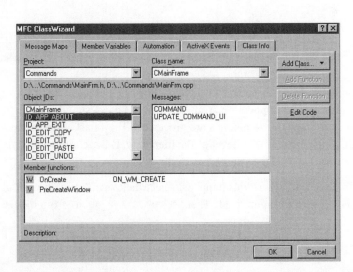

Looking at the ClassWizard, you can see that there isn't a function defined for the COMMAND message for the ID_APP_ABOUT resource ID, yet when you click the Help, About Commands menu item, it works.

If you examine the ClassWizard more closely, you can see that the class name selected is probably CMainFrame. Select the class name CCommandsApp from the drop-down list of class names. Select the ID_APP_ABOUT resource ID. This time, you should see the COMMAND message is in bold, meaning that the handler has been defined for this class.

Note

If you only see the current class name in the list of Object IDs, you should close the ClassWizard, making sure something such as a dialog resource or menu resource is the currently selected item in the editor. You should then be able to go into the ClassWizard and see the list of resource IDs (see Figure 5.12).

FIGURE 5.12

ClassWizard with
ID_APP_ABOUT
resource ID selected in
the CCommandsApp
class.

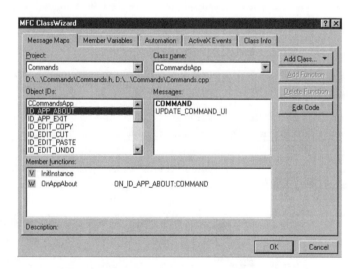

So, what does this mean? This means that you can handle the commands in different places of your application. You just need to be careful where you place it. There is a hierarchy to how the commands are processed. They start at the highest level and "fall through" to the lowest level of the hierarchy. If the command is not processed by the application, it is then passed on to the system.

To demonstrate how this happens, select the CMainFrame class from the ClassWizard as shown back in Figure 5.11. Then, select ID_APP_ABOUT from the list of Object IDs.

After you have the resource ID selected, double-click the COMMAND message to create a new function. The default name of OnAppAbout is fine, so click OK. The new function has been created in the CMainFrame class as shown in Figure 5.13.

FIGURE 5.13

ClassWizard showing the newly created function, OnAppAbout, *in the* CMainFrame *class.*

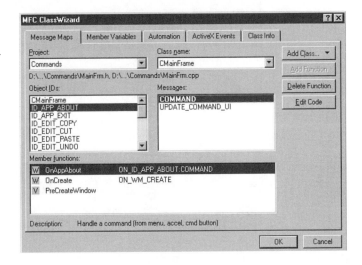

Looking at Figure 5.13, you can see that ClassWizard has created the function and added it to the list of Member functions for the CMainFrame class. Double-click the newly created OnAppAbout member function to bring up the MainFrm.cpp file in your editor. Add the following line of code to the OnAppAbout function:

```
AfxMessageBox("Hello Interactive World!");
```

The entire procedure should look like the following code segment after you add your line of code:

```
void CMainFrame::OnAppAbout()
{
    // TODO: Add your command handler code here
    AfxMessageBox("Hello Interactive World!");

}
```

Now that you have coded the message handler, build and execute the application. When the program is running, compare what happens when you click the Help, About Commands menu item to Figure 5.14.

5

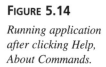

Figure 5.14

Running application after clicking Help, About Commands.

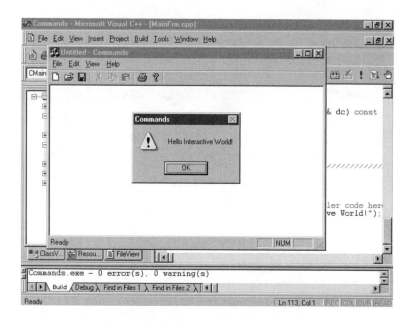

You should have gotten a message box stating `Hello Interactive World!`. What happened when you clicked OK? Did it display the actual About box?

The reason the original About box was not displayed is because of the order in which the message maps were processed. Because `CMainFrame`'s message map is scanned before `CCommandsApp`'s and there is a message mapped for `ID_APP_ABOUT`, it gets processed. Determining the order in which the message maps are processed can be tricky for a novice. For this SDI application, the order is as follows:

1. `CCommandsView`
2. `CCommandsDoc`
3. `CMainFrame`
4. `CCommandsApp`

The thing to be careful about when setting up these message maps to process commands is not to step on another class's message map. For example, you could easily add a function for `ID_FILE_SAVE` in `CCommandsView` that would prevent the MFC's message map from catching and processing the command.

Command Updates

Earlier in this lesson when you ran the Commands application for the first time, the fact that the Edit menu's items were disabled was pointed out.

One important function of commands is command updates. This tells you when a menu item, speed button, and so on is enabled or disabled. For the purpose of the lesson, you will be using menu items.

It used to be that in order to keep track of whether items were enabled or disabled, a large table would be maintained. This is not the approach used in the MFC. The items are updated on demand, meaning that they are enabled and disabled just before they are displayed.

This reflects back to earlier in this lesson when you saw that the CDocument class was managing the File, Save menu item. This means that the object itself knows when to enable and disable menu items. For example, if a document has been modified, then the Save menu item will be enabled; otherwise, it will be disabled.

Unfortunately, the MFC doesn't take care of all instances for you. If you are programming in your own functionality to the application, you will need to manage the states yourself, although the MFC has provided an easy mechanism for doing this.

The MFC has a special object called CCmdUI that is given to objects that are set up to process a CN_UPDATE_COMMAND_UI message. You can use the ClassWizard to set up an object to process the UPDATE_COMMAND_UI message.

To do this, display the ClassWizard for the CMainFrame class. Select the ID_APP_ABOUT Object ID. You should see the COMMAND and UPDATE_COMMAND_UI messages. The COMMAND message is the one you previously defined to show the Hello Interactive World! message.

Using Figure 5.15 as a guide, create a member function for the UPDATE_COMMAND_UI message by double-clicking the message name. You will be prompted for the function name; just click OK.

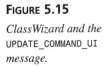

FIGURE 5.15

ClassWizard and the
UPDATE_COMMAND_UI
message.

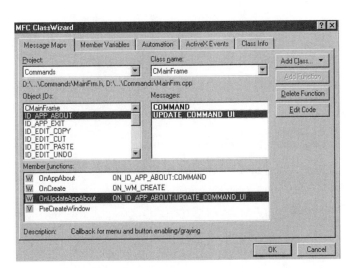

ClassWizard will then update the list of Member functions with the new function, OnUpdateAppAbout. Notice the name of the function. It has the prefix OnUpdate. This is another convention used by the MFC for update commands.

Click the Edit Code button to display the MainFrm.cpp in your editor and add the following line of code:

```
pCmdUI->Enable(FALSE);
```

The complete function should look like the following:

```
void CMainFrame::OnUpdateAppAbout(CCmdUI* pCmdUI)
{
    // TODO: Add your command update UI handler code here
    pCmdUI->Enable(FALSE);
}
```

The line of code you added is what determines if the command should be enabled or disabled. The Enable() function of the CCmdUI class takes one parameter. This parameter can be anything that returns a TRUE or FALSE value. In this example, it is explicitly set to FALSE to disable the menu item.

To see this in action, build, then run, the application. Compare the Help menu to the one in Figure 5.16 and make sure that your Help, About Commands menu item is disabled.

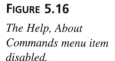

FIGURE 5.16

The Help, About Commands menu item disabled.

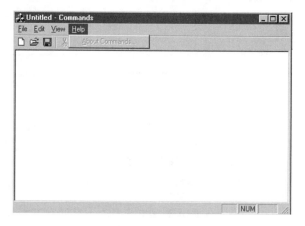

The CCmdUI class has some useful members:

- Enable()—Enables or disables the item.
- SetCheck()—Checks or unchecks the item.
- SetRadio()—Same as SetCheck(), except it's used like option buttons.
- SetText()—Sets the text of the interface item.

The following listing shows the message map from MainFrm.cpp.

```
BEGIN_MESSAGE_MAP(CMainFrame, CFrameWnd)
    //{{AFX_MSG_MAP(CMainFrame)
    ON_WM_CREATE()
    ON_COMMAND(ID_APP_ABOUT, OnAppAbout)
    ON_UPDATE_COMMAND_UI(ID_APP_ABOUT, OnUpdateAppAbout)
    //}}AFX_MSG_MAP
END_MESSAGE_MAP()
```

Looking at this message map, you can see the two macros that effect the Help, About Commands, ON_COMMAND and ON_UPDATE_COMMAND_UI.

Lesson Summary

This lesson focused on how the MFC implements command processing. Even though the MFC hides a lot of the implementation details of how commands are processed, it is important to have an understanding of what is going on "under the hood" (at least to some degree).

You learned about a new macro, ON_COMMAND that is used to map commands to functions using the interface item's resource ID. You also learned that to control the command updating, a special class, CCmdUI is used by the MFC to enable and disable controls.

Quiz 3

1. What macro function is used for command updating?

   a. ON_UPDATE_COMMAND

   b. CCmdUI

   c. UPDATE_COMMAND_UI

   d. ON_UPDATE_COMMAND_UI

2. What macro function is used to link resource IDs to a member function for command processing?

   a. ON_COMMAND

   b. WM_COMMAND

   c. ON_OBJECT_COMMAND

   d. UPDATE_COMMAND_UI

3. What function of the CCmdUI class is used to enable and disable an interface item?

   a. SetEnabled()

   b. Enable()

5

    c. `SetValid()`

    d. `Valid()`

4. Which resource ID is typically used for the File, Save menu item?

    a. `IDC_FILE_SAVE`

    b. `IDD_FILE_SAVE`

    c. `ID_FILE_SAVE`

    d. `IC_FILE_SAVE`

Exercise 3

Complexity: Easy

1. Create a new SDI-based application named "Exercise 1." This program should have a function handler for the Help, About Exercise 1 menu item that will prevent the default function from being called. Have this menu item display the message, `Hello Interactive World!` when chosen.

   Add a message handler that will disable the Help, About Exercise 1 menu item using the `CCmdUI` class.

LESSON 4

Standard Windows Messages

So far, all the messages that you have provided message handlers for have been the MFC's interpretation of the messages. You can actually have your program process standard Windows messages.

In the previous lessons, you were using the message map to process messages that were caused by actions such as clicking a button or selecting a menu item. In this lesson, you will learn how to process Windows messages as well.

Deciding on what messages you want to trap and process is probably the hard part. There are literally hundreds of messages that can be generated and trapped. Thankfully, the MFC ClassWizard and other dialog boxes help you out by filtering out messages that are not pertinent to the class on which you are working.

Normally, the Windows messages that you will want to trap start with the standard prefix of `WM_` followed by the message name. These message names are defined by the system and hold a specific numeric value.

For example, to trap the message that says this window has just been resized, you would trap the WM_SIZE message. The important thing to know is where to add the message handler. In this case, it could be added to any of the CMainFrame, CCommandsApp, or CCommandsView classes. For the purpose of this lesson, you will be adding it to the CMainFrame class, because it's the window's frame that actually gets resized by the user.

One handy tool in VC++ 6 that hasn't been talked about much so far is the New Windows Message and Event Handlers dialog box that enables you to add functions to classes. The easy way to access this dialog box is to use the Class View tab of the Project Workspace.

Click the Class View tab in the Project Workspace. In this view, you will see the different classes defined within your project. Right-click the CMainFrame class and select Add Windows Message Handler from the pop-up context menu. You should recognize this dialog box from an earlier lesson in this chapter.

Select the WM_SIZE message from the list of available messages and then click the Add and Edit button to create the function. Figure 5.17 shows the New Windows Message and Event Handlers for class CMainFrame dialog box with the WM_SIZE message selected.

FIGURE 5.17

The New Windows Message and Event Handlers for class CMainFrame *dialog box.*

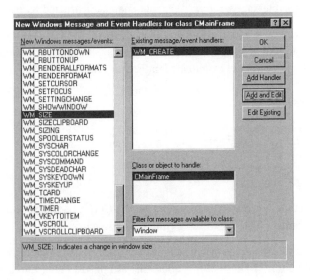

After you click the Add and Edit button, the code editor takes you to the newly created event procedure named, conveniently enough, OnSize. Enter the following line of code into this message handler just after the //TODO comment line:

```
SetWindowText("Window Size Changed");
```

The entire message handler should look like the following code segment after you entered the preceding line of code:

```
void CMainFrame::OnSize(UINT nType, int cx, int cy)
{
    CFrameWnd::OnSize(nType, cx, cy);

    // TODO: Add your message handler code here
    SetWindowText("Window Size Changed");
}
```

There is something about this message handler that is different from the others created so far. This one has a call to `CFrameWnd::OnSize()` in it. This is here so that the default behavior of this message is carried out. If you want to override it, you can comment this line out to prevent the function from doing its normal behavior, but in this case, it wouldn't be a good idea. That action would prevent the window from being resized properly. For the purpose of this lesson, you will leave it as it is. The line of code you entered simply changes the window's title after you move the window.

If you haven't done so already, build and execute the application. When the application is running, change the size of the window. After you do so, the window's title should change to the message Window Size Changed as instructed by the OnSize function.

Now that you have added a function that processes the WM_SIZE message, it would be a good time to look at how the message map has been changed. The following listing shows the message map from the MainFrm.cpp file.

```
BEGIN_MESSAGE_MAP(CMainFrame, CFrameWnd)
    //{{AFX_MSG_MAP(CMainFrame)
    ON_WM_CREATE()
    ON_COMMAND(ID_APP_ABOUT, OnAppAbout)
    ON_UPDATE_COMMAND_UI(ID_APP_ABOUT, OnUpdateAppAbout)
    ON_WM_SIZE()
    //}}AFX_MSG_MAP
END_MESSAGE_MAP()
```

Notice that the last macro added is `ON_WM_SIZE()`. This macro follows the convention of being preceded by `ON_` followed by the message name.

Looking at this macro, you can see that there are no parameters. So how does it find the OnSize function? To answer this question, you need to look into how the macro for this function is defined. This is contained in the afxmsg_.h file in the MFC\Include directory of VC++ 6. The following listing is the code segment from that file that defines the ON_WM_SIZE macro:

```
#define ON_WM_SIZE() \
  { WM_SIZE, 0, 0, 0, AfxSig_vwii, \
    (AFX_PMSG)(AFX_PMSGW)(void (AFX_MSG_CALL CWnd::*)
    ➥(UINT, int, int))&OnSize },
```

Looking at this code segment, you can see that the `#define` gives the macro its name. The next line gives the macro the information it needs about which message it is trapping. The last line is responsible for pointing the macro to the `OnSize` function. The important part of the line is the `&OnSize`. This is what links the `ON_WM_SIZE` macro to the `OnSize` function in the class the message map is in.

To expand on what you have learned so far in this lesson, you are going to add a couple more functions that will trap the `WM_CLOSE` and `WM_MOVE` messages.

To start with, use either the ClassWizard or the New Windows Message and Event Handlers message box to create the new functions for the `CMainFrame` class. Figure 5.18 shows the ClassWizard after the two new member functions have been created.

FIGURE 5.18

The ClassWizard after the two new member functions.

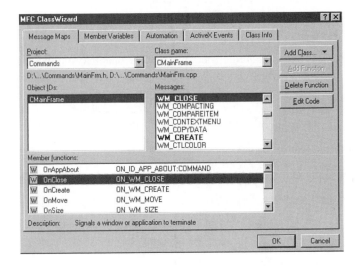

Even though you've defined functions for these messages, they have a normal behavior that will be executed even if you don't add any lines of code.

These two messages were chosen because of where you need to place code in the message handler. In the `OnMove` function, you will add code after the message has been processed, and in `OnClose`, you will add code before the message gets processed.

To start with, add the following lines of code after the `//TODO` comment in the `OnMove` function you just created:

```
CString caption;
caption.Format("Window Moved to :%d,%d",x,y);
SetWindowText(caption);
```

The complete function should look like the following:

```
void CMainFrame::OnMove(int x, int y)
{
    CFrameWnd::OnMove(x, y);

    // TODO: Add your message handler code here
    CString caption;
    caption.Format("Window Moved to :%d,%d",x,y);
    SetWindowText(caption);
}
```

Notice that in this procedure, CFrameWnd::OnMove gets called before your code does. This is the default behavior for processing this message. This allows the window to be redrawn before you do any of your processing. If your program needs to do something before the window is updated, in this case, you would add the code before the call to CFrameWnd::OnMove.

Next, you need to edit the OnClose message handler. Add the following line of code after the //TODO comment, but before the CFrameWnd::OnClose statement:

```
AfxMessageBox("The window is closing");
```

Now, add the following line of code *after* the CFrameWnd::OnClose statement:

```
AfxMessageBox("This line does not get executed");
```

The complete function should look like the following code segment:

```
void CMainFrame::OnClose()
{
    // TODO: Add your message handler code here and/or call default
    AfxMessageBox("The window is closing");
    CFrameWnd::OnClose();
    AfxMessageBox("This line does not get executed");
}
```

In this message handler, you added a line of code before and after the default function is called. Build and execute the application. This time, when the program is running, move the window around. When you are done moving it, the window's title will be updated with a message stating where its new location is.

When you are done moving and sizing the window, close it. You should get a message stating The window is closing as instructed by the OnClose message handler. Click the OK button. Does the next message appear? No.

The reason the next message, This line does not get executed, does not get executed is that it comes after the call to CFrameWnd::OnClose, which closes the window, hence terminating the program.

This means that it's important to make sure you add your code in the necessary spot when processing messages; otherwise, undesired behavior might occur.

Now that you have defined two more message handlers, take a look at the message map in the following code segment:

```
BEGIN_MESSAGE_MAP(CMainFrame, CFrameWnd)
    //{{AFX_MSG_MAP(CMainFrame)
    ON_WM_CREATE()
    ON_COMMAND(ID_APP_ABOUT, OnAppAbout)
    ON_UPDATE_COMMAND_UI(ID_APP_ABOUT, OnUpdateAppAbout)
    ON_WM_SIZE()
    ON_WM_CLOSE()
    ON_WM_MOVE()
    //}}AFX_MSG_MAP
END_MESSAGE_MAP()
```

As expected, two macros were added: ON_WM_CLOSE for the WM_CLOSE message and ON_WM_MOVE for the WM_MOVE message. These two macros don't take parameters just like the ON_WM_SIZE macro didn't need to. This is for the same reason as the ON_WM_SIZE macro: The function name has been defined by the macro ahead of time. If you think back to when you created the functions, the ClassWizard did not ask you for a function name—it created one by default.

Lesson Summary

In this lesson, you learned that besides processing messages that the MFC has interpreted, you can process actual Windows messages. By being able to process Windows messages, you can add additional functionality to your programs.

This lesson focused on just three of the many Windows messages available to Windows programs. You learned that even though you were processing the messages with your own message handlers, the MFC and VC++ 6 has built-in mechanisms that make them integrate seamlessly into your application without losing the basic functionality of the default behaviors.

Quiz 4

1. Which Windows message is sent to a window when its size has changed?

    a. WM_SIZE_CHANGED

    b. WM_SIZE

    c. SIZE_WM

    d. WM_WINDOW_SIZE_CHANGED

2. Which tools will enable you to add message handlers for standard Windows messages?

    a. The MFC ClassWizard dialog box

    b. The New Windows Message and Event Handlers dialog box

    c. The Add Windows Handler dialog box

    d. All of the above

3. Which statement(s) best describes handling the WM_CLOSE message?

    a. You must pass the OnClose a TRUE or FALSE value to determine whether or not the window gets closed.

    b. You should not comment out the default OnClose statement, because it might prevent your application from being closed properly.

    c. WM_CLOSE message can only be handled by the MFC and can't be changed.

    d. You should not put any statements after the default OnClose statement.

4. Which statement(s) best describe the macros added to the message map when processing standard Windows Messages?

    a. The macro's name is comprised of the resource ID and the function name.

    b. The macro takes two parameters: the resource ID of the interface item issuing the command and the function name of the function that handles the command.

    c. The macro has no parameters.

    d. The same macro name, ON_WM_MESSAGE, is used with the message as the first parameter and the function to be mapped to as the second parameter.

Exercise 4

Complexity: Easy

1. Create a new dialog-based application named "Exercise 1" that traps the WM_MOVE message and shows the window's new coordinates in the dialog box's title.

Complexity: Moderate

2. Create a new dialog-based application named "Exercise 2" that traps the WM_MOUSEMOVE message and changes the dialog box's caption to the location of the mouse.

LESSON 5

Custom Windows Messages

Throughout this chapter, you've read about Windows messages. You've seen that they come in several flavors, but what you haven't seen so far is how to create your own messages.

First, you might ask, why would you need to create your own messages when Windows has predefined so many? The reason is that Windows' messages have a specific function they were designed to accomplish, and you might not find one to meet your needs.

In your own application, an incident may arise when you may need to notify another part of your program that something has happened. Granted, a lot of programs that you write will probably not need to have their own messages, but learning how to create your own messages will give you a better understanding of how the message process works. Besides, up until now, all you've seen is how to receive a message. In this lesson, you will also see how to send messages.

Actually, a message, such as WM_MOVE, is only a number. Each of Windows' messages have been defined in header files so that as you program, you can refer to these messages by name, not by number. This undoubtedly makes working with messages a lot simpler.

Windows has defined five ranges of messages. These ranges themselves translate into a group or range of numbers. Table 5.3 explains the different message ranges.

TABLE 5.3 Message Ranges

Range	Description
0 through WM_USER - 1	This range is used by Windows for its default set of messages. This would include messages such as the WM_MOVE and WM_SIZE messages that you trapped in the last lesson.
WM-USER through 0x7FFF	This range is used for private windows class messages. This range contains messages for controls in a window as well as messages defined privately for this class. This is typically the range you define your messages in. The 0x7FFF is a hex number which is 32767 in decimal.
0x8000 through 0xBFFF	This range has been reserved for future versions of Windows. The decimal equivalents are 32768 through 49151.
0xC000 through 0xFFFF	This range is used for private messages that have been registered with the system using the RegisterWindowMessage API call. The decimal equivalents are 49152 through 65535.
0xFFFF and up	Anything above 0xFFFF is reserved by the system.

5

From looking at Table 5.3, you see a special message, WM_USER. Windows defines the value of this message. This is the starting point at which one less is where the Windows range ends and where the class definable range begins. At the time of this writing, this value is 0x400 in hex, or 1024 in decimal.

Also in this table is the range 0xC000 through 0xFFFF. This range is typically used when you are writing an application that talks to another application. This can be two different applications, or the same application running more than once. Using RegisterWindowMessage is beyond the scope of this book, but it is important to understand how this function works.

RegisterWindowMessage takes a single parameter, a pointer to a null terminated string. This string is registered with Windows and is given a guaranteed unique number. This unique number is returned if the call was successful; otherwise, a 0 (zero) value is returned.

After the message has been registered with the system, any subsequent calls to RegisterWindowMessage with the same message name will return the value previously registered. This registered message will last during the current Windows session.

Looking back to Table 5.3, you can see that the range WM_USER through 0x7FFF is used for private messages. This is where you will typically define your messages. When using this range, it is important to note that controls within that window's class will also use this range for messages. To avoid conflicting with the messages used for these controls, it's common to add a "padding" to the WM_USER value when defining your own messages. A "padding" of 100 is usually safe.

For the example in this lesson, you need to create a new workspace with the name "Custom." Create this project as a dialog-based application. All of the defaults are fine.

After AppWizard has created the application framework for your "Custom" Dialog application, change the main dialog box by completing the following steps:

1. Remove the "TODO" static text control from the main dialog box.

2. Add a list box control with the resource ID of IDC_LBMSSG. This control should be sized to take up the majority of the left side of the dialog box.

3. Add a button control below the "Cancel" button. Give this button the resource ID of IDC_BSEND and a caption of Message.

Figure 5.19 shows what your dialog resource should look like after you have completed the above steps.

FIGURE 5.19

Dialog resource with list box and button controls.

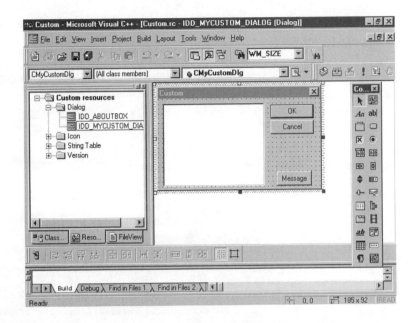

With the dialog box's appearance done, now you need to add a member variable for the list box control and an event procedure for when the Message button gets clicked.

Using Figure 5.20 as a guide, use the ClassWizard to create a member variable for the list box control with the resource ID of IDC_LBMSG. Name this member variable m_lbmsg_control with the category of Control and a variable type of CListBox.

FIGURE 5.20

Adding a member variable with the ClassWizard.

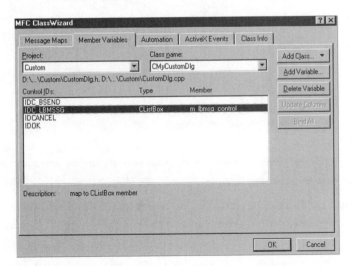

5

Now, using Figure 5.21 as a guide, create a member function for the BN_CLICKED message for the IDC_BSEND resource ID.

FIGURE 5.21

Adding a member function with the ClassWizard.

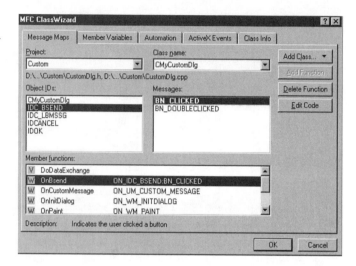

After you have the m_lbmsg_control member variable defined and the message handler created for the Message button, you can modify the message handler to send a message when clicked.

To do this, click the Edit Code button for the OnBsend function that was just created. Add the following line of code just below the //TODO comment:

```
SendMessage(UM_CUSTOM_MESSAGE,0,0);
```

The entire function should look like the following block of code after you have that line of code added:

```
void CMyCustomDlg::OnBsend()
{
    // TODO: Add your control notification handler code here
    SendMessage(UM_CUSTOM_MESSAGE,0,0);
}
```

Right away, there are a couple things to note about this procedure. First is the function SendMessage(), and then the class name, CMyCustomDlg.

Because the CMyCustomDlg was derived from the CDialog class, it inherits its functions. One of them is the SendMessage() function.

The SendMessage function is used to send a message to the class' window. Another function that does virtually the same thing is PostMessage. PostMessage will send a message to the window and immediately return, whereas the SendMessage function will send the message and wait for it to be processed.

Looking closer at the SendMessage function, you can see that it is passing three parameters: a message, a WPARAM and a LPARAM. The message will be the user-defined message that you create. The other two parameters are used to pass data.

In this example, you are sending the message, UM_CUSTOM_MESSAGE. This message name can be virtually anything you want it to be, barring reserved words and invalid characters.

Defining the message can be done almost anywhere before the message is first used, just like any other constant. Because this message is only valid for the dialog's class, it would make sense to define it at the beginning of the class' header file, CustomDlg.h.

Add the following three lines of code to the beginning of the CustomDlg.h file just after the //CustomDlg.h comment line:

```
#if !defined(UM_CUSTOM_MESSAGE)
#define UM_CUSTOM_MESSAGE WM_USER + 0xFF
#endif
```

Looking at these three lines, you can see that a compiler directive is being used to see if this message has already been defined. If it has, the definition is ignored; if it hasn't, the new constant is defined.

The value assigned to UM_CUSTOM_MESSAGE is the value of WM_USER + 0xFF. The value of WM_USER is defined within the MFC to make room for windows messages. The 0xFF is the "padding" that was mentioned earlier. The hex value 0xFF has a decimal equivalent of 255. Because WM_USER is 1024, this means that UM_CUSTOM_MESSAGE has a value of 1279.

Note When building applications with your own messages, never hard code a value. Always use a message name that has been defined with WM_USER + a padding value. If the MFC value of WM_USER gets changed, a recompile of your project will automatically re-create the new value for your message.

Now that the message has been defined, build and execute the application. While the application is executing, click the Message button. Does anything happen?

Actually, yes. When you click the button, the UM_CUSTOM_MESSAGE is sent. Unfortunately, nothing is listening for it, so it goes unheard.

The next step is to add the necessary code to process the message. This step will be done manually, because this is not one of MFC's normal messages.

Remembering earlier lessons in this chapter, you used ClassWizard to add entries to the message map. Three things were achieved when using the ClassWizard for this purpose:

1. An entry was made in the class' header file for the function that processed the message.
2. An entry was made in the class' message map that linked the message to the function that processed the message.
3. A stub function was created for the message if it didn't already exist.

Taking these steps in turn, you will have to accomplish these tasks to process your message. This might seem like a daunting task, but after you get the hang of it, you'll see that it is really quite simple.

First, you need to add the function declaration to the class' definition. This is done in the class' header file. In this example, this would be in CustomDlg.h. This is the same file that you defined the message in earlier.

The hard part of this step is knowing where to add the function declaration. You know that it's going to be a part of class' declaration, but that is what this file is for. The key is to look for the comment //Generated message map functions. Because this file is rather short, it should be relatively easy to find.

After you find the location, you can see that there are two comments used by VC++ 6 that section off the functions used for message mapping, //{{AFX_MSG() and //}}AFX_MSG.

You need to add the following line of code to the list of message mapped functions:

```
afx_msg void OnCustomMessage();
```

Because this file is relatively short, the entire contents are listed below:

```
// CustomDlg.h : header file
//

#if !defined(UM_CUSTOM_MESSAGE)
#define UM_CUSTOM_MESSAGE WM_USER + 0xFF
#endif

#if !defined(AFX_CUSTOMDLG_H__B6938587_9C90_
➥11D1_9B29_A8F9B04B2E60__INCLUDED_)
#define AFX_CUSTOMDLG_H__B6938587_9C90_
➥11D1_9B29_A8F9B04B2E60__INCLUDED_

#if _MSC_VER > 1000
#pragma once
#endif // _MSC_VER > 1000
```

```
/////////////////////////////////////////////////////////////////
// CMyCustomDlg dialog

class CMyCustomDlg : public CDialog
{
// Construction
public:
    CMyCustomDlg(CWnd* pParent = NULL);  // standard constructor

// Dialog Data
    //{{AFX_DATA(CMyCustomDlg)
    enum { IDD = IDD_MYCUSTOM_DIALOG };
    CListBox    m_lbmsg_control;
    //}}AFX_DATA

    // ClassWizard generated virtual function overrides
    //{{AFX_VIRTUAL(CMyCustomDlg)
    protected:
    virtual void DoDataExchange(CDataExchange* pDX);    // DDX/DDV
                                                        // support

    //}}AFX_VIRTUAL

// Implementation
protected:
    HICON m_hIcon;

    // Generated message map functions
    //{{AFX_MSG(CMyCustomDlg)
    virtual BOOL OnInitDialog();
    afx_msg void OnSysCommand(UINT nID, LPARAM lParam);
    afx_msg void OnPaint();
    afx_msg HCURSOR OnQueryDragIcon();
    afx_msg void OnBsend();
    afx_msg void OnCustomMessage();
    //}}AFX_MSG
    DECLARE_MESSAGE_MAP()
};

//{{AFX_INSERT_LOCATION}}
// Microsoft Visual C++ will insert additional declarations
// immediately before the previous line.

#endif // !defined(AFX_CUSTOMDLG_H__B6938587_9C90_
➥11D1_9B29_A8F9B04B2E60__INCLUDED_)
```

Looking at the contents of this file, you should see the #define statement you set up earlier (at the top of the file), and the line of code that you just added in the list of message
mapped functions. Following conventions learned so far, the function was named
OnCustomMessage.

The next step is to add a message map entry that will link the message to a function that processes the message. This happens right in the class's source code file, CustomDlg.cpp. You need to locate the message map for the CMyCustomDlg class.

After you locate the message map, add the following line of code to the bottom of this list:

```
ON_MESSAGE(UM_CUSTOM_MESSAGE, OnCustomMessage)
```

The complete message map after you have added the preceding line of code for the CMyCustomDlg class is as follows:

```
BEGIN_MESSAGE_MAP(CMyCustomDlg, CDialog)
    //{{AFX_MSG_MAP(CMyCustomDlg)
    ON_WM_SYSCOMMAND()
    ON_WM_PAINT()
    ON_WM_QUERYDRAGICON()
    ON_BN_CLICKED(IDC_BSEND, OnBsend)
    ON_MESSAGE(UM_CUSTOM_MESSAGE, OnCustomMessage)
    //}}AFX_MSG_MAP
END_MESSAGE_MAP()
```

With the function declaration and the message map in place, the last thing to create is the actual event procedure that processes the message. As stated previously, the function will be named OnCustomMessage. Because this function is a member of the CMyCustomDlg class, it will reside in the CustomDlg.cpp file as well.

The following code listing is the entire message handler. You need to add it at the end of the file:

```
void CMyCustomDlg::OnCustomMessage()
{
    m_lbmsg_control.AddString("Got Message");
}
```

Looking at the preceding code segment, its purpose is quite short. When a message is processed, a line of text is added to the list box. Build and run the application. While it is running, click the Message button a couple of times. Figure 5.22 shows the application running after pressing the Message button several times.

If you haven't done so already, close the application.

Earlier, it was mentioned that you could pass values along with the message. This could be useful if you had a generic message that when processed, accomplished several tasks dependent upon the values passed with it. In fact, this is how the majority of Windows' messages are processed.

FIGURE 5.22

Custom messages being processed.

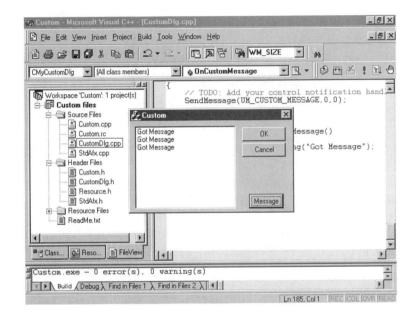

Processing messages with values isn't any more difficult to set up than processing messages with parameters. In fact, you go through all the same steps. The only difference is what you do with the values.

In order to demonstrate this, you are going to add some more functionality to the program that you have been building in this lesson. This time, when a second button is pressed, a message will be sent that has two values. These values will consist of a counter and its previous value.

Two variables will need to be created in the CMyCustomDlg class. One will be for the counter and the other for the previous value. To complete this step, you will need to add these variables to the class' definition, which is in CustomDlg.h. Add the following two lines of code to the public section, under the // Dialog Data comment:

```
int m_counter;
int m_previous;
```

This declares the two values. The next step is to initialize them when the class is initialized. This is done in the class's OnInitDialog function. This is in the CustomDlg.cpp file. Add the following two lines of code just before the return statement at the end of the function:

```
m_counter = 0;
m_previous = 0;
```

This will initialize both variables to 0 (zero). The complete `OnInitDialog` function follows. Use it to make sure that you entered the lines above in the proper location:

```
BOOL CMyCustomDlg::OnInitDialog()
{
    CDialog::OnInitDialog();

    // Add "About..." menu item to system menu.

    // IDM_ABOUTBOX must be in the system command range.
    ASSERT((IDM_ABOUTBOX & 0xFFF0) == IDM_ABOUTBOX);
    ASSERT(IDM_ABOUTBOX < 0xF000);

    CMenu* pSysMenu = GetSystemMenu(FALSE);
    if (pSysMenu != NULL)
    {
        CString strAboutMenu;
        strAboutMenu.LoadString(IDS_ABOUTBOX);
        if (!strAboutMenu.IsEmpty())
        {
            pSysMenu->AppendMenu(MF_SEPARATOR);
            pSysMenu->AppendMenu(MF_STRING, IDM_ABOUTBOX,
            ➥strAboutMenu);
        }
    }

    // Set the icon for this dialog. The framework does this
    // automatically when the application's main window isn't a dialog
    SetIcon(m_hIcon, TRUE);         // Set big icon
    SetIcon(m_hIcon, FALSE);        // Set small icon

    // TODO: Add extra initialization here

    m_counter = 0;
    m_previous = 0;
    return TRUE;  // return TRUE  unless you set the focus to
                  // a control
}
```

Now that the variables needed are defined, you can start adding the necessary items to create and process a new message. This time, you need to create a message named `UM_CREATE_MSG_PARAM`. This should be done just like the one you defined earlier at the beginning of the CustomDlg.h file. Add the following lines of code just below the other message you defined earlier:

```
#if !defined(UM_CUSTOM_MSG_PARAM)
#define UM_CUSTOM_MSG_PARAM WM_USER + 256
#endif
```

Notice that this time, the decimal value of 256 was added to `WM_USER`. This is actually just one higher than the hex value 0xFF, which is 255.

Because you are already in this file making changes, now would be a good time to add the function declaration for the function that will process the message. Locate the function declarations for the CMyCustomDlg class and add the following line just below the one you added earlier:

```
afx_msg void OnCustomMsgParam(WPARAM wParam, LPARAM lParam);
```

After you have added the above line of code, the list should look like the following:

```
// Generated message map functions
    //{{AFX_MSG(CMyCustomDlg)
    virtual BOOL OnInitDialog();
    afx_msg void OnSysCommand(UINT nID, LPARAM lParam);
    afx_msg void OnPaint();
    afx_msg HCURSOR OnQueryDragIcon();
    afx_msg void OnBsend();
    afx_msg void OnCustomMessage();
    afx_msg void OnCustomMsgParam(WPARAM wParam, LPARAM lParam);
    //}}AFX_MSG
    DECLARE_MESSAGE_MAP()
```

The difference between this entry and the one you coded previously should be apparent. This time, you are stating that the function has two parameters. This is the mechanism that provides passing values with the message.

Next, you need to add the message map entry in the CustomDlg.cpp file that links the message to a function. This should go just below the one you added to that message map as well. Add the following line of code:

```
ON_MESSAGE(UM_CUSTOM_MSG_PARAM, OnCustomMsgParam)
```

The complete message map should look like the following after you add the preceding line of code:

```
BEGIN_MESSAGE_MAP(CMyCustomDlg, CDialog)
    //{{AFX_MSG_MAP(CMyCustomDlg)
    ON_WM_SYSCOMMAND()
    ON_WM_PAINT()
    ON_WM_QUERYDRAGICON()
    ON_BN_CLICKED(IDC_BSEND, OnBsend)
    ON_MESSAGE(UM_CUSTOM_MESSAGE, OnCustomMessage)
    ON_MESSAGE(UM_CUSTOM_MSG_PARAM, OnCustomMsgParam)
    //}}AFX_MSG_MAP
END_MESSAGE_MAP()
```

Now, the last thing that needs to be added is the function that will actually process the message. Again, this function will be a member of the CMyCustomDlg class, therefore, it will go in the CustomDlg.cpp file. The following lines of code are the entire function. Add them to the end of the file.

5

```
void CMyCustomDlg::OnCustomMsgParam(WPARAM wParam, LPARAM lParam)
{
    CString caption;
    caption.Format("Values W:%d L:%d",wParam,lParam);
    m_lbmsg_control.AddString(caption);
}
```

This function processes the UM_CUSTOM_MSG_PARAM message. First, it creates a variable to build a message. Next, it formats the variable using CString's Format function. This function takes the two passed values and plugs them into the string. After that, a line is added to the list box that shows what values were passed.

Well, all the pieces are in place to process the message. The only problem is that nothing is sending the new message. To send the new message, add a new button to the dialog box just above the Message button.

Give this new button a resource ID of IDC_BPARAMS and the caption of "Params." Figure 5.23 shows the new dialog box and the properties for the new button.

FIGURE 5.23

Main dialog box resource with the new button and properties.

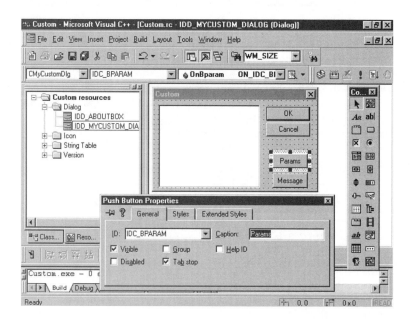

Next, add an event handler for the button. In the OnBparam function, add the following lines of code just below the //TODO comment:

```
m_previous = m_counter;
m_counter++;
SendMessage(UM_CUSTOM_MSG_PARAM,m_counter,m_previous);
```

The first line of code assigns the current value of m_counter to m_previous. Next, m_counter is increased by one. The last line sends the new message with the two variables as parameters.

With all of these code changes complete, build and execute the application. While it is running, click the Message button and then the Params button a couple times. You will see that the two messages are processed as planned and that the parameters are being incremented as instructed to do so. Figure 5.24 shows the running application.

FIGURE 5.24

Custom application running.

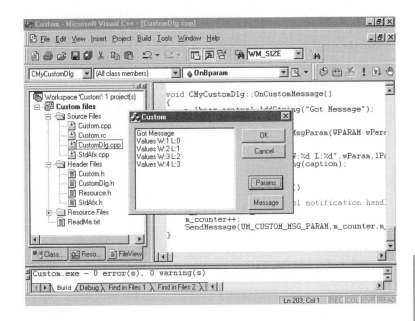

Lesson Summary

This lesson concentrated on creating and processing custom messages. During this process, you were introduced to the ranges Windows enables you to use for your messages.

You learned that one special message is reserved in Windows, WM_USER. This message is used to define the starting point where you can create messages.

You were also introduced to another range of messages that enable you to register a message by a name so that other applications or instances of the same application can use the same message.

You also saw that you could process messages with or without parameters, and that doing so really doesn't take any extra effort on your part. The only difference is how you want to process the parameters and making sure you declare them in the message map.

Quiz 5

1. What functions are used to send messages?

   a. PostMessage

   b. SendMessage

   c. MessagePost

   d. WM_USER

2. Of the choices below, which macro is used to map user-defined messages?

   a. ON_USER_MESSAGE

   b. ON_UM_MESSAGE

   c. ON_MESSAGE

   d. ON_USER_COMMAND

3. Assume that you have a message defined as UM_MAX_COUNT and that you want to send two numbers with the message. If the two values to be passed to the OnMaxCount function are MAX_COUNT and CUR_COUNT, which message map macro below will accomplish the link?

   a. ON_MESSAGE(UM_MAX_COUNT, OnMaxCount(WPARAM MAX_COUNT, LPARAM CUR_COUNT)

   b. OnMaxCount)

   c. ON_MESSAGE(UM_MAX_COUNT, OnMaxCount)

   d. ON_USER_MESSAGE(UM_MAX_COUNT, OnMaxCount)

4. Using the same information from Question 3: Assuming the class that the message was defined for is named CItemCountDlg, which function header will work for the OnMaxCount function?

   a. ItemCountDlg::OnMaxCount()

   b. CItemCountDlg::OnMaxCount(WPARAM MAX_COUNT, LPARAM CUR_COUNT)

   c. CitemCountDlg::OnMaxCount(WPARAM MAX_COUNT, LPARAM CUR_COUNT)

   d. None of the above

Exercise 5

Complexity: Easy

1. Create a new dialog-based application named "Exercise 1." Place a button on the dialog resource.

   The purpose of the button is to send a user-defined message. When this message is received, display a message stating its arrival.

Complexity: Moderate

2. Create a new dialog-based application named "Exercise 2." Place a button on the dialog resource as well as two list box controls.

The purpose of this button is to send a user-defined message. The message sent should contain two parameters. These two parameters should be added to the list in the list boxes.

Chapter Summary

This chapter covered a topic that is at the heart of every Windows program—messages. Whether you deal with the message processing in your application or let the MFC do it all for you, it is important that you understand what is going on "under the hood."

First, you learned about Message maps and macros. Here you discovered that the MFC has built in mechanisms that make dealing with making sure that messages get processed a simple task. Without such a tool, the task of writing message loops would be mind-numbing. In fact, in the days of C, message loops were coded without the aid of the tools used now.

After seeing how the MFC helps in managing messages, you saw how the MFC ClassWizard hid even more of the messy details from you by giving you a nice GUI that allowed you to point-and-click your way to message handlers.

Even though the MFC is very thorough, there are times that you will want to process Windows messages by yourself. Knowing this ahead of time, the people that gave us VC++ 6 and MFC have given us a mechanism for processing such tasks.

But when Windows messages aren't enough to get the job done, you can create and process your own messages. Using this feature depends solely on your need to add it to an application. Even though the MFC is quite complex, it's still flexible enough to give you the freedom to create and process your own messages.

Understanding this chapter is important, if not crucial, to your success at writing programs with VC++ 6 simply because Windows revolves around messages.

5

CHAPTER 6

Customizing the User Interface

Even when DOS was the standard programming platform for PCs, the user interface for an application was crucial to an application's success. The problem was that there was no standard way to implement common features into the interface.

Menus have been around since the earliest of programs. They were as simple as a list of options or as complicated as drop-down styles.

Adding to the concept of drop-down menus the concept of status bars in a DOS-based application, you would have one of the nicer programs. But, not too many DOS-based applications had the capability of docking toolbars. Sure, there were applications that created and used their own graphics libraries to build this type of functionality, but that feature came at an expensive price—performance and overhead.

Then came Windows. Applications programmed for Windows could make use of these elements with little effort. In this chapter, you learn how to give your application the needed functionality that is now taken for granted by many Windows users—menus, toolbars, and status bars. You will see that it's relatively easy in Visual C++.

LESSON 1

Building Menus

To put it simply, building menus in VC++ 6 is rather simple. The most difficult concept to grasp when building menus is organizing them properly.

Users of your application will expect that menu items common to nearly all Windows programs will be in the same position in each program. Some of these include the File, Edit, and Help menus. If you stray from normality, it's quite possible that the users of your application will get lost, or not even know that a certain menu item exists.

Taking this into consideration, you can see how important it is that you give some fore-thought into how you create and organize your menu items.

Visual C++ 6 takes on a lot of this responsibility itself. When you create a new MDI- or SDI-based application, the common menu items are built for you. Typically, all you have to do is add your own custom menu items. For a dialog-based application, you need to create the entire menu from scratch or import the resource.

Menus in Windows are considered resources. They are considered resources because actual C++ code is not needed to build them. VC++ 6 manages menu resources in the Resource View of the project workspace.

Menu Resources and the Menu Designer

One of the handy tools in VC++ 6 is the menu resource editor. This editor makes light work of editing resource files. What used to be done by hand can be accomplished visually.

To get a firsthand look at how menus are built and how to edit them, you need to create a new MFC application. Because the AppWizard creates the basic framework with menus for an SDI or an MDI application, you should choose one of these. For the purpose of this lesson, you'll need to use MDI.

Go ahead and create an MDI application. Because the menus will be created automatical-ly, create the application with all of the default settings. To keep synchronized with this chapter, name the application "GUI."

Using Figure 6.1 as a guide, locate and expand the Menu resources branch of the Resource View in the project workspace.

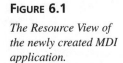

FIGURE 6.1

The Resource View of the newly created MDI application.

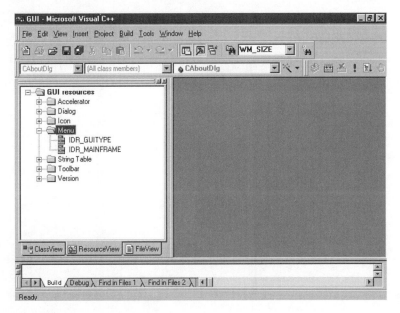

Looking at the menu resources, you can see that two resources were created, IDR_GUITYPE and IDR_MAINFRAME. Notice that they too have a naming convention. They both have the prefix IDR_.

Because this is an MDI application, there are two sets of menus. IDR_MAINFRAME is used when there are no child (or document) windows open, and IDR_GUITYPE is used when a child window is open. The menu options needed when a document is open are different from those needed when no documents are open; hence, there are two menus.

The simplest way to activate the menu editor is to double-click the resource ID of the menu on which you want to work. Go ahead and double-click the IDR_GUITYPE menu resource. Figure 6.2 shows how the menu editor should look.

Looking at this resource, you can see that from left to right the menu items are File, Edit, View, Window, and Help. These are called *static* menu bar items. They get this name from the fact that they remain at the top on the menu bar. When clicked, they display a list of menu items.

To see what menu items were created by default, click the top-level menu. Figure 6.3 shows what menu items are available on the File menu after you click it in the menu editor.

6

FIGURE 6.2

The IDR_GUITYPE *menu resource.*

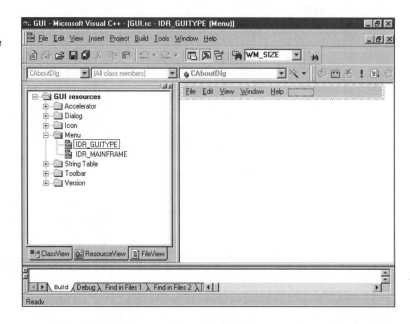

FIGURE 6.3

The File menu and menu items.

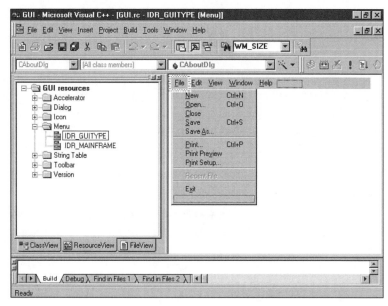

To control how a menu item appears and its fundamental behavior, you set its properties. To display the properties for a menu or one of its items, right-click the item and select Properties from the pop-up context menu. Figure 6.4 shows the properties dialog for the File, New menu item.

FIGURE 6.4

The Menu Item Properties dialog box for the File, New menu item.

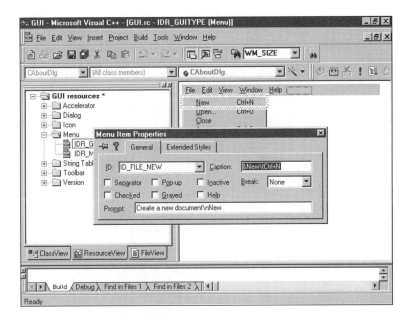

Note

As with any properties dialog box, you can click the pushpin in the top left corner to toggle whether the properties dialog box stays on top of the screen.

Table 6.1 outlines the properties for menu items.

TABLE 6.1 Menu Properties

Property	Description
ID	This property assigns a resource ID to the menu item. This resource ID is used by message maps to link the item to a function. Typically, these resource IDs consist of the prefix ID_ plus the menu name plus the item's name. For example, File, Save is typically ID_FILE_SAVE.
Caption	This property contains the text that is displayed in the menu item. Preceding a letter with an ampersand (&) will underline that letter. That letter then becomes the shortcut key for that menu item. The text after the \ shows that an accelerator key has been assigned to this menu item.

6

continues

TABLE 6.1 continued

Property	Description
Separator	Indicates that this menu item is to be used as a separator. A separator is a menu item that has no function, but is represented by a solid horizontal line. This is used to organize the menu items into logical sections.
Pop-up	When used on the top row, it indicates that this item is a menu, such as the File menu. When used as a menu item, it indicates that the item will display a submenu when selected. When this property is selected, the ID property is disabled.
Inactive	Works in conjunction with the Grayed property. Inactive determines whether the menu item is initially active or not. If Grayed is true, then so is Inactive.
Break	This menu item controls how the menu items are organized vertically. This menu item presents one of three choices: None, Column, and Bar. None (default) does nothing to the menu. When column is set for a static menu bar item, it places the item on the next line. When used in a pop-up menu item, it separates the items into columns with no dividing line. Bar is the same as Column except that it displays a bar between the old and new columns.
Checked	Indicates whether or not the menu item has a check mark to its left.
Grayed	Sets the menu item's initial enabled state. This property is represented on the menu item by visually changing its color to gray. Because an item is inactive when it's grayed, setting this property disables the inactive property.
Help	Right justifies the menu item on the menu bar. Using this property can have undesired results on the look of your menu items. Typically, Help can be used if the Help menu is the last menu and you want it aligned on the right-hand side of the menu bar.
Prompt	The value entered into this property is displayed on the application's status bar when the menu item is highlighted. An entry is created in the application's string table under the resource ID.
Right-to-left	This is found on the Extended Styles page. When selected, the menus will be displayed right-to-left for languages that are read from right to left, such as Hebrew.

As you can see, there are quite a few things that you can do to control the basic appearance of a menu item.

Navigating, adding, and removing menu items are quite easy. To navigate the menu items, you can simply click an item or use the cursor keys. Up and down will traverse through the menu items, whereas right and left move back and forth through the menus.

To add a menu on the menu bar, place the cursor where you want to insert the menu and press the insert key on your keyboard. The newly created blank menu will be inserted into that spot, pushing the selected, as well as the following, menu items to the right.

To add a menu item, press the insert key where you want to add the item. The newly created item will be added in the spot that you selected, and will push any following menu items down the list.

To remove a menu or an item, select and press the delete key. You do not get the opportunity to confirm the removal of an item, so you need to be sure before deleting an item.

For practice, add a new menu just before the Help menu on the IDR_GUITYPE menu resource. Give it the caption Hell&o. Figure 6.5 shows the new menu.

FIGURE 6.5

The modified IDR_GUI-
TYPE *menu resource
and properties.*

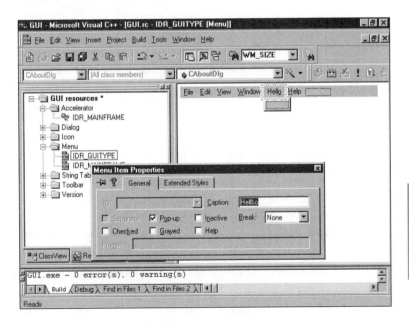

Looking at this item, you can see that it doesn't have a resource ID. This is because the Pop-up property was set by default, because the menu item was created on the menu bar. The Pop-up property tells VC++ 6 that this menu item has no action other than display menu items. If you wanted to assign a resource ID and code to this menu item (on the menu bar), you would need to de-select the Pop-up property.

With the static menu bar item created, add two menu items. The first should have the caption &Interactive and an ID of ID_HELLO_INTERACTIVE. The second should have the caption &World and an ID of ID_HELLO_WORLD. Figure 6.6 shows the menu with the two newly created menu items.

FIGURE 6.6

The IDR_GUITYPE menu resource with the newly created menu items.

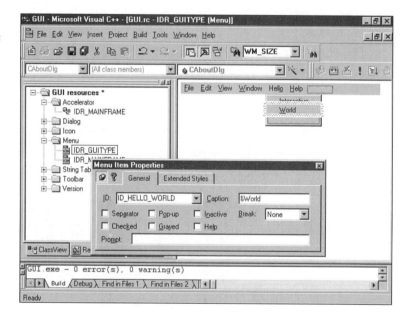

After you have created the menu items, build and execute the program. While the application is running, explore the menus, including the two items you added.

By creating these two menu items, you got the feel for editing the menus. Now, you need to create a new menu from scratch. For the purpose of this lesson (and the next), create a new dialog resource. Give this dialog resource an ID of IDD_INTERACTIVE. Figure 6.7 shows what the new dialog resource should look like with its properties dialog shown.

After the dialog resource has been created, create a new menu resource. To do this, right-click the Menu branch in the Resource View of the project workspace. When the pop-up context menu appears, select Insert Menu. A blank menu will be created for you. Give this menu resource an ID of IDR_INTERACTIVE. Figure 6.8 shows the newly created blank menu resource.

FIGURE 6.7

The new
IDD_INTERACTIVE
*dialog resource and
properties.*

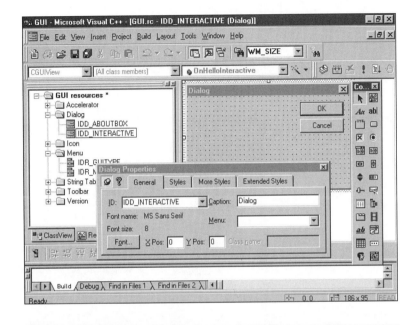

FIGURE 6.8

The new
IDR_INTERACTIVE
menu resource.

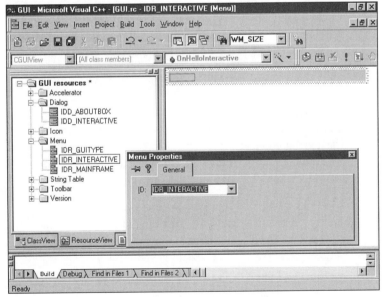

6

Now that the menu resource has been created, you can manipulate the menus and their items. Add elements to this resource by following these steps:

1. Add a static menu bar menu with the caption "&Window." This will create the menu with the shortcut key of Alt+W.

2. Add a menu item with the caption "E&xit" and a resource ID of ID_WINDOW_EXIT.

Figure 6.9 shows the results.

FIGURE 6.9

New IDR_INTERACTIVE
menu resource with
menu items.

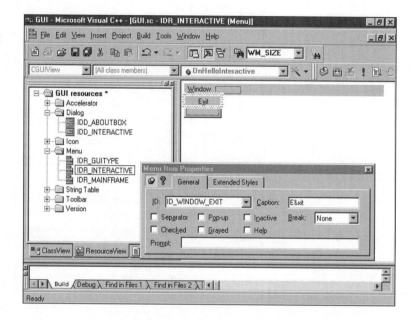

Looking at this process, it's easy to tell that creating the menus and their items is rather quick and painless. Although, there is one "gotcha" that you need to be cautious about when creating menu items—having menu items with the same short-cut key. VC++ 6 refers to these as mnemonics. Luckily enough, VC++ 6 has a built-in tool that checks your mnemonics to make sure they are not duplicated.

To see an example of this, add another menu item just below the Exit menu item you created in the previous two steps. This time, use the exact same caption, E&xit. After you have that complete, right-click the menu resource and select Check Mnemonics from the pop-up context menu. You should get an error message stating that duplicates were found as shown in Figure 6.10.

As you can see from Figure 6.10, VC++ 6 will tell you which mnemonic has duplicates, and will offer to select them in your menu for you. Some programmers say that it's little things such as this that set VC++ 6 apart from other development tools.

FIGURE 6.10

*The check Mnemonics
error.*

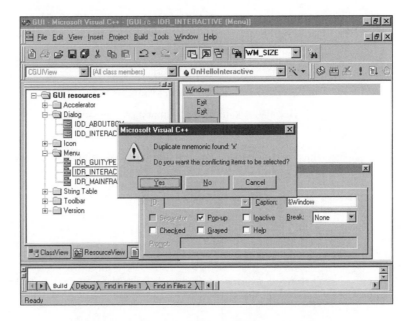

Remove the duplicate menu item by selecting it in the menu editor and pressing your
delete key. You now have a perfectly operating menu (aside from no code attached to the
menu item).

Because the goal of this menu was to be attached to the new dialog resource, you must
take one more step to link the menu to the dialog resource. Display the IDD_INTERACTIVE
dialog resource in your editor and view its properties window.

To make the link, select the IDR_INTERACTIVE resource ID from the drop-down list of
IDs for the dialog's menu property. This will not have an effect in the designer, but will
show up when the app is running. Displaying the dialog resource with the menu will be
covered in the next lesson.

Lesson Summary

This lesson focused on the concepts of editing and building menu resources. You learned
how to edit a menu resource that was automatically created by the AppWizard, and to
create your own menu resources from scratch.

During this process, you learned about how to assign shortcut keys to menu items and
how to check to make sure you didn't have duplicates.

You also reviewed the properties that control the initial visual appearance of the menu
items, and how to use some of the special features that VC++ 6 adds to menu items.

6

Quiz 1

1. Why is a menu considered a resource?

    a. It's not considered a resource.

    b. Because it is interpreted at runtime and is not added to the program.

    c. Because it's not actually made of C++ code.

    d. Because it's not object oriented.

2. Which menu property will enable you to display text in the status bar when a menu item is highlighted?

    a. The `caption` property

    b. The `status` property

    c. The `text` property

    d. The `prompt` property

3. What menu property is used to discolor the item and indicate that it is not usable?

    a. Inactive

    b. Disabled

    c. Ghosted

    d. Grayed

4. When adding a menu to a dialog resource, which property needs to be defined, and for which resource?

    a. The `menu` property for the dialog resource.

    b. The `dialog` property for the menu resource.

    c. The `window` property for the menu resource.

    d. You can't link a menu resource to a dialog resource.

Exercise 1

Complexity: Easy

1. Create a new MDI application named "Exercise 1." When the application framework has been created, modify the main menu so that it will include a Tools menu with a single Options menu item.

Complexity: Moderate

2. Create a new dialog-based application named "Exercise 2." Next, create a new menu resource with File and Help menus.

The File menu should have a single menu item titled Exit with an appropriate shortcut key. The Help menu should have a single menu item labeled About with a shortcut key as well.

After you have the menu resource, make it appear with the dialog when the program is executed.

LESSON 2

Working with Menus

Now that you've seen how easy it is to build a menu resource, it's time to learn how to implement it in your program.

While working through Chapter 5, "Processing Windows Messages and Commands," you saw that the MFC has predefined the behavior of quite a few of the menu items. In most circumstances, this is good. Even though the MFC has gone to great lengths to implement the details of the menus and items it creates automatically, it's up to you to make sure that they perform as expected. This includes writing event handlers for your own menu items.

Behind the Scenes of a Menu Resource

An important thing to know about menus is that they are resources, as was mentioned in Lesson 1. They are considered resources because they aren't built from C++ code. They are compiled and linked into your application while it's being built. Unlike resources such as icons, menus are assembled and maintained in text files automatically by VC++ 6.

The following code segment is from the GUI.rc file. This file belongs to the application built in the previous lesson.

```
/////////////////////////////////////////////////////////////////////
//
// Menu
//

IDR_MAINFRAME MENU PRELOAD DISCARDABLE
BEGIN
    POPUP "&File"
    BEGIN
        MENUITEM "&New\tCtrl+N",            ID_FILE_NEW
        MENUITEM "&Open...\tCtrl+O",         ID_FILE_OPEN
        MENUITEM SEPARATOR
        MENUITEM "P&rint Setup...",          ID_FILE_PRINT_SETUP
```

6

```
            MENUITEM SEPARATOR
            MENUITEM "Recent File",                 ID_FILE_MRU_FILE1, GRAYED
            MENUITEM SEPARATOR
            MENUITEM "E&xit",                       ID_APP_EXIT
        END
        POPUP "&View"
        BEGIN
            MENUITEM "&Toolbar",                    ID_VIEW_TOOLBAR
            MENUITEM "&Status Bar",                 ID_VIEW_STATUS_BAR
        END
        POPUP "&Help"
        BEGIN
            MENUITEM "&About GUI...",               ID_APP_ABOUT
        END
END

IDR_GUITYPE MENU PRELOAD DISCARDABLE
BEGIN
    POPUP "&File"
    BEGIN
        MENUITEM "&New\tCtrl+N",                ID_FILE_NEW, HELP
        MENUITEM "&Open...\tCtrl+O",            ID_FILE_OPEN
        MENUITEM "&Close",                      ID_FILE_CLOSE
        MENUITEM "&Save\tCtrl+S",               ID_FILE_SAVE
        MENUITEM "Save &As...",                 ID_FILE_SAVE_AS
        MENUITEM SEPARATOR
        MENUITEM "&Print...\tCtrl+P",           ID_FILE_PRINT
        MENUITEM "Print Pre&view",              ID_FILE_PRINT_PREVIEW
        MENUITEM "P&rint Setup...",             ID_FILE_PRINT_SETUP
        MENUITEM SEPARATOR
        MENUITEM "Recent File",                 ID_FILE_MRU_FILE1, GRAYED
        MENUITEM SEPARATOR
        MENUITEM "E&xit",                       ID_APP_EXIT
    END
    POPUP "&Edit"
    BEGIN
        MENUITEM "&Undo\tCtrl+Z",               ID_EDIT_UNDO
        MENUITEM SEPARATOR
        MENUITEM "Cu&t\tCtrl+X",                ID_EDIT_CUT
        MENUITEM "&Copy\tCtrl+C",               ID_EDIT_COPY
        MENUITEM "&Paste\tCtrl+V",              ID_EDIT_PASTE
    END
    POPUP "&View"
    BEGIN
        MENUITEM "&Toolbar",                    ID_VIEW_TOOLBAR
        MENUITEM "&Status Bar",                 ID_VIEW_STATUS_BAR
    END
    POPUP "&Window"
    BEGIN
        MENUITEM "&New Window",                 ID_WINDOW_NEW
        MENUITEM "&Cascade",                    ID_WINDOW_CASCADE
```

```
        MENUITEM "&Tile",                ID_WINDOW_TILE_HORZ
        MENUITEM "&Arrange Icons",       ID_WINDOW_ARRANGE
    END
    POPUP "Hell&o"
    BEGIN
        MENUITEM "&Interactive",         ID_HELLO_INTERACTIVE
        MENUITEM "&World",               ID_HELLO_WORLD
    END
    POPUP "&Help"
    BEGIN
        MENUITEM "&About GUI...",        ID_APP_ABOUT
    END
END

IDR_INTERACTIVE MENU DISCARDABLE
BEGIN
    POPUP "&Window"
    BEGIN
        MENUITEM "E&xit",                ID_WINDOW_EXIT
        MENUITEM "E&xit",                ID_WINDOW_EXIT
    END
END
```

Looking through this listing, you can see that there are three menus, IDR_MAINFRAME, IDR_GUITYPE, and IDR_INTERACTIVE. The BEGIN...END block segments each menu resource. Inside these blocks are POPUP tags that are followed by the caption of the static menu bar item. Then, for each menu bar item that has menus, another BEGIN...END block segments the MENUITEM tags. The MENUITEM tag is used to create the menu item. The menu's caption, its resource ID, and any other property settings follow this tag.

Typically, you won't need to modify the menus directly. VC++ 6's menu editor does an excellent job of managing this task for you. Although, if the need arises, it's nice to know where an application's resources are defined.

Note   The resource file (in this case, GUI.rc) also contains other resource information. Details about icons, version info, and string tables are among the items that can be found in this file. Dialog resources are also defined here.

6

Adding Function Handlers to Menu Items

When selecting an item from a menu, you are essentially commanding the application to perform some function. For example, when you select the File, Exit menu item that is found in virtually all Windows applications, you are commanding that the application closes.

Adding a member function to a menu item is pretty much the same process as adding a member function for other controls. The normal method is to use the ClassWizard to accomplish this task. To activate the ClassWizard with the proper object ID selected, right-click the menu item for which you want to create the function and select ClassWizard from the pop-up context menu.

If you don't already have it loaded, load the GUI application created in Lesson 1 of this chapter. After you have loaded it, display the ClassWizard for the Hello, Interactive menu item from the IDR_GUITYPE menu resource.

When the ClassWizard is displayed, you can see that the resource ID, ID_HELLO_INTER-ACTIVE, is selected from the list of object IDs. In the Messages section, there are two messages available to create a function against, COMMAND and UPDATE_COMMAND_UI.

COMMAND is used when an item is selected from a menu. UPDATE_COMMAND_UI is used to control the updating of the menu item before it is displayed. This message was covered in Lesson 3 of Chapter 5.

Create a message handler for the COMMAND message by selecting the message and clicking the Add Function button. When you are creating a new function for the COMMAND message, you are asked for a function name. The function name OnHelloInteractive is fine; click the OK button to complete the creation of the function. Figure 6.11 shows the ClassWizard with the newly created function defined.

FIGURE 6.11

The ClassWizard with the new function handler defined.

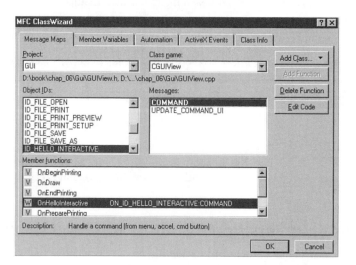

The purpose of this function is to show the IDD_INTERACTIVE dialog created in Lesson 1 of this chapter. Before you can add code to create and display the dialog box, you need to create a class for it. Do this by selecting and displaying the IDD_INTERACTIVE dialog resource from the Dialog branch of the Resource View in the project workspace.

After you have the dialog resource in the editor, display the ClassWizard. This will bring up a dialog box that asks you to create a class for this dialog. Make sure the Create a New Class option is selected and click the OK button. The New Class dialog will then be displayed asking for information about this class. Enter `CInteractiveDlg` for the class name and click OK to create the class. Figure 6.12 shows the New Class dialog box with the proper values selected.

FIGURE 6.12

The New Class dialog box for the `IDD_INTERACTIVE` *dialog resource.*

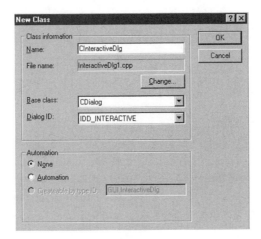

With the ClassWizard still displayed, select the `CGUIView` class from the list of available classes. Next, locate the `ID_HELLO_INTERACTIVE` object ID. Next, you should see where you just defined a function handler for the `COMMAND` message. Select `COMMAND` from the list of messages and click the Edit Code button. This will open and display the GUIView.cpp file in the `OnHelloInteractive` function handler.

After you are in the editor, add the following lines of code to the `OnHelloInteractive` function:

```
CInteractiveDlg myDialog;
    myDialog.DoModal();
```

The complete function handler should look like the following section of code:

```
void CGUIView::OnHelloInteractive()
{
    // TODO: Add your command handler code here
    CInteractiveDlg myDialog;
    myDialog.DoModal();
}
```

The first line of code declares a variable, `myDialog`, of type `CInteractiveDlg`. This is the class name assigned to the `IDD_INTERACTIVE` dialog resource. The second lines calls the inherited `DoModal()` function to show the dialog box modally.

6

After you add the code to your function handler, you need to tell the application where to find the declaration for the `CInteractiveDlg` class. This is accomplished by adding an `#include` statement towards the beginning of the same file, GUIView.cpp. Go to the beginning of this file and add the following `#include` statement after the other two includes for the GUIDoc.h and GUIView.h files:

```
#include "InteractiveDlg.h"
```

The following section of code is from the GUIView.cpp file and shows where to insert the preceding `#include` line of code. Notice its location.

```
#include "stdafx.h"
#include "GUI.h"

#include "GUIDoc.h"
#include "GUIView.h"
#include "InteractiveDlg.h"
```

Now that the function handler has been defined and the header file has been included, go ahead and build and execute the application. While it is running, select the Hello, Interactive menu item to display the `IDD_INTERACTIVE` dialog resource. Figure 6.13 shows the application running with the `IDD_INTERACTIVE` dialog resource displayed after the Hello, Interactive menu item has been selected.

FIGURE 6.13

The GUI application running with `IDD_INTERACTIVE` *dialog resource displayed.*

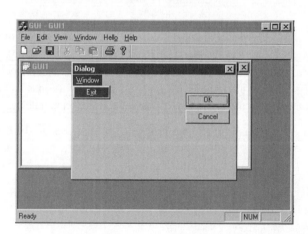

While the `IDD_INTERACTIVE` dialog is displayed, you can see that the `IDR_INTERACTIVE` menu resource is being used by the dialog. Selecting the Window, Exit menu item at this point won't do anything. In order for that menu item to operate, you need to add a function handler.

The purpose of the Window, Exit menu item in the `IDR_INTERACTIVE` menu is to close the dialog box when the menu item is selected. But before you can add the function handler, the menu resource must be defined in a class. This step is necessary for this menu resource, because it was built manually.

Define the IDR_INTERACTIVE menu in a class by selecting and displaying it from the Menu branch of the Resource View in the project workspace. After the menu editor is displayed using this resource, right-click the editor and select ClassWizard from the pop-up context menu.

When the ClassWizard is displayed, it will notice that this menu resource hasn't been defined in a class. This time, the selected default is Select an existing class.

Because this menu resource is only used for the IDD_INTERACTIVE dialog, you should leave the Select an existing class option selected and press OK. This will bring up the Select Class dialog, as shown in Figure 6.14.

FIGURE 6.14

The Select Class dialog box.

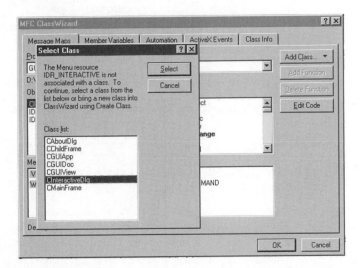

The IDD_INTERACTIVE dialog resource is defined in the CInteractiveDlg class. Considering this, you should select this class from the list of classes presented by the Select Class dialog box. After you have selected the class, click OK to complete the process.

With the menu resource associated with a class, you can now define function handlers for the menu items. The ClassWizard now reflects the new association by listing the resource IDs of the menu items in the list of object IDs. In this case, the only object ID added was ID_WINDOW_EXIT. Create a function handler for the COMMAND message for this object ID, just as you did earlier in this lesson. Figure 6.15 shows the ClassWizard after the function handler has been defined.

6

FIGURE 6.15

The MFC ClassWizard dialog box with the OnWindowExit *function handler.*

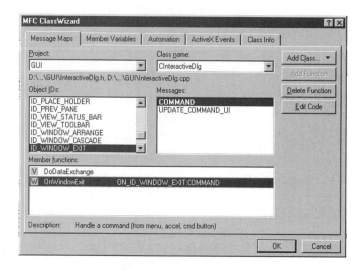

With the function handler created, add the following line of code:

```
SendMessage(WM_CLOSE,0,0);
```

The complete function handler for OnWindowExit should look like the following section of code:

```
void CInteractiveDlg::OnWindowExit()
{
    // TODO: Add your command handler code here
    SendMessage(WM_CLOSE,0,0);
}
```

The purpose of the line you added was to close the dialog box. Looking at the function's header, you can see that it's a member of the CInteractiveDlg class. SendMessage is a derived function that sends a message to the object's message queue. In this case, you are sending it the WM_CLOSE message. This is a system message used to tell a window to close.

Go ahead and build and execute the program. This time, while the application is running, select the Hello, Interactive menu item to display the IDD_INTERACTIVE dialog box. When that dialog box is displayed, click the Window, Exit menu item. This will close the dialog box and return you to the application.

In Chapter 5, you learned about messages and commands. You can examine the message maps for this application to see how what you've done so far synchronizes with the concepts learned in Chapter 5.

The following section of code is the message map from the GUIView.cpp file.

```
BEGIN_MESSAGE_MAP(CGUIView, CView)
    //{{AFX_MSG_MAP(CGUIView)
    ON_COMMAND(ID_HELLO_INTERACTIVE, OnHelloInteractive)
    //}}AFX_MSG_MAP
    // Standard printing commands
    ON_COMMAND(ID_FILE_PRINT, CView::OnFilePrint)
    ON_COMMAND(ID_FILE_PRINT_DIRECT, CView::OnFilePrint)
    ON_COMMAND(ID_FILE_PRINT_PREVIEW, CView::OnFilePrintPreview)
END_MESSAGE_MAP()
```

As you can see in this message map, an `ON_COMMAND` macro has been added that links your `ID_HELLO_INTERACTIVE` resource ID to the `OnHelloInteractive` function handler. You can also see that AppWizard created several others when it built your application.

The following section of code is the message map from the InteractiveDlg.cpp file.

```
BEGIN_MESSAGE_MAP(CInteractiveDlg, CDialog)
    //{{AFX_MSG_MAP(CInteractiveDlg)
    ON_COMMAND(ID_WINDOW_EXIT, OnWindowExit)
    //}}AFX_MSG_MAP
END_MESSAGE_MAP()
```

Looking at this section of code, you can see that an `ON_COMMAND` macro for the `ID_WINDOW_EXIT` resource ID has been linked to the `OnWindowExit` function.

Even though the MFC has hidden quite a few of the menu items' implementations from you, every menu item needs to be linked to a function somewhere in a message map. In the case of the menu items you create, you will see them in their respective classes.

Menu Items and Command Updating

In Chapter 5, you were introduced to a special class, `CCmdUI`, which is used by the MFC just prior to a command interface item being displayed or updated. For menu items, this is triggered when the menu item receives the `UPDATE_COMMAND_UI` message.

When a menu item receives this message, the MFC passes it the `CCmdUI` object. This object can then be used to manage the appearance of the menu item. Common usage of this would be to check the state of some process or status inside of your application and update the menu item accordingly.

To demonstrate this feature in action, you will be making the necessary code additions to your application that will toggle a check mark on the Hello, World menu item. To keep track of the menu item's current state, you need to create a member variable.

In this case, the member variable will be named `m_world_checked`. This will need to be declared in the GUIView.h file because that is where the `CGUIView` class is defined. Add the following line of code in the `//Attributes` public section of the `CGUIView` class declaration:

6

```
BOOL m_world_checked;
```

Because the class declaration is extensive, only the header and a few immediate lines of code are listed below. The last line of this list is the one you should have added.

```
class CGUIView : public CView
{
protected: // create from serialization only
    CGUIView();
    DECLARE_DYNCREATE(CGUIView)

// Attributes
public:
    CGUIDoc* GetDocument();
    BOOL m_world_checked;
```

With the variable created to hold the state of the menu item's checked property, you can add the necessary code that will toggle its value. To accomplish this task, create a function handler for the COMMAND message for ID_HELLO_WORLD resource ID.

After you have created the function handler, add the following line of code to toggle the variable's state:

```
m_world_checked = !m_world_checked;
```

The following section of code shows the complete function handler after you entered your line of code:

```
void CGUIView::OnHelloWorld()
{
    // TODO: Add your command handler code here
    m_world_checked = !m_world_checked;
}
```

The line of code you added is quite simple. It uses the logical NOT operator (!) to switch between TRUE and FALSE values.

The program would work at this point, but the menu wouldn't reflect the state of the variable. Just before the menu item is drawn, it will process the UPDATE_COMMAND_UI message if defined.

The steps to define a function handler for the UPDATE_COMMAND_UI message are the same as those used to define the COMMAND message. Go ahead and use ClassWizard to create the needed function handler. After it is created, add the following line of code:

```
pCmdUI->SetCheck(m_world_checked);
```

The entire function handler that processes the UPDATE_COMMAND_UI message is as follows:

```
void CGUIView::OnUpdateHelloWorld(CCmdUI* pCmdUI)
```

```
{
    // TODO: Add your command update UI handler code here
    pCmdUI->SetCheck(m_world_checked);

}
```

The line of code is quite simple. It calls the CCmdUI object's SetCheck function. In this example, you pass it the value of m_world_checked, which is toggled each time the menu item is selected. This means that the check mark on the Hello, World menu item should be displayed every other time that it is selected.

Go ahead and build and execute the program. Figure 6.16 shows the application running with the Hello, World menu item selected.

FIGURE 6.16

The GUI application running with Hello, World checked.

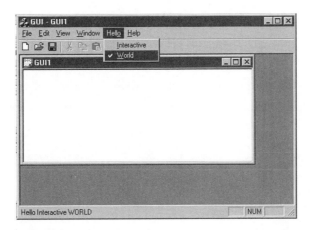

Lesson Summary

This lesson focused on implementing code when a menu item is clicked. In the process of learning more about menus, you saw that menus are built by simple commands in an applications resource file.

You learned that when adding menu items to a dialog resource, not only did you have to set the menu property in the dialog resource, you also had to create a class for the menu resource. After the class was created for the menu resource, you were able to start coding function handlers for when the menu items were selected.

After learning about how to create the menu functions, you reviewed what you learned about the MFC class, CCmdUI, and how to use this class.

6

Quiz 2

1. What message map macro is used to link a menu item to a function?

    a. `ON_MENU_ITEM`

    b. `ON_COMMAND`

    c. `WM_COMMAND`

    d. `ON_MENU_COMMAND`

2. Of the following choices, which step is necessary when adding function handlers to menu items after you have created a new menu resource?

    a. The menu resource must be linked to a dialog resource through the dialog resource's menu property.

    b. The menu resource's class property must be assigned.

    c. The menu resource's ID must be linked in a message map to a dialog resource's menu property.

    d. The menu resource needs to be associated with a class.

3. What member function of the `CCmdUI` class is used to set the state of the menu item's check mark?

    a. `SetCheck()`

    b. `Checked()`

    c. `SetChecked()`

    d. `SetCheckmark()`

4. Considering that you wanted to edit a menu's resource manually without the aid of VC++ 6's tools, which statement below is most accurate?

    a. You would use any text-based editor to edit the project's RESOURCE.H file.

    b. You would use any text-based editor to edit the project's .rc file(s).

    c. You would use any text-based editor to edit the project's .RES file(s).

    d. Menu resources for a VC++ 6 project can only be edited by VC++ 6's menu editor tool.

Exercise 2

Complexity: Easy

1. Create a new MDI-based application named "Exercise 1." Edit the main menu to add a "Hello" menu option to the Help menu. When clicked, this menu item should display a message such as `Hello Interactive World`.

Complexity: Moderate

2. Create a new dialog-based application named "Exercise 2." Create a menu resource and attach it to the dialog resource. The menu should have a "Help" menu with an "About" menu item. When the menu item is clicked, it should display the default About box generated by the AppWizard.

LESSON 3

Customizing the Toolbar

User interface items such as menus are definitely important to your program, but they are not the only resource you can use. One of the next most popular interface items is the toolbar. Toolbars are typically rows of buttons that have a direct correlation to a menu item, and they tend to be grouped by common functionality. Even though each button usually ties directly to a menu item, that behavior is not carved in stone.

The original definition of a toolbar has changed considerably over the last several years. Toolbars aren't limited to just buttons. You can add other controls to the toolbar as well, one of which is the drop-down combo box. Your application can even have more than one toolbar—in fact, as you've seen in VC++ 6, it has quite a few of them.

It used to be that toolbars were placed just below the application's menu bar. This is still the common practice, but you now have the freedom to place the toolbar along any of the window's edges or in a window all to itself.

The buttons on the toolbar have several names, some of which are tool buttons, speed buttons, or even toolbar buttons. Typically, each button links directly to a menu item, but you can create buttons that call their own functions.

VC++ 6 Toolbar Editor

Yet again, VC++ 6 has provided a visual tool to help you create and manage the toolbars in your application.

To display the toolbar editor, expand the Toolbar branch in the Resource View of the project workspace. This will show you the list of toolbars that are included in your program. Double-click the IDR_MAINFRAME resource ID. Figure 6.17 shows the toolbar resource editor.

6

FIGURE 6.17

The Toolbar resource editor.

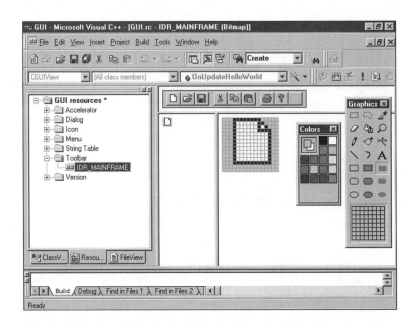

Looking at Figure 6.17, you can see that the toolbar resource editor comprises three panes and two windows.

The top pane shows the images for the toolbar's buttons. The pane on the left shows the selected image in its actual size. The pane on the right shows the image in a zoomed state, which makes the image easier to edit. The two windows that work with the editor are used to select a painting color and a painting tool.

On the top pane are buttons that are segmented into groups. This empty space between the images represents where a separator is displayed. When the application is running, a thin vertical line will represent the separator.

This area of the edit has several hidden capabilities. You can rearrange the images and add separators or you can remove unwanted images. To move an image, you simply click it and drag it to its new location. To add a separator, click and drag an image away from its neighboring image and release. To remove an image, click and drag it off the top pane. You can also click a button to display its properties.

When creating toolbars, there are a couple things you need to keep in mind: the size of the image and what happens when it is selected.

Creating a new button is quite simple. Looking back to Figure 6.17, you can see an empty button on the far right of the toolbar images. VC++ 6 always displays an empty image on the right so that there are no special steps needed to add an image. As soon as you start editing the image, VC++ 6 will add another empty button.

Looking at the standard toolbar, you can see that there are three groups totaling eight buttons. Each of these buttons has its predefined functions within the application. Double-click the first button to display its properties dialog box. Figure 6.18 shows this dialog box.

FIGURE 6.18

The Toolbar Button Properties dialog box.

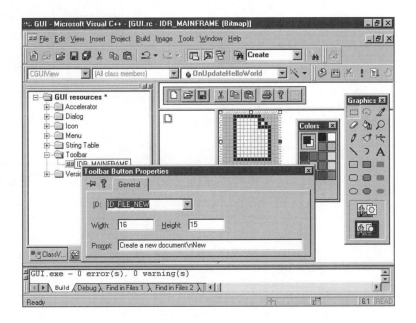

Looking at Figure 6.18, you can see that there aren't too many properties for a toolbar button. The following list describes each of the properties:

- ID—This property specified the resource ID for the toolbar button.
- Width—This property specifies the width of the images for entire toolbar.
- Height—This property specifies the height of the images for the entire toolbar.
- Prompt—Specifies the text for the status bar and the ToolTip.

You should be careful changing the width or height properties. Changing either one of these properties will change the width or height for all buttons on the toolbar.

The resource ID has a special function for toolbar buttons. You can either define a new resource ID for the toolbar button, or you can select an ID that has already been defined by your application or by the MFC. This is the mechanism used to link a toolbar button to a menu item.

To demonstrate how this works, modify the button's image and link it to the ID_APP_EXIT. Figure 6.19 shows an example image and the button's properties.

6

FIGURE 6.19

*The new Toolbar
Button Properties dia-
log box.*

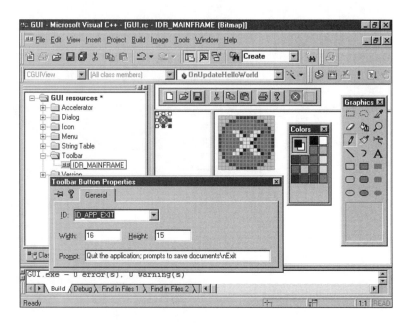

The figure in the book is in black and white. The color toolbar image was created using
the following steps:

1. Click the empty button.

2. Select red from the color palette.

3. Select maroon as the background color by right-clicking the color in the color
   palette.

4. Select the outlined ellipse drawing tool.

5. Start circle from top left corner towards the bottom right until the circle touches all
   four sides.

6. Select the yellow color from the palette.

7. Select the Text drawing tool and type the letter x (lowercase) into the window that
   appears.

8. Drag the yellow x to the middle of the circle.

9. Close the Text dialog box.

10. Select black from the color palette.

11. Outline the right edges of the x to give it a shadowed appearance.

12. Add a separator before the new image by clicking and dragging it to the right until
    it barely touches the empty button.

With the image created, double-click either the new image in the top pane on the left pane. This will display the properties dialog box. Select ID_APP_EXIT from the list of available resource IDs.

With the image added, build and execute the application. Figure 6.20 shows the application running with the new button added to the toolbar.

FIGURE 6.20

The new toolbar button and properties.

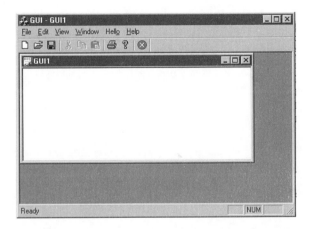

Clicking the newly created button while the application is running will close the application. This happens because the toolbar was linked to the ID_APP_EXIT resource ID. If you look at the menu properties in Figure 6.21, you will see that the File, Exit menu item has the same resource ID.

FIGURE 6.21

The File, Exit Menu Item Properties dialog box.

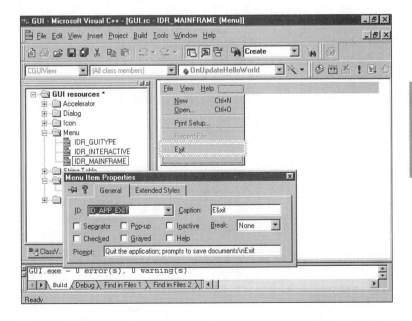

6

External Painting Programs and the Clipboard

The toolbar resource editor that comes with VC++ 6 has its pros and cons. It's easy to move and arrange the buttons and separators, but the drawing tools are quite basic. If you have experience with other drawing tools, then you might want to use them to create the images.

Fortunately enough, Windows comes with a slightly more advanced drawing tool that makes creating the images a little easier—Paint. However, there are some special considerations when using external programs to create the images.

When working with an image at a time, you want to make sure your new image's dimensions are the same as other images in the toolbar. When working on the toolbar's image resource directly, you need to be careful of not only the size of the new image, but the entire toolbar as well.

VC++ 6 has included an image gallery for common images found on toolbars. If the image you need isn't in this gallery (or another gallery that you have), then you will need to draw it yourself.

To demonstrate using an external tool, you will need to make sure that you have Microsoft's paint program installed on your system, This should have been installed for you automatically. Figure 6.22 shows the default location of the Paint program.

FIGURE 6.22

The default location of Paint program's shortcut.

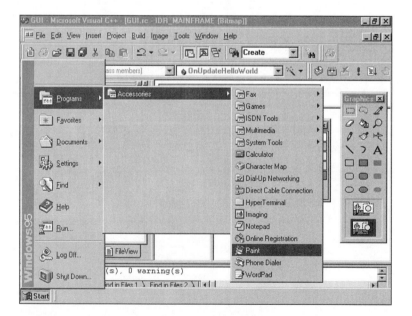

The main feature that Paint supports that VC++ 6 doesn't is loading (and saving) images. Use Paint to load the Delete.bmp file from the VC++ 6 image gallery. The image gallery is stored in the "common" directory inside of your Visual Studio directory. An example path would be C:\PROGRAM FILES\VS6\COMMON\GRAPHICS\BITMAPS\ TLBR_W95\DELETE.BMP. The exact path to the gallery would depend on how your VC++ 6 was installed. Figure 6.23 shows the Paint program with the DELETE.BMP file opened.

FIGURE 6.23

*The DELETE.BMP file
loaded into Paint.*

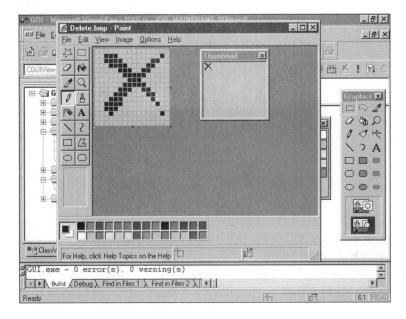

To get an image from Paint into VC++ 6, select Paint's Edit, Select All menu item to select the entire image. Next, copy the image to Windows' clipboard by selecting Paint's Edit, Copy menu item.

With the image copied to the clipboard, return to VC++ 6 and select the empty toolbar button. After it is selected, use VC++ 6's Edit, Paste menu item to copy the contents of the clipboard to the toolbar editor. Voila! You now have an image created outside of VC++ 6's toolbar editor in the toolbar.

Now that you have the image in the toolbar, display the properties dialog box by double-clicking any of the toolbar editor's three panes (found on the new button in the top pane).

Assign the new button the resource ID that was given to the Hello, Interactive menu item, ID_HELLO_INTERACTIVE. Figure 6.24 shows the new toolbar button and its properties.

6

FIGURE 6.24

*The new toolbar button
and properties.*

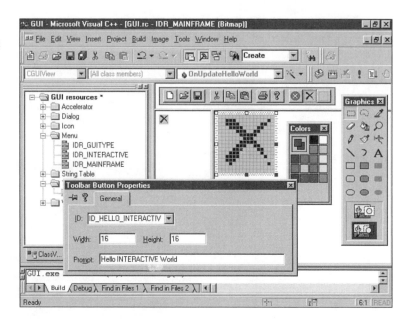

With the new button added and linked to a menu item, what do you think its behavior
will be when the program is executed? Go ahead and build and execute the program.
Figure 6.25 shows the program running with the newly added button and what happens
when it is clicked.

FIGURE 6.25

*The application run-
ning with the new but-
ton clicked.*

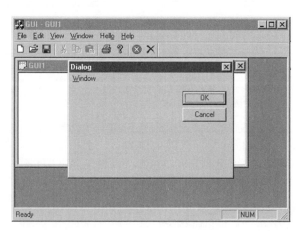

If you guessed that the dialog box created in Lessons 1 and 2 of this chapter would be
displayed, then you were right! The dialog box was displayed because the toolbar button
was linked directly to menu item that is told to display the dialog in code, Hello,
Interactive.

Editing the Toolbar Image Resource Directly

So far in this lesson, you saw how to edit the toolbar's images by using the toolbar editor to manipulate an image. You also saw how to use tools such as Paint to copy images to the clipboard and then paste them with the toolbar editor.

In most circumstances, those methods will be more than adequate for designing the toolbar. There are, however, times when you might want to design a toolbar in an external paint program with more than one image at a time.

Before jumping right into a paint program to edit images, it's important to know what is going on behind the scenes with the toolbar editor.

As you build and manage an application's toolbar resources with the toolbar editor, VC++ 6 is managing the images. These images are being managed in one single bitmap file. All the images are being kept side by side. As you move or delete items, VC++ 6 makes the necessary adjustments to the bitmap to keep it in sync with the toolbar editor.

For each button on the toolbar, there is an image represented in this bitmap. Because this bitmap is in a common format, it can be manipulated with external programs, again, such as Paint.

An important thing to remember is that before you jump out to edit the bitmap, make sure you have saved your latest changes within VC++ 6.

Finding the .BMP file to edit is quite simple too. There is one file per toolbar. For the program used in this chapter, it's in the GUI\RES directory with the filename TOOLBAR.BMP. Go ahead and load this file into Paint. Figure 6.26 shows Paint with the resource file, Toolbar.bmp, loaded.

FIGURE 6.26

Paint with the Toolbar.bmp file loaded.

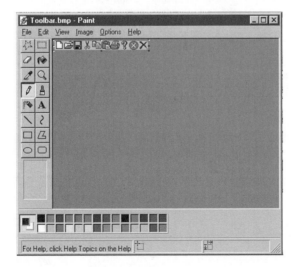

6

Looking at Figure 6.26, you can see that the image is one long array of images. Because all the images are concatenated together, it's important that they all remain the same size.

The default size of each image as created by the AppWizard is 16 by 15 pixels. If you count the number of images, you should come up with 10. Because there are 10 images at 16 pixels wide each, the total width of Toolbar.bmp should be 160. To verify this, select Paint's Image, Attributes menu item. Figure 6.27 shows the Attributes dialog box in Paint.

FIGURE 6.27

The Toolbar.bmp Attributes dialog box in Paint.

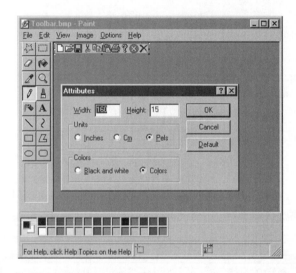

Before you manipulate this file, you should add a "placeholder" to the toolbar resource. You do this by simply giving the empty button a bogus resource ID or by editing the image. Because you want the image to be blank, you might want to just use the resource ID. When you assign the resource ID, the toolbar will be updated and the empty button will move.

Go ahead and change the resource ID of the empty button to ID_PLACE_HOLDER. This isn't a predefined ID, so you'll need to type it in instead of looking in the drop-down list of IDs.

When you change the resource ID, you should notice that the empty button moves and you now have a button that has no image. Figure 6.28 shows the modified toolbar.

In Figure 6.28, you can see the properties for the button with no image, the button itself, and the empty button.

With the image-less button created, reload the Toolbar.bmp file in Paint. Figure 6.29 shows the modified Toolbar.bmp image.

FIGURE 6.28

*The Toolbar editor—
the properties for a
button with no image.*

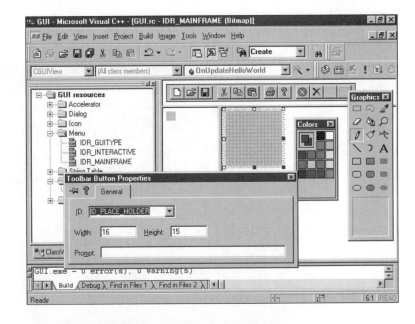

FIGURE 6.29

*The Toolbar.bmp file in
Paint and its Attributes
dialog box.*

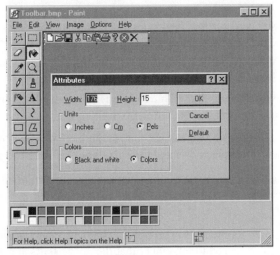

6

Looking at Figure 6.29, you can see where the image-less button was added to the end of the image. You can also see that the attributes for the image have changed. The new width is 176, up from 160. If you calculate the difference, you will see that it's 16 pixels—the width of the new image.

Working with Paint has its advantages and drawbacks too. One of its advantages is its zooming feature.

In Figure 6.30, you can see that the image has been zoomed. To get Paint to match Figure 6.30, follow these steps:

FIGURE 6.30

The Toolbar.bmp file zoomed and new image highlighted.

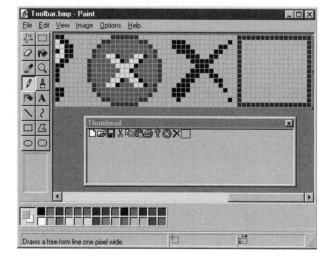

1. Select View, Zoom, Custom.

2. Select 800 percent from the Zoom dialog that appears from step 1. This will increase the size of the image in the editor—not the size of the image in pixels.

3. Select View, Zoom, Show Grid. This will turn on the grid lines in the image. This makes it easier to see where a pixel exists in the image.

4. Select View, Zoom, Show Thumbnail. This will display another window in Paint that shows the image at its normal size.

As shown in Figure 6.30, you can see that an outline has been added to the image. This outline was added manually to show the boundaries for the new button's image.

What you can't see in Figure 6.30 is the mouse cursor pointing to the top-left corner of the outline, but you can see in Paint's status bar the number 160,0. This tells the location of the cursor.

By applying some simple math, you can find out where an icon begins and ends. When doing this math, you need to remember that the image starts at pixel 0,0, not 1,1.

A simple equation would be (Image number * 16) - 16. For example, if you wanted to work on the 11th image, as is the case in this lesson, it's (11 * 16) - 16.

11 * 16 = 176. 176 - 16 = 160. That is the starting point. The ending point is the same equation without subtracting 16, or (Image number * 16). If you had a toolbar where your image width was wider, you'd need to substitute that width for 16.

Now that you know where you need to edit for the new image, you can go ahead and draw the image you want. Figure 6.31 shows the image after it has been modified. It resembles a flag. If you want your image to look like the one used in this lesson, use Figure 6.31 as a model.

FIGURE 6.31

The Toolbar.bmp with modified image.

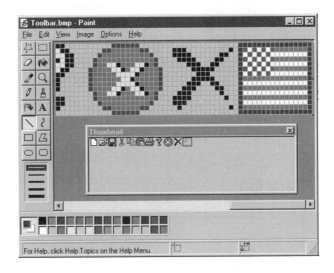

When you get the image edited and you are happy with the results, you need to save it. To do this in Paint, select the File, Save menu item. Now that the newly edited images have been saved, you can go back into VC++ 6.

When you go back into VC++ 6, it will recognize that the file Toolbar.bmp has been changed outside of its environment. When it detects these changes, it will ask you if you want to reload the resource. Figure 6.32 shows VC++ 6 when it recognizes this change.

You'll want to click the Yes button so that the toolbar resource editor will be updated.

 Note

Sometimes, when you perform this operation, VC++ 6 will display a different resource in the editor, such as a menu. To get back to the toolbar resource editor, simply double-click the resource ID in the Resource View of the project workspace that you are working on. You should see the changes at that point.

6

FIGURE 6.32

VC++ 6 when it recognizes the changes in Toolbar.bmp.

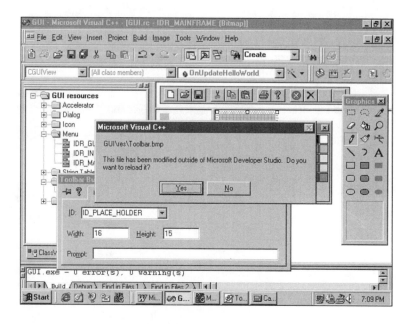

Now that you have saved and refreshed the toolbar resource editor in VC++ 6, you should see the new image in the toolbar. Figure 6.33 shows the button previously defined as ID_PLACE_HOLDER selected and its image.

FIGURE 6.33

The Toolbar resource editor with the ID_PLACE_HOLDER selected.

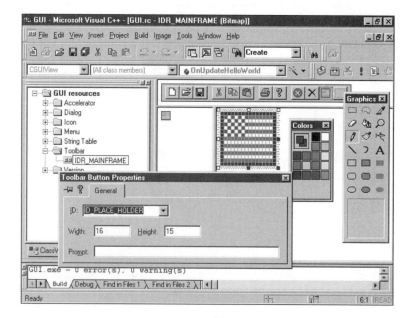

Before you run the application, what do you think the behavior will be for the new button? Go ahead and build and execute the program. Figure 6.34 shows the GUI application running.

FIGURE 6.34

The GUI application running.

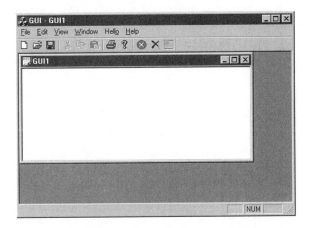

If you said that the button would be disabled, you were correct. Why was it disabled? The reason the button was disabled was because no function handler has been assigned to the ID_PLACE_HOLDER resource ID. In fact, if any toolbar button (or menu item) has a resource ID that is not linked to code via its COMMAND message, it will appear as disabled.

A key point to this section was that you created the "placeholder" resource before editing the image resource. This makes managing the toolbar resource much simpler and allows you to do it while VC++ 6 is running.

If you were creating a completely new resource, it would be to your benefit to create the menu resource first in VC++ 6 not only to get the actual image file, but also to define the series of buttons you want on the toolbar. After you have the image-less buttons defined, it is a lot easier to edit the image file, because the width and height of the file will be created automatically.

Lesson Summary

In this lesson, you learned that VC++ 6 provides yet another visual tool. This time, the tool is used to manage toolbar resources. With all of these visual tools, it's getting clearer and clearer how VC++ 6 got its name.

Using the toolbar resource editor, you learned that you can directly manipulate the images that appear in the buttons on a toolbar as well as arrange the location and spacing of the buttons.

6

You also learned how to use external programs such as Paint to copy an image to the clipboard and then use VC++ 6 toolbar editor to paste that image to a button.

Another main topic about external image editors covered editing the entire toolbar image file at once. This enables you to use an image editor that you are more familiar with that could give you more design tools.

Quiz 3

1. Assume that you created a new SDI application with AppWizard and added your own toolbar resource. If you wanted to call the predefined menu item, File, Save's function handler, to which resource ID would you link your button?

    a. `ID_DOCUMENT_SAVE`

    b. `ID_SERIALIZE_SAVE`

    c. `ID_DOCUMENT_SERIALIZE_OUT`

    d. `ID_FILE_SAVE`

2. Of the following statements, which is (are) true about creating toolbar buttons?

    a. A button on a toolbar can only link to items that are defined in menus.

    b. A button on a toolbar can be linked either to a menu item's resource ID or to one of its own.

    c. If a toolbar button's resource ID does not link to a resource ID that has been mapped, it will be disabled on the toolbar.

    d. You can have images on the same toolbar with different sizes.

3. What is the default image size for toolbar buttons when an SDI application is created with the AppWizard?

    a. 16×16 pixels

    b. 16×15 pixels

    c. 16 pixels wide × 32 pixels high

    d. 320 pixels

4. Which of the equations listed can help you find the starting point of an image in a toolbar's image file?

    a. (image number * image width) - image width

    b. (image width * image number) - image width

    c. (image number - 1) * image width

    d. image width * (image number - 1)

Exercise 3

Complexity: Easy

1. Create a new SDI application named "Exercise 1." After you have the application framework built, modify the default toolbar by adding another button to it.

Complexity: Moderate

2. Expanding upon the program you built in the first part of Exercise 3, create the necessary link with a resource ID that will toggle the visibility of the application's status bar when clicked.

LESSON 4

Using the Toolbar

Now that you know how to create toolbar resources, it's time that you learned how to use them in your application. Using a toolbar is quite similar to using menu items with only a few changes. The difficulty is more apparent when you want to use more than one toolbar. This not only requires creating the toolbar resource, but telling your application to create and use it.

You've seen how to link a toolbar button to a menu item that already has a function handler defined. You simply select the resource ID of the menu item in the toolbar button's properties. If you select a resource ID or create one that isn't linked to a function handler, then the toolbar button will be disabled when the program executes.

Creating Function Handlers for a Toolbar Button

You create function handlers for toolbar buttons in essentially the same way you do so for a menu item—you use the MFC ClassWizard.

In the last lesson, you added a button that used the resource ID ID_PLACE_HOLDER. When you ran the application, you couldn't click the button simply because it had no function handler defined.

For continuity between the previous lesson and this lesson, the name of the resource ID, ID_PLACE_HOLDER, will remain the same, although it's good practice to use resource IDs that are meaningful.

To define a function handler for a toolbar button, you select the button in the toolbar editor and select View, ClassWizard from VC++ 6's menu. There is no pop-up context menu in the toolbar editor because the right mouse button is used for other purposes. Go ahead

6

and select the ID_PLACE_HOLDER button and display the ClassWizard. Figure 6.35 shows
the ClassWizard with the ID_PLACE_HOLDER button resource selected.

FIGURE 6.35

The ClassWizard for
ID_PLACE_HOLDER
toolbar button.

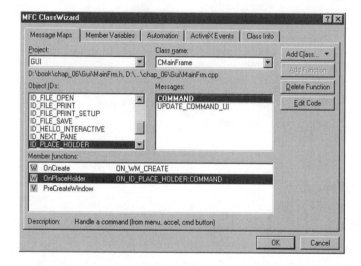

In the ClassWizard in Figure 6.35 you can see that the toolbar button ID_PLACE_HOLDER
has two messages that it can respond to: COMMAND and UPDATE_COMMAND_UI. Just like
menu items, COMMAND is used when the interface item is selected, and the
UPDATE_COMMAND_UI is used to manage the appearance of the button.

To define a function handler for when the user clicks a button, double-click the COMMAND
message and accept the default name given for the function handler. After the function
handler's header has been added to the list of member functions, you can either double-
click it or select the Edit Code button to write code.

Go ahead and add a function handler for the COMMAND message for the ID_PLACE_HOLDER
object ID. After you create the function handler, add the following line of code after the
TODO comment:

```
AfxMessageBox("Hello Interactive World");
```

The complete function handler should look like the following section of code:

```
void CMainFrame::OnPlaceHolder()
{
    // TODO: Add your command handler code here
    AfxMessageBox("Hello Interactive World");
}
```

What do you think the program will do when executed, and what will the state of the
ID_PLACE_HOLDER button be? Go ahead and build and execute the program after you have
the function handler complete to answer these questions.

Now that you have a function handler defined for the ID_PLACE_HOLDER button, it will be
enabled when the program is executed. When clicked, it will do as instructed and display
the Hello Interactive World message. Figure 6.36 shows the running program after
the ID_PLACE_HOLDER button was clicked.

FIGURE 6.36

*The running applica-
tion after the
ID_PLACE_HOLDER but-
ton has been clicked.*

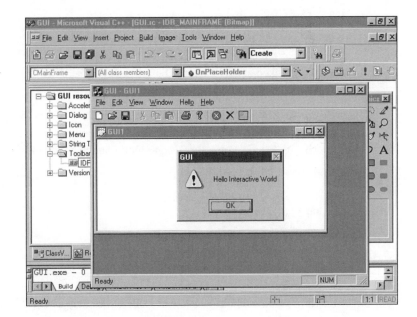

Following that example, you can see that it would be quite easy to write a function handler for a block of code when a button is clicked. The function handler could also be
linked to a menu item, thus making it a snap to create graphical shortcuts to menu items.

Toolbar buttons also have another visual capability. They can show when an item is
selected by appearing recessed. This is essentially the same as a menu item being
checked. To see an example of this, you need to add some code to the GUI program and
create a function handler for the ID_PLACE_HOLDER's UPDATE_COMMAND_UI message.

First, you need to create a variable that will hold the state of the toolbar button. Add the
following line of code to the CMDIFrameWnd class declaration in the MainFrm.h file, just
after the public statement in the //Attributes section:

```
BOOL m_flag;
```

Your change to the CMDIFrameWnd class should look like the following:

```
// Attributes
public:
    BOOL m_flag;
```

After you define your variable, you need to set its default value. This is done in the CMainFrame's OnCreate function. This function is in the MainFrm.cpp file. Add the following line just before the return 0; statement at the end of the CMainFrame::OnCreate function:

```
m_flag = FALSE;
```

With the default value set, your next step is to decide where and how this variable is to be changed. For the purpose of this lesson, the ID_PLACE_HOLDER button should toggle between the checked state. When the button gets checked, the Hello Interactive World message should be displayed.

Because the ID_PLACE_HOLDER's COMMAND message is already being processed, all you have to do is change the function handler to accommodate the new behavior. Change the CMainFrame::OnPlaceHolder function to look like the following:

```
void CMainFrame::OnPlaceHolder()
{
    // TODO: Add your command handler code here
    m_flag = !m_flag;
    if (m_flag)
    {
      AfxMessageBox("Hello Interactive World");
    }
}
```

This function first switches the boolean value of the flag. Then, if it was set to TRUE, it shows the Hello Interactive World message.

With the code in place to manage the variable and show the message, all you have to do now is add the functionality to manage the appearance of the button. Adding a function handler for the UPDATE_COMMAND_UI message for the ID_PLACE_HOLDER button accomplishes this task.

Next, create the function handler for the UPDATE_COMMAND_UI message for the ID_PLACE_HOLDER toolbar button. Modify the function handler so it looks like the following section of code:

```
void CMainFrame::OnUpdatePlaceHolder(CCmdUI* pCmdUI)
{
    // TODO: Add your command update UI handler code here
    pCmdUI->SetCheck(m_flag);
}
```

Notice that the only line of code you had to add was the last one, pCmdUI->SetCheck(m_flag);.

This line of code uses the special object passed by the MFC to control the appearance of the interface item. In this case, the value of the m_flag variable is being passed to the

SetCheck function. If the value is true, the button will appear as if it has been pressed; otherwise, it appears normal.

Go ahead and build and execute the program. While it is running, use the ID_PLACE_HOLDER button. The first time you select it, you will get the Hello Interactive World message. The next time, it will simply reset the button. This cycle will continue as long as the application is running. Figure 6.37 shows the application running after the ID_PLACE_HOLDER button was clicked.

FIGURE 6.37

The GUI application running with ID_PLACE_HOLDER *button in the pushed position.*

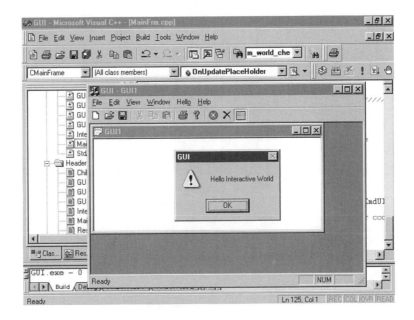

Creating a Custom Toolbar Resource

So far, you've seen plenty of examples in this and the last lesson on how to modify a menu resource that already exists—or was automatically created by the AppWizard. There will be plenty of times when you will want to create a new toolbar resource of your own.

Creating a new toolbar resource is similar to creating a new menu resource. There are several ways to do it. You can right-click the Toolbar branch of the Resource View and select Insert or Insert Toolbar from the pop-up context menu, or you can select the Insert, Resource Menu item and select Toolbar from the Insert Resource dialog. Either way, the end result is the same.

Go ahead and add a new toolbar resource to the application. The default resource name of IDR_TOOLBAR1 is fine for this lesson. After the new toolbar resource has been created,

6

it should appear in the toolbar editor. The new toolbar will consist of a single empty button at this time. Figure 6.38 shows the new toolbar resource and the toolbar editor.

FIGURE 6.38

The newly created
IDR_TOOLBAR1 *toolbar resource.*

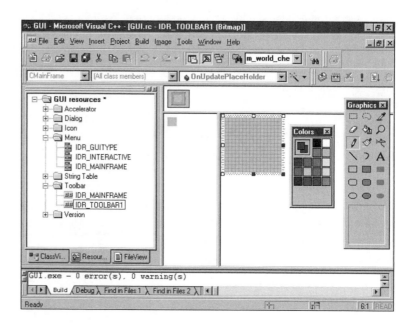

Note

Before saving the project, VC++ 6 will look at a toolbar resource. If it has no buttons defined, the resource will be removed from the project. To prevent this from happening, give at least one button a resource ID.

Because the GUI application is an MDI-based application, it will manage several documents at once. Some of the most common toolbar buttons defined when dealing with documents are left, center, and right justify.

Create three buttons on the IDR_TOOLBAR1 toolbar by completing the following steps:

1. Name the first button ID_DOC_LEFT with a prompt of "Align Text to Left Edge\nLeft."

2. Use Paint (or some other tool) to copy the LFT.BMP image to the clipboard. This image resides in VC++ 6's common directory (...COMMON\GRAPHICS\BITMAPS\TLBR_W95). Then paste the image into the newly created button in VC++ 6. Because this bitmap (as well as the following two bitmaps) is 16 by 16 pixels, VC++ 6 will ask you to resize the toolbar's height. Answer NO. The bottom line of the image will be cropped.

3. Create a second button with the resource ID of ID_DOC_CENTER and a prompt of "Align Text in Center\nCenter."

4. Use CNT.BMP as the second button's image. The image is located in the same place as step 2.

5. Create a third button with the resource ID of ID_DOC_RIGHT and a prompt of "Align Text to Right Edge\nRight."

6. Use RT.BMP as the third button's image. The image is located in the same place as Steps 2 and 4.

Now that you have created the toolbar resource, make sure your work is saved. Figure 6.39 shows the edited toolbar resource.

FIGURE 6.39

The edited
IDR_TOOLBAR1 *toolbar*
resource.

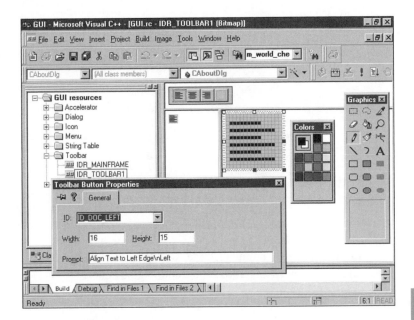

Displaying the Toolbar

Creating the toolbar resource isn't all you need to do to have your application make use of the new resource. You need to have your application create the toolbar, set the toolbar's style, and define its behavior. Even though this sounds like a lot of work, it's actually quite simple.

Your first step is to tell your application which class to associate your new toolbar resource with. This is where some forethought comes in. Because the purpose of the three buttons on this toolbar is to align the text, it should be associated with the application's document class. In this example, it's CGUIDoc.

To associate the toolbar with a class, you use the ClassWizard. Make sure that you have the toolbar resource in the editor pane of VC++ 6 and display the ClassWizard.

When the ClassWizard pops up, it will recognize that the new resource hasn't been associated with a class, and it will prompt you to either define a new class for the toolbar or to select an existing class. Go ahead and choose Select an existing class and press the OK button. This will bring up the Select Class dialog box. As mentioned a few moments ago, you need to associate this toolbar with the CGUIDoc class. Select it from the list of classes and click the Select button. Figure 6.40 shows the ClassWizard after this step is complete.

FIGURE 6.40

ClassWizard after new toolbar has been associated with the CGUIDoc *class.*

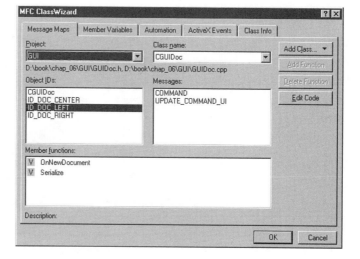

Because you're not quite ready to code the function handlers for the buttons, click the OK button on the ClassWizard to return to the editor.

The action you performed above doesn't really make the toolbar a part of the GUIDoc class; it merely lets the MFC ClassWizard know what to associate the toolbar resource with. This makes tracking down the button's COMMAND and UPDATE_COMMAND_UI messages quite a bit simpler and lets ClassWizard know where to create the message map and member functions.

Note

To see how the ClassWizard associated this toolbar to the CGUIDoc class, look in the GUI.CLW file located in your project's directory. The format of this file is like a standard Windows INI file. Look for the section header, [TB:IDR_TOOLBAR1]. To see how the resource is defined, look at the GUI.RC file.

After you associate the toolbar, add the necessary lines of code that will show the toolbar when the program runs.

Considering that toolbars are considered part of the application's window and not a part of its view or document, the changes you will be making affect the CMainFrame class. This class is housed in the MainFrm.cpp and MainFrm.h files.

In order to get access to a toolbar resource, you need to create a variable of a toolbar's class, CToolBar. This is accomplished by adding a member variable to CMainFrame's class declaration. This is in the MainFrm.cpp file. Add the following line of code to the class' public variables in its // Attributes section:

```
CToolBar m_ToolBar1;
```

The modified public variables should look like the following section of code:

```
// Attributes
public:
    BOOL m_flag;
    CToolBar m_ToolBar1;
```

This defines the member variable. Now, you need use this variable to create and display the toolbar when the application is created. Listing 6.1 shows the OnCreate function for the CMainFrame class, which is housed in the MainFrm.cpp file.

LISTING 6.1   CMainFrame::OnCreate in MainFrm.cpp

```
int CMainFrame::OnCreate(LPCREATESTRUCT lpCreateStruct)
{
    if (CMDIFrameWnd::OnCreate(lpCreateStruct) == -1)
        return -1;

    if (!m_wndToolBar.CreateEx(this, TBSTYLE_FLAT, WS_CHILD
        ¦ WS_VISIBLE ¦ CBRS_TOP ¦ CBRS_GRIPPER
        ¦ CBRS_TOOLTIPS ¦ CBRS_FLYBY ¦ CBRS_SIZE_DYNAMIC) ¦¦
        !m_wndToolBar.LoadToolBar(IDR_MAINFRAME))
    {
        TRACE0("Failed to create toolbar\n");
        return -1;      // fail to create
    }

    if (!m_wndStatusBar.Create(this) ¦¦
        !m_wndStatusBar.SetIndicators(indicators,
          sizeof(indicators)/sizeof(UINT)))
    {
        TRACE0("Failed to create status bar\n");
        return -1;      // fail to create
    }
```

6

continues

LISTING 6.1   continued

```
    // TODO: Delete these three lines if you don't want the toolbar
    // to be dockable
    m_wndToolBar.EnableDocking(CBRS_ALIGN_ANY);
    EnableDocking(CBRS_ALIGN_ANY);
    DockControlBar(&m_wndToolBar);

    m_flag = FALSE;

    return 0;
}
```

Before rushing right into creating the toolbar, you should look over Listing 6.1. In this listing, you can see that the toolbar created by the AppWizard is being created. That toolbar has been given the member variable name of m_wndToolBar. The following section of code comes from Listing 6.1 and is responsible for the application's main toolbar creation:

```
if (!m_wndToolBar.CreateEx(this, TBSTYLE_FLAT, WS_CHILD
    ¦ WS_VISIBLE ¦ CBRS_TOP ¦ CBRS_GRIPPER
    ¦ CBRS_TOOLTIPS ¦ CBRS_FLYBY ¦ CBRS_SIZE_DYNAMIC) ¦¦
    !m_wndToolBar.LoadToolBar(IDR_MAINFRAME))
{
    TRACE0("Failed to create toolbar\n");
    return -1;      // fail to create
}
```

This block of code accomplishes several tasks. First, it creates the toolbar by calling the CToolBar class' CreateEx function. Next, it loads the toolbar's resource into the toolbar. If either of these steps fails, it exits this function with a -1 value and continues to close the program.

The two important elements to discuss here are the CreateEx and LoadToolBar functions.

CreateEx is responsible for creating the toolbar and setting its initial style. This function takes four parameters:

- CWnd* pParentWnd—This parameter specifies which window will be the toolbar's parent.

- DWORD dwCtrlStyle—This parameter specifies the initial appearance of the buttons on the toolbar. Multiple control styles can be used.

- DWORD dwStyle—This parameter controls the style, alignment and docking capabilities of the toolbar. Multiple control styles can be used.

- UINT nID—This parameter is the resource ID of the toolbar to use.

Note The CToolBar class also has a Create function that has all but the second parameter from above (DWORD dwCtrlStyle). When using Create, the standard 3D style buttons are used by default, whereas the TBSTYLE_FLAT as used in CreateEx will create flat toolbar buttons.

Table 6.2 lists some of the available styles that can be used for the dwCtrlStyle parameter of the CreateEx function.

TABLE 6.2 Common Button Styles

Style	Description
TBSTYLE_BUTTON	Standard 3D style buttons
TBSTYLE_FLAT	Buttons without borders

Table 6.3 lists some common styles that can be used for the dwStyle parameter in both Create and CreateEx.

TABLE 6.3 Common Toolbar Styles

Style	Description
CBRS_BOTTOM	Places toolbar at the bottom of the window
CBRS_TOP	Places toolbar at the top of the window
CBRS_ALIGN_ANY	Enables the toolbar button to be docked on any of the window's borders
CBRS_FLOATING	Places toolbar in its own floating window
CBRS_TOOLTIPS	Enables the toolbar to display ToolTips
CBRS_FLYBY	Enables the application's status bar to display the toolbar's description

The LoadToolBar function is responsible for loading the toolbar resource into the toolbar. It takes only one parameter—the resource ID of a toolbar resource.

Looking down a bit further in Listing 6.1, you will see the following block of code:

```
m_wndToolBar.EnableDocking(CBRS_ALIGN_ANY);
EnableDocking(CBRS_ALIGN_ANY);
DockControlBar(&m_wndToolBar);
```

The first line of code tells the toolbar that it can be docked anywhere along the frame of the application's window. Next, the CMainFrame class' EnableDocking function tells the

6

application to allow toolbars to be docked. Without these two lines, the toolbar can't be displayed, because there would be nowhere to put it.

The last line, `DockControlBar`, docks the passed toolbar to the window. Without first docking the toolbar, its position will be fixed and can't be moved.

Now that you've seen what code is necessary to create and display your toolbar, it's time to add some code.

First, you need to add the code to create and load the toolbar. For the purpose of this lesson, and to see it in action, use the `Create` function in place of the `CreateEx` function. It's a good idea to follow VC++ 6's guide and create the toolbar in the same manner in which AppWizard created the main toolbar. Add the following lines of code just before the return statement at the end of the `OnCreate` function:

```
if (!m_ToolBar1.CreateEx(this, TBSTYLE_FLAT, WS_CHILD
    | WS_VISIBLE | CBRS_TOP | CBRS_GRIPPER
    | CBRS_TOOLTIPS | CBRS_FLYBY | CBRS_SIZE_DYNAMIC) ||
    !m_ToolBar1.LoadToolBar(IDR_TOOLBAR1))
{
    TRACE0("Failed to create toolbar\n");
    return -1;      // fail to create
}
m_ToolBar1.EnableDocking(CBRS_ALIGN_ANY);
DockControlBar(&m_ToolBar1);
```

The complete `OnCreate` function handler should look like the following section of code after you add the previous lines of code:

```
int CMainFrame::OnCreate(LPCREATESTRUCT lpCreateStruct)
{
    if (CMDIFrameWnd::OnCreate(lpCreateStruct) == -1)
        return -1;

    if (!m_wndToolBar.CreateEx(this, TBSTYLE_FLAT, WS_CHILD
        | WS_VISIBLE | CBRS_TOP | CBRS_GRIPPER
        | CBRS_TOOLTIPS | CBRS_FLYBY | CBRS_SIZE_DYNAMIC) ||
        !m_wndToolBar.LoadToolBar(IDR_MAINFRAME))
    {
        TRACE0("Failed to create toolbar\n");
        return -1;      // fail to create
    }

    if (!m_wndStatusBar.Create(this) ||
        !m_wndStatusBar.SetIndicators(indicators,
          sizeof(indicators)/sizeof(UINT)))
    {
        TRACE0("Failed to create status bar\n");
        return -1;      // fail to create
```

```
    }

    // TODO: Delete these three lines if you don't want the toolbar
    // to be dockable
    m_wndToolBar.EnableDocking(CBRS_ALIGN_ANY);
    EnableDocking(CBRS_ALIGN_ANY);
    DockControlBar(&m_wndToolBar);

    m_flag = FALSE;

    if (!m_ToolBar1.Create(this, WS_CHILD | WS_VISIBLE | CBRS_TOP
        | CBRS_GRIPPER | CBRS_TOOLTIPS | CBRS_FLYBY
        | CBRS_SIZE_DYNAMIC) ||
        !m_ToolBar1.LoadToolBar(IDR_TOOLBAR1))
    {
        TRACE0("Failed to create toolbar\n");
        return -1;       // fail to create
    }
    m_ToolBar1.EnableDocking(CBRS_ALIGN_ANY);
    DockControlBar(&m_ToolBar1);
    return 0;
}
```

Now that the necessary code has been added that will display the toolbar, go ahead and build and execute the program. While it is running, you will see that the three buttons are disabled. This happens because no functions have been linked to these buttons yet. Figure 6.41 shows the application with the new toolbar after it has been moved and docked beside the application's main toolbar.

FIGURE 6.41

The GUI application running with the new toolbar resource displayed.

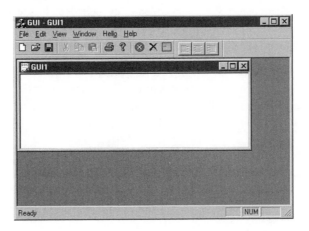

6

Finishing the Toolbar

Now that the toolbar is being displayed, it's time to add the code that will make the buttons work. In this example, the three buttons are used to align the text inside the documents.

Because Chapter 7, "Saving, Loading, and Printing Your Documents," covers the document class in more detail, only the necessary steps to implement the toolbar's functions will be discussed in this section.

Because this (GUI) application is based upon the MDI model, it has the capability of managing several documents at a time. In order to keep track of values for each document, it's quite common to add member variables to the application's document class. For this application, the class is CGUIDoc. This is the same class that you associated the IDR_TOOLBAR1 resource with. This class is housed in the GUIDoc.h and GUIDoc.cpp files.

To add a member variable, you need to add a line of code to the class' declaration. Add the following line after the public statement in the // Attributes section of the CGUIDoc class:

```
int m_alignment;
```

The // Attributes section should look like the following block of code:

```
// Attributes
public:
    int m_alignment;
```

Because this member variable was added to the CGUIDoc class, each time an object is created from this class, it will contain that member variable. Because each document in this MDI application is derived from this class, they will contain this member variable.

The next step is to give the m_alignment member variable a default value. This is done in the CGUIDoc's OnNewDocument function, which is in the GUIDoc.cpp file. This function gets called each time a new document is created. Add the following line of code before the return statement at the end of this function:

```
m_alignment = DT_LEFT;
```

The complete OnNewDocument function is listed below:

```
BOOL CGUIDoc::OnNewDocument()
{
    if (!CDocument::OnNewDocument())
        return FALSE;

    // TODO: add reinitialization code here
    // (SDI documents will reuse this document)
```

```
    m_alignment = DT_LEFT;

    return TRUE;
}
```

Now, each time a document is created, the m_alignment variable will be assigned a default value. In this case, it's assigned to DT_LEFT. This is yet another of the many predefined constants found in VC++ 6.

So far, so good. The only problem up until this point is that there is no text to display. This brings you to another class, CGUIView. This class is responsible for displaying a document's contents. Again, this class is discussed in more detail in Chapter 7. This class resides in GUIView.h and GUIView.cpp.

Inside of the CGUIView class is a function that controls the drawing of the document, named appropriately enough, OnDraw. Locate that function and add the following lines of code just before the return statement at the end of the OnDraw function:

```
CRect rect;
GetClientRect(&rect);
pDC->DrawText("Hello Interactive World",&rect,pDoc->m_alignment);
```

The complete OnDraw function handler should look like the following block of code after you make your changes:

```
void CGUIView::OnDraw(CDC* pDC)
{
    CGUIDoc* pDoc = GetDocument();
    ASSERT_VALID(pDoc);

    // TODO: add draw code for native data here
    CRect rect;
    GetClientRect(&rect);
    pDC->DrawText("Hello Interactive World",&rect,pDoc->m_alignment);

}
```

Each time the document needs to be drawn on the screen, this function gets called. The first two lines of code you added get the area that it has to draw. The third line draws the text on the screen.

At this point, if you were to build and run the application, each document created would display the message Hello Interactive World aligned to the left edge of the document's window.

To complete the application, you need to add the necessary function handlers that will change the document's alignment and manage the updating of the toolbar buttons.

6

With the `IDR_TOOLBAR1` toolbar resource selected in the toolbar editor, display the
ClassWizard and create the necessary function handlers for the three button's `COMMAND`
messages. Using the following listing of code as a guide, complete the function handlers:

```
void CGUIDoc::OnDocLeft()
{
    // TODO: Add your command handler code here
    CGUIDoc* pDoc = this;
    pDoc->m_alignment = (DT_LEFT);
    UpdateAllViews(NULL);
}

void CGUIDoc::OnDocCenter()
{
    // TODO: Add your command handler code here
    CGUIDoc* pDoc = this;
    pDoc->m_alignment = (DT_CENTER);
    UpdateAllViews(NULL);

}

void CGUIDoc::OnDocRight()
{
    // TODO: Add your command handler code here
    CGUIDoc* pDoc = this;
    pDoc->m_alignment = (DT_RIGHT);
    UpdateAllViews(NULL);
}
```

All three of the function's codes are virtually the same. Only the value assigned to
`m_alignment` is changed.

At this point, the toolbar buttons will accomplish their task. In some scenarios, this
would be all that needs to be done. In this case, the buttons should visually reflect which
alignment a document has. Processing the `UPDATE_COMMAND_UI` message will accomplish
this task.

Again, with the `IDR_TOOLBAR1` resource selected in the toolbar editor, display the
ClassWizard and create the three necessary function handlers that will process the
`UPDATE_COMMAND_UI` message for each button. Using the following listing of code as a
guide, complete these new function handlers:

```
void CGUIDoc::OnUpdateDocLeft(CCmdUI* pCmdUI)
{
    // TODO: Add your command update UI handler code here
    CGUIDoc* pDoc = this;
    pCmdUI->SetCheck(pDoc->m_alignment == (DT_LEFT));
}
```

```
void CGUIDoc::OnUpdateDocCenter(CCmdUI* pCmdUI)
{
    // TODO: Add your command update UI handler code here
    CGUIDoc* pDoc = this;
    pCmdUI->SetCheck(pDoc->m_alignment == (DT_CENTER));
}

void CGUIDoc::OnUpdateDocRight(CCmdUI* pCmdUI)
{
    // TODO: Add your command update UI handler code here
    CGUIDoc* pDoc = this;
    pCmdUI->SetCheck(pDoc->m_alignment == (DT_RIGHT));

}
```

Each of these functions will check the value of the current document's m_alignment variable and set the button's check state accordingly.

This is all the code that is needed to fully implement the IDR_TOOLBAR1 resource. With that in mind, go ahead and build and execute the program. While it is running, create a couple documents and set the alignment property different for each. Notice that as you switch between the documents, the toolbar buttons are updated accordingly. Figure 6.42 shows the running application with several documents open.

FIGURE 6.42

IDR_TOOLBAR1 *fully implemented with several documents open.*

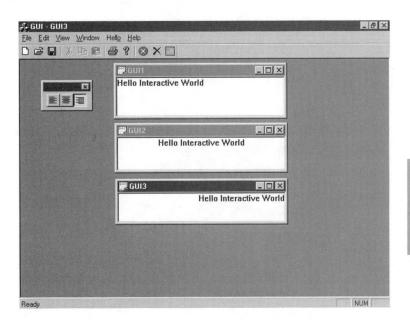

6

Lesson Summary

This lesson covered the necessary steps involved with bringing toolbar buttons to life.

Working with toolbar buttons is similar to menu items in the sense that you process the same messages. However, when creating a new toolbar, you need to follow certain steps to ensure its proper operation. The following list summarizes steps used when creating a new toolbar:

1. Create the toolbar resource. You should group buttons by logical function. This process includes assigning good resource IDs to each button.

2. Associate the toolbar with a class. This is done using a ClassWizard. A good rule of thumb when associating a toolbar with a class is to pick a class that should contain the message map and functions for the toolbar's buttons.

3. Create a member variable in your applications main frame class that will be the toolbar.

4. Add the necessary code in the main frame's `OnCreate` function to create and load the toolbar resource. This includes setting the toolbar's styles and docking capabilities.

5. Add function handlers as necessary that process the toolbar buttons' `CREATE` and `UPDATE_COMMAND_UI` messages.

There are definitely many ways to create the toolbar and to implement it in your application. As you gain experience by using toolbar resources, you can modify the preceding list as necessary to accommodate your needs.

Quiz 4

1. Which message is processed for a toolbar button when clicked?

   a. `ON_COMMAND`

   b. `WM_COMMAND`

   c. `COMMAND`

   d. `TB_COMMAND`

2. What member function of the `CCmdUI` class would be used to show a toolbar button as if it were pressed?

   a. `SetPressed`

   b. `SetChecked`

   c. `SetCheck`

   d. `SetRadioButton`

3. What member function for the `CToolBar` class is used to create a toolbar?

    a. `Create`

    b. `CreateToolbar`

    c. `OnCreate`

    d. `CreateEx`

4. Which toolbar button style is used by the `EnableDocking` member function of the `CToolBar` class to specify that docking can take place on all borders?

    a. `CBRS_DOCK_ALL`

    b. `CBRS_ALIGN_ANY`

    c. `CBRS_ALIGN_ALL`

    d. `BUTTON_ALIGN_ANY`

Exercise 4

Complexity: Easy

1. Create a new MDI application named "Exercise 1." Modify the application's toolbar with three new buttons. Add function handlers for each button that will display a message when clicked.

Complexity: Moderate

2. Building upon part one of Exercise 4, add the necessary code that will enable the toolbar to be dockable.

LESSON 5

Keeping the User Informed with a Status Bar   6

Among user interface items such as the menu bar and the toolbar, a typical Windows application contains a status bar. A status bar's role in a Windows application is normally quite clear—it shows the status of actions or system states.

When using the AppWizard to create an SDI or MDI application's framework, one of the options is to include a status bar that is turned on by default. Because the GUI application used in this chapter is an MDI application with all the default settings, it includes a status bar. Figure 6.43 shows the GUI application. At the bottom of the application's window is its status bar.

FIGURE **6.43**

*Examining GUI's
status bar.*

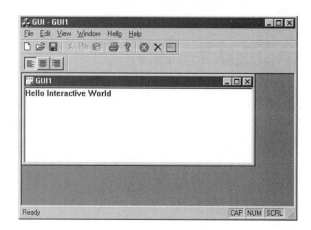

Each section of a status bar is called a *pane*. As you can see from Figure 6.43, the GUI application has four panes:

- A text pane that shows application activity and prompt information.
- A recessed box that indicates when the Caps Lock button is pressed.
- A recessed box that indicates when the Num Lock button is pressed.
- A recessed box that indicates when the Scrl Lock button is pressed.

On the surface, the MFC does a good job of hiding the implementation of the status bar from you. These default panes are fine for some applications, but is not perfect for every program. For that reason, the MFC gives you the flexibility to customize it if needed through the CStatusBar class.

The CStatusBar Class

The MFC's CStatusBar class is used to customize the status bar. This class has several functions that aid in the process of customizing your application's status bar. Table 6.4 lists some of the methods of the CStatusBar class.

TABLE 6.4   Common Functions for MFC's CStatusBar Class

Function	Description
Create()	Used to create the status bar
CommandToIndex()	Used to get a pane's index by specifying an ID
GetItemID()	Used to get a pane's ID by specifying an index
GetItemRect()	Used to get a pane's display area by its index
GetPaneInfo()	Used to get information about a pane
SetPaneInfo()	Used to set a pane's information
GetPaneStyle()	Used to get a pane's style

Function	Description
SetPaneStyle()	Used to set a pane's style
GetPaneText()	Used to get a pane's text
SetPaneText()	Used to set a pane's text
SetIndicators()	Used to set the status bar's indicator IDs

Customizing the Status Bar

Quite often, the status bar created automatically won't have all the functionality that your application requires. Using the GUI application as an example, it would be nice to indicate the text's alignment status in the status bar.

There are several things to consider when adding a pane to the status bar. The most important of which is what you want to display. For this application, the status should be "Left," "Center," or "Right."

Unfortunately, the status bar isn't a resource like menus or toolbars, and VC++ 6 doesn't have a visual tool to help you design it. This means that in order to customize the status bar, you have to do it manually.

One thing that is common throughout VC++ 6 is the use of resource symbols. Most of the resource symbols you've used so far have been represented by resource IDs. VC++ 6 does have a dialog box that helps you manage these resource symbols. Go ahead and display the Resource Symbols dialog box by selecting the View, Resource Symbols menu item in VC++ 6's environment. Figure 6.44 shows the Resource Symbols dialog box.

FIGURE 6.44

The Resource Symbols dialog box.

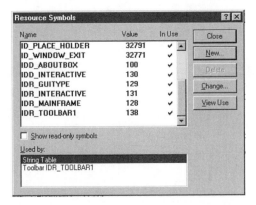

6

To begin creating the new status bar pane, you need to use this dialog box to create a resource symbol. To create a new symbol, click the New button. This will display the New Symbol dialog box that asks you for the symbol name and its value. Figure 6.45 shows the New Symbol dialog box.

FIGURE **6.45**

*The New Symbol dia-
log box.*

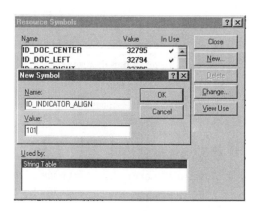

Using Figure 6.45 as a guide, create a new resource symbol named
ID_INDICATOR_ALIGN. VC++ 6 will automatically create a value for each new symbol.
Very rarely will you need to change its computed value. Click the New Symbol's OK
button to create the symbol and then close the Resource Symbol dialog box by clicking
its Close button.

Next, to indicate to VC++ 6 that this is a used symbol, you need to assign a string to it.
This is accomplished by expanding the String Table branch of the Resource View in the
project workspace. After you expand this branch, double-click the String Table element
to display the table in its editor. Figure 6.46 shows the String Table resource in the editor.

FIGURE **6.46**

*The String Table
resource.*

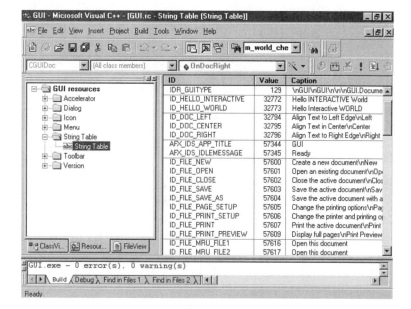

With the string table resource as the selected element in VC++ 6, select the Insert, New String menu item. This will display the String Properties dialog box. To use this dialog box, you need to select the resource symbol you just created from the drop-down list and enter a default caption.

Select the `ID_INDICATOR_ALIGN` resource symbol and give it a caption of "Align Status."

When the AppWizard constructed the application's status bar, it created four default panes. You now have to add your pane to the list of panes for the status bar. Because the status bar is part of the main window, you will find the list of panes in the MainFrm.cpp file. The following code segment is the status bar's default panes:

```
static UINT indicators[] =
{
    ID_SEPARATOR,           // status line indicator
    ID_INDICATOR_CAPS,
    ID_INDICATOR_NUM,
    ID_INDICATOR_SCRL,
};
```

On this list are the resource symbols for the four panes. This list is in the order in which the panes will be drawn on the status bar. Usually, you will want to make your changes after the `ID_SEPARATOR` symbol. Go ahead and modify the list of indicators to look like the following code segment:

```
static UINT indicators[] =
{
    ID_SEPARATOR,           // status line indicator
     INDICATOR_ALIGN,
    ID_INDICATOR_CAPS,
    ID_INDICATOR_NUM,
    ID_INDICATOR_SCRL,
};
```

By following those three steps, the status bar will show your new pane—although at this point, you don't have any code that tells the status bar what to display.

With that in mind, the purpose of adding this pane was to show the alignment of the current document. An easy way to keep track of each document's status with a string would be to add a new member variable to the document's class. Go ahead and add a member variable to the document's class by adding the following line of code to the `CGUIDoc` class declaration in GUIDoc.cpp:

```
CString m_alignstatus;
```

The modified `// Attributes` section of the `CGUIDoc` class should look as follows:

```
// Attributes
public:
    int m_alignment;
    CString m_alignstatus;
```

6

Remembering back to the last lesson, this is where you placed the member variable that holds the document's alignment. Following good programming practice, you should assign this member variable a default value. This is done in the CGUIDoc's OnNewDocument function in the GUIDoc.cpp file. Add the following line of code below where you assigned m_alignment an initial value:

```
m_alignstatus = "Left";
```

With the default value set, you need to assign this variable a status each time it changes. Because your toolbar buttons already control the document's alignment in their COMMAND function handler, this would be a good place to update the m_alignstatus member variable. Using the following listing as a guide, modify your existing COMMAND message handlers to set the m_alignstatus value:

```
void CGUIDoc::OnDocLeft()
{
    // TODO: Add your command handler code here
    CGUIDoc* pDoc = this;
    pDoc->m_alignment = (DT_LEFT);
    m_alignstatus = "Left";
    UpdateAllViews(NULL);
}

void CGUIDoc::OnDocCenter()
{
    // TODO: Add your command handler code here
    CGUIDoc* pDoc = this;
    pDoc->m_alignment = (DT_CENTER);
    m_alignstatus = "Center";
    UpdateAllViews(NULL);

}

void CGUIDoc::OnDocRight()
{
    // TODO: Add your command handler code here
    CGUIDoc* pDoc = this;
    pDoc->m_alignment = (DT_RIGHT);
    m_alignstatus = "Right";
    UpdateAllViews(NULL);
}
```

With these code changes complete, the last thing you have to do is process your new resource symbol's UPDATE_COMMAND_UI message. Unfortunately, the ClassWizard doesn't process this message for you when working with the status bar, but considering the MFC's great flexibility, it enables you to add the code that will.

In Chapter 5, you learned how to work with message maps. You need to use those concepts to complete the modification of the status bar.

When creating a message map, you needed to accomplish three steps:

1. Define the function in the class' header file.
2. Add a message map macro to link the resource ID to a function.
3. Code the function handler.

This process remains the same when working with status bars. Modify the CGUIDoc's class declaration by adding the following function definition to the class' protected section:

```
afx_msg void OnUpdateIndicatorAlign(CCmdUI *pCmdUI);
```

Examining this line, you can see that the function name was built by using the standard prefix of OnUpdate followed by the resource symbol's name (without the prefix or underscores).

Because this function processes the UPDATE_COMMAND_UI message, it is given the CCmdUI object by the MFC when processed.

Next, you need to modify the message map within the GUIDoc.cpp file. Add the following line of code just before the END_MESSAGE_MAP macro:

```
ON_UPDATE_COMMAND_UI(ID_INDICATOR_ALIGN, OnUpdateIndicatorAlign)
```

As you can see, the ON_UPDATE_COMMAND_UI macro is utilized to link the resource symbol to the yet-to-be-created function. The entire message map is as follows:

```
BEGIN_MESSAGE_MAP(CGUIDoc, CDocument)
    //{{AFX_MSG_MAP(CGUIDoc)
    ON_COMMAND(ID_DOC_LEFT, OnDocLeft)
    ON_COMMAND(ID_DOC_CENTER, OnDocCenter)
    ON_COMMAND(ID_DOC_RIGHT, OnDocRight)
    ON_UPDATE_COMMAND_UI(ID_DOC_LEFT, OnUpdateDocLeft)
    ON_UPDATE_COMMAND_UI(ID_DOC_CENTER, OnUpdateDocCenter)
    ON_UPDATE_COMMAND_UI(ID_DOC_RIGHT, OnUpdateDocRight)
    //}}AFX_MSG_MAP
    ON_UPDATE_COMMAND_UI(ID_INDICATOR_ALIGN, OnUpdateIndicatorAlign)
END_MESSAGE_MAP()
```

In the message map above, you can see that the new macro was added after the //}}AFX_MSG_MAP line. The message maps before this line are the ones created automatically. Even though you could have put the new macro inside that block, it's good practice to keep the ones you add manually out of the way.

Last but not least, you need to add code for the OnUpdateIndicatorAlign function. This should go at the end of the GUIDoc file, which you should be currently editing. The entire function is as follows—add it to your program:

```
void CGUIDoc::OnUpdateIndicatorAlign(CCmdUI* pCmdUI)
{
```

6

```
    pCmdUI->Enable(TRUE);
    pCmdUI->SetText(m_alignstatus);
}
```

As you can see, this function is quite short, as it should be. First, it enables the indicator and then sets its text to the current value in the m_alignment member variable.

> **Note**
>
> This function could have coded a series of if statements or a switch to check the value of the m_alignment member variable and update accordingly, but this function needs to execute quickly. With that in mind, you should always make any functions that process the UPDATE_COMMAND_UI message as short as possible.

With all the code necessary to implement the modified status bar, go ahead and build and execute the program. While it is running, create several documents and change the alignment for each of them. As you change alignments and switch documents, the new indicator on the status bar is updated accordingly. Figure 6.47 shows the completed application with several documents showing different alignments.

FIGURE 6.47

The completed GUI application.

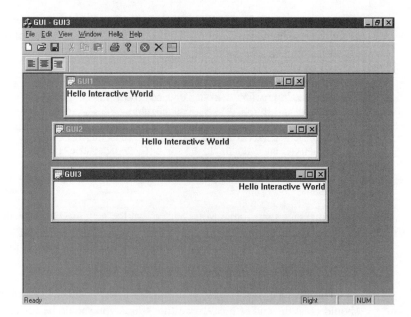

Lesson Summary

In this lesson, you learned that the MFC has gone to great lengths to hide the implementation details of the status bar from you. You also saw that it is still flexible enough that you can customize it if it doesn't meet the application's needs.

During this process, you saw how to create a new resource symbol that represents a status bar indicator, and that you need to manually add the code necessary for its implementation.

To implement a custom pane in the status bar, you follow these steps:

1. Create a resource symbol that will represent the new pane.
2. Add an item to the string table resource that links a string to the newly created resource symbol.
3. Modify the status bar's indicator list to include the newly created resource symbol.
4. Add the necessary code to update the status.

Quiz 5

1. Which member function of the `CStatusBar` class is used to get an indicator's current text value?

   a. `GetCaption`

   b. `SetCaption`

   c. `GetText`

   d. `GetPaneText`

2. Which message map macro is used when processing updates for status bar panes?

   a. `ON_COMMAND_UI`

   b. `WM_UPDATE_COMMAND_UI`

   c. `ON_UPDATE_COMMAND_UI`

   d. `WM_UPDATE`

3. Which statement(s) below is one of the steps needed when customizing the status bar?

   a. The toolbar resource must be linked to the status bar.

   b. A resource symbol must be created for the new pane.

   c. A string table entry needs to be created for the new pane.

   d. A new class needs to be created that is derived from the default status bar. This new class is then modified with the new panes.

6

4. Which statement(s) is true about an indicator's update function handler?

   a. The function needs to execute quickly.

   b. The function should be as short as possible.

   c. The function handler must redraw the entire status bar.

   d. The function handler is called only once during an application's session.

Exercise 5

Complexity: Easy

1. Create a new SDI application named "Exercise 1." Add a status bar indicator to the default status bar.

Complexity: Moderate

2. Modify the program from the first step in Exercise 1 to display the coordinates of the mouse as the mouse moves over the document.

Chapter Summary

This chapter focused on two key interface elements—the toolbar and the status bar. These two interface elements, along with menus, give the user the highest level of inter-action and feedback to and from your application. Utilizing these elements efficiently and effectively is the key to creating a great application.

VC++ 6 includes many tools that ease the development process, one of which enables you to manage the layout and appearance of toolbar resources.

Occasionally, you need more than the default toolbar created by the AppWizard. The MFC rises to the occasion by being flexible enough to let you create as many toolbar resources as your application needs.

When implementing your custom toolbar, you need to create, load, and define its style and functionality. This is made possible by easy-to-use function calls to the `CToolBar` class.

It seems that almost all Windows applications now include a status bar. The default SDI and MDI applications that the AppWizard creates are no exceptions. Even though the default toolbar that is created is quite basic, it does provide some useful feedback to the user.

Realizing that the default status bar won't fit every application's needs, the MFC has built in the flexibility to customize the status bar to add your own indicators. This is made possible through the `CStatusBar` class within the MFC.

CHAPTER 7

Saving, Loading, and Printing Your Documents

One of the major capabilities that you will need to add to the applications you write is the capability for the user to load and save his or her data. You will also need to provide a way for the user to display, edit, and print this data. Each of these functions is an essential part of many applications, and all are considered standard features for applications that process information.

In this chapter, you learn how to load, save, view, and print data. You will accomplish this by learning about the document and view classes that are created for you when you create an SDI or an MDI application.

The document class provides you with a good majority of the functionality you need to manage data. The view class will be used to present the data to your user, either on screen or on a printer.

LESSON 1

Working with Documents and Views

Before you learn about loading, saving, and printing data, you should understand how the document and view classes work together. This lesson will teach you how the document class is organized to manage your data and how the view class is used to display it.

Creating a Document/View Example Application

To examine the document and view classes, you need to create an application with which to play. Go ahead and create an SDI application named "DocExample." The purpose of this example is to display a message that is stored in the document in the view window.

To make this example application a little more functional, you will need to add a dialog box that will enable you to enter the text that will be displayed on the view. Using Figure 7.1 as a guide, create the necessary dialog box. After the dialog box is created, change the caption of the dialog box and the static text to "Enter Message."

FIGURE 7.1

The dialog box used to enter the message.

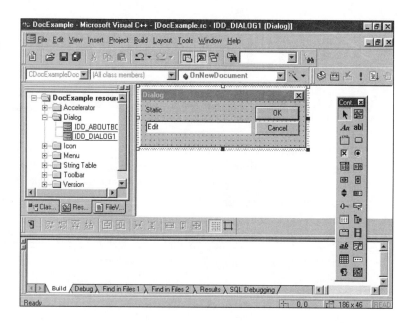

With the necessary dialog box created, you will need to create a member variable for the edit box. However, before you can create the member variable, you need to create a class for the new dialog box. The ClassWizard easily handles both of these tasks.

When you start the ClassWizard, a dialog box is displayed that asks if you want to add a class for the dialog box. You do want to create a class for this dialog box, so go ahead and click the OK button. After you click OK, you are presented with the New Class dialog box. Go ahead and name this class CMessageDlg, as shown in Figure 7.2. After you type in the name, click the OK button to create the class.

FIGURE 7.2

Creating the CMessageDlg class.

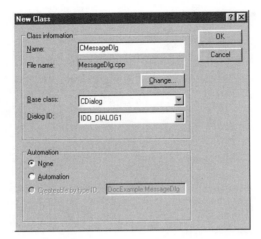

Now that a class represents the dialog box, you can go ahead and create the member variables for that dialog. The only member variable that you are going to need for this example is a variable for the IDC_EDIT1 control. Using Table 7.1 as a guide, create a member variable for this control.

TABLE 7.1 Member Variable for the Edit Control

ID	Type	Member Variable
IDC_EDIT1	CString	m_edit_message

Examining the Document and View Classes

Now that you have an SDI application created with a dialog box that enables you to change the displayed message, you can start examining the document and view classes.

Click on the Classes tab of the Workspace panel and expand the DocExample class, as shown in Figure 7.3. The two classes that you are going to concentrate on in this lesson are the CDocExampleDoc class and the CDocExampleView class. The CDocExampleDoc class is derived from CDocument, and the CDocExampleView class is derived from CView.

The CDocExampleDoc class is responsible for managing the application's data. To store data in the document, you will add data members to the CDocExampleDoc class. If you double-click on the CDocExampleDoc class, the associated header file, DocExampleDoc.h shows in the code editor. Listing 7.1 is a listing of this header file.

7

FIGURE 7.3

The generated classes for DocExample.

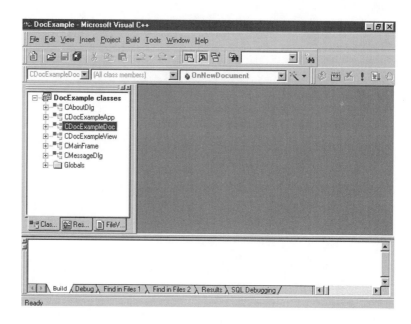

LISTING 7.1   The DocExampleDoc.h Header File

```
// DocExampleDoc.h : interface of the CDocExampleDoc class
//
/////////////////////////////////////////////////////////////////////

#if
!defined(AFX_DOCEXAMPLEDOC_H__952D860B_A25A_11D1_A949_80B279B52165_
➥_INCLUDED_)
#define
AFX_DOCEXAMPLEDOC_H__952D860B_A25A_11D1_A949_80B279B52165__INCLUDED_
#if _MSC_VER > 1000
#pragma once
#endif // _MSC_VER > 1000


class CDocExampleDoc : public CDocument
{
protected: // create from serialization only
    CDocExampleDoc();
    DECLARE_DYNCREATE(CDocExampleDoc)
// Attributes
public:

// Operations
public:
```

```
// Overrides
    // ClassWizard generated virtual function overrides
    //{{AFX_VIRTUAL(CDocExampleDoc)
    public:
    virtual BOOL OnNewDocument();
    virtual void Serialize(CArchive& ar);
    //}}AFX_VIRTUAL

// Implementation
public:
    virtual ~CDocExampleDoc();
#ifdef _DEBUG
    virtual void AssertValid() const;
    virtual void Dump(CDumpContext& dc) const;
#endif
protected:
// Generated message map functions
protected:
    //{{AFX_MSG(CDocExampleDoc)
        // NOTE - the ClassWizard will add and remove member functions
        // here.   DO NOT EDIT what you see in these blocks
        // of generated code !
    //}}AFX_MSG
    DECLARE_MESSAGE_MAP()
};

//////////////////////////////////////////////////////////////////

//{{AFX_INSERT_LOCATION}}
// Microsoft Visual C++ will insert additional declarations immediately
// before the previous line.
#endif // !defined(AFX_DOCEXAMPLEDOC_H__952D860B_A25A_
➥11D1_A949_80B279B52165__INCLUDED_)
```

Near the beginning of Listing 7.1, you will see the Attributes section. You will declare your data members in this section. For this example program, go ahead and declare a string variable named m_doc_message, as shown here:

```
//Attributes
public:
    CString m_doc_message;
```

A little later in this lesson, you will use this variable to pass some text back and forth from the dialog box that you created.

Also in this header file are two member functions overrides. The first is the OnNewDocument() function. This function is called whenever a user selects File, New from the menu or from a toolbar. This function is used to perform initialization to the

7

document data. The second function, Serialize(), is responsible for saving and loading the data for your application. You will learn more about serialization in the next lesson.

Because the OnNewDocument() function is called when a new document is created, you need to add a small piece of code in this function to initialize the m_doc_message string. Go ahead and expand the CDocExampleDoc class and double-click on the OnNewDocument() function to bring it into the code editor. Modify this class so that the m_doc_message variable is initially set to a default value when the document is created, as shown in Listing 7.2.

LISTING 7.2   The OnNewDocument() Function—Initializing the m_doc_message String

```
BOOL CDocExampleDoc::OnNewDocument()
{
    if (!CDocument::OnNewDocument())
        return FALSE;
    // TODO: add reinitialization code here
    // (SDI documents will reuse this document)
    m_doc_message = "Hello Interactive World";

    return TRUE;
}
```

If you were to execute this example application at this time, the application still wouldn't have any real functionality. You can take care of this by using the view to display a message on the document. To examine the view, double-click on the CDocExampleView class to bring it into the code editor. This will open the DocExampleView.h header file, which is shown in Listing 7.3.

LISTING 7.3   The DocExampleView.h Header File

```
// DocExampleView.h : interface of the CDocExampleView class
//
/////////////////////////////////////////////////////////////////

#if _!defined(AFX_DOCEXAMPLEVIEW_H__952D860D_A25A_
➥11D1_A949_80B279B52165__INCLUDED_)
#define
AFX_DOCEXAMPLEVIEW_H__952D860D_A25A_11D1_A949_80B279B52165__INCLUDED_
#if _MSC_VER > 1000
#pragma once
#endif // _MSC_VER > 1000

class CDocExampleView : public CView
{
protected: // create from serialization only
    CDocExampleView();
```

```
    DECLARE_DYNCREATE(CDocExampleView)
// Attributes
public:
    CDocExampleDoc* GetDocument();
// Operations
public:

// Overrides
    // ClassWizard generated virtual function overrides
    //{{AFX_VIRTUAL(CDocExampleView)
    public:
    virtual void OnDraw(CDC* pDC);   // overridden to draw this view
    virtual BOOL PreCreateWindow(CREATESTRUCT& cs);
    protected:
    virtual BOOL OnPreparePrinting(CPrintInfo* pInfo);
    virtual void OnBeginPrinting(CDC* pDC, CPrintInfo* pInfo);
    virtual void OnEndPrinting(CDC* pDC, CPrintInfo* pInfo);
    //}}AFX_VIRTUAL

// Implementation
public:
    virtual ~CDocExampleView();
#ifdef _DEBUG
    virtual void AssertValid() const;
    virtual void Dump(CDumpContext& dc) const;
#endif
protected:
// Generated message map functions
protected:
    //{{AFX_MSG(CDocExampleView)
        // NOTE - the ClassWizard will add and remove member functions
        // here.   DO NOT EDIT what you see in these blocks
        // of generated code !
    //}}AFX_MSG
    DECLARE_MESSAGE_MAP()
};

#ifndef _DEBUG  // debug version in DocExampleView.cpp
inline CDocExampleDoc* CDocExampleView::GetDocument()
   { return (CDocExampleDoc*)m_pDocument; }
#endif


/////////////////////////////////////////////////////////////////////

//{{AFX_INSERT_LOCATION}}
// Microsoft Visual C++ will insert additional declarations
// immediately before the previous line.
#endif // !defined(AFX_DOCEXAMPLEVIEW_H__952D860D_A25A_
➥11D1_A949_80B279B52165__INCLUDED_)
```

7

Looking towards the top of Listing 7.3, you will see the Attributes section for the view. In this section, the GetDocument() function is declared as a pointer to a CDocExample object. This function enables you to access the document data from anywhere within the view. This will easily enable you to work with the data throughout your application.

Examining Listing 7.3 further, you will notice that the view also overrides the following functions:

- OnDraw()
- PreCreateWindow()
- OnPreparePrinting()
- OnBeginPrinting()
- OnEndPrinting()

Because the OnDraw() function is used to display the document data to the view, this is where you will put the necessary code to display the m_doc_message string to the view. To do this, you need to bring the OnDraw() function into the code editor by expanding the CDocExampleView class and double-clicking on the function. After you have the function in the editor, modify the OnDraw() function so that it matches the code listed in Listing 7.4.

LISTING 7.4 The OnDraw() Function Modified to Draw the String to the View

```
void CDocExampleView::OnDraw(CDC* pDC)
{
    CDocExampleDoc* pDoc = GetDocument();
    ASSERT_VALID(pDoc);
    // TODO: add draw code for native data here
    pDC->TextOut(0,10,pDoc->m_doc_message);
}
```

When the OnDraw() function is called, one of its passed parameters is the Device Context (DC) of the view. You will learn more about the DC and other graphics programming topics in Chapter 8, "Working with Graphics and Sound." For this example, all you need to know is that the TextOut() function is used to display a string variable at a specific location on the screen. For this example, the contents of m_doc_message, which is of type CString, will be displayed at pixel 0,10 on the view.

After you enter the line of code to display the text message, you can execute the application. When you do, a message will automatically be displayed in the view upon execution. This is because you assigned a value to the string in the OnNewDocument() function and then displayed it in the OnDraw() function. When you run the application, your screen should look similar to Figure 7.4.

FIGURE 7.4

The DocExample application.

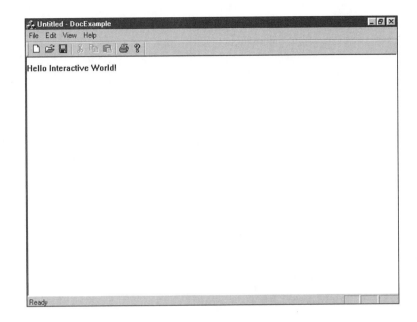

Now that the message is displayed onscreen, you need a way to modify the message. This is why you added a dialog box earlier in this lesson. To access the dialog box, you must create a menu option that calls the dialog box. Go ahead and add a menu option on the Edit menu with a caption of "Message." The ID of the message should be ID_EDIT_MESSAGE. If you don't remember the exact procedure to modify a menu, refer to Chapter 6, "Customizing the User Interface," which covers menus.

After you have added the Message menu option to the Edit menu, call the dialog box when this menu option is chosen. To do this, you need to capture the command message sent out when you select this option from the menu. To capture the right message, bring up the ClassWizard and click the Message Map tab.

Before actually capturing the message, you need to determine where to capture it. If you change the Class Name drop down, you will notice that the ID_EDIT_MESSAGE ID is available for each class. Which class should you choose? Because the variable is owned by the document, you need to use the document class, which is the CDocExampleDoc class. To create the necessary message handler, follow these simple steps:

1. Set the Class name to CDocExampleDoc.

2. Select the ID_EDIT_MESSAGE ID.

3. Select the COMMAND message.

4. Click the Add Function button.

7

5. Accept the default name of the function by clicking on the OK button.

6. Double-click the newly added function to open it into the code editor.

Now that you have a message handler for the Edit, Message menu option, display the dialog box to allow the text message to be altered. Modify the CDocExampleDoc::OnEditMessage() function to look like Listing 7.5.

LISTING 7.5   Displaying the Dialog Box When the Edit, Message Menu Option Is Selected

```
void CDocExampleDoc::OnEditMessage()
{
    // TODO: Add your command handler code here
    CMessageDlg dlg;
    dlg.m_edit_message = m_doc_message;
    if(dlg.DoModal() == IDOK)
    {
        m_doc_message = dlg.m_edit_message;
        SetModifiedFlag(TRUE);
        UpdateAllViews(NULL);

    }
}
```

The first line of code simply creates a dialog box named dlg from the dialog class CMessageDlg that you created earlier. The next line of code copies the value of the data member in the document, which is a string, to the edit box in the dialog box so that it can be edited. After the text is copied to the edit box, the dialog box is then displayed in modal form. If you click the OK button to close the dialog box, the new contents of the edit box will be copied back to the document data member m_doc_message. The SetModifiedFlag() function sets an internal flag for the document that determines if the document has been modified since it was last loaded or saved. By setting this flag to TRUE, when you try to load another document or close the application, you will be prompted with a dialog box that asks if you want to save the changes.

The last thing that is performed is a call to the UpdateAllViews() function which tells the view to do a redraw.

There is one more thing you need to add. If you were to compile the application at this point, you would receive several error messages stating that the CMessageDlg is an undeclared identifier. In order to use the dialog class that you created, you need to move to the top of the DocExampleDoc.cpp file and add the necessary include file. Listing 7.6 shows the added #include "MessageDlg.h" line.

LISTING 7.6   Adding the Necessary include for the Dialog Box Class

```cpp
// DocExampleDoc.cpp : implementation of the CDocExampleDoc class
//

#include "stdafx.h"
#include "DocExample.h"

#include "DocExampleDoc.h"
#include "MessageDlg.h"

#ifdef _DEBUG
#define new DEBUG_NEW
#undef THIS_FILE
static char THIS_FILE[] = __FILE__;
#endif
```

Now you can compile and execute your application. If everything compiles and executes properly, your application should look like Figure 7.5 when the Edit, Message menu option is selected.

FIGURE 7.5

Calling the Enter Message dialog box.

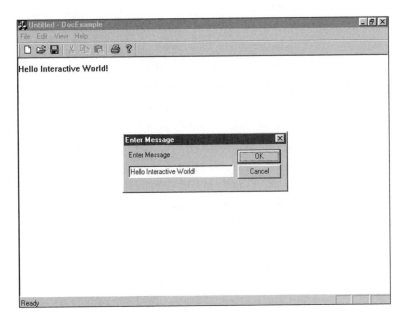

Lesson Summary

In this lesson, you learned that there are two classes that work together that enable you to work with documents. These two classes are the CDocument class and the CView class.

The CDocument class accomplishes the following:

- Manages the data for the application.
- Calls the OnNewDocument() function when a new document is to be created.
- Calls the Serialize() function to load and save data. You will learn more about this function in the next lesson.

The CView class accomplishes the following:

- Retrieves information about the CDocument class through the use of the GetDocument() function.
- Draws the output.
- Prints functions of your application.

Quiz 1

1. Which class is responsible for managing the data in a document?

    a. CDocumentManager

    b. CView

    c. CDocumentData

    d. CDocument

2. Which of the following is true about the CView class?

    a. It manages the document's data.

    b. It is responsible for drawing the display.

    c. This class is derived from CViewClass.

    d. The OnDrawDoc() function is a member of this class.

3. Using the DocExample application, where do you declare member variables for the document?

    a. In the attributes section of DocExampleDoc.h header file

    b. In the attributes section of the DocExampleDoc.cpp file

    c. In the OnNewDocument() function

    d. In the attributes section of the DocExampleView.h header file

4. Which function in the CView class enables you to access the CDocument object, such as the CDocExample object the DocExample application?

    a. GetDocClass()

    b. GetDocument()

    c. GetViewDocument()

    d. OnNewDocument()

Exercise 1

Complexity: Easy

1. Create an SDI application named "Exercise 1." This application will print two messages on the screen that can be edited. Create a dialog box and add two edit controls to it. These two edit controls will be used to change the displayed messages. This dialog box should be called from the Edit, Messages menu, which you will need to create. The messages should have the default values of Message 1 and Message 2.

Complexity: Moderate

2. Create an MDI application named "Exercise 2." This application will print several items on the view. Create a dialog box and add two edit controls to it. The first edit box will be used to enter a string value and the second edit box will be used to enter a long value. This dialog box should be displayed when the Edit, Messages menu option is selected, which you will need to create. The message should have the default values of Message1 and 2000.

When creating the data members (attributes) for the document, declare the first message as type CString and the second message as long. When displaying the numerical value in the OnDraw() function, you will need to create a variable of type CString and then call the Format() function of that string, passing it the value of message 2.

LESSON 2

Loading and Saving Data

The two of the most important functions of your application are loading and saving the user's data. If your application doesn't contain these capabilities, your users will be required to enter their data each time they use your application.

When you create an SDI or MDI application with the MFC AppWizard, by default, you create an application that is capable of easily storing and retrieving data. For an SDI and an MDI application, this functionality is provided by the document class, also known as the *document object*. The capability for an object to load and save its state is known as *persistence*.

7

Using the Document to Load and Save Data

To look at the way the document class is used to load and retrieve data, you will need to build a small example program. This example program will be pretty much like the one you wrote in the last lesson, except that it will allow you to load and save the message entered.

To build the necessary application for this example, follow these easy steps:

1. Create a new SDI application named "LoadSave."

2. Insert a dialog box, using Figure 7.6 as a guide. Notice that this dialog box has an edit box and a static text control on it. The caption of the dialog box has been changed as well.

FIGURE 7.6

Inserting the dialog box.

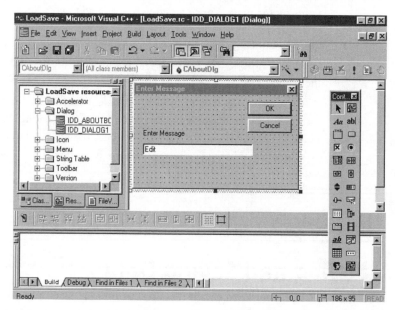

3. Start the ClassWizard.
4. Choose OK to create a new class for the dialog.
5. Name the class CMsgDlg and click OK.
6. Click on the Member Variables tab.
7. Create a member variable for ID_EDIT1. Name the variable m_dlg_message. Its category should be a value. Click OK to create the variable.
8. Close the ClassWizard by clicking on OK.
9. Add a menu option to the menu bar. The option should be under the Edit menu. Its ID should be ID_EDIT_MESSAGE and its caption should be Message.

10. Right-click the menu and select ClassWizard from the context menu to bring up the ClassWizard.

11. Click the Message Map tab.

12. Change the Class name to CLoadSaveDoc.

13. Click the ID_EDIT_MESSAGE Object ID.

14. Double-click the COMMAND message to bring up the Add Member Function dialog box.

15. Accept the default name for the message handler function by clicking OK.

Now that you have created the menu and dialog box, you need to add some code to make the message display on the screen. You will also need to add the code that will enable you to change the message from the dialog box. So far, everything in this lesson has been pretty much just like the last lesson. The same goes for adding this portion of code. So, using the following steps, add the necessary code to the application:

1. In the CLoadSaveDoc header, declare a variable in the attribute section. Name this variable m_message with a type of CString.

2. In the OnNewDocument() function of the CLoadSaveDoc class, set the default value of the m_message variable to "Hello Interactive World."

3. In the OnDraw() function of the CLoadSaveView class, display m_message to the screen at pixel position 0,10.

4. In the OnEditMessag() of CLoadSaveDoc, display the dialog box, and if the user chooses OK from the dialog, change m_message to the contents entered into the edit box on the dialog.

5. Add #include MsgDlg.H to LoadSaveDoc.cpp.

At this point, if you were to execute this application, you would have the same functionality as the application you created in the last lesson. Now that you do have an application that enables you to enter some sort of data, you need to provide a way to save and load the data entered.

Saving Data

By using the MFC AppWizard to generate your application for you, you have eliminated a lot of the hard work in working with storing objects. When your application was created, a member function named Serialize() was automatically added for you, which is shown in Listing 7.7.

LISTING 7.7 The Serialize() Member Function

```
void CLoadSaveDoc::Serialize(CArchive& ar)
{
    if (ar.IsStoring())
    {
```

7

continues

LISTING 7.7 continued

```
        // TODO: add storing code here
    }
    else
    {
        // TODO: add loading code here
    }
}
```

This is the empty shell generated by the MFC AppWizard. This shell contains a simple If statement that determines if the application is currently saving or loading the document's data. Because you only have one data member, which is defined as a CString, you can directly transfer the string into the archive, thus saving the value. To do this, modify the Serialize() function so that it looks like Listing 7.8.

LISTING 7.8 Saving the Data

```
void CLoadSaveDoc::Serialize(CArchive& ar)
{
    if (ar.IsStoring())
    {
        // TODO: add storing code here
        ar << m_message;
    }
    else
    {
        // TODO: add loading code here
    }
}
```

Now, when you choose the File, Save As menu option, you will actually have something to save, as shown in Figure 7.7.

FIGURE 7.7

The Save As dialog box.

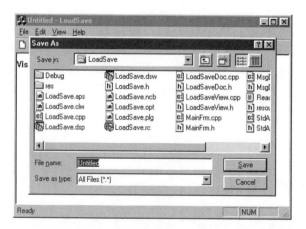

Before you actually save the file, you might want to change the path so that it doesn't
save the file in the same directory as your project source code. To do this, change your
path to a temporary directory or somewhere on your machine that you don't keep valuable data. Type in text1.vci as the name of the file to save, as shown in Figure 7.8, and
click the OK button.

FIGURE 7.8

Saving the text1.vci file.

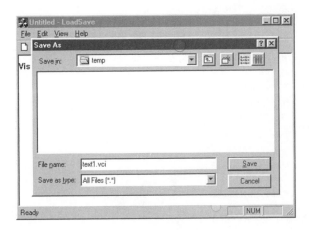

If you were to go to a DOS shell and get a directory from your temp directory, you
would see the text1.vci file listed, as shown in Figure 7.9.

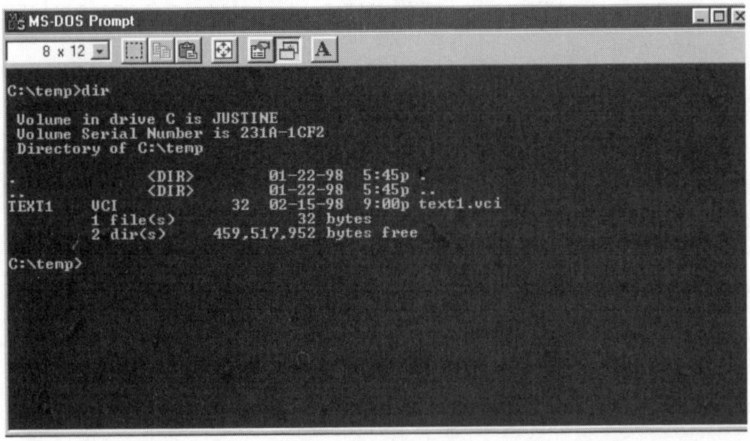

FIGURE 7.9

*The text1.vci file on
disk.*

Loading Data

Now that you have your document file saved to disk, you need a way to load the data
when a user wants to modify or view it. This is just as easy as saving the data.

7

In the previous part of this lesson, you saved a file named text1.vci. You are now going to add the code to your application that enables the user to load the file when they select File, Open from the menu. To do this, modify the Serialize() function again, this time for loading data. The necessary code change is shown in Listing 7.9.

LISTING 7.9   Loading the Data

```
void CLoadSaveDoc::Serialize(CArchive& ar)
{
    if (ar.IsStoring())
    {
        // TODO: add storing code here
        ar << m_message;
    }
    else
    {
        // TODO: add loading code here
        ar >> m_message;
    }
    SetModifiedFlag(FALSE);
}
```

If you look at the second half of the If statement, you will see where you are using the archive to populate the m_message variable. Also, after the If statement, a new line was added, the line with SetModifiedFlag(FALSE) call. This call clears the document's modified flag, which indicates whether or not the document has been modified since the last load or save.

Compile and execute the example application. When you choose File, Open from the menu, the open dialog box is presented. Go ahead and change the path to which you originally saved a document and select text1.vci, as shown in Figure 7.10.

FIGURE 7.10

Loading the text1.vci file.

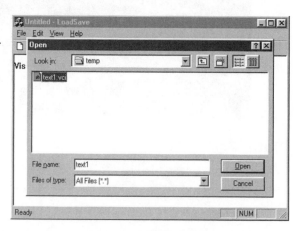

When you select the file and choose OK to load it, nothing will happen visually. This is because you saved the text1.vci file with the default value. Now, to show that something is actually happening, go ahead and change the message to Learning is fun. When you click the OK button, your screen should now look like Figure 7.11.

FIGURE 7.11

Changing the message shown onscreen.

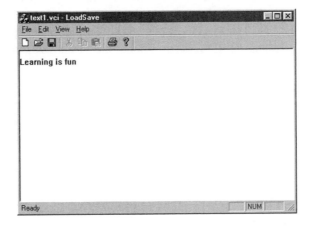

Save the new message as text2.vci in the same directory as the first message. After you save it, load text1.vci; you will notice that the document now has the default message again, as saved in the first file. Another way to tell which file was opened is to look at the caption bar of the application window. It now has the name of the document opened (text1.vci) rather than Untitled, as shown in Figure 7.12.

FIGURE 7.12

The dialog box shown after loading a document.

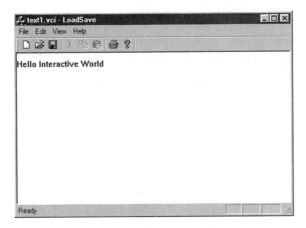

7

Lesson Summary

In this lesson, you learned how the document class is used to store information through the use of the `Serialize()` function.

By using the `Serialize()` function to save and retrieve your data, you are enabling the MFC to manage the majority of the workload of saving and loading data. The MFC will automatically give the user a dialog box when a load or save request is sent. After a file-name is selected, the `Serialize()` function is called and you then pass your data into the archive for storage or retrieve it for use.

Quiz 2

1. Which function in the `CDocument` class is responsible for saving and loading data?

   a. `Save()`

   b. `Load()`

   c. `Serialize()`

   d. `ProcessData()`

2. What function is used to tell a document that it has been modified?

   a. `SetModifiedFlag()`

   b. `UpdateDocument()`

   c. `Serialize()`

   d. `ModifyDocument()`

3. Which statement is true about the `Serialize()` function?

   a. This function is called only for loading data.

   b. This function is called only for saving data.

   c. This function is used to display the data to the screen.

   d. This function is responsible for both loading and saving the data.

4. When is the `Serialize()` function called?

   a. When the application first starts up

   b. When a request is made to load or save a document

   c. When a new document is created

   d. When the application is closed

Exercise 2

Complexity: Easy

1. Create an SDI application named "Exercise 1." This application will print two messages on the screen that can be edited. Add the necessary code to the `Serialize()` function to enable the user to save the two strings to disk.

   This application should use a dialog box with two edit controls that are used to edit the two messages. This dialog box should be called from the Edit, Messages menu, which you will need to create. The messages should have the default values of `Message 1` and `Message 2`.

Complexity: Moderate

2. Create an MDI application named "Exercise 2." This application will print several items on the view. Add the necessary code to the `Serialize()` function to enable the user to save and load the data.

   This application should use a dialog box with two edit controls that are used to edit the two messages. The first edit box will be used to enter a string value while the second edit box will be used to enter a long value. This dialog box should be called from the Edit, Messages menu, which you will need to create. The messages should have the default values of `Message 1` and `2000`.

   When creating the data members (attributes) for the document, declare the first message as type `CString` and the second message as `long`.

LESSON 3

Loading and Saving Persistent Classes

In the previous lesson, you learned how to store and retrieve a single string object. This is fine if all you need to store is a single item, but in most cases, you will need to manage more data than that. In this lesson, you will learn how to define a persistence class and then store and retrieve it.

Creating a Persistence Class

By defining a custom class that holds more than one piece of data, you can easily create an application that can store a complex document without writing an enormous amount of code. To learn how to do this, you will need to build an SDI application. Go ahead and create an SDI application named `Persistence`.

7

After you create the basic framework, you need to create a dialog box. This dialog box will be used to enter the information that will be stored to disk. Using Figure 7.13 as a guide, create the necessary dialog box. After you have created the dialog box, go ahead and bring up the ClassWizard and give this dialog box a class name of CaddressDlg.

FIGURE 7.13

The Edit Address dialog box.

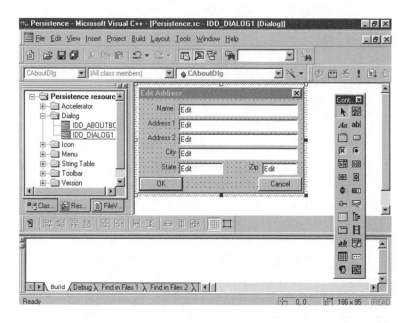

After the dialog box is created, you need to create member variables for each of the edit boxes you placed on the control. Using Table 7.2 as a guide, create the member variables for the controls.

TABLE 7.2   Member Variables for the Address Dialog Box

ID	Type	Member Variable
IDC_EDIT1	CString	m_dlg_name
IDC_EDIT2	CString	m_dlg_address1
IDC_EDIT3	CString	m_dlg_address2
IDC_EDIT4	CString	m_dlg_city
IDC_EDIT5	CString	m_dlg_state
IDC_EDIT6	CString	m_dlg_zip

After you create the member variables, you need to create an option under the Edit menu that will call this dialog box. Go ahead and create this menu option with an ID of ID_EDIT_ADDRESS and a caption of Address.

You already know that you are going to need a message handler for the menu option, so go ahead and bring up the ClassWizard by right-clicking on the menu and selecting it from the presented context menu. Click the Message Map tab to create the message handler. Just don't forget to change the Class Name drop-down to CPersistenceDoc. Go ahead and create a handler for the COMMAND message, just like you have done in the previous lessons. Now you should be ready to start coding the example application.

One of the first things that you class. You should already be familiar with this file; it's the file in which you defined the document variables in the previous lessons. You are going to define your custom class in this file. To define this class, modify the header file using the code in Listing 7.10. Add this class definition just before the class definition of the CPersistenceDoc class.

LISTING 7.10 The Modified Portion PersistenceDoc.h File

```
class CAddress : public CObject
{
    DECLARE_SERIAL(CAddress)
    CAddress(){};
public:
    CString m_name;
    CString m_address1;
    CString m_address2;
    CString m_city;
    CString m_state;
    CString m_zip;
};
```

Your class will be derived from the CObject class. Toward the top of the definition, you will see the DECLARE_SERIAL macro. This macro will provide the additional functions and members needed to implement persistence. After this macro, a constructor is created for the class. MFC needs this constructor so that it can create objects of this class when loading data. For this example, all of the data members for the class are defined in the public area.

To finish adding the serial capabilities of the class, use the IMPLEMENT_SERIAL() macro. This macro works in conjunction with the DECLARE_SERIAL macro. For this example, place this macro in the PersistenceDoc.cpp file. Go ahead and open this file into the code editor.

Toward the top of the PersistenceDoc.cpp file, you will see the IMPLEMENT_DYNCREATE(CPersistenceDoc, CDocument) macro. Go ahead and add the following line of code just after the IMPLEMENT_DYNCREATE macro.

```
IMPLEMENT_SERIAL(CAddress, CObject, 0);
```

7

This macro takes three parameters. The first is the name of the class that uses the serial functions, which is CAddress in this case. The second parameter is the type base class that the CAddress object is derived from, which is CObject. The last parameter is a *schema number*. For this example, leave this value as 0. The schema number is like a version number for the data stored in the archive.

After you have inserted this line of code, along with the class definition, you have a class that can load and save its own data. With this class defined, you can declare a variable of this type to use in the program. Create a data member named NewAddress of type CAddress in PersistenceDoc.h. The following code shows where you should add this data member, just in case you need a reminder.

```
// Attributes
public:
    CAddress NewAddress;
```

Now that you have defined the data member for the document, declare the default values for the variable. Using Listing 7.11 as a guide, modify the OnNewDocument() function.

LISTING 7.11 The Modified OnNewDocument() Function

```
BOOL CPersistenceDoc::OnNewDocument()
{
    if (!CDocument::OnNewDocument())
        return FALSE;
    // TODO: add reinitialization code here
    // (SDI documents will reuse this document)
    NewAddress.m_name     = "Kirsten";
    NewAddress.m_address1 = "123 ABC St.";
    NewAddress.m_address2 = "Apt. Z";
    NewAddress.m_city     = "Anytown";
    NewAddress.m_state    = "US";
    NewAddress.m_zip      = "12345";

    return TRUE;
}
```

As in the previous lessons, you will display the data to the screen using the OnDraw() event of CPersistentView. Using Listing 7.12 as a guide, modify the OnDraw() function.

LISTING 7.12 The Modified OnDraw() Function

```
void CPersistenceView::OnDraw(CDC* pDC)
{
    CPersistenceDoc* pDoc = GetDocument();
    ASSERT_VALID(pDoc);
    // TODO: add draw code for native data here
```

```
    pDC->TextOut(0,10,pDoc->NewAddress.m_name);
    pDC->TextOut(0,26,pDoc->NewAddress.m_address1);
    pDC->TextOut(0,42,pDoc->NewAddress.m_address2);
    pDC->TextOut(0,58,pDoc->NewAddress.m_city + ", " +
    ➥pDoc->NewAddress.m_state);
    pDC->TextOut(0,74,pDoc->NewAddress.m_zip);
}
```

The previous code should look familiar to you by now, with only a few differences. The first difference is that more than one line of text is being displayed; therefore, the Y position on the screen is incremented for each TextOut() call. Also, the city and state data members are printed on the same line separated by a comma. Because both data members are of type CString, you can concatenate them by using the plus (+) sign. If you want to run the application at this point to see what the output will look like, you can go ahead and do so. If you do, your screen should look similar to Figure 7.14.

FIGURE 7.14

Output with multiple lines of text.

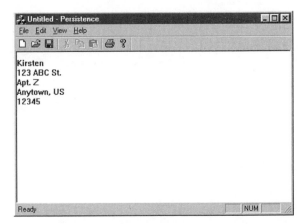

Now that the data is displaying correctly, you need to make your application bring up the dialog box so that the data can be changed. You already created the message handler for the Edit, Address menu option, so go ahead and modify the OnEditAddress() function so that it looks like the code in Listing 7.13.

LISTING 7.13 The Modified OnEditAddress() Function

```
void CPersistenceDoc::OnEditAddress()
{
    // TODO: Add your command handler code here
    CAddressDlg dlg;
    dlg.m_dlg_name     = NewAddress.m_name;
    dlg.m_dlg_address1 = NewAddress.m_address1;
```

7

continues

LISTING 7.13   continued

```
            dlg.m_dlg_address2 = NewAddress.m_address2;
            dlg.m_dlg_city     = NewAddress.m_city;
            dlg.m_dlg_state    = NewAddress.m_state;
            dlg.m_dlg_zip      = NewAddress.m_zip;

            if(dlg.DoModal() == IDOK)
            {
                NewAddress.m_name     = dlg.m_dlg_name;
                NewAddress.m_address1 = dlg.m_dlg_address1;
                NewAddress.m_address2 = dlg.m_dlg_address2;
                NewAddress.m_city     = dlg.m_dlg_city;
                NewAddress.m_state    = dlg.m_dlg_state;
                NewAddress.m_zip      = dlg.m_dlg_zip;

                SetModifiedFlag(TRUE);
                UpdateAllViews(NULL);
            }
        }
```

Before you try to execute this example, don't forget to make sure that the necessary #include statement has been added to the top of the PersistenceDoc.cpp file, which is the file you should be in right now. If you haven't added the #include statement for the dialog class, go ahead and do so now by moving to the top of this file and adding the following line of code:

```
#include "AddressDlg.h"
```

The only portion of your program that you have left to do is implement the loading and saving of your class. Just like in the previous lesson, you will accomplish this by adding the necessary code to the Serialize() function of CPersistenceDoc class. Using Listing 7.14 as a guide, go ahead and modify the Serialize() function.

LISTING 7.14   The Modified Serialize() Function

```
void CPersistenceDoc::Serialize(CArchive& ar)
{
    if (ar.IsStoring())
    {
        // TODO: add storing code here
        ar << NewAddress.m_name     << NewAddress.m_address1
           << NewAddress.m_address2 << NewAddress.m_city
           << NewAddress.m_state    << NewAddress.m_zip;
    }
    else
    {
        // TODO: add loading code here
```

```
        ar >> NewAddress.m_name      >> NewAddress.m_address1
            >> NewAddress.m_address2 >> NewAddress.m_city
            >> NewAddress.m_state    >> NewAddress.m_zip;
    }
    SetModifiedFlag(FALSE);
}
```

In this example application, to store the information, each member of the NewAddress object is passed into the archive. To load the data members, each member is pulled from the archive.

After you enter this code you are ready to execute the application. When you first execute the application, you will have a screen similar to Figure 7.15. This is the output for the default data.

FIGURE 7.15

The output of the default data.

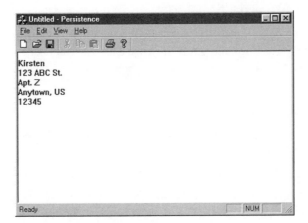

Before you change this data, go ahead and save it to your temp directory with the filename of Kirsten.vci. Now, choose Edit, Address from the menu and change the name and address so that it is different from the default data. After you have changed the data, the new data will be displayed on the screen. Now save this document as Changed.vci. After you save the new data, load in the Kirsten.vci file. The data that you saved in the Kirsten.vci file is back in the document. If you load in the Changed.vci document, its values will be loaded, as shown in Figure 7.16.

7

FIGURE 7.16

The output of the
Changed.vci *data.*

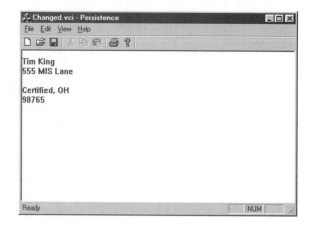

Lesson Summary

In this lesson, you learned how easy it is to store multiple pieces of information through the use of a persistence class. A persistence class is capable of storing and retrieving its current state from disk. You also learned about the macros needed to implement a persistence class.

The key steps to creating a persistence class are as follows:

1. Define the class in the document's header file (PersistenceDoc.h for the example).
2. Include the DECLARE_SERIAL() macro in the class.
3. Declare data members or member functions for the class.
4. Add the IMPLEMENT_SERIAL() function. For the example in this lesson, this was done in the PersistenceDoc.cpp file.
5. Declare a data member in the document based on your new class.
6. Add the necessary code to the Serialize() function to store and retrieve data.

Quiz 3

1. Which of the following is a capability of a persistence class?

    a. Formatting output

    b. Storing and retrieving its current state

    c. Validating data

    d. Displaying the save dialog box

2. Which macro must you include when defining a persistence class?

    a. `DECLARE_SERIAL()`

    b. `DECLARE_PERSISTENCE()`

    c. `ALLOW_SAVELOAD()`

    d. `MAKE_PERSISTENCE()`

3. When defining a persistence class, from what base object do you derive?

    a. `CPersistence`

    b. `CDocClass`

    c. `CObjectPersistence`

    d. `CObject`

4. What is the first parameter passed into the `IMPLEMENT_SERIAL()` macro?

    a. The class that you created which uses serial functions

    b. The base object for which your class is derived

    c. The schema number

    d. A pointer to the `Serialize()` function

Exercise 3

Complexity: Moderate

1. Create an SDI application named "Exercise 1." This application will use a persistence object to store a name and a phone number. Name this class `CName`. Both variables will be of type `CString`. You will use a dialog box to edit the name and phone number. Add the necessary code to the `Serialize()` function to enable the user to save and load the data. The variables should have default values of `Joe Doe` and `(999) 555-1212`.

LESSON 4

Previewing and Printing the Document

One of the most common features of many Windows applications is printed output. Printed output provides a way for a user to generate a hard copy of a document that was created in your application.

It used to be that programming your application to print output to a printer required a great amount of knowledge. This knowledge was only gained through experience and a

7

lot of hard work, especially if you wanted anything more than normal text printed. Programmers had to write custom drivers or purchase expensive libraries for their applications just so they could support the numerous printers on the market.

Now, thanks to the MFC, adding printing capabilities to your application is a simple task and should be considered when designing your application. By using MFC, you can easily add these capabilities without a lot of hard work.

Building an Application with Print Capabilities

The first thing you will learn to do is add the printing capabilities to your application. For this lesson, you will create an SDI application that supports these printing capabilities by default.

To make sure that everything is set up properly when you create the example program, follow these steps:

1. Start by closing any open workspaces that you might have open.
2. Start the MFC AppWizard by choosing the File, New menu option.
3. Select MFC AppWizard(exe) from the Project types, name the application Print, and click the OK button.
4. Choose SDI as the application type to create and then click the Next button.
5. You don't need any database support for this example, so go ahead and click the Next button again.
6. You don't need to use compound document support, so click the Next button again.
7. This next step in the creation process is the important step. Make sure that the Printing and Print Preview check box is checked, as shown in Figure 7.17. This will tell MFC to add the necessary framework to implement printing capabilities into your application.

FIGURE 7.17

Make sure that print capabilities are selected.

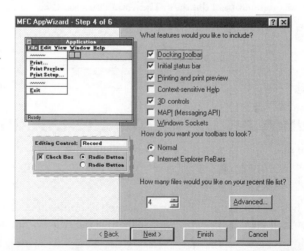

8. If the check box is checked, you can go ahead and click the Finish button to finish creating the application.

Now, by default, printing capabilities are automatically created because the check-box was checked by default. However, it's a good idea to make sure things are set up properly when you create your program as it could be a monstrous task to implement a feature of this nature later.

If you were to run this application at this point, you wouldn't have anything to print. Why? You only created the basic framework for an application. You will need to add some code that displays something on the document so that it will have something to print.

Something to Print

Earlier in this chapter, you learned that the place to display data is in the view's `OnDraw()` function. Go ahead and modify the `OnView()` function so that it matches Listing 7.15.

LISTING 7.15 Adding Something to Print

```
void CPrintView::OnDraw(CDC* pDC)
{
    CPrintDoc* pDoc = GetDocument();
    ASSERT_VALID(pDoc);
    // TODO: add draw code for native data here
    pDC->Ellipse(0,0,50,50);
}
```

To display something on the screen to print, a circle is drawn starting at pixel location 0,0 with a width of 50 and height of 50. With both the width and height the same, the ellipse will form a circle. When you run the application, your screen looks like Figure 7.18.

FIGURE 7.18

Placing something on the document to print.

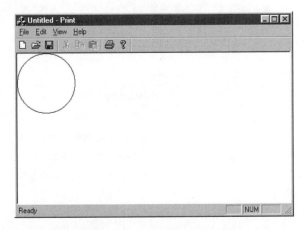

7

Now that you have an application with something to print, you can choose the File, Print Preview option from the menu. This enables you to preview your document before printing, as shown in Figure 7.19. If the document seems a little small while viewing it, you can always zoom in by clicking on the Zoom button. Some of the other options that you can perform from this screen include printing, changing pages, and displaying multiple pages.

FIGURE 7.19

Examining the document with Print Preview.

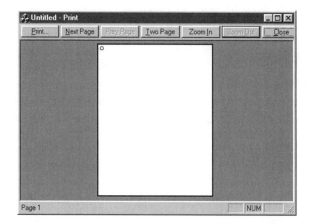

While looking at the print preview, you might notice that the simulated output's circle is much smaller than the one shown on the screen in Paint. This is caused by the difference in the size of a pixel on your screen and the size of a dot on the printer. Even though the circle is 100 pixels wide on both the screen and the printer, each device displays them differently. Through the use of different mapping modes, you can change the way the document is displayed on the screen.

Adjusting the Mapping Mode

The default mapping mode for the display is the MM_TEXT mode. There are a few mapping modes that you can use that affect the way information is presented on the display. Table 7.3 lists the common modes that you can use.

TABLE 7.3   Different Mapping Modes

Mode	Description
MM_HIENGLISH	Each unit is converted to 0.001 inch.
MM_HIMETRIC	Each unit is converted to 0.01 millimeter.
MM_ISOTROPIC	Each unit is converted to 0.01 inch.
MM_LOMETRIC	Each unit is converted to 0.1 millimeter.

Mode	Description
MM_TEXT	Each unit is converted to one device pixel. Unlike the other modes, the y-axis moves downward and the other modes move upward.
MM_TWIPS	Each logical unit is converted to 1/20 of a point.

Listing 7.16 shows the modified OnDraw() function that sets the mapping mode for the device context. For now, you won't delve too deep into the device context. You will learn more about them in Chapter 8. Also, the line that draws the ellipse has changed. The MM_TEXT mapping method has a Y value that increases as it moves down the screen. With the MM_LOENGLISH mapping mode, the further you move down the screen, the lower the number is. Figure 7.20 shows both mapping modes as they would be on a 640×480 screen. Notice that the bottom right of the MM_LOENGLISH mode has a negative Y value.

LISTING 7.16 Changing the Mapping Mode

```
void CPrintView::OnDraw(CDC* pDC)
{
    CPrintDoc* pDoc = GetDocument();
    ASSERT_VALID(pDoc);
    // TODO: add draw code for native data here
    pDC->SetMapMode(MM_LOENGLISH);
    pDC->Ellipse(0,0,50,-50);
}.
```

FIGURE 7.20

The MM_TEXT and MM_LOENGLISH mapping modes.

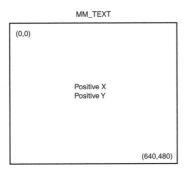
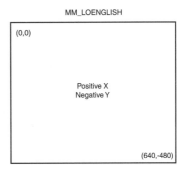

Now, when you go to print the document to the printer or preview it with the print preview, you will get a more accurate representation of what will be printed to the printer.

7

Lesson Summary

One of the key elements to many applications is printing capabilities. You learned that the CView class is responsible for printing your document, as well as viewing it onscreen.

Even though the OnDraw() function is responsible for drawing and printing, you learned that there are differences in the way that the printer handles output versus the way the screen displays output. Through the use of mapping modes, you learned how to better accommodate these differences.

Quiz 4

1. Which function is responsible for printing your document?
   a. The OnDraw() function of CDocument
   b. The PrintDoc() function
   c. The OnNewDocument() function
   d. The OnDraw() function of CView

2. Which mapping mode is the default mapping mode for the display?
   a. MM_LOENGLISH
   b. MM_DEFAULT
   c. MM_TEXT
   d. MM_LOMETRIC

3. Which statement is false about print previewing?
   a. You can zoom in on a page.
   b. You can select a range of pages to print from the Print Preview display.
   c. You can view multiple pages at a single time.
   d. You can print the document from within the Print Preview display.

4. Which statement is true about the MM_TEXT mapping mode?
   a. Units are measured at 0.01 millimeters.
   b. Each logical unit is converted to 1/20 of a point.
   c. Units are measured in one device pixel.
   d. Each unit represents 1 inch.

Exercise 4

Complexity: Easy

1. Create an SDI application and name it "Exercise 1." This application should display a message of `Hello Interactive World` two times. The first one should be drawn on the view at coordinates (0,0) and the second should be drawn at coordinates (0,-100). You will need to set the mapping mode to `MM_LOENGLISH` so that the two lines of text print properly.

Complexity: Moderate

2. Create an MDI application and name it "Exercise 2." A message is to be displayed with a default value of "Hello Interactive World." Add a dialog box to enable the user to change the message. The application should be able to load and save the documents.

    To test your application, change the message twice, saving each change under a different filename. Load each file and print it to view the results. Because you will only be printing one line of text, you will not have to adjust the mapping mode.

LESSON 5

Advanced Printing Capabilities

Printing single-page documents are a breeze when you use the MFC AppWizard. All you need to do is add code to the `OnDraw()` function to display your data. Unfortunately, not every application will be able to print its data onto one page. If your application is going to print data to multiple pages, you need to account for this and add the code necessary to handle the task.

In this lesson, you will learn about the different printing functions of the view class along with building an application that creates output that spans across multiple pages.

Understanding How MFC Handles Printing

Before you create an application that takes advantage of the advanced printing features provided by MFC, you will briefly look at the functions available and how they are used to print your document. Table 7.4 outlines the functions that you can use when working with the `CView` class.

7

TABLE 7.4   The CView Class Printing Functions

Function	Description
OnBeginPrinting()	Called when a print job starts
OnDraw()	Called to render output to the display, printer, or when print previewing
OnEndPrinting()	Called when a print job finishes
OnEndPrintPreview()	Called when the print preview option is closed
OnPrepareDC()	Called before the OnPrint function is called when printing or previewing, or is called before the OnDraw function when displaying
OnPreparePrinting()	Called before the document is previewed or printed
OnPrint()	Called to print or preview the document

When the MFC goes to print a document, it will call these functions in a certain order. The following list shows you the order in which the functions are called:

1. OnPreparePrinting()—You can use this function to retrieve or set the attributes of the print job. Inside this function, the DoPreparePrinting() function is called, as shown in Listing 7.17. The DoPrepreparePrinting() will display the Print dialog box and will create a device context for the printer.

LISTING 7.17   The OnPreparePrinting() Function

```
BOOL CPrint2View::OnPreparePrinting(CPrintInfo* pInfo)
{
    // default preparation
    return DoPreparePrinting(pInfo);
}
```

2. OnBeginPrinting()—By default, this function does nothing; however, you can add code to this function if you need to allocate any GDI resources, such as pens, fonts, and so on. You can also perform some initializations in this function, depending on the device context of the printer.

3. OnPrepareDC()—This function does nothing if it is called for a screen display; however, if it is called for printing, it will examine the page information in the pInfo structure. By default, the document is assumed to have only one page; therefore, the m_bContinuePrinting member is set to False. You need to override this function if you plan to print multiple pages, which is covered later in this lesson. This function is responsible for calling the OnPrint() function to print the actual page.

4. `OnEndPrinting()`—This function is called after the last page is printed. You can release any resources that you created for this printing job here.

When working with these functions, one of the classes with which you will become familiar is the `CPrintInfo` class. Several of these functions pass this class to you as a parameter. This class provides you with the information you need about your printing job. Table 7.5 outlines several of the more common function members of this class, and Table 7.6 outlines the member variables.

TABLE 7.5 Commonly Used `CPrintInfo` Function Members

Function	Description
GetFromPage()	Returns the starting page to print
GetMaxPage()	Returns the last page number
GetMinPage()	Returns the first page number
GetToPage()	Returns the number of the last page to print
SetMaxPage()	Sets the number of the last page of a document
SetMinPage()	Sets the number of the first page of a document

TABLE 7.6 Commonly Used `CPrintInfo` Data Members

Member	Description
m_bContinuePrinting	A flag that determines if the print loop should continue.
m_bDirect	A flag that indicates if the docment is being printed without displaying the print dialog box.
m_bPreview	A flag that indicates if the document is being previewed.
m_lpUserData	A pointer to a user created structure.
m_nCurPage	The number of the page currently being printed.
m_nNumPreviewPages	The number of pages shown in the print preview. This is can have a value of 1 or 2.
m_pPD	A pointer to the `CPrintDialog` box.
m_rectDraw	A rectangle that specifies the usable page area.
m_strPageDesc	Holds a string for formatting the page number.

7

Printing Multiple Pages

Now that you know how MFC handles printing, you are going to build an example program that will use some of the mentioned functions to print a document that spans across multiple pages. To get started, you are going to build a simple program with which to work.

Start by building an SDI application with the name of Print2. When building the application, you might want to double check just to make sure that the option to include printing capabilities is checked.

After you have the application built, you will need to add a small amount of code to the OnDraw() function of the CPrint2View class. Using Listing 7.18 as guide, go ahead and modify the code.

LISTING 7.18   The OnDraw() Function of the CPrint2View Class

```
void CPrint2View::OnDraw(CDC* pDC)
{
    CPrint2Doc* pDoc = GetDocument();
    ASSERT_VALID(pDoc);
    // TODO: add draw code for native data here
    pDC->SetMapMode(MM_LOENGLISH);
    for (int y = 0; y<20; y++)
    {
        pDC->Ellipse(  0,-y*100,100,-y*100+100);
        pDC->Ellipse(100,-y*100,200,-y*100+100);
        pDC->Ellipse(200,-y*100,300,-y*100+100);
    }
}
```

Because the MM_LOENGLISH mapping mode is measured in 1/100 of an inch (0.01), the circles were drawn with a width and height of 100 units, which makes the circle's diameter 1 inch (100 * 0.01 = 1.0).

At this point, you can compile and execute the Print2 example program. When executed, you should have a screen that looks like Figure 7.21.

While you have the application running, go into the Print preview option. If you only have one page showing in the preview, click the Two Page button to show two pages at a time, as shown in Figure 7.22.

FIGURE 7.21

The Print2 example program.

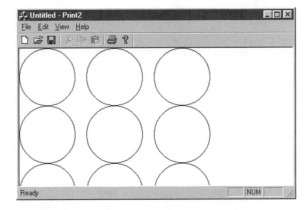

FIGURE 7.22

Print Preview showing two pages.

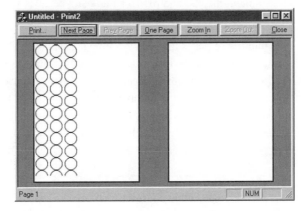

Determining the Number of Pages to Print

Looking at the Print Preview screen, you will notice that the circles run off the bottom of the first page but don't continue onto the next page. By default, MFC assumes that your document only has one page, therefore, you must add the necessary code to inform MFC how many pages are in your document. Because you want to adjust the page count before the document prints or previews, you should add the code in the OnBeginPrinting() function of the CPrin2View class. Bring this function into the code editor and use Listing 7.19 to modify the function.

LISTING 7.19 Setting the Page Count

7

```
void CPrint2View::OnBeginPrinting(CDC* pDC, CPrintInfo* pInfo)
{
    // TODO: add extra initialization before printing
    int iHeight = pDC->GetDeviceCaps(VERTRES);
```

continues

LISTING 7.19   continued

```
        int iPixels = pDC->GetDeviceCaps(LOGPIXELSY);
        int iPages  = 20 * iPixels / iHeight + 1;

        pInfo->SetMaxPage(iPages);
    }
```

Before learning what the code inside the function accomplishes, you will need to uncomment the parameters passed into the function. By default, these two parameters are commented to avoid compiler warnings. Originally, the code looked like the following line:

```
void CPrint2View::OnBeginPrinting(CDC* /*pDC*/, CPrintInfo* /*pInfo*/)
```

You need to uncomment the pDC and pInfo parameters because you need to calculate the page size. After you uncomment these parameters, you can start calculating the page size.

To calculate the number of pages that this example spans, you will need to get a couple pieces of information from the device context (DC) of the printer. To retrieve information about a DC, call the GetDeviceCaps() function, and pass it a constant telling it what specific information to return. To get the number of vertical units for the printer (the number of dots from top to bottom), you will pass the VERTRES constant. After you know how many vertical units are on a page, you will need to determine how many vertical units are in an inch (dots per inch). You can retrieve this value by passing the LOGPIXELSY constant.

> **Note**   There are many other constants that you can pass into this function to gather details about a DC, such as PLANES for the number of color planes and NUMCOLORS for the number of entries in the color table. You will learn more about the device context in Chapter 8.

Because the mapping mode was set to MM_LOENGLISH, the unit measurement was set to 1/100 per unit, or 0.01 inches. It's not an accident that the circles drawn on the screen were drawn with a diameter of 100. This makes calculating the number of circles on the page easy.

For this example, to get the page count, you will need to determine the height of one circle. You already know this to be 1 inch. Next, you need to multiply the number of circles drawn by its height, which would be 20 * 1. To get the number of circles per page, you then divide by the height of the page and then add 1 to the result. You now have the value that determines the number of pages used.

Just to have a second example, assume that the diameter of the circle was 75, which would be 0.75 of an inch. Now, assume that there was a small gap after each circle of 30 units, which would be 0.3 of an inch. To get the total height of the circle, the actual height plus the gap, you would add the two values together. This would result in 1.05 inches. You would then multiply this value with the number of circles draw, which is 20. The result would be 21. You then take this result and divide it by the height of the page, then add 1 to that result.

Now you know why it is so important that you know exactly what is in your document. With the page count calculated, you can run the application. After you run the application, go into Print Preview and examine it to see what the new code accomplished. Your screen should look like Figure 7.23.

FIGURE 7.23

Print preview showing both pages filled with circles.

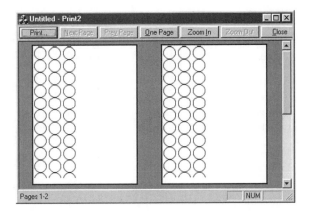

Printing Subsequent Pages Properly

While examining the print preview screen, you will notice that something just doesn't look quite right. In case you didn't notice, the two pages are exactly alike. They both start drawing the circles from the top of the page and continue downward, cutting off some circles at the bottom.

For the subsequent pages to print correctly, you must inform MFC where each new page starts. To do this, you must override the `OnPrepareDC()` function. Just follow these steps to set up the necessary override:

1. Start the ClassWizard.
2. Click the Message Maps tab.
3. Select `CPrint2View` from the Class Name drop-down list.
4. Click the `CPrint2View` Object ID.
5. Scroll down the Messages list and double-click on the `OnPrepareDC` message.
6. Double-click the `OnPrepareDC` member function to bring it up in the code editor.

After you have created the override, modify the code so that it looks like the code in Listing 7.20.

LISTING 7.20   Setting the Page Count

```
void CPrint2View::OnPrepareDC(CDC* pDC, CPrintInfo* pInfo)
{
    // TODO: Add your specialized code here and/or call the base class
    if (pDC->IsPrinting())
    {
        int iHeight = pDC->GetDeviceCaps(VERTRES);
        int iPos    = iHeight * (pInfo->m_nCurPage -1);
        pDC->SetViewportOrg(0, -iPos);
    }

    CView::OnPrepareDC(pDC, pInfo);
}
```

The first thing you want to do is to make sure that a printing process in under way. If it is, you can go ahead and calculate the starting position of each page.

First, start by getting the number of vertical units (dots) for the page. You then multiply this value to the current page, which is represented by a data member in pInfo. So that you get the right position for the current page, you need to subtract 1 from the current page number so that it computes properly when you multiply it by the page height. For example, if you left it at 1 and multiplied it by the height of the page, you would actually begin at page 2. Page 1 starts at position zero (0).

After you calculate the new position, make a call to the SetViewportOrg() function to adjust from where the DC starts drawing. The first parameter adjusts the horizontal offset and the second parameter adjusts the vertical offset. Because you changed the mapping mode to MM_LOENGLISH, you need to use the negative value of the position to move it properly, because the *y* coordinate is now measured in negative numbers when moving down the page.

You can now compile and execute the Print2 example application. After you do, go ahead and go into the print preview. The printed output should now flow properly across the pages, as shown in Figure 7.24.

FIGURE 7.24

Properly printed output, at last.

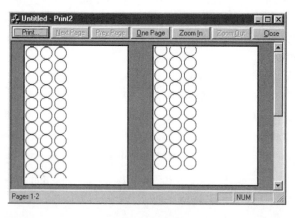

Lesson Summary

As you learned in this chapter, there is a good bit of information that you need to manage when dealing with applications that print multiple pages. You also learned that the CView class has extensive printing capabilities that enable you to easily control the way documents are printed in your application.

The MFC has a specific order in which it executes the printing functions in an application. Each step of the way, you can intervene and modify or change the way the document is printed. The following is a list in order of execution:

- OnPreparePrinting()
- OnBeginPrinting()
- OnPrepareDC()
- OnEndPrinting()

To work with the information about a document, you learned about the CPrintInfo class. You learned how to use the functions and data members of this class to manage multiple page printing. You also learned how to calculate the number of pages that need to be printed along with properly setting the origin so that subsequent pages print properly.

Quiz 5

1. What function of the CPrintInfo class do you call to set the maximum number of pages to print?

    a. SetPageCount()

    b. SetBottomPage()

    c. AdjustPageCount()

    d. SetMaxPage()

2. Which function is the first to be called when a print job is started? This function is called before the document is previewed or printed.

    a. OnPreparePrinting()

    b. BeforePrinting()

    c. OnPrepareDC()

    d. PreparePrinter()

3. What function is called from within the OnPreparePrinting() function?

    a. SetMaxPage()

    b. GetPageCount()

7

    c. `DoPreparePrinting()`

    d. `OnPrepareDC()`

4. What data member of the `CPrintInfo` class returns the current page number?

    a. `m_nCurPage`

    b. `m_CurrentPageNo`

    c. `m_iPagesPrinted`

    d. `m_nNumPrintedPages`

Exercise 5

Complexity: Easy

1. Create an SDI application named "Exercise 1." This application should draw 25 circles down the view. Each circle should be 1/2 inch in diameter. Correct the output so that multiple pages are printed correctly.

Complexity: Moderate

2. Create an MDI application named "Exercise 2." By default, only five circles with 2.5-inch diameters will be drawn. By selecting a menu option named Count from the Edit menu, the user can adjust the number of circles drawn. They will do this by entering in a value into an edit box on a dialog. Limit the value that the user can enter to the range of 1 through 10. Page correction should be accounted for.

Chapter Summary

This chapter outlined the great flexibility of the `CDocument` and `CView` classes. Using these two classes together, you can easily manage your data. With these two classes, you use the same code to display your document as you do to print it, all with very little coding on your part.

You started out by learning how the two classes worked together. You then moved on to using the document class to load and save data. After learning the basic principal of loading and saving data through the `Serialize()` function, you went on to create a persistence class that enabled you to save multiple data items easily.

You learned that printing a single document was very easy to accomplish by using the functionality supplied by the MFC when you generated your program. Printing multiple pages takes a little extra work on your part and you learned how to manage it properly.

CHAPTER 8

Working with Graphics and Sound

Graphics have always been a fundamental aspect of Windows programming. The term *graphics* covers a wide range of topics, from simple text objects to complex animations. Even though it doesn't seem like much, displaying a simple line of text in a window is a form of graphics programming. In order to get that line of text on the display, you must make a call to a graphic function that displays the text.

When programming graphics in the Windows environment, you will use a device context (DC) to display what you need. A *device context* (DC) is a structure that contains information about the drawing attributes of a device, such as the printer or the display. Using the Windows API with a device context, you can easily draw shapes, lines, text, and other graphic objects.

A device context is derived from the CDC class. There are four main DC objects that are derived from the CDC class that you can use:

- CPaintDC—This is the most common DC object that you use while developing Windows applications. This object starts by calling the BeginPaint() function, then drawing the DC, then the EndPaint() function.

- CClientDC—This object encapsulates a DC that represents the client area of a window.

- `CWindowDC`—This object encapsulates a DC that represents the whole window, which includes the frame.

- `CMetaFileDC`—This object encapsulates drawing into a Windows metafile. You will have to call the `OnPrepareDC()` function manually, unlike the `CPaintDC` object.

For all the classes derived from `CDC`, you will use the function members of the `CDC` class to do all drawing. There are member functions for working with drawing tools, GDI objects, palettes, regions, mapping modes, shapes, text, fonts, and many more.

Adding simple graphics is not the only way to enhance your application. You might want to consider adding sound effects to your application. You can add sounds for a variety of reasons, from playing a chime every hour, to playing a message when a new email arrives. In the last lesson of this chapter, you will learn how easy it is to play sound files from within your application.

LESSON 1

Working with Fonts

Back in the days of DOS programming, a programmer didn't have a whole lot of choices for displaying information to users. You were usually stuck with a system-defined generic font and all you could do was change the color or style in which you displayed the text.

For PC programmers, this all changed with the introduction of Windows. It was finally possible for a programmer to enhance the visual appeal of his application by using various styles and sizes along with multiple colors and shapes, making his application much more appealing.

In this lesson, you will learn how to use fonts to enhance your application.

Creating the Fonts Application

To get started with this lesson, you will need to create a basic application, so go ahead and create an SDI application named Fonts using the MFC AppWizard. With this application, you will learn how to change font styles, sizes, colors, and even how to rotate fonts.

Before you can use a different font in your application, you must create a `LOGFONT` structure and fill it in with the settings for your font. Listing 8.1 shows you the `LOGFONT` structure.

LISTING 8.1 The LOGFONT Structure

```
typedef struct tagLOGFONTA
{
    LONG        lfHeight;
    LONG        lfWidth;
    LONG        lfEscapement;
    LONG        lfOrientation;
    LONG        lfWeight;
    BYTE        lfItalic;
    BYTE        lfUnderline;
    BYTE        lfStrikeOut;
    BYTE        lfCharSet;
    BYTE        lfOutPrecision;
    BYTE        lfClipPrecision;
    BYTE        lfQuality;
    BYTE        lfPitchAndFamily;
    CHAR        lfFaceName[LF_FACESIZE];
} LOGFONTA, *PLOGFONTA, NEAR *NPLOGFONTA, FAR *LPLOGFONTA;
typedef LOGFONTA LOGFONT;
```

By looking at this structure, you can see the great flexibility that you have when working with fonts. The following list briefly describes what each field represents:

- lfHeight—The height of the font.
- lfWidth—The width of the font. By setting this to zero, Windows will calculate the width for you.
- lfEscapement—The angle to use for displaying the font. The default is 0, which is horizontal. The angle is measured in 0.1-degree units. So, a value of 900 would be 90 degrees.
- lfOrientation—This field is supposed to affect the angle at which individual characters are printed, but it is not implemented at this time.
- lfWeight—This field determines the font weight, which is also known as bold. The allowable range is 0 through 1000. There are some predefined constants that you can use, and you will read about them when you create the example application for this lesson.
- lfItalic—Setting this value to 1 will turn on italics. A setting of 0 will turn it off.
- lfUnderline—Setting this value to 1 will turn on the underline. A setting of 0 will turn it off.
- lfStrikeout—Setting this value to 1 will turn on the strikeout. A setting of 0 will turn it off.
- lfCharset—This value determines the characters used by the font. You will learn about the constants that you can use for this field when you build the example application for this lesson.

- lfOutPrecision—This value defines how closely the output must match the requested font.
- lfClipPrecision—This value defines how to clip characters that are clipped by the clipping region.
- lfQuality—This value defines the font's output quality.
- lfPitchAndFamily—This value defines the pitch and family of the font.
- lfFaceName—This value is a pointer to a null terminated string that contains the name of the font to use, not to exceed 30 characters.

Now that you know about the LOGFONT structure, you can add the necessary code to your application to create the font that you want to use. Your first step is to declare a variable of the LOGFONT type. Add the following line of code to the Attributes section of the CFontsDoc class:

```
// Attributes
    LOGFONT font;
```

This will declare a variable for the LOGFONT structure. Now, modify the OnNewDocument() function so that it matches Listing 8.2.

LISTING 8.2 Populating the LOGFONT Structure

```
BOOL CFontsDoc::OnNewDocument()
{
    if (!CDocument::OnNewDocument())
        return FALSE;

    // TODO: add reinitialization code here
    // (SDI documents will reuse this document)
    font.lfHeight         = 20;
    font.lfWidth          = 0;
    font.lfEscapement     = 0;
    font.lfOrientation    = 0;
    font.lfWeight         = FW_NORMAL;
    font.lfItalic         = 0;
    font.lfUnderline      = 0;
    font.lfStrikeOut      = 0;
    font.lfCharSet        = ANSI_CHARSET;
    font.lfOutPrecision   = OUT_DEFAULT_PRECIS;
    font.lfClipPrecision  = CLIP_DEFAULT_PRECIS;
    font.lfQuality        = PROOF_QUALITY;
    font.lfPitchAndFamily = VARIABLE_PITCH | FF_SWISS;
    strcpy(font.lfFaceName, "Verdana");

    return TRUE;
}
```

The first thing that you've done was set the font's height to 32. By setting the `lfWidth` field to 0, you are telling Windows to calculate the width of the font. Skipping down to the `lfWeight` field, this is how you tell Windows to display the text. There are several constants that you can use for this field and they are listed in Table 8.1.

TABLE 8.1 `lfWeight` Constants

Constant	Value
FW_DONTCARE	0
FW_THIN	100
FW_EXTRALIGHT	200
FW_ULTRALIGHT	200
FW_LIGHT	300
FW_NORMAL	400
FW_REGULAR	400
FW_MEDIUM	500
FW_SEMIBOLD	600
FW_DEMIBOLD	600
FW_BOLD	700
FW_EXTRABOLD	800
FW_ULTRABOLD	800
FW_BLACK	900
FW_HEAVY	900

Note
Not all fonts support every one of these constants; therefore, these values are approximate values. Some fonts only use FW_NORMAL and FW_BOLD.

At this time, the italic, underline, and strikeout fields are not being used in this example. You will use these fields later in this lesson.

The `lfCharset` field defines the font's character set. Table 8.2 lists the constants that you can use for this field.

TABLE 8.2   lfCharset Constants

Constant	Value
ANSI_CHARSET	0
DEFAULT_CHARSET	1
SYMBOL_CHARSET	2
SHIFTJIS_CHARSET	128
OEM_CHARSET	255

The most common value for this field is ANSI_CHARSET. The DEFAULT_CHARSET constant might seem like the logical choice, but you should stick with the ANSI_CHARSET.

There are a couple of constants associated with the lfOutPrecision field, but in most cases you will use the OUT_DEFAULT_PRECIS constant.

The lfClipPrecision field has a couple constants as well, but you will generally use the CLIP_DEFAULT_PRECIS constant.

The lfQuality determines the output quality. The constants for this field are the following: DEFAULT_QUALITY, which is used when the appearance of the font doesn't matter. DRAFT_QUALITY is used when the appearance is less important than PROOF_QUALITY, which is used when the character quality of the font is more important than the exact matching of the logical font attributes.

The lfPitchAndFamily helps Windows pick a typeface if the requested face isn't available. Depending on your need, you can use VARIABLE_PITCH, DEFAULT_PITCH, or FIXED_PITCH for the pitch. Table 8.3 lists the values that you can use to set the family of the font.

TABLE 8.3   Family Values for lfPitchAndFamily

Constant	Description
FF_DECORATIVE	Novelty fonts
FF_DONTCARE	Let Windows decide
FF_MODERN	Fonts with fixed-width strokes
FF_ROMAN	Fonts with variable-width strokes with serifs
FF_SCRIPT	Fonts designed to look like writing
FF_SWISS	Proportional fonts without serifs

The last field, lfFaceName, declares the name of the font to use. In this example, you are going to use the Verdana font.

After you have the necessary font structure populated, you need to create the font, select it into the DC, draw some text, and then release the font. A good place to do this is in the `CFontsView::OnDraw()` member function. Go ahead and modify your `OnDraw()` function so that it looks like the one listed in Listing 8.3.

LISTING 8.3   Creating the Font in the `OnDraw()` Function

```
void CFontsView::OnDraw(CDC* pDC)
{
    CFontsDoc* pDoc = GetDocument();
    ASSERT_VALID(pDoc);

    // TODO: add draw code for native data here

    CFont* MyFont = new CFont();
    MyFont->CreateFontIndirect(&pDoc->font);
    CFont* OldFont = pDC->SelectObject(MyFont);

    pDC->TextOut(100,100,"Hello Interactive World");

    pDC->SelectObject(OldFont);
    delete MyFont;
}
```

First, create a new font object derived from `CFont`. In this example, the new font object will be named `MyFont`. Now, using the `LOGFONT` structure that you defined in the document's attributes section, call the `CreateFontIndirect()` function. This function takes the `LOGFONT` structure, in this example the font member variable of the document, and tries to create a font matching the values in the structure. If an exact match cannot be created, the `LOGFONT` structure will be populated with the values from the font that is created.

The next step is the important step. When the `SelectObject()` function is called with the new font object, the existing font object is returned. Store this pointer so that you can restore the original font when you are done. This holds true for all graphical objects. You cannot use the objects directly. You must select them into the DC and then use the DC to do your work. The pointer returned is used to restore the DC when you are done.

After you have selected the new font into the DC, you draw text on the view using the new font. In this example, the `TextOut()` function of the DC is used to draw text at pixel location (100,100) with a string stating `"Hello Interactive World"`.

After you display the text that you need with the font you created, you need to select the old font object back into the DC to restore it. After you restore the old font, you need to release the resource that you created when you created the font. The last line of code accomplishes this task.

Note

> In a larger application, you could create your fonts at the beginning of your application and select them into the DC when needed. You would then release the fonts after the application is closed. Creating fonts on-the-fly could slow down your application, but for these small examples, it's not noticeable. The important thing to remember is to release the object before your application terminates.

After you have entered all of the code, you can execute the application. Your output should have the text message "Hello Interactive World" displayed with a 20-point font in the middle of the view, as shown in Figure 8.1.

FIGURE 8.1

The Fonts sample application.

Bold, Underline, Italics, and Strikeout

One of the nice things about working with TrueType fonts is the capability to change the appearance of the font on the screen. By changing some of the values in the LOGFONT structure when defining your font, you can easily change the way the font is displayed to the screen.

To see how easy it is to change the appearance of the font, simply modify the OnNewDocument() member function so that it matches Listing 8.4.

LISTING 8.4   Changing the Font Appearance

```
BOOL CFontsDoc::OnNewDocument()
{
    if (!CDocument::OnNewDocument())
        return FALSE;
```

```
// TODO: add reinitialization code here
// (SDI documents will reuse this document)
font.lfHeight          = 20;
font.lfWidth           = 0;
font.lfEscapement      = 0;
font.lfOrientation     = 0;
font.lfWeight          = FW_BOLD;
font.lfItalic          = 1;
font.lfUnderline       = 1;
font.lfStrikeOut       = 1;
font.lfCharSet         = ANSI_CHARSET;
font.lfOutPrecision    = OUT_DEFAULT_PRECIS;
font.lfClipPrecision   = CLIP_DEFAULT_PRECIS;
font.lfQuality         = PROOF_QUALITY;
font.lfPitchAndFamily  = VARIABLE_PITCH | FF_SWISS;
strcpy(font.lfFaceName, "Verdana");

    return TRUE;
}
```

Notice that the only fields you modified were the `lfWeight`, `lfItalic`, `lfUnderline`, and `lfStrikeOut` fields. The different values for the `lfWeight` field were discussed earlier in this lesson. As for the other three fields, you can toggle each one by changing their values to either 0 for off, or 1 for on. You can go ahead and execute the modified application. Your screen should now look similar to Figure 8.2.

FIGURE 8.2

Bold, underline, italics, and strikethrough.

You don't have to set all the values at the same time. If you only wanted underline on, that would be the only field that you need to set. They were all set in this example just so you could see them all working together.

Rotating Fonts

At first, you might think that there is a lot involved with getting text to display on the screen at an angle. One thing that you should have learned by now is that Windows can be pretty easy to program, and at the same time very hard. However, with fonts, a lot of the hard work is hidden from you. You simply provide the settings and Windows does the rest.

Rotating the font is just as easy as setting the font to underline. Font rotation is controlled by the lfEscapement field. By default, text is drawn at zero degrees, which is straight across the display. By simply changing the value in lfEscapement, you can change the angle in which the text is displayed. Go ahead and change the lfEscapement field in the sample application to match the following line of code:

```
font.lfEscapement    = 150;
```

This small change tells Windows to draw the text at a 15-degree angle. To see this in action, recompile and execute the sample application. Your screen should now look like Figure 8.3.

FIGURE 8.3

Rotating fonts.

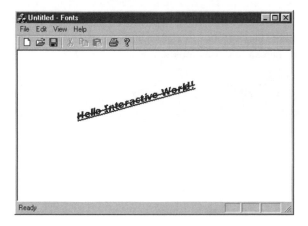

Because the display angle is measured in tenths, you will need to multiply the desired angle by 10. The preceding example displays the text at 15 degrees. Multiplying this value by 10 gives a value of 150 for the lfEscapement field.

Lesson Summary

Working with the device context can be rather simple if you use the proper functions for the tasks that you want to complete. To get used to the device context, you learned how to create fonts and display them on the screen.

You started by creating a font structure and then the font. You then selected the new font into the device context and stored a pointer to the old one. After you displayed the desired message on the screen, you then restored the device context and released the created font.

After learning how to create and use fonts, you learned how simple it is to use some of the advanced options of fonts, such as underlining and rotating.

Quiz 1

1. Which field in the LOGFONT structure would you use to set a font to use bold?

   a. lfBold

   b. lfWidth

   c. lfWeight

   d. lfStyles

2. When selecting a font into the DC with the SelectObject() function, what value is returned?

   a. A pointer to the new font

   b. The size, in pixels, of the font

   c. The handle of the DC

   d. A pointer to the old font

3. What happens when you set the lfWidth property to 0?

   a. Windows determines the width of the font.

   b. The font will be displayed in a fixed font mode.

   c. You cannot set the value of lfWidth to 0.

   d. Windows determines the height of the font.

4. Which statement is true about using fonts?

   a. You can work with the font directly, bypassing the DC.

   b. You can rotate the font.

   c. The font object that you create will automatically be released when you are done with it.

   d. All fonts support all of the weights specified by the constants used for the lfWeight field.

Exercise 1

Complexity: Easy

1. Create an SDI application named "Exercise 1." Using the Times New Roman font with a size of 16, display `Hello Interactive World!` down the left edge of the document.

Complexity: Moderate

2. Create an SDI application named "Exercise 2." Using the Arial font, display `Hello` at location (10,10) with a font size of 20. Second, use the Verdana font to display `Interactive World` at location (10,30) with a font size of 20 as well. Also, this line should be in italics and bold.

LESSON 2

Pens and Brushes

Drawing to the device context is done using pens and brushes. The pen is used to draw the actual shape or line on the view. When drawing shapes, the brush is used to fill in the shape, if desired.

Working with pens and brushes is a lot easier than working with the more complicated objects, such as fonts. With pens and brushes, you don't have to play around with complicated data structures if you don't want to. To create a pen, all you need to do is specify the style, thickness, and color. Brushes can be created using the default shapes provided by the GUI or you can create your own custom brushes from a bitmap, giving you great flexibility.

The goal of this lesson is to teach you how to use pens and brushes to enhance the output of your application.

Creating the PenBrush Application

To get started with this lesson, you will need to create a standard SDI application. Go ahead and create this application and give it a name of PenBrush. You will add the necessary code to this application to display the different line and brush patterns.

After you get the application created, you can get right down to work. Open up the `OnDraw()` function of the view and modify the code so that it looks like the code in Listing 8.5.

LISTING 8.5 The `OnDraw` Function of the PenBrush Application

```cpp
void CPenBrushView::OnDraw(CDC* pDC)
{
    CPenBrushDoc* pDoc = GetDocument();
    ASSERT_VALID(pDoc);

    // TODO: add draw code for native data here
    CPen pen1(PS_SOLID,     1, RGB(0,0,0));
    CPen pen2(PS_DASH,      1, RGB(0,0,0));
    CPen pen3(PS_DOT,       1, RGB(0,0,0));
    CPen pen4(PS_DASHDOT,   1, RGB(0,0,0));
    CPen pen5(PS_DASHDOTDOT, 1, RGB(0,0,0));

    CPen* oldpen = pDC->SelectObject(&pen1);
    pDC->MoveTo( 10,10);
    pDC->LineTo(450,10);

    pDC->SelectObject(&pen2);
    pDC->MoveTo( 10,20);
    pDC->LineTo(450,20);

    pDC->SelectObject(&pen3);
    pDC->MoveTo( 10,30);
    pDC->LineTo(450,30);

    pDC->SelectObject(&pen4);
    pDC->MoveTo( 10,40);
    pDC->LineTo(450,40);

    pDC->SelectObject(&pen5);
    pDC->MoveTo( 10,50);
    pDC->LineTo(450,50);

    pDC->SelectObject(oldpen);

    CBrush brush1(HS_HORIZONTAL, RGB(0,0,0));
    CBrush brush2(HS_VERTICAL,   RGB(0,0,0));
    CBrush brush3(HS_CROSS,      RGB(0,0,0));
    CBrush brush4(HS_FDIAGONAL,  RGB(0,0,0));
    CBrush brush5(HS_BDIAGONAL,  RGB(0,0,0));
    CBrush brush6(HS_DIAGCROSS,  RGB(0,0,0));
    CBrush brush7(RGB(0,0,0));

    CBrush* oldbrush = pDC->SelectObject(&brush1);
    pDC->Rectangle(10,70,450,90);

    pDC->SelectObject(&brush2);
    pDC->Rectangle(10,100,450,120);
```

8

continues

LISTING 8.5   continued

```
pDC->SelectObject(&brush3);
pDC->Rectangle(10,130,450,150);

pDC->SelectObject(&brush4);
pDC->Rectangle(10,160,450,180);

pDC->SelectObject(&brush5);
pDC->Rectangle(10,190,450,210);

pDC->SelectObject(&brush6);
pDC->Rectangle(10,220,450,240);

pDC->SelectObject(&brush7);
pDC->Rectangle(10,250,450,270);

pDC->SelectObject(oldbrush);

}
```

There may be a lot of code here, but it's straightforward. The code is broken down into two major sections. The first section deals with pens and the second section deals with brushes.

 Note   Although this code is straightforward and good for learning purposes, it is inefficient for production applications. For a production application, you should consider creating the pens and brushes at the beginning of your application and releasing them when your application is terminated, freeing up valuable processing time in the OnDraw() function.

Starting off, there are five different pens created, which are derived from the CPen class. Creating a pen is very easy; three parameters are used. The first parameter is used to define what the brush style should look like. The available pen styles are listed below.

- PS_SOLID—A solid pen.
- PS_DASH—A dashed pen. The thickness of this pen can only be set to 1.
- PS_DOT—A dotted pen. The thickness of this pen can only be set to 1.
- PS_DASHDOT—A pen with alternating dashes and dots. The thickness of this pen can only be set to 1.
- PS_DASHDOTDOT—A pen with alternating dashes and double dots. The thickness of this pen can only be set to 1.

8

- PS_NULL—Creates a null pen (invisible).
- PS_INSIDEFRAME—A pen that draws a line inside the frame of GDI shapes, such as rectangles, ellipses, and so on.

The second parameter determines the thickness of the pen. You will notice that some of the pens can only accept a thickness value of 1. If you set the thickness value to anything else, they will be drawn as solid.

The last parameter sets the color of the pen. In the example, the RGB macro is used to calculate the color used. The RGB macro makes it very easy to calculate a color. It takes three parameters, a red intensity, a green intensity, and a blue intensity. In this example, (0,0,0) is used, which is black. Setting the value to (255,0,0) produces a red pen.

Note | The higher intensity a pen is set to, the brighter the color. A value of (0,0,0) represents black and a value of (255,255,255) represents white.

After the pens are created, the next step is to get a pointer to the current pen being used by the DC and selecting in the first pen.

After the first pen is selected into the DC, a call is made to the MoveTo() function which positions the current drawing position. After setting the drawing position, a line is drawn using the LineTo() function. The LineTo() function draws a line from the current drawing position to the coordinates specified in the function call. After the line is drawn, the new drawing position is set to where the end of the line was drawn. When the line is drawn, it will use the pen that is currently selected into the DC. Listing 8.5 shows a series of code blocks that select a pen into the DC, move to a new position, and draw a line. Each section draws a different style line. After all of the lines are drawn, the old pen style is restored into the DC.

Now that different line styles are drawn, it's time to draw the different brushes. Brushes are used to fill in a shape that is drawn to the view. There are several different predefined brush styles from which you can choose. When defining a brush style to use, two parameters are used. The first parameter is used to tell the style of the brush. The following list briefly describes each predefined brush style.

- HS_HORIZONTAL—Horizontal hash
- HS_VERTICAL—Vertical hash
- HS_CROSS—Horizontal and vertical crosshatch
- HS_FDIAGNOL—A 45-degree, from left to right, upward hash

- `HS_BDIAGNOL`—A 45 degree, from left to right, downward hash
- `HS_DIAGCROSS`—Crosshatch at 45 degrees

The second parameter defines the brush color, just as the color of a pen was defined. You might have noticed that there are seven brushes in the example application and only six styles listed. Looking at the seventh brush, you will notice that it has only passed one parameter, the color parameter. If you omit the style parameter, the brush created is a solid brush.

After the brushes are created, the next step is to get a pointer to the current brush being used by the DC and selecting in the first brush.

After the first brush is selected into the DC, a rectangle is drawn using the `Rectangle()` function. This function has four parameters. These parameters specify the bounding area to be drawn. The first two parameters specify the top-left corner and the last two parameters specify the bottom-right corner of the rectangle. Looking at Listing 8.5, you will notice that there is a series of code blocks that select a brush into the DC and draw a rectangle. Each section draws a different style rectangle.

After all of the rectangles are drawn, the old brush style is restored to the DC. At this time, you compile and execute the example application. When you do, your screen should look like Figure 8.4.

Figure 8.4

The PenBrush application.

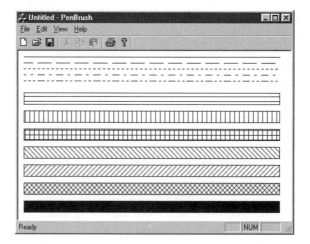

Creating Your Own Patterns

Even though there is a good selection of patterns to use for filling in shapes, you might have the need to create your own. Creating your own pattern is rather easy, but there are a couple things that you need know before creating a pattern:

- The size of your pattern can only be 8×8 pixels.
- The patterns are created from a bitmap, which will usually be stored as a resource, a bitmap, or as an icon.
- If your bitmap is larger than 8×8 pixels, only the top-left 8×8 of the bitmap will be used as the pattern.

 Note

> The 8×8 pixel restriction only applies to Windows 95, not Windows NT.

Now that you know the rules for creating a pattern, it's time to add one to the example program that you have worked on in this lesson.

The first thing that you will need to do is create the bitmap patterns. For your convenience, a simple bitmap has been supplied and is in the RES directory for this example program on the CD that is provided with this book. You can load this bitmap into a resource or create a new one, just as long as you have an 8×8 bitmap to use for the example.

After you create the bitmap resource, which should be named IDB_BITMAP1, you can add the necessary code to create the patterned brush. Towards the bottom of the OnDraw() function, change the code so that it looks like the code listed in Listing 8.6. Notice that this isn't a complete listing of the OnDraw() function, just the bottom portion that has changed.

LISTING 8.6   The OnDraw Function of the PenBrush Application

```
pDC->SelectObject(&brush7);
pDC->Rectangle(10,250,450,270);

CBitmap* checker;
checker = new CBitmap;
checker->LoadBitmap(IDB_BITMAP1);

CBrush brush8(checker);

pDC->SelectObject(&brush8);
pDC->Rectangle(460,10,480,270);

pDC->SelectObject(oldbrush);
delete checker;

}
```

The first two lines already exist; they are just here for alignment. The important code comes next.

The first thing you created was a `CBitmap` object named checker. After creating the bitmap, you called the `LoadBitmap()` function with the ID of the bitmap that you created. After the bitmap is loaded, you created a brush that uses a bitmap for a pattern by passing the checker `CBitmap` as the parameter when you created `brush8`.

To use the new checkered pattern, you selected the brush into the DC. You then drew a rectangle down the right side of the screen by calling the `Rectangle()` function. After you were done with the checkered pattern, you selected the old brush into the DC and then released the checkered `CBitmap` that you created.

Now, if you were to execute the application, your screen would look similar to Figure 8.5.

FIGURE 8.5

The PenBrush application with the checker pattern.

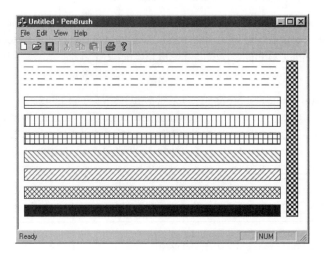

Lesson Summary

In this lesson, you learned how to create pens and brushes and how to use them together to create various styles of presenting lines and filled rectangles on the view. You also learned how to create and use a bitmap as the pattern for your brush for those instances when the available brushes just don't give you the look that you want.

Quiz 2

1. Which of the following is not a valid pen style?

    a. `PS_DASH`

    b. `PS_DOTDOT`

c. PS_NULL

d. PS_SOLID

2. If you wanted an invisible line, which pen style would you use?

    a. PS_CLEAR

    b. PS_INVISIBLE

    c. PS_NONE

    d. PS_NULL

3. Which statement is not true about brushes?

    a. You can create a brush pattern from a bitmap.

    b. You can create a brush pattern from an icon.

    c. Brush patterns can only be 16×16 pixels.

    d. Brush patterns are used to fill in shapes.

4. Which of the following is not a valid brush style?

    a. HS_VERTICAL

    b. HS_LEFTRIGHT

    c. HS_FDIAGNOL

    d. HS_CROSS

Exercise 2

Complexity: Easy

1. Create an SDI application named "Exercise 1." In this application, draw three different lines across the document. Each line drawn should use a different pen style. For each line you draw, use a different color.

Complexity: Moderate

2. Create an SDI application named "Exercise 2." Using a custom bitmap, build your own pattern and draw a rectangle to the document using your new pattern. You can create whatever pattern you want. The rectangle should have a bounding rectangle of (10,10) to (100,100).

LESSON 3

Drawing Shapes

The CDC class provides a magnitude of drawing functions to make drawing shapes a lot easier for you. It used to be that if a programmer wanted to draw a circle on the screen, he or she had to actually calculate the circle, pixel-by-pixel. But that wasn't the hardest part; the programmer also had to write code to fill in the circle with a color. By using the DC's functions, you can accomplish these drawing feats with very little code.

The goal of this lesson is to teach you how to use some of the more common shape functions so that you can use them in your applications.

The Different Drawing Functions of the CDC Class

With all the different functions available to choose from when drawing onto the DC, it is a lot easier to look at the different functions by a group classification. Tables 8.4, 8.5, and 8.6 outline the more common drawing functions by their functionality groups.

TABLE 8.4 The Line Output Functions of the CDC Class

Function	Description
AngleArc	Draws a line segment and an arc. The drawing position is updated to the end position of the arc.
Arc	Draws an arc.
ArcTo	Draws an arc and updates the drawing position.
GetArcDirection	Returns the current arc direction.
GetCurrentPosition	Returns the current logical position of the pen.
LineTo	Draws a line from the current position to a new position.
MoveTo	Moves the pen position to a new location.
PolyLine	Draws a set of line segments connecting the specified points.
PolyLineTo	Draws one or more straight lines and updates the pen position.
SetArcDirection	Sets the drawing direction for arc and rectangle functions.

TABLE 8.5   Simple Drawing Functions

Function	Description
Draw3DRect	Draws a three-dimensional rectangle.
DrawDragRect	Erases and draws a rectangle as it is being dragged.
DrawEdge	Draws the edges of a rectangle.
DrawFrameControl	Draws a frame control onto the DC.
DrawIcon	Draws an icon onto the DC.
FillRect	Draws a filled rectangle using a specified brush.
FillSolidRect	Draws a solid rectangle with a specific color.
FrameRect	Draws a border around a rectangle.
InvertRect	Inverts the contents of a rectangle.

TABLE 8.6   Ellipse and Polygon Functions

Function	Description
Chord	Draws a chord.
Ellipse	Draws an ellipse.
Pie	Draws a pie shape.
Polygon	Draws a polygon consisting of two or more points.
Rectangle	Draws a rectangle. The rectangle is drawn with the current pen and is filled with the current brush.
RoundRect	Just like the rectangle except that the corners are rounded off.

Tables 8.4, 8.5, and 8.6 give you an idea of the great flexibility the DC offers you for drawing shapes. These tables are not a complete list of the functions available for you to use but they are the most commonly used ones.

Creating the Shapes Application

To get started with this lesson, you will need to create a standard SDI application. Go ahead and create this application and give it a name of Shapes. You will add the necessary code throughout this lesson to draw different shapes on the view. This application is going to use the toolbar that changes the shape drawn on the view.

To keep track of the shape being drawn, you need to add a member variable to the document. Add the following line of code to the Attributes section of the document:

```
// Attributes
public:
    int shape;
```

To draw the different shapes for this application, you need to modify the toolbar so that you can click an icon and change the shape drawn. If you look at the toolbar in Figure 8.6, you will notice that six icons were added. The first four are normal shapes, representing a box, a circle, a line, and a pie shape. The next two icons draw a filled box and a filled ellipse.

FIGURE 8.6

The modified toolbar for Shapes.

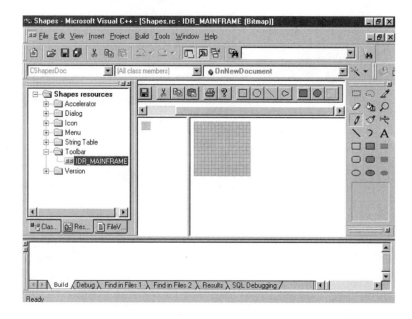

After you have drawn the icons, you can give them an ID that better represents what each one does. Use Table 8.7 to give each of the icons their IDs.

TABLE 8.7   Toolbar Icon IDs

Icon	ID
Square	ID_DRAW_SQUARE
Ellipse	ID_DRAW_ELLIPSE
Line	ID_DRAW_LINES
Pie	ID_DRAW_PIE
Filled Square	ID_FILLED_BOX
Filled Ellipse	ID_FILLED_ELLIPSE

8

After you have renamed all the IDs, you need to create the necessary message handlers. When you go to create the message handlers, make sure the Class name for the handler is set to CShapesDoc.

After all six message handlers are set up, you need to add code to each of the handlers to update the shape drawn. Using Listing 8.7, modify each of the functions.

LISTING 8.7   The Icon Message Handler Functions

```
// CShapesDoc commands

void CShapesDoc::OnDrawSquare()
{
    // TODO: Add your command handler code here
    shape = 1;
    UpdateAllViews(NULL,0,NULL);
}

void CShapesDoc::OnDrawEllipse()
{
    // TODO: Add your command handler code here
    shape = 2;
    UpdateAllViews(NULL,0,NULL);
}

void CShapesDoc::OnDrawLines()
{
    // TODO: Add your command handler code here
    shape = 3;
    UpdateAllViews(NULL,0,NULL);
}

void CShapesDoc::OnDrawPie()
{
    // TODO: Add your command handler code here
    shape = 4;
    UpdateAllViews(NULL,0,NULL);
}

void CShapesDoc::OnFilledBox()
{
    // TODO: Add your command handler code here
    shape = 5;
    UpdateAllViews(NULL,0,NULL);
}

void CShapesDoc::OnFilledCircle()
{
    // TODO: Add your command handler code here
    shape = 6;
    UpdateAllViews(NULL,0,NULL);
}
```

Each message handler is pretty much identical. The only difference for each handler is the value assigned to the shape member variable. The call to the UpdateAllViews() function tells the view that it needs to redraw its contents. You will need to do this if you want to see the changes when you click on one of the icons.

With all of the icons in place, you need to add the code to actually draw the desired shapes. This is accomplished in the OnDraw() function of the view. Go ahead and modify the OnDraw() function so that it looks like Listing 8.8.

LISTING 8.8   Drawing the Shapes in the OnDraw Function

```
void CShapesView::OnDraw(CDC* pDC)
{
    CShapesDoc* pDoc = GetDocument();
    ASSERT_VALID(pDoc);

    // TODO: add draw code for native data here
    switch (pDoc->shape)
    {
        case 1: //Rectangle
            pDC->Rectangle(10,10,400,250);
            break;
        case 2: //Ellipse
            pDC->Ellipse(10,10,400,250);
            break;
        case 3: //Lines
            pDC->MoveTo(10,10);
            pDC->LineTo(400,250);
            pDC->MoveTo(400,10);
            pDC->LineTo(10,250);
            break;
        case 4: //Arch
            pDC->Pie(10,10,400,250,10,10,10,250);
            break;
        case 5: //Filled Box
            pDC->FillSolidRect(10,10,400,250,RGB(255,0,0));
            break;
        case 6: //Filled Circle
            CBrush brush(RGB(255,0,0));
            CBrush* oldbrush = pDC->SelectObject(&brush);
            pDC->Ellipse(10,10,400,250);
            pDC->SelectObject(&oldbrush);
            break;
    }
}
```

The code used to determine which shape to draw is pretty straightforward. A switch statement is used to determine the value of the shapes variable. Depending on its value, the appropriate block of code is executed.

When the value is 1, a rectangle is drawn to the screen. The `Rectangle()` function requires four parameters. The first two parameters specify the top-left corner of the rectangle, and the last two parameters specify the bottom-right corner.

When the value is 2, an ellipse is drawn. An ellipse can be used to draw circles and ovals. The `Ellipse()` function requires four parameters as well. Just like the rectangle, the first two parameters define the top-left corner of the bounding area and the last two parameters specify the bottom right of the bounding area. Even though you put in coordinates like you would for a rectangle, the ellipse will be rounded, and its size will be determined by the values you enter.

When the value is 3, two lines are drawn. Before drawing a line, you need to set the starting position of the line. This is accomplished by the `MoveTo()` function. The `MoveTo()` function accepts two parameters, which is a pair of coordinates. After moving to the desired starting location, the `DrawTo()` function is used to draw the line. The two parameters passed to this function specify the ending point to draw the line to. After the line is drawn, the position is updated to the end-point of the line. After the first line is drawn, the starting position is repositioned and a second line is drawn. When these two lines are drawn on the view, they will form an X pattern.

When the value is 4, a pie shape is drawn by using the `Pie()` function. The `Pie()` function requires six parameters. The first two parameters specify the top-left portion of the bounding rectangle. The next two parameters specify the bottom-right portion of the bounding rectangle. The next two parameters specify the arc's starting point and the last two parameters specify the arc's ending point. The arc points do not have to lie exactly on the arc.

When the value is 5, a solid rectangle is drawn on the screen by calling the `FillSolidRect()` function. This function requires five parameters. The first four parameters specify the bounding edges for the rectangle, and the last parameter specifies the color to use when filling the rectangle.

When the value is 6, a filled ellipse is drawn. Looking at Listing 8.7, you will notice that there is a little bit of extra code in this section. In order to draw the filled ellipse, you need to change the brush style. For this example, a solid brush with a red color was created. With the brush created, a normal call to the `Ellipse()` function draws a filled ellipse.

When you first run the application, your screen will look like Figure 8.7, which has a rectangle drawn on the view. If you were to click the filled ellipse icon, your screen would look like Figure 8.8.

FIGURE 8.7

The rectangle shape.

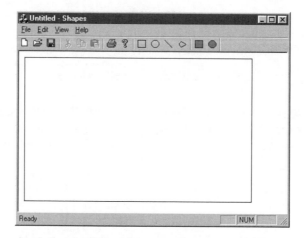

FIGURE 8.8

The filled ellipse shape.

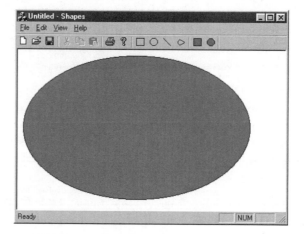

Lesson Summary

It is very easy to see that the CDC class provides you with enough capabilities to draw just about any type of shape that you need. By building the example program, you learned that it can be very easy to draw many different shapes on the view.

Quiz 3

1. Which function is not a valid shape function of the CDC class?

    a. Pie()

    b. Rectangle()

8

c. Chart()

d. Ellipse()

2. Which function is used to draw a rectangle filled with a specific color, not with a brush?

   a. FillRect()

   b. FillSolidRect()

   c. Rectangle()

   d. ColorRect()

3. What is the purpose of the MoveTo() function?

   a. To move the pen position to a new location

   b. To move the position of a line

   c. To set the starting position of a rectangle

   d. To draw a line to a specific location

4. To draw a solid shape, such as an ellipse, what must you do to make the shape solid?

   a. Call the SetSolidFill() function.

   b. Call the FillShape() function.

   c. Create a solid brush and select it into the DC.

   d. Specify the brush to use as one of the parameters when calling the function to draw the ellipse.

Exercise 3

Complexity: Easy

1. Create an SDI application named "Exercise 1." In this application, draw two rectangles and an ellipse anywhere on the document. Each shape should use a unique-colored brush style.

Complexity: Moderate

2. Create an SDI application named "Exercise 2." In this application, you are going to build the infamous smiley face. Draw a yellow ellipse so that it forms a circle, then draw two smaller black ellipses to create the eyes. Then draw an arc for the mouth.

LESSON 4

Displaying Bitmaps

One of the most powerful graphic objects for Windows is a bitmap. Bitmaps are used to display graphical images in a view. You can use bitmaps for many different reasons. In business applications, such as database applications, bitmaps can be used to display a picture of a product or pictures of employees working at your company.

There are many different approaches to working with bitmaps, but if all you need to do is display a simple bitmap on this DC, you can use the general bitmap functions in the CDC class. In this lesson, you will learn what it takes to display a bitmap on the DC and then how to display a bitmap and stretch it at the same time.

The Bitmap Functions of the CDC Class

When working with bitmaps, the CDC provides several useful functions for manipulating and displaying the bitmaps onto the DC. Table 8.8 lists the CDC bitmap functions.

TABLE 8.8 The CDC Bitmap Functions

Function	Description
BitBlt	Copies a bitmap from a device context to a specified location.
ExtFloodFill	Fills an area with the current brush and provides more flexibility than the normal FloodFill function.
FloodFill	Fills an area with the current brush.
GetPixel	Returns an RGB value of a specified pixel.
MaskBlt	Combines the color data for the source and destination bitmaps using a mask and the specified raster operations.
PatBlt	Creates a bit pattern.
SetPixel	Changes the specified pixel to an RGB value. This function returns the color value of the pixel before the change.
SetPixelV	Changes the specified pixel to an RBG value. This function is faster than the SetPixel function, because it doesn't return the previous pixel color value.
StretchBlt	Copies a bitmap from a source bitmap onto the current bitmap. This function will either shrink or enlarge the bitmap to fill the specified destination rectangle.

Creating the Bitmaps Application

To get started with this lesson, you need to create a standard SDI application. Go ahead and create this application and give it a name of Bitmaps. Throughout this lesson, you will add code to the program to learn how to manage and manipulate bitmaps.

After a generic application is created, the next step is to insert a bitmap into the resources to use for this example program. If you don't have a little bitmap handy, you can use the one in the bitmap named bezone.bmp in the RES directory on the CD for this project. You can easily create a bitmap resource by using the Import feature. Just browse to where your bitmap is located and import it. If you imported the eZone logo, your screen should look like Figure 8.9. By looking at the Workspace panel in Figure 8.9, you will notice that the resource was renamed to better reflect the name of the bitmap. Go ahead and do so yourself.

FIGURE 8.9

The eZone bitmap as a resource.

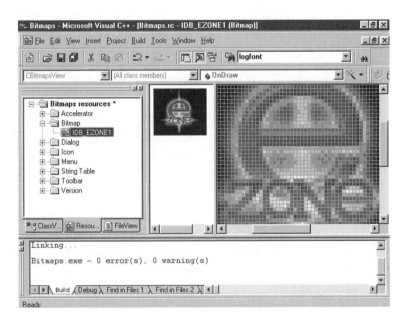

With the bitmap stored as a resource, it's time to add the necessary code to display the bitmap. As you should well know by now, you will display your output from the OnDraw() function of the view class. Go ahead and bring this function into the code editor and modify it so that the code matches the code in Listing 8.9.

LISTING 8.9   The Code to Display a Bitmap

```
void CBitmapsView::OnDraw(CDC* pDC)
{
    CBitmapsDoc* pDoc = GetDocument();
    ASSERT_VALID(pDoc);

    // TODO: add draw code for native data here
    CBitmap* eZone;
    eZone = new CBitmap;
    eZone->LoadBitmap(IDB_EZONE1);

    CDC myDC;
    myDC.CreateCompatibleDC(pDC);
    CBitmap* oldbitmap = myDC.SelectObject(eZone);
    pDC->BitBlt(0,0,90,78,&myDC, 0,0, SRCCOPY);
    myDC.SelectObject(oldbitmap);

    delete eZone;
}
```

To display the bitmap that you created as a resource, you will need to create a CBitmap object to hold the actual bitmap image. After constructing the CBitmap object, make a call to the LoadBitmap() function. This function initializes the newly created CBitmap object and copies in the bitmap image from the resource, all in one easy step.

The following code shows the declaration for the BltBit() function.

```
BOOL BitBlt( int x, int y, int nWidth, int nHeight, CDC* pSrcDC,
➥int xSrc, int ySrc, DWORD dwRop );
```

The BltBit() function requires several parameters. The parameter in which you are interested at this point is the pSrcDC parameter. You will look at the other parameters when you actually do the blitting (bit block transfer), but for now, you need to work on satisfying the requirement for this one.

The pSrcDC parameter requires that you pass along the DC for the source bitmap that you will be blitting to the DC of the current view. To send a valid value for this parameter, you need to create a DC for the new bitmap manually. The CDC class has a function just for this reason.

To create a DC manually, you will need to create a variable of type CDC. After declaring the variable, you need to call the constructor of that variable. There are several ways to create a DC manually, but the easiest way is to create a DC that is directly compatible with the current DC. This is easily accomplished by calling the CreateCompatibleDC() constructor. By passing in the current DC as the parameter for this constructor, you will create a DC that is device-compatible with the DC that you need.

After creating the DC, you need to select the bitmap into the DC. This is accomplished by using the SelectObject() function, passing in the new bitmap and storing the old.

After you have the new bitmap selected into the new DC, you can use the BitBlt() function to copy it. As discussed a few minutes ago, the BitBlt() function has several parameters. Table 8.9 lists these parameters and gives you a brief description.

TABLE 8.9 The BitBlt() Function Parameters

Parameter	Description
x	The left edge of the destination area.
y	The top edge of the destination area.
nWidth	The width of the destination area. If this value is less than the actual width of the source bitmap, the destination area will clip the results to this specified width.
nHeight	The height of the destination area. If this value is less than the actual height of the source bitmap, the destination area will clip the results to this specified height.
pSrcDC	This is a pointer to the source device context. You just created this pointer. Without this pointer, the current DC wouldn't know from where to copy the bitmap.
xSrc	The left edge of the source bitmap. By adjusting this value along with the width of the destination area, you can copy a portion of a bitmap rather than the whole image.
ySrc	The top edge of the source bitmap. By adjusting this value along with the height of the destination area, you can copy a portion of a bitmap rather than the whole image.
dwRop	This parameter specifies how the bitmap is to be copied into the DC. By changing the value of this parameter with the defined constants, you can change the way the bitmap appears while it is being copied into the display. Table 8.10 lists the common raster operation constants that you can choose from.

TABLE 8.10 Raster Operation Constants

Constant	Description
BLACKNESS	All output is turned to black.
DSTINVERT	Destination bitmap is inverted.
MERGECOPY	Combines the current pattern and the source bitmap. The AND operator is used for this operation.

continues

TABLE 8.10 continued

Constant	Description
MERGEPAINT	Combines the inverted source bitmap with the destination bitmap. The OR operator is used for this operation.
NOTSRCCOPY	Copies the inverted source bitmap to the destination.
NOTSRCERASE	Inverts the result of combining the destination and source bitmaps. The OR operator is used for this operation.
PATCOPY	Copies the current pattern to the destination bitmap.
PATINVERT	Combines the destination bitmap with the current pattern using the XOR operator.
PATPAINT	Combines the inverted source bitmap with the current pattern using the OR operator. Combines the result of this operation with the destination bitmap using the OR operator.
SRCAND	Combines the destination and source bitmaps using the AND operator.
SRCCOPY	Copies the source bitmap directly to the destination bitmap.
SRCERASE	Inverts the destination bitmap and combines the result with the source bitmap using the AND operator.
SRCINVERT	Combines the destination bitmap and the source bitmap using the XOR operator.
SRCPAINT	Combines the destination bitmap and the source bitmap using the OR operator.
WHITENESS	All output is turned white.

As you can tell by looking at Listing 8.8, you will be copying the eZone logo to the screen with a direct copy.

After you code the BitBlt() function, all that is left is the little bit of cleanup work. After releasing the bitmap by selecting in the original bitmap, the DC that you created is freed.

At this point, you can actually execute the application to see what the output looks like. Once you execute the application, your screen should look like Figure 8.10.

FIGURE 8.10

The Bitmaps application shows the eZone logo.

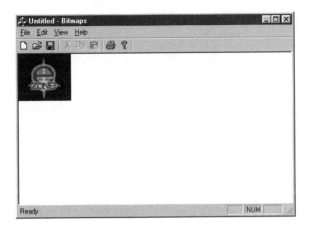

One of the other nice bitmap functions of the CDC class is the StretchBlt() function. This function operates much like the BitBlt() function except that it can resize the bitmap as it is being copied into the current DC. The following is the declaration for the StretchBlt() function:

```
BOOL StretchBlt( int x, int y, int nWidth, int nHeight,
➥CDC* pSrcDC, int xSrc, int ySrc, int nSrcWidth,
➥int nSrcHeight, DWORD dwRop );
```

As you can tell by looking at this declaration, it has several extra parameters. Table 8.11 describes each of the parameters for this function.

TABLE 8.11 The StretchBlt() Function Parameters

Parameter	Description
x	The left edge of the destination area.
y	The top edge of the destination area.
nWidth	The width of the destination area. If this value is less than the actual width of the source bitmap, the destination area will clip the results to this specified width.
nHeight	The height of the destination area. If this value is less than the actual height of the source bitmap, the destination area will clip the results to this specified height.
pSrcDC	This is a pointer to the source device context.
xSrc	The left edge of the source bitmap. By adjusting this value along with the width of the destination area, you can copy a portion of a bitmap rather than the whole image.

continues

TABLE 8.11   continued

Parameter	Description
ySrc	The top edge of the source bitmap. By adjusting this value along with the height of the destination area, you can copy a portion of a bitmap rather than the whole image.
nSrcWidth	The width of the source bitmap to be copied.
nSrcHeight	The height of the source bitmap to be copied.
dwRop	This parameter specifies how the bitmap is copied into the DC. By changing the value of this parameter with the defined constants, you can change the way the bitmap appears while it is being copied into the display. Table 8.10 (earlier in the chapter) lists the common raster operation constants that you can choose from.

To draw a stretched bitmap to the view, go ahead and add this line of code after the BitBlt() line:

```
pDC->StretchBlt(100,0,180,156, &myDC, 0,0,90,78,SRCCOPY);
```

This line of code copies the bitmap to pixel location (100,0). The resulting width and height of the blit is 180×156 pixels. After adding this line of code and executing the application, your screen will look like Figure 8.11.

FIGURE 8.11

Stretching bitmaps.

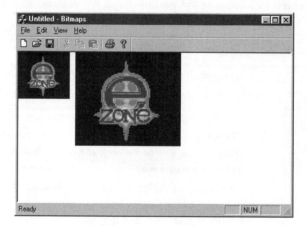

Lesson Summary

By using the CDC bitmap functions, you learned how easy it is to display bitmaps to a device context. By displaying a bitmap on the DC, you learned how to manually create a DC.

The functions that you used in the example program are the two most common functions used for drawing bitmaps. With these two functions, you can easily copy a portion of a bitmap, or even the entire bitmap, to a DC. While copying the bitmap, you can choose from several raster operations that create different results as the bitmaps are copied. By using the StretchBlt() function, not only can you copy a bitmap to the DC, you can resize it in the process.

Quiz 4

1. What MFC structure is used to manage a bitmap?

   a. CMFCBitmap

   b. CBitBlt

   c. CView

   d. CBitmap

2. What parameter of the BitBlt() function determines how the bitmap is copied to the DC?

   a. dwRop

   b. dwRasterOp

   c. dwDestStyle

   d. BLACKNESS

3. Which statement is true when copying a bitmap to a DC?

   a. You must call the BitBlt() function to create the bitmap object.

   b. You can only copy an entire bitmap, not just a portion.

   c. The source bitmap must be selected into the destination DC by using the SelectBitmap() function.

   d. In order to use the BitBlt() function to copy a bitmap, you must create a DC for the source bitmap.

4. Which raster operation is used to make a direct copy of the source bitmap?

   a. SRCCOPY

   b. DIRECTCOPY

   c. SOURCECOPY

   d. SRCERASE

Exercise 4

Complexity: Easy

1. Create an SDI application named "Exercise 1." This application should draw a bitmap from a resource to the current display context. When drawing the bitmap to the DC, it should be stretched to fit within a bounding rectangle of (0,0) to (380,380).

Complexity: Moderate

2. Create an SDI application named "Exercise 2." This application should draw a bitmap from a resource to location (0,0) without stretching the bitmap. Draw the bitmap a second time to location (50,50), but this time use one of the raster operations to change the way the bitmap is drawn to the DC.

LESSON 5

Adding Audio to Your Application

Using graphics in your application is a good way to enhance the cosmetic portion of your application; however, pretty pictures and words might not be enough. For example, you might want to inform the user that a task has completed by sounding an audible alarm.

Of course there are many different reasons why you might want to add an audio clip to your application; therefore, in this lesson, you will build a small application that will easily enable you to play the most common type of audio files, those .WAV files.

Building the PlayWavs Application

To play a .WAV file, you need to build a dialog-based application. This application is going to enable you to select a .WAV file from your hard drive and then, by pressing a button on the dialog box, the sound will magically begin to play. Well, it's not really magic; you will have to add a little bit of code to make it work. So, to get started with this application, go ahead and use the MFC AppWizard to create a dialog-based application named PlayWavs.

After you have created the dialog box, add some controls. Using Figure 8.12 as a guide, add the following controls:

- An edit box control—Used to enter the name of the .WAV file to play.
- A button control—Used to locate a .WAV file by browsing around your hard drive.

- A button control—Used to start the sound when one is selected.
- A button control—Used to stop a sound that is playing.
- A check box control—Used to determine whether looping should be used when playing the sound.

FIGURE 8.12

Aligning the controls for PlayWavs.

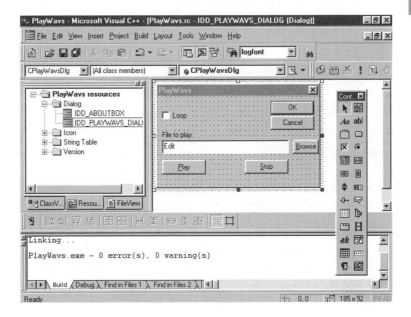

After you have all the necessary controls on the dialog box, you can use Table 8.12 as a guide to setting the properties.

TABLE 8.12 The Control Properties for PlayWav

Control	Property	Value
ID_STATIC	Caption	File to play:
IDC_BUTTON1	Caption	&Browse
IDC_BUTTON2	Caption	&Play
IDC_BUTTON3	Caption	&Stop
IDC_CHECK1	Caption	Loop

I'm sure you could have done without the last table, but when you add the member variables and message handlers, it's nice to make sure that the right block of code will be executed. After all, you wouldn't want the Stop button calling the OnButton1 message handler, would you?

Speaking of member variables and message handlers, you need to create these now. Go ahead and bring up the Class Wizard. Add the three necessary message handlers for each of the three button IDs. If you are unsure how to do this, you can always refer back to Chapter 5, "Processing Windows Messages and Commands."

After you have set the three message handlers up, you need to create the member variables for each of the controls. Using Table 8.13 as a guide, create the necessary member variables.

TABLE 8.13   The Member Variables for the PlayWav Controls

ID	Type	Member
IDC_BUTTON1	CButton	m_browse
IDC_BUTTON2	CButton	m_play
IDC_BUTTON3	CButton	m_Stop
IDC_CHECK1	CButton	m_looping
IDC_EDIT1	CEdit	m_wav_name

After you have created all of the necessary member variables, you can add the code for the message handlers. The first handler which you will add the necessary code is the Browse button. Using Listing 8.10 as a guide, modify the message handler, which is the OnButton1() function.

LISTING 8.10   The Code for the Browse Feature of PlayWav

```
void CPlayWavsDlg::OnButton1()
{
    //http://nic2000.com/james/_vbtips/00000015.htm

    // TODO: Add your control notification handler code here

    CFileDialog openwav(TRUE, ".WAV", "*.WAV",0,"*.WAV",    NULL);
    if (openwav.DoModal() == TRUE)
    {
        m_wav_name.SetWindowText(openwav.GetPathName());
    };
}
```

The first part of the browse feature is pretty simple. A CFileDialog is constructed with the necessary parameters to specify that you want to look for .WAV files. The dialog box is then shown in the modal state. If the user selects a valid .WAV file, the complete path of the file will be copied into the edit box.

If you were to execute the application at this time and clicked the Browse button, your screen would look like Figure 8.13. While you have the file dialog open, notice that the specified file type that you are browsing for is a .WAV file because this is what you specified in the dialog constructor. I'm pretty sure you don't want to browse for other types of files, such as text files, when you want to listen to some audio files.

FIGURE 8.13

Browsing for .WAV
files.

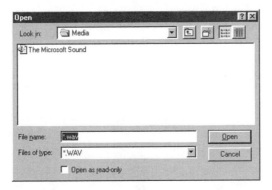

Now that the browsing feature is implemented, you can add the necessary code to play the selected .WAV file. To do this, you will need to modify the OnButton2() message handler function. Go ahead and modify your function so that it matches Listing 8.11.

LISTING 8.11   The Code That Actually Plays the .WAV File

```
void CPlayWavsDlg::OnButton2()
{
    // TODO: Add your control notification handler code here
    CString filename;
    UINT fuSound;

    if (m_looping.GetCheck() == 1)
        fuSound = SND_ASYNC ¦ SND_LOOP;
    else
        fuSound = SND_ASYNC;

    m_wav_name.GetWindowText(filename);
    if (sndPlaySound(filename, fuSound) == FALSE)
        AfxMessageBox("Error");
}
```

Before you play the sound file, you need to make sure that you account for the looping option so you will want to check the status of the check box to see if the user selected it or not. The state of the check box will determine how the sound is played. The fuSound variable inside the if statement is used to build up the selected options.

Before going any further with discussing the code, we will discuss the sndPlaySound()
function that is being used. The following line of code is the declaration for this function:

```
BOOL sndPlaySound(LPCSTR lpszSound, UINT fuSound);
```

This is a multimedia command that enables you to easily play standard .WAV files. This
function requires two parameters. The first parameter, lpszSound, specifies the filename
of the .WAV file to play and the second parameter, fuSound, is used to pass along the
specified flags on how to play the sound. Table 8.14 lists the available flag constants for
the fuSound parameter.

TABLE 8.14   Valid Values for fuSound

Value	Description
SND_ASYNC	Plays the sound asynchronously. Does not wait for the sound to stop playing before giving control back to your application.
SND_LOOP	Plays the loop continuously.
SND_MEMORY	Indicates that the lpszSound parameter points to a waveform in memory.
SND_NODEFAULT	If the specified sound is not found, no sound is to be played.
SND_NOSTOP	If a sound is already playing, do not play this sound.
SND_SYNC	Plays the sound synchronously. The sound will play all the way through before returning control back to your application.

Note   If the sound specified is not found and the SND_NODEFAULT flag is not used,
the system default sound will be played (if it is available). If it is not, the
function will return with a value of FALSE.

Now that you know what the parameters are for the sndPlaySound() function, you can
examine the rest of the code.

Note   For a .WAV to be played with the sndPlaySound() function, the whole sound
file must fit into physical memory.

Before the sndPlaySound() function is called, the current text in the edit box is copied
into a CString variable that will be passed into the sndPlaySound() function. Next
comes the actual call to the sndPlaySound() function. Depending on the value of
m_looping, the sound will either be played with or without looping. Notice that the

SND_ASYNC option was used on both options. This was done so that the application wouldn't hang around waiting for the sound to quit playing. Can you imagine what would happen if you played the sound synchronously with looping?

 Note If you are using the SND_ASYNC option when playing sounds, when you make a call to the sndPlaySound() function with a new sound to play and a sound is currently playing, you will stop the first sound because you can only play one sound at a time. If you have the SND_NOSTOP option specified, the sound will not be interrupted.

Now that you have the necessary code in place to play the actual .WAV file, you will need to add the necessary code to stop the sound. Using Listing 8.12 as a guide, go ahead and modify the OnButton3() function.

LISTING 8.12 The Code That Stops the .WAV File

```
void CPlayWavsDlg::OnButton3()
{
    // TODO: Add your control notification handler code here
    sndPlaySound(NULL, SND_ASYNC);
}
```

Well, there really isn't much code here. By passing a NULL value as the name of the sound to play, the sound that is currently playing will stop.

Now that you have the necessary code to locate, play, and stop a .WAV file, you will need to do two more things before the application will compile and execute. Because the sndPlaySound() function is defined in the mmsystem.h file, you will need to go to the top of the PlayWavsDlg.cpp file and add the necessary include statement.

After you have the include statement inserted, you also need to add the winmm.lib file to the linker settings. To do this, select Project, Settings and then click the Link tab. Click in the Object/Library Modules and add winmm.lib. You are now able to compile and execute the PlayWav application.

Well, it really doesn't do any good to include a figure here with the results of this application, so you'll just have to take my word and trust that it works.

Lesson Summary

Adding sound capabilities to your application is a delightful feature for any application, and with as little code as it takes to implement it, it is something that should be considered.

By using the standard multimedia `sndPlaySound()` function, you easily created an application that could locate and play sounds. You also learned how to play a .WAV file continuously.

Quiz 5

1. Which statement is true about the `sndPlaySound()` function?

    a. You can play multiple .WAV files at a single time.

    b. You can play a sound waveform that already exists in memory.

    c. You cannot stop a sound that is currently playing.

    d. You can play a sound backwards.

2. Which `fuSound` constant is used to tell the sound to play completely before returning control back to your application?

    a. `SND_NOSTOP`

    b. `SND_ASYNC`

    c. `SND_SYNC`

    d. `SND_COMPLETE`

3. How do you stop a sound when it is playing?

    a. Pass a `NULL` string as the `fuSound` parameter.

    b. Use `SND_STOP` as the `fuSound` parameter.

    c. Call the `sndStopSnd()` function.

    d. Pass a `NULL` string in the `lpszSound` parameter.

4. How many .WAV files can you play at one time?

    a. 256

    b. 16

    c. 1

    d. Only limited by memory.

Exercise 5

Complexity: Easy

1. Create a dialog-based application named "Exercise 1." This application enables you to browse through your hard drive. After a .WAV file is selected, go ahead and play it synchronously so that the application plays the complete sound file before returning control back to your application.

Complexity: Moderate

2. Create a dialog-based application named "Exercise 2" that is based on the application created in the previous exercise. This application will have the same functionality as the first application except that it will play the sound asynchronously. If you try to start another sound while one is playing, the new sound should not play. The first sound must complete before starting a new sound.

Chapter Summary

The CDC class provides you with a lot of flexibility when it comes to drawing standard graphic objects, such as fonts, shapes, and bitmaps. You learned how easy it is to enhance the look of your application by using different fonts. You learned how to change the typeface to bold, italics, underline, and strikeout. You also learned how to change the size and angle in which the font is drawn.

By using the pens and brushes, you learned how easy it is to change the way the graphic objects are drawn to the screen. You also learned how to create your own custom brushes from bitmap images. With the use of the shape-drawing functions, you learned how easy it can be to draw some of the most common shapes, such as rectangles, ellipses, and lines.

After learning about the general graphic objects, you learned how to copy bitmaps into the device context. By doing so, you learned how you can do partial transfers as well as stretching the bitmap to fit within a region.

After you mastered the graphics stuff, you learned how simple it is to play the most common audio media for the PC, a .WAV file. By adding audio to your application, you can literally add the bells and whistles to your application.

CHAPTER 9

An Introduction to ActiveX Programming

Programming ActiveX containers, servers, and controls is a very in-depth topic and usually requires a good understanding of Windows programming, not to mention the fact that it would take more than an entire book by itself to fully explore the topic. However, MFC gives you a tremendous head start by fully supporting most of the ActiveX technologies.

In this chapter, you will learn the very basics of ActiveX programming. You will start by learning about ActiveX and how to use pre-designed controls in your own applications. You will then move on to create your very own ActiveX control.

After learning about ActiveX controls in general, you will learn about container and server applications. You will build an application with container capabilities; then you will build an application with server capabilities.

By building all of the example applications in this chapter, you will gain a general knowledge about ActiveX and MFC, and how you can use this technology to improve your applications.

LESSON 1

Working with ActiveX

Before Microsoft changed its name, ActiveX was commonly known as Object Linking and Embedding, or OLE for short. This technology enabled programmers to write smaller components that could easily be used within other applications. This effectively enabled programmers to reuse code that was already written and tested in another application, saving a tremendous amount of time on their new application.

ActiveX controls can be used in numerous ways. One of the more common uses of ActiveX controls is to embed spreadsheets into text documents, or vice versa. But the use of these controls doesn't stop there. It's very easy to incorporate these controls into your own programs or even into a Web page.

To start off this lesson, you will learn about two different ways of using ActiveX objects, linking and embedding. You will then build an application that actually uses an ActiveX control.

Linking Objects

As the name implies, linking an object from within an application creates a physical link to a file. Figure 9.1 shows a bitmap object that was linked into a Word document.

FIGURE 9.1

A bitmap linked in a Word document.

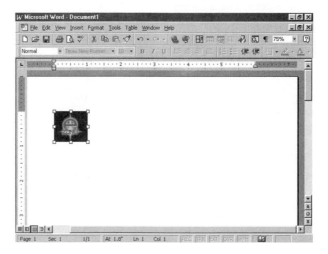

If you have Word installed, go ahead and start it up and insert a bitmap object. If you are unsure of the steps involved, you can follow these simple steps:

1. Start Word, or any other application that will allow you to link objects, such as Excel.

2. In a new document, choose the Insert, Object menu, as shown in Figure 9.2. You will be presented with a dialog box that will enable you to select which type of object to insert, as shown in Figure 9.3.

FIGURE 9.2

Inserting an object into Word.

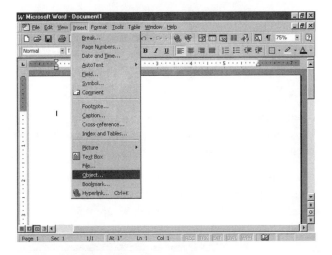

FIGURE 9.3

Selecting the type of object to insert.

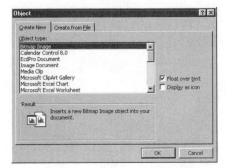

3. Click the Create from File tab. This will change the dialog to enable you to browse for a specific file and will present you with a couple of options from which to select.

4. Browse your hard drive and select a bitmap.

5. After you have the bitmap selected, check the option Link to File, as shown in Figure 9.4.

FIGURE 9.4

*Selecting a specific file
and setting the Link
option.*

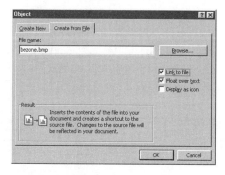

6. Click OK.

You should now have a document that is similar to the one in Figure 9.1. Your document
will now have a linked bitmap. If you were to make a modification to the bitmap outside
of your document, the change would be reflected from within your document.

If you want to modify the bitmap, you can right-click the bitmap and select the Linked
Bitmap Image Object, Open link context menu option to open the associated application
for the bitmap, which is Paint, as shown in Figure 9.5.

FIGURE 9.5

*Opening Paint from the
linked object.*

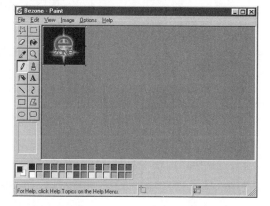

Note   For some objects, you can double-click the object to start its associated
application.

Embedding Objects

Embedding an object is accomplished in the same manner as linking an object, with one major difference. When you embed an object into your document, a copy of the original object is stored along with your document. If you were to modify the original object outside of the document, no changes would be reflected within the document.

Another notable difference is that, when you double-click the object to edit it, the toolbars and menus that are being used by Word are replaced with the menus and tool bars from the associated application, which is Paint in this example. This change is shown in Figure 9.6.

FIGURE 9.6

Editing an embedded object.

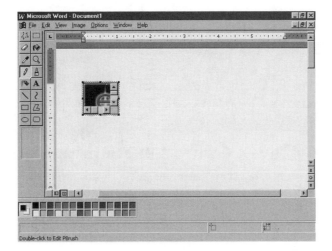

If you make changes to the embedded object, the changes will only be saved within the document, not to the original object that you embedded.

Where Did ActiveX Controls Come From?

ActiveX controls were previously known as *OLE custom controls*These controls were developed to replace the VBX controls that were used in earlier versions of Visual C++ and Visual Basic. OLE controls were stored on disk with the .OCX file extension and were referred to as *OCX controls*. As technology progressed, so did the name of OLE and OLE controls. These controls are still saved on disk as .OCX files, but they are now called ActiveX controls. Figure 9.7 shows some of the .OCX files that exist in my C:\WINDOWS\SYSTEM directory.

FIGURE 9.7

*Existing ActiveX
(.OCX) components.*

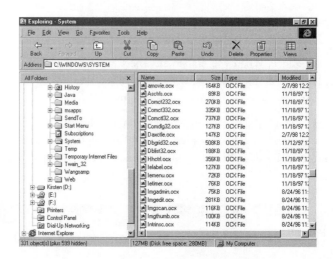

As time and technology moved on, so did the complexity of the controls being developed by programmers. Now, ActiveX controls are used to help ease the process of building powerful and complex applications.

Using ActiveX Controls in Your Application

ActiveX controls are very popular amongst software developers. By using a control that someone else developed, you can add a magnitude of features into your application in only a few minutes.

Think about this: What would it take for you to build an application that included calendar capabilities? Depending on your programming experience, you could spend a couple days, maybe even a couple weeks, developing calendar functions for your application. What if someone else had already developed a control that you could simply include in your application, giving you these functions in only a couple minutes? Wouldn't you want to know how to use it? That is exactly what you are going to do in the next example application. You are going to build a dialog-based application that uses an ActiveX control that displays a calendar.

Building the Calendar Application

To get started, use the MFC AppWizard to build a dialog-based application named Calendar. Before you get too far along, you will need to make sure that your application is capable of using ActiveX controls. After you decide to create a dialog-based application, click the Next button to move on to the next set of options.

The next group of options is where you will determine if you want to allow ActiveX controls in your application. Looking at the dialog box, as shown in Figure 9.8, you will see that one of the options enables you to include ActiveX control support. By default, this option is already checked, but it's a good idea to check, just to make sure. With the ActiveX Controls option checked, you can now click the Finish button to build your application.

FIGURE 9.8

The option that allows ActiveX controls in your application.

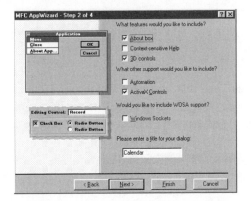

Adding an ActiveX Control

After your application is built, you have the infamous empty dialog box that you must work with. Adding ActiveX controls to dialog-based applications is a breeze. To see how easy it is, right-click the dialog box. You will be presented with the normal context menu, as shown in Figure 9.9. The menu option that you are looking for is Insert ActiveX Control. Go ahead and select this menu option.

FIGURE 9.9

The menu option to insert ActiveX controls.

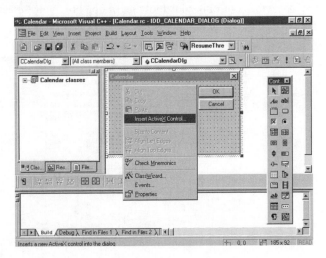

After you click the Insert ActiveX Control menu option, you will be presented with a new dialog box, as shown in Figure 9.10. This dialog box will enable you to select one of the ActiveX controls that are installed on your system.

FIGURE 9.10

The Insert ActiveX Control dialog box.

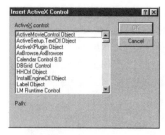

Scroll down the list until you find Microsoft MonthView Control, version 6. Because this dialog box is a fixed size, you might not be able to see the complete name of the control. Looking at Figure 9.11, you can see which control you need to select.

FIGURE 9.11

Selecting the Date and Time Picker control.

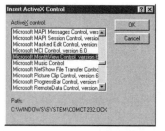

Also on this dialog box, you will see the path to the `.OCX` file that houses this control. This control belongs to `COMCT232.OCX`. After you find the control, go ahead and click the `OK` button. After the control is added to your dialog box, your screen should look something like the one shown in Figure 9.12.

FIGURE 9.12

The Date and Time Picker control on your dialog box.

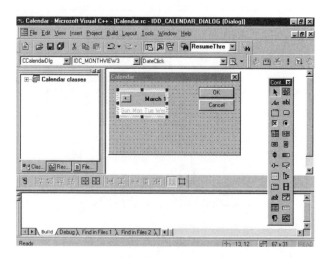

As with many other controls that you will work with, you need to position and resize the control to your liking. Using Figure 9.13 as a guide, reposition and resize the control.

FIGURE 9.13

Making the control more suitable for display.

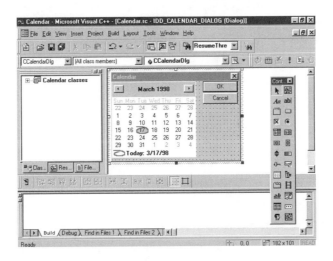

Usually, an ActiveX control will have associated properties. You can easily access the properties of this control , by right-clicking the control and selecting Properties MonthView Object. This brings up the property dialog box for the control, as shown in Figure 9.14. You can click through the various tabs of properties to get a good feel for all the options that this control provides for you.

FIGURE 9.14

The properties for the MonthView ActiveX control.

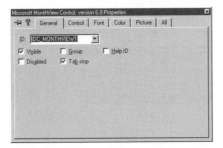

At this point, if you were to compile the Calendar application, your screen would look something like Figure 9.15. Notice that the calendar looks just as it did when you were designing the dialog box. It's amazing. You have a complete calendar in your application with absolutely no coding on your part, another nice feature of Visual C++ programming.

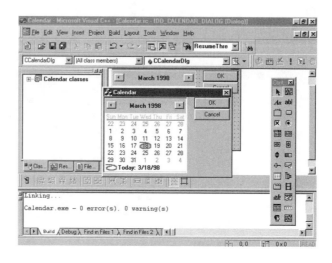

ActiveX Controls and Events

The MonthView ActiveX control that you are using has several events associated
with it. Go ahead and right-click the control and then choose ClassWizard. After the
ClassWizard dialog box , is presented, click the IDC_MONTHVIEW1 object ID to see the list
of events that you can override. Click the DateClick message, as shown in Figure 9.16.
Go ahead and create the necessary message-handler function for this message.

FIGURE **9.16**

*The MonthView event
messages.*

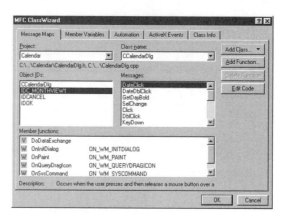

After you have created the message handler function, go ahead and modify it so that it
matches Listing 9.1.

LISTING 9.1 Displaying the Date That Was Clicked

```
void CCalendarDlg::OnDateClickMonthview1(DATE DateClicked)
{
    // TODO: Add your control notification handler code here
    CString MyDate;
    MyDate.Format("%f",DateClicked);
    AfxMessageBox(MyDate);
}
```

9

When this event is triggered,, it will pass along the date that was clicked on the calendar by the user. If you have ever used the DATE type, then you are aware that the date is passed back as an 8-byte floating point number, which doesn't mean anything to a user until it is converted into readable form. If you were to run the application at this time and clicked on a date, you would see a dialog box similar to Figure 9.17.

FIGURE 9.17

Displaying the date.

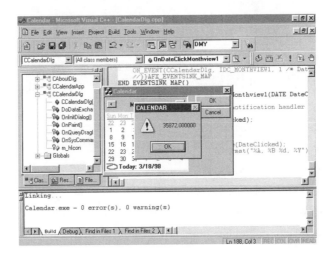

You can easily convert a DATE type to a more friendly value by using the COleDateTime class provided by MFC. Go ahead and modify the function so that it now matches Listing 9.2.

LISTING 9.2 Displaying the Date That Was Clicked in a Readable Form

```
void CCalendarDlg::OnDateClickMonthview1(DATE DateClicked)
{
    // TODO: Add your control notification handler code here
    COleDateTime* MyDate;
    MyDate = new COleDateTime(DateClicked);
    AfxMessageBox(MyDate->Format("%A, %B %d, %Y"));
    delete MyDate;
}
```

This time, when you run the application, click a day in the calendar; you will get a dialog box that looks like Figure 9.18.

FIGURE 9.18

Displaying the date in readable form.

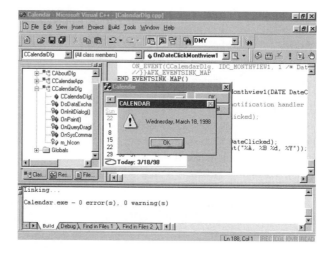

The following is a list of several of the formatting values for the Format() function , just in case you would ever need to know them:

- %a—Abbreviated weekday name
- %A—Full weekday name
- %b—Abbreviated month name
- %B—Full month name
- %d—Day of month as decimal number (01 - 31)
- %H—Hour in 24-hour format (00 - 23)
- %I—Hour in 12-hour format (01 - 12)
- %j—Day of year as decimal number (001 - 366)
- %m—Month as decimal number (01 - 12)
- %M—Minute as decimal number (00 - 59)
- %p—Current A.M./P.M. indicator for 12-hour clock
- %S—Second as decimal number (00 - 59)
- %U—Week of year as decimal number, with Sunday as first day of week (00 - 53)
- %w—Weekday as decimal number (0 - 6; Sunday is 0)
- %W—Week of year as decimal number, with Monday as first day of week (00 - 53)
- %y—Year without century, as decimal number (00 - 99)
- %Y—Year with century, as decimal number

Lesson Summary

In this lesson, you learned that linking an object enables you to make a physical connection with an object. If you make a change to an object that is linked, the change will be reflected in the original object as well. If you embed an object, a copy of that object is copied into your document and any changes that you make to that object do not affect the original object.

After learning about ActiveX controls, you learned how to enhance your application by inserting a pre-developed ActiveX control. By using these pre-developed controls, you learned that you can quickly add great features to your applications in only a matter of minutes, something that could take you a great deal of time if you tried to write the same functionality.

Quiz 1

1. What was ActiveX formally known as before its name was changed to ActiveX?

    a. Active controls

    b. Active OLE

    c. Object controls

    d. Object Linking and Embedding (OLE)

2. What file extension is used when storing ActiveX controls?

    a. `.ACX`

    b. `.OLE`

    c. `.OCX`

    d. `.CPP`

3. Which statement is true about linking objects?

    a. The linked object is saved in your document, and removed from your hard drive.

    b. If you make a change to the original object, the change is also reflected in the linked object.

    c. You cannot make modifications to a linked object.

    d. You can only link bitmap images.

4. Which statement is true about embedding objects?

    a. A copy of the source object is made, but it is not stored with your document.

    b. If you make a change to the original object, the change is also reflected in the embedded object.

c. The changes you make to an embedded object do not affect the original object.

d. Embedded objects are not stored with your document; only modifications or changes to the object are stored.

Exercise 1

Complexity: Easy

1. Create a dialog-based application named "Exercise 1." After created, remove the TODO: Static Text control and insert the Microsoft Forms 2.0 Image control onto the dialog box. After the control is in place, use the `Picture` property of the control to load in a bitmap for display.

Complexity: Moderate

2. Create a dialog-based application named "Exercise 2." After created, remove the TODO: Static Text control and insert the Microsoft MonthView control onto the dialog box. Using the properties of the control, turn off the option to show today's date and turn on the option to show the week numbers. When a date is clicked, show the date in a message box with the format `MM/DD/YY`.

LESSON 2

Building Your Own ActiveX Control

There are many different reasons that you might want to build your own ActiveX controls. You could be designing a user interface that requires a specific look and you want to use this interface across multiple applications. A simple solution would be to build a custom control that you could simply plug into each application. Or, one of the common controls might not function properly for your application, so you decide to rewrite it to suit your needs. Whatever your reason, you will need a place to start.

In this lesson, you are going to build a small ActiveX control that will respond to specific events and will have an associated property page.

The Smile ActiveX Control

To get started with this lesson, you will need to create the necessary framework for an ActiveX control. To build this framework, follow these simple steps:

1. Close any other projects that you might have open at this time.

2. Choose File, New menu option.

3. Type `Smile` for the name of the project, and then select MFC ActiveX
   ControlWizard from the list of project types, as shown in Figure 9.19.

FIGURE 9.19

Selecting MFC ActiveX ControlWizard.

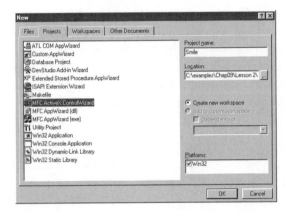

9

4. Click the OK button.

5. Accept the default options on this dialog box and click the Next button.

6. On this next dialog box, make sure that the Available in "Insert Object" Dialog
   option is checked, as shown in Figure 9.20.

FIGURE 9.20

Select Available in "Insert Object" Dialog.

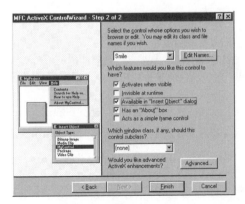

7. The rest of the default options are fine, so click the Finish button.

You have the very basic framework for your ActiveX control. All you need to do now is
write your control.

Inside the Smile ActiveX Control

When you used the MFC ActiveX ControlWizard to generate your control, it generated three base classes. To get a better understanding of what was created, each of these classes will be briefly discussed.

The CSmileApp Class

This class provides you with two overrides, which are InitInstance() and ExitInstance(). These two override functions are in the Smile.cpp file. The most important piece of code in this class is your unique ID for the control. Along with the global ID, you will find two other variables that hold the major and minor versions for your control. Listing 9.3 shows you the ID and the global variables for the Smile ActiveX control.

LISTING 9.3 The Unique ID and Version Numbers for the Smile ActiveX Control

```
const GUID CDECL BASED_CODE _tlid =
        { 0xf322e323, 0xbe86, 0x11d1, { 0xa9, 0x4a, 0xe1, 0x12,
        ➡0x7b, 0x77, 0xeb, 0x6b } };
const WORD _wVerMajor = 1;
const WORD _wVerMinor = 0;
```

The CSmileCtrl Class

Along with the constructor and destructor, this class has four other functions that were created:

- AboutBox()—This function displays the about box to the user.
- DoPropExchange()—This function is used to initialize your control's properties. This function allows your control's settings to be saved and loaded from a document.
- OnDraw()—This function is used to draw your control onto a DC.
- OnResetState()—This function will reset your control to its default state.

Along with these functions, this class will hold the event maps for your control.

The CSmilePropPage Class

This class is used to manage the property page associated   with your control. There are two functions in this class:

- CSmilePropPage()—This function is used to display the property page for your control.
- DoDataExchange()—This function exchanges data for the property page.

Drawing the Smile Control

Because the Smile control will be displaying graphics, one of the first things that you will want to do is add the necessary code to draw the smile face. This will be done in the `OnDraw()` function, like always. Go ahead and bring this function into the code editor and modify it so that it matches Listing 9.4.

LISTING 9.4 Drawing the Smile Face

```
void CSmileCtrl::OnDraw(
            CDC* pdc, const CRect& rcBounds, const CRect& rcInvalid)
{
    // TODO: Replace the following code with your own drawing code.
    CPen smile(PS_SOLID, 4, RGB(0,0,0));

    CBrush white(RGB(255,255,255));
    CBrush yellow(RGB(255,255,0));
    CBrush black(RGB(0,0,0));

    CBrush* oldbrush = pdc->SelectObject(&white);
    pdc->Rectangle(rcBounds);

    int xsize = rcBounds.Width() / 12;
    int ysize = rcBounds.Height() / 12;
    int top   = rcBounds.left;
    int left  = rcBounds.top;

    pdc->SelectObject(&yellow);
    pdc->Ellipse(left,top,left+12*xsize,top+12*ysize);

    CPen* oldpen = pdc->SelectObject(&smile);
    pdc->SelectObject(&black);
    pdc->Ellipse(left+ 2 * xsize,top+ 2 * ysize,
                 left+ 5 * xsize,top+ 5 * ysize);
    pdc->Ellipse(left+ 7 * xsize,top+ 2 * ysize,
                 left+10 * xsize,top+ 5 * ysize);

    pdc->Arc(left +2 * xsize,top+ 2 * ysize,
             left+10 * xsize,top+10 * ysize,
             left    * xsize,top+ 7 * ysize,
             left+12 * xsize,top+ 7 * ysize);

    pdc->SelectObject(oldpen);
    pdc->SelectObject(oldbrush);
}
```

There is nothing in this function that you shouldn't already know. This function draws a smiley face using standard pens, brushes, and shapes. The only things that might look different are the calculations for drawing the shapes.

Because the control can be placed anywhere within a document, the position and size of the control must be accounted for. The simple calculations for drawing the shapes take into consideration the position and size of the control.

At this point, you actually have an ActiveX control. The control serves no real purpose yet but to draw a smiley face. However, before you go any further, you should learn how to test your control while developing it.

To test the Smile control, follow these simple steps:

1. Choose Tools, ActiveX Control Test Container from the main menu. This will bring up a small utility that will allow you to test your controls, as shown in Figure 9.21.

FIGURE 9.21

The ActiveX Control Test Container application.

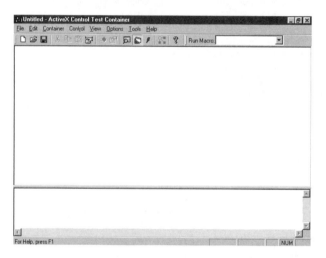

2. Choose Edit, Insert New Control from the menu. This will bring up a dialog box that will enable you to select a control to insert.

3. Select Smile Control, as shown in Figure 9.22.

FIGURE 9.22

Selecting your Smile control.

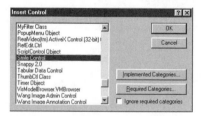

4. Click the OK button. This will bring your control into the test container application. If you resize the control, you should have a smiley face control similar to Figure 9.23.

FIGURE 9.23

Looking at the Smile control.

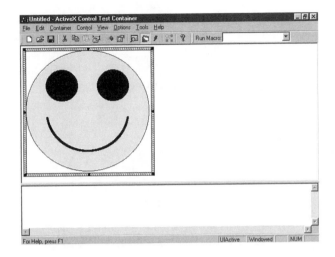

Adding Custom Properties

No ActiveX control would be complete if it didn't have properties for the user to change. Properties are used to change the behavior, look, or operations of a control. For this example, you will add properties that will allow the user to change the color of the smiley face as well as the type of smile.

The property that you are going to implement is the SmileState property. This property will have a BOOL value, and whenever this property is set to TRUE, the smiley face will smile. Whenever the SmileState property is set to FALSE, the smiley face will frown.

To add the SmileState property, you will need to use the ClassWizard, so go ahead and bring it up. After you have the ClassWizard up, you will need to select the Automation tab, as shown in Figure 9.24.

FIGURE 9.24

The Automation page of ClassWizard.

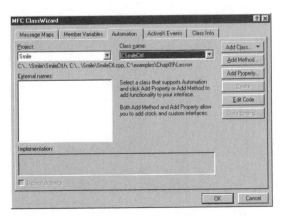

To create the property, click the Add Property button. This will bring up a dialog box that enables you to specify items about the property. Using Figure 9.25 as a guide, go ahead and fill the Add Property dialog box.

FIGURE 9.25

Creating properties.

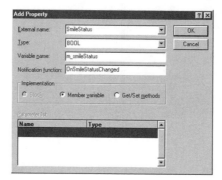

Whenever you create a property, you should also give it a default value. You can do this in the DoPropExchange() function. Modify your DoPropExchange() function so that it matches Listing 9.5.

LISTING 9.5   Setting the Default Value for the FaceColor Property

```
void CSmileCtrl::DoPropExchange(CPropExchange* pPX)
{
    ExchangeVersion(pPX, MAKELONG(_wVerMinor, _wVerMajor));
    COleControl::DoPropExchange(pPX);

    // TODO: Call PX_ functions for each persistent custom property.
PX_Bool( pPX, "SmileStatus", m_smileStatus, TRUE);
}
```

The PX_Bool() function is a property-exchange function. There is a property-exchange function for each of the supported property types. The following is a list of these functions:

- PX_Blob()
- PX_Bool()
- PX_Color()
- PX_Currency()
- PX_DATAPATH()
- PX_Double()

- PX_Float()
- PX_Font()
- PX_IUnknown()
- PX_Long()
- PX_Picture()
- PX_Short()
- PX_String()
- PX_ULong()
- PX_UShort()

These functions take four parameters. The first parameter is the pointer that was passed to you in the DoPropExchange() function, pPX. The next parameter is the external name of the property. The next parameter is the member variable name, and the last property is the default value for the property.

Because the SmileStatus property is of type BOOL, you will use the PX_Bool() property-exchange function. You will also assign a default value of TRUE so that the face starts off with a smile.

To make the Smile control use the property that you just created, you will need to modify the OnDraw() function. Locate the function that draws the arc for the mouth and replace it with the following code in Listing 9.6.

LISTING 9.6   Using the SmileStatus Property to Draw a Smile or a Frown

```
if (m_smileStatus = TRUE)
    {
        pdc->Arc(left +2 * xsize,top+ 2 * ysize,
        left+10 * xsize,top+10 * ysize,
        left    * xsize,top+ 7 * ysize,
        left+12 * xsize,top+ 7 * ysize);
    }
    else
    {
        pdc->Arc(left+ 2 * xsize,top+ 7 * ysize,
        left+10 * xsize,top+14 * ysize,
        left+12 * xsize,top+ 7 * ysize,
        left    * xsize,top+ 7 * ysize);
    }
```

Now, depending on the value of the m_smileStatus member variable, which is the SmileStatus property, either a smile or a frown will be drawn.

Now that you have the property implemented in code, you need to create the property page that will enable you to change the property.

When you created the Smile control using the MFC ActiveX ControlWizard, a dialog resource for the property page was created. Go ahead and open the IDD_PROPAGE_SMILE dialog so that you can make modifications to it.

First, remove the TODO: Static Text control. Then, add a check box to the dialog and set the caption to Smile?, as shown in Figure 9.26.

FIGURE 9.26

Setting the caption.

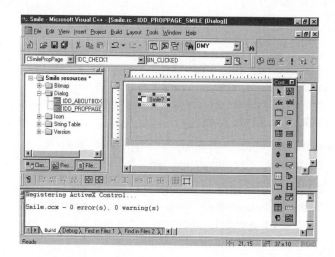

Now that you have a check box that represents the property, you will need to tie the check box with the actual property. You will use the ClassWizard to make this connection. Just follow these simple steps:

1. With the dialog box open, right-click ClassWizard from the context menu.

2. Click the Member Variables tab and make sure CSmilePropPage is selected in the Class name drop-down list.

3. Click the Add Variable button.

4. Fill in the dialog box to match the values in Figure 9.27. The Member Variable Name option is the member variable name that you assigned to the property, which is m_smileStatus for this example. The Variable Type should be set to BOOL, just like the member variable, and the Optional Property Name should be the external name you gave to the property, which is SmileStatus.

FIGURE 9.27

Creating a member variable that links with a property.

5. Click the OK button.

If you have a custom property that has a visual effect on the control, such as this control does, the control's OnDraw() function will not be called until the control needs to be redrawn. Changing a property is not an indication for the control to be redrawn; therefore, you must manually cause the control to be redrawn. The easiest way to accomplish this is to invalidate the control. Bring up the ClassWizard and click the Automation tab. Now, double-click the SmileStatus external name. This will bring the OnSmileStatusChanged() function into the code editor. Add the following line of code after the call to SetModifiedFlag():

```
Invalidate();
```

This will cause the control to be redrawn. At this time, you can build the ActiveX control and load it into the Test Container application. After you insert the control, choose the Edit, Properties menu option. You will be presented with a property dialog box like the one shown in Figure 9.28.

FIGURE 9.28

The properties for the Smile control.

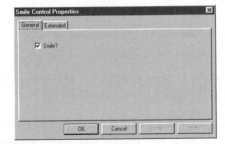

Go ahead and uncheck the Smile? property and click the Apply button. The smile face will change from a smile to a frown, as shown in Figure 9.29.

FIGURE 9.29

Mr. Smiley is no longer happy.

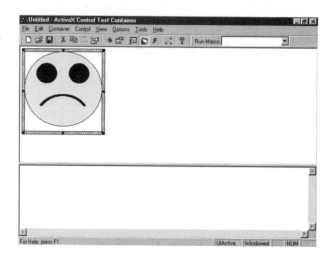

Stock and Ambient Properties

When you create an ActiveX control, some default properties are generated. These properties are known as Stock properties and Ambient properties. The following list is a complete list of the Stock properties to which you have access:

- Appearance—The general appearance of the control.
- BackColor—The background color of the control.
- BorderStyle—The style of the border used by the control.
- Caption—The caption of the control.
- Enabled—Determines if the control is allowed to be used.
- Font—The default font for the control.
- ForeColor—The foreground color of the control.
- hWnd—The window handle of the control.
- ReadyState—The readiness of the control. For example, loading or already loaded.
- Text—The caption or text of a control.

Ambient properties are properties that describe the surrounding environment of the control. You cannot change these properties, but you can use them to make adjustments in your control if needed. Table 9.1 lists some of the more common Ambient functions.

TABLE 9.1 Functions That Return Ambient Properties

Function	Return Type
AmbientBackColor()	OLE_COLOR
AmbientDisplayName()	CString
AmbientFont()	LPFONTDISP
AmbientForeColor()	OLE_COLOR
AmbientTextAlign()	short
AmbientUserMode()	BOOL

You are going to use the Stock properties BackColor and ForeColor to determine the colors used in drawing Mr. Smiley. To do this, you will need to use the ClassWizard. Go ahead and bring it up and click the Automation tab. Double check to make sure that CSmileCtrl is selected in the Class name drop-down list. Now click the Add Property button to bring up the Add Property dialog box.

For the External name of the property, select BackColor from the drop-down list, as shown in Figure 9.30. Click the OK button to create the property. Create a property for the ForeColor in the same manner.

FIGURE 9.30

Adding Stock properties.

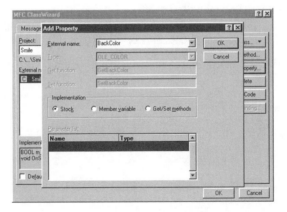

Now that you have added the Stock properties, you will need to add them to your property page dialog box. This is very easy to implement, because there are stock property pages that you can use. To use one of the stock property pages, you need to add the appropriate ID to the code that initializes the control's array of property pages. This code is located in the implementation file for the control, which is the SmileCtl.cpp file. Scroll down the code listing until you see the code presented in Listing 9.7.

LISTING 9.7   The Property Page Definition

```
// Property pages

// TODO: Add more property pages as needed.
// Remember to increase the count!
BEGIN_PROPPAGEIDS(CSmileCtrl, 1)
    PROPPAGEID(CSmilePropPage::guid)
END_PROPPAGEIDS(CSmileCtrl)
```

Modify this block of code to match Listing 9.8.

LISTING 9.8   Adding the `CColorPropPage` Property Page

```
// Property pages

// TODO: Add more property pages as needed.
// Remember to increase the count!
BEGIN_PROPPAGEIDS(CSmileCtrl, 2)
    PROPPAGEID(CSmilePropPage::guid)
    PROPPAGEID(CLSID_CColorPropPage)
END_PROPPAGEIDS(CSmileCtrl)
```

Just in case you overlooked it, in the `BEGIN_PROPPAGEIDS()` macro, the second parameter was changed to 2. This value indicates the number of property pages that you are defining. You then added the `CLSID_CColorPropPage` ID as a property page for your control.

There are two other property pages that you can use, and their IDs are

- `CLSID_CFontPropPage`
- `CLSID_CPicturePropPage`

Now, when you bring up the properties for the control, there will be a Colors tab on the property page, as shown in Figure 9.31.

FIGURE 9.31

The new Colors property tab.

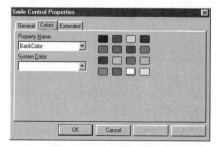

Now, these new properties don't mean a thing if you don't modify your code to use them. Go ahead and modify the `OnDraw()` function with the changes in Listing 9.9.

LISTING 9.9 Changing the `OnDraw()` Function to Use the `BackColor` and `ForeColor` Properties

```
// TODO: Replace the following code with your own drawing code.
   CPen smile(PS_SOLID, 4, GetForeColor());

   CBrush white(RGB(255,255,255));
   CBrush yellow(GetBackColor());
   CBrush black(GetForeColor());
```

The smile pen was changed to use the `ForeColor` property. To get the color in `ForeColor`, a call is made to the `GetForeColor()` function. The black brush was changed to use the `ForeColor` property as well, and the yellow brush was changed to use the `BackColor` property. This time, when you examine the control in the test container application, you will be able to change the colors of the smiley face. Although you probably won't be able to tell in the black and white Figure 9.32, the smiley face is now red with a yellow mouth and eyes.

FIGURE 9.32

Mr. Smiley is blushing.

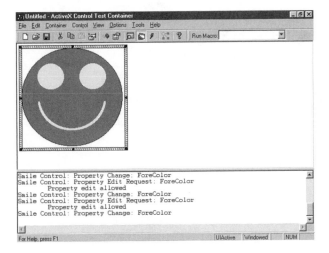

Lesson Summary

In this lesson, you learned how to build your very own custom ActiveX control. By using the MFC ActiveX ControlWizard, you basically built a self-contained ActiveX control. After creating a control, you learned how to incorporate a property page with custom properties.

You then moved on, learning about the standard properties and property pages that are available to all ActiveX controls.

Quiz 2

1. Which of the following is not one of the property-exchange functions?

    a. `PX_Bool()`

    b. `PX_Intiger()`

    c. `PX_Long()`

    d. `PX_IUnknown()`

2. Which of the following is not one of the stock property pages that you can use as a property page in an ActiveX control?

    a. `CLSID_CFontPropPage`

    b. `CLSID_CPicturePropPage`

    c. `CLSID_CExtendedPropPage`

    d. `CLSID_CColorPropPage`

3. To easily build the framework for an ActiveX control, which wizard do you use?

    a. MFC AppWizard Control

    b. MFC ActiveX Control

    c. MFC AppWizard (dll)

    d. MFC ActiveX ControlWizard

4. Which of the following functions would cause a control to be redrawn?

    a. `Invalidate()`

    b. `RedrawControl()`

    c. `UpdateView()`

    d. `DrawControl()`

Exercise 2

Complexity: Easy

1. Create an ActiveX control named "Exercise 1." This control should display the text message `Welcome Interactive World`. This control should have a property that will enable the color of the text to be changed to use the `ForeColor` stock property. Before you draw the text on the control, draw a rectangle filled with the `BackColor` stock property.

Complexity: Moderate

2. This exercise is closely modeled after the previous exercise. Create an ActiveX control named "Exercise 2." Along with the properties mentioned in the previous exercise, add a custom property that will enable you to change the text that is displayed on the control.

LESSON 3

Developing an ActiveX Container Application

An ActiveX container application is an application that will enable a user to link or embed objects into its document. By enabling a user to link or embed objects into your application's documents, you are giving the user the capability to use your application to its fullest extent.

By including container capabilities in your application, you open your application up to a great deal of flexibility. Could you imagine trying to code every feature that a user would want into your application? By simply including container support in your application, you give your users the capability to insert just about any type of object they will need into their documents. In this lesson, you are going to build an application that has container capabilities.

Building the MyContainer Application

To get started with this lesson, you will need to build an example application. Follow these steps to build the MyContainer application:

1. Close any open projects.

2. Choose File, New from the menu to create a new project.

3. Name the project MyContainer and select MFC AppWizard (exe).

4. Click OK to begin selecting options for the program.

5. Accept the default application type as MDI and click the Next button.

6. You don't need database support for this application, so just click the Next button.

7. On this next page, select Container as the compound document support that you want to include, as shown in Figure 9.33.

FIGURE 9.33

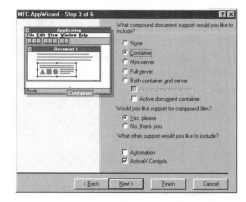

*Selecting to include
container capabilities.*

8. After selecting Container, you can click the Finish button because no other changes
   are needed.

Inside the MyContainer Application

You have built standard MDI applications in previous chapters. By selecting the container option, some changes are made in the way that the MFC AppWizard generates your
code. The following is a list of the classes that were generated:

- CAboutDlg
- CChildFrame
- CMainFrame
- CMyContainerApp
- CMyContainerCntrItem
- CMyContainerDoc
- CMyContainerView

Other than the CMyContainerCntrItem class, everything looks the same. Well, the class
names are the same, but there are some changes internally. The following sections will
outline the changes so that you will know the differences between a standard MDI application and an MDI container application.

The CMyContainerApp Class

The InitInstance() function in this class has a couple of small changes. The first
noticeable change in this function is the initialization of the OLE libraries, as shown in
Listing 9.10.

LISTING 9.10 Initializing the OLE Libraries in the `InitInstance()` Function

```
// Initialize OLE libraries
    if (!AfxOleInit())
    {
        AfxMessageBox(IDP_OLE_INIT_FAILED);
        return FALSE;
    }
```

9

Before the `AddDocTemplate()` function is called in the `InitInstance()` function, another line of code is added. The following line of code is used to register the menu used for editing embedded objects:

```
pDocTemplate->SetContainerInfo(IDR_MYCONTTYPE_CNTR_IP);
```

The resource that this function is referring to is a menu resource that was generated by the AppWizard. If you were to look at your resources tab and expand the Menu branch, you will see that there are now three menu resources. The third menu, as shown in Figure 9.34, is the menu that will be used when objects are being edited "in-place."

FIGURE 9.34

A menu for in-place editing of contained objects.

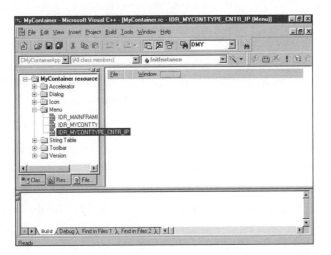

Looking at the menu in Figure 9.34, you will see two vertical separators. This is where a server application, which you will learn about in the next lesson, adds its menu options.

Because you are looking at the menus, click the `IDR_MYCONTTYPE` menu resource. There are a few changes here as well, which are shown in Figure 9.35.

FIGURE 9.35

The Object menu items for UDR_MYCONTTYPE.

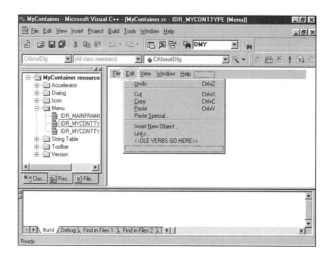

- The Paste Special menu option—This is used to paste an object from the clipboard into the container application.

- The Insert New Object menu option—This option brings up the Insert Object dialog box.

- The Links menu option—Choosing this option brings up the Links dialog box, which enables you to control the way the object is updated.

- The <<OLE VERBS GO HERE>> menu option—When an object has focus within the container application, it has associated verbs that will be placed in this area.

The CMyContainerCntrItem Class

This class is used to describe an item that is contained in the document. Other than the normal constructor and destructor for a class, this class has eight override functions for you to use:

- GetActiveView()—Returns the member variable for the view.

- GetDocument()—Returns the member variable for the document.

- OnActivate()—This function is called when the object is double-clicked. This function makes sure that the current view is valid, and activates the item.

- OnChange()—When the contained item has changed, the server notifies the container that the change has occurred. This function then calls the UpdateAllViews() to refresh the screen.

- OnChangeItemPosition()—This function is called when the item is moved during in-place editing.

- `OnDeactivateUI()`—This function is called when an object is deactivated.
- `OnGetItemPosition()`—This function is called from the `OnActivate()` function. This function is used to determine the placement of the object.
- `Serialize()`—This function is called by the document's `Serialize()` function.

The `CMyContainerDoc` Class

The biggest difference for this class is the fact that it now inherits from the `COleDocument` class rather than the `CDocument` class. The message map has been expanded to enable the menu options that were discussed in the last section of this lesson. You can see the expanded message map by looking at Listing 9.11.

LISTING 9.11 The Expanded Message Map for the Document Class

```
BEGIN_MESSAGE_MAP(CMyContainerDoc, COleDocument)
    //{{AFX_MSG_MAP(CMyContainerDoc)
        // NOTE - the ClassWizard will add and remove mapping
        // macros here.   DO NOT EDIT what you see in these blocks
        // of generated code!
    //}}AFX_MSG_MAP
    // Enable default OLE container implementation
    ON_UPDATE_COMMAND_UI(ID_EDIT_PASTE,
COleDocument::OnUpdatePasteMenu)
    ON_UPDATE_COMMAND_UI(ID_EDIT_PASTE_LINK,
COleDocument::OnUpdatePasteLinkMenu)
    ON_UPDATE_COMMAND_UI(ID_OLE_EDIT_CONVERT,
COleDocument::OnUpdateObjectVerbMenu)
    ON_COMMAND(ID_OLE_EDIT_CONVERT, COleDocument::OnEditConvert)
    ON_UPDATE_COMMAND_UI(ID_OLE_EDIT_LINKS,
COleDocument::OnUpdateEditLinksMenu)
    ON_COMMAND(ID_OLE_EDIT_LINKS, COleDocument::OnEditLinks)
    ON_UPDATE_COMMAND_UI_RANGE(ID_OLE_VERB_FIRST, ID_OLE_VERB_LAST,
    ➥COleDocument::OnUpdateObjectVerbMenu)
END_MESSAGE_MAP()
```

The `CMyContainerDoc()` function of this class has a new line of code in it as well. A call to the `EnableCompoundFiles()` is called to turn on support for compound files.

The `Serialize()` function has a new line, too. A call to the `COleDocument::Serialize()` function is called, which takes care of serializing all of the objects in the document.

The `CMyContainerView` Class

The `CMyContainerView` class has several new functions added:

- `IsSelected()`—This function is used to test for selected items.
- `OnCancelEditCntr()`—This function is called when the Esc key is pressed while an object is being edited in-place.

- `OnInitialUpdate()`—This function is called before the first time the view is to be displayed. This function calls the base `OnUpdate()` function.
- `OnInsertObject()`—This function is called when an object is to be inserted into the document. It starts by displaying the Insert Object dialog box. If an object is selected, a container item is then created. After the item is successfully created, the new item is selected and the view is updated.
- `OnSetFocus()`—This function is called whenever the view receives focus.
- `OnSize()`—This function is called whenever the application is resized.

The message map of this class has been modified as well, as shown in Listing 9.12.

LISTING 9.12   The Expanded Message Map for the View Class

```
BEGIN_MESSAGE_MAP(CMyContainerView, CView)
    //{{AFX_MSG_MAP(CMyContainerView)
        // NOTE - the ClassWizard will add and remove mapping macros
        // here.   DO NOT EDIT what you see in these blocks
        // of generated code!
    ON_WM_DESTROY()
    ON_WM_SETFOCUS()
    ON_WM_SIZE()
    ON_COMMAND(ID_OLE_INSERT_NEW, OnInsertObject)
    ON_COMMAND(ID_CANCEL_EDIT_CNTR, OnCancelEditCntr)
    //}}AFX_MSG_MAP
    // Standard printing commands
    ON_COMMAND(ID_FILE_PRINT, CView::OnFilePrint)
    ON_COMMAND(ID_FILE_PRINT_DIRECT, CView::OnFilePrint)
    ON_COMMAND(ID_FILE_PRINT_PREVIEW, CView::OnFilePrintPreview)
END_MESSAGE_MAP()
```

The new entries into this message map are

- `ON_WM_SETFOCUS()`
- `ON_WM_SIZE()`
- `ON_COMMAND(ID_OLE_INSERT_NEW, OnInsertObject)`
- `ON_COMMAND(ID_CANCEL_EDIT_CNTR, OnCancelEditCntr)`

If you look at the constructor for this class, `CMyContainerView::CMyContainerView()`, you will see that there is now a variable being initialized, as shown in Listing 9.13.

LISTING 9.13   The m_pSelection in the Constructor

```
CMyContainerView::CMyContainerView()
{
    m_pSelection = NULL;
    // TODO: add construction code here

}
```

This variable is declared in the Attributes section of the `MyContainerView.h` file, which is shown here in Listing 9.14. The variable is used to communicate with the currently selected object.

LISTING 9.14   Declaring the `m_pSelection` Member Variable

```
// Attributes
public:
    CMyContainerDoc* GetDocument();
    // m_pSelection holds the selection to the current
CMyContainerCntrItem.
    // For many applications, such a member variable isn't adequate
    // to represent a selection, such as a multiple selection or a
    // selection of objects that are not CMyContainerCntrItem objects.
    // This selection mechanism is provided just to help
    // you get started.

    // TODO: replace this selection mechanism with one
    // appropriate to your app.
    CMyContainerCntrItem* m_pSelection;
```

The `OnDraw()` function has been modified a great deal as well. Listing 9.15 shows you the new `OnDraw()` function.

LISTING 9.15   The New `OnDraw()` Function

```
void CMyContainerView::OnDraw(CDC* pDC)
{
    CMyContainerDoc* pDoc = GetDocument();
    ASSERT_VALID(pDoc);

    // TODO: add draw code for native data here
    // TODO: also draw all OLE items in the document

    // Draw the selection at an arbitrary position.  This code should
    // be removed after your real drawing code is implemented.  This
    // position corresponds exactly to the rectangle returned by
    // CMyContainerCntrItem, to give the effect of in-place editing.

    // TODO: remove this code when final draw code is complete.

    if (m_pSelection == NULL)
    {
        POSITION pos = pDoc->GetStartPosition();
        m_pSelection = (CMyContainerCntrItem*)pDoc->
        ➥GetNextClientItem(pos);
    }
    if (m_pSelection != NULL)
        m_pSelection->Draw(pDC, CRect(10, 10, 210, 210));
}
```

The code in the `OnDraw()` function is only here as a rudimentary way of drawing a contained object. You will be changing this code a little later in this lesson.

Resizing and Moving Objects

To illustrate this next topic, go ahead and follow these steps to view a problem with the standard framework generated for MyContainer.

1. Build and execute the MyContainer application. When you run the application, it will look just like a normal MDI application.

2. Choose the Edit, Insert New Object menu option, as shown in Figure 9.36. This will bring up the Insert Object dialog box, which is shown in Figure 9.37.

FIGURE 9.36

Inserting a new object into the document.

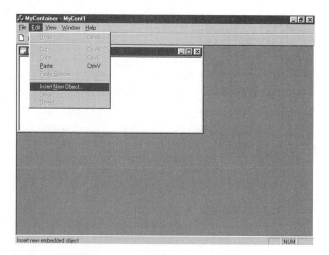

FIGURE 9.37

The Insert Object dialog box.

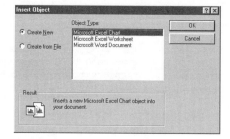

3. Select the Create from File option and browse around your hard drive to find a bitmap picture.

4. After you find a bitmap, go ahead and click the OK button to insert the bitmap into the document. Your screen should look similar to Figure 9.38, except for the fact that you might have used a different bitmap than the one shown here.

FIGURE 9.38

A bitmap was inserted into the document.

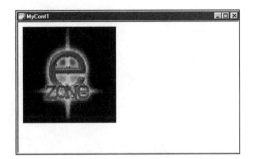

Now, unless the bitmap you inserted was exactly 200×200 pixels, it will be stretched to fill this size. This is because the OnDraw() function is coded to draw the contained object in a rectangle of (10,10,210,210). This is only one problem. Choose Edit, Bitmap Image Object, Edit from the menu. The MyContainer menu options will be changed to the menu options of Paint. Go ahead and resize and move the object as shown in Figure 9.39.

FIGURE 9.39

Moving and resizing the bitmap object.

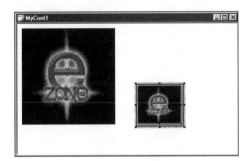

You will notice that the object is still drawn at its original position and you also resized and moved it as well. Now, hit the Esc key to go back to the normal menu system. Did you notice that the object didn't change? It stayed in the same place and position. You will need to add the necessary code that will allow your user to move and resize objects after they have been inserted.

Before you add the code to resize and move the object, you should add a tracking rectangle. A tracking rectangle is basically a dashed outline that represents the object's size and position while moving or resizing.

To implement a tracking rectangle, you will need to create a member variable for the container item, which is the CMyContainerCtnrItem class. In the ClassView panel, right-click the CMyContainerCtnrItem class and then select Add Member Variable, as shown in Figure 9.40.

FIGURE 9.40

Adding a member variable to the MyContainerCtnrItem *class.*

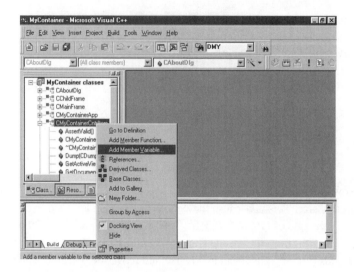

The Add Member Variable dialog box will be presented (see Figure 9.41). Go ahead and enter CRect as the variable type and enter m_ItemRect as the variable name. Leave the access set to Public and then click the OK button.

FIGURE 9.41

The Add Member Variable dialog box.

Now that you have the member variable created, you will want to initialize it to the default size as the object, which is a 200×200 rectangle. You will need to do this when the object is first initialized, so go ahead and click the CMyContainerCtnrItem() constructor and modify it so that it matches Listing 9.16.

LISTING 9.16 Initializing the Tracking Outline

```
CMyContainerCntrItem::CMyContainerCntrItem(CMyContainerDoc* pContainer)
    : COleClientItem(pContainer)
{
    // TODO: add one-time construction code here
    m_ItemRect = CRect(10,20,210,210);

}
```

Now, to make the `OnDraw()` function use this variable when moving or resizing the object, which you will do shortly, modify the line that calls the `Draw()` function to the following:

```
m_pSelection->Draw(pDC, m_pSelection->m_ItemRect);
```

Now, when the object is drawn, it will be drawn within the rectangle specified in `m_ItemRect`. However, in order to actually change this value, you will need to add a few lines of code to the `OnChangeItemPosition()` function of the `CMyContainerCtnrItem` class. Go ahead and modify this function so that it matches Listing 9.17.

LISTING 9.17   Changing the Size of the Tracking Outline When an Item Is Resized

```
BOOL CMyContainerCntrItem::OnChangeItemPosition(const CRect& rectPos)
{
    ASSERT_VALID(this);

    // During in-place activation
    // CMyContainerCntrItem::OnChangeItemPosition is called by the
    // server to change the position of the in-place window.
    // Usually, this is a result of the data in the server document
    // changing such that the extent has changed or as a result
    // of in-place resizing.
    //
    // The default here is to call the base class, which will call
    // COleClientItem::SetItemRects to move the item
    // to the new position.

    if (!COleClientItem::OnChangeItemPosition(rectPos))
        return FALSE;

    // TODO: update any cache you may have of the item's
    // rectangle/extent
    m_ItemRect = rectPos;
    GetDocument()->SetModifiedFlag();
    GetDocument()->UpdateAllViews(NULL);
    return TRUE;
}
```

The code that you need to add is at the bottom of the function, just before the return `TRUE` line. When the object is resized or moved, the new values will be captured into `m_ItemRect` and the view will be redrawn. Now, this time when you edit the object and you press the Esc key, the new size and position will be used to draw the object in the view, as shown in Figure 9.42.

FIGURE 9.42

The bitmap object has been resized and repositioned.

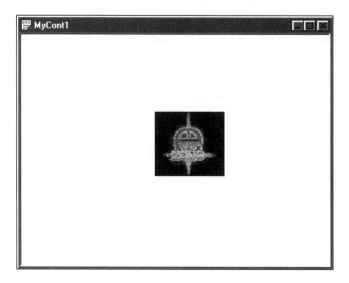

Now, you need to draw the tracking rectangle. First, you need to modify the If statement that draws the object rectangle in the OnDraw() function. Modify it so that it matches Listing 9.18.

LISTING 9.18 Drawing the Tracking Rectangle

```
if (m_pSelection != NULL)
    {
        m_pSelection->Draw(pDC, m_pSelection->m_ItemRect);
        CRectTracker tracker;
        DoTracker(m_pSelection, &tracker);
        tracker.Draw(pDC);
    }
```

After drawing the object, a variable named tracker is constructed. This variable is then passed into a function named DoTracker() along with m_pSelection. After this function returns, the tracker rectangle is then drawn to the view.

So, where did this DoTracker() function come from? Well, you need to write it. Before you can write the function, you need to declare it in the CMyContainerView class. Go ahead and double-click the CMyContainerView in the ClassView panel to bring it into the editor. Using Listing 9.19 as a guide, add the declaration for the DoTracker() function.

LISTING 9.19 Declaring the `DoTracker()` Function

```
// Implementation
public:
    virtual ~CMyContainerView();
    void CMyContainerView::DoTracker(CMyContainerCntrItem* item,
    ➥CRectTracker* tracker);
#ifdef _DEBUG
    virtual void AssertValid() const;
    virtual void Dump(CDumpContext& dc) const;
#endif
```

A little extra code was presented here to help you find the spot you were looking for. The line you added is the second line in the public area of the Implementation section.

Now that you have the function declared, you need to code the actual function. Open the `CMyContainerView` class branch and double-click the `~CMyContainerView()` destructor. Now, scroll down past the end of this function and add the `DoTracker()` function, which is shown in Listing 9.20.

LISTING 9.20 The `DoTracker()` Function

```
void CMyContainerView::DoTracker(CMyContainerCntrItem* item,
➥CRectTracker* tracker)
{
    tracker->m_rect = item->m_ItemRect;
    if (item == m_pSelection)
    {
        tracker->m_nStyle |= CRectTracker::resizeOutside;
    }
    if (item->GetType() == OT_LINK)
    {
        tracker->m_nStyle |= CRectTracker::dottedLine;
    }
    else
    {
        tracker->m_nStyle |= CRectTracker::solidLine;
    }
    if (item->GetItemState() == COleClientItem::openState ||
        item->GetItemState() == COleClientItem::activeUIState)
    {
        tracker->m_nStyle |= CRectTracker::hatchedBorder;
    }
}
```

This function's pretty straightforward. First, it captures the rectangle of the item. It then checks to see if the pointers to this item and the currently selected item are the same. If so, the item gets the resize handles. This function then checks to see if the item is linked or embedded. If it is linked, it will use a dotted line for the tracking rectangle. If it is embedded, it will use a solid line for the tracking rectangle. If the item is active, it sets the border to hatched marks.

Go ahead and compile and execute the MyContainer application. Now, when you insert an object, you will see the tracking rectangle around the edge of the bitmap, as shown in Figure 9.43.

FIGURE 9.43

The object now has the tracking rectangle.

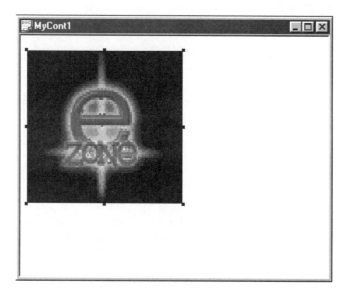

Working with Multiple Objects

Currently, the MyContainer example application only works with one object, and you must use the menu options to edit the object. Now, you are going to modify the application to allow you to work with multiple items. This includes clicking an item to activate it and double-clicking an item to edit it.

The first thing that you will need to do is add the necessary code that will tell you which object is currently selected. This is best handled by a small helper function, much like the DoTracker() function you added. So, go ahead and add the following function declaration just after the declaration you added for the DoTracker() function:

```
CMyContainerCntrItem* CMyContainerView::WhichObject(CPoint point);
```

Now, add the WhichObject() function just after the DoTracker() function in MyContainerView.cpp. The WhichObject() function is shown in Listing 9.21.

LISTING 9.21　The WhichObject() Function

```
CMyContainerCntrItem* CMyContainerView::WhichObject(CPoint point)
{
```

```
CMyContainerDoc* pDoc = GetDocument();
CMyContainerCntrItem* pItem = NULL;

POSITION pos = pDoc->GetStartPosition();
while(pos)
{
    CMyContainerCntrItem* pCurrItem =
        (CMyContainerCntrItem*) pDoc->GetNextClientItem(pos);
    if(pCurrItem->m_ItemRect.PtInRect(point))
    {
        pItem = pCurrItem;
    }
}
return pItem;
}
```

This function will go through all of the objects in the document checking to see if the click was within the rectangle for the object. If it was, that object that was clicked on will be returned; otherwise a NULL value will be returned. This function is set up to handle several objects in the document and MyContainer only supports one object. You will correct this after you add support for mouse clicks.

Single Clicks

To handle a single-click, you will need to capture the WM_LBUTTONDOWN message. Go ahead and create the message handler function by using the ClassWizard. Make sure that the Class name drop-down list is set to CMyContainerView. Scroll through the list of messages until you find the WM_LBUTTONDOWN. Double-click it to create the message-handler function, as shown in Figure 9.44.

FIGURE 9.44

Creating a message handler for the WM_LBUTTONDOWN *message.*

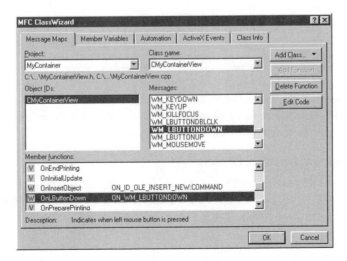

After you have the message-handler function created, go ahead and modify it to match Listing 9.22.

LISTING 9.22   The `OnLButtonDown()` Message-Handler Function

```
void CMyContainerView::OnLButtonDown(UINT nFlags, CPoint point)
{
    // TODO: Add your message handler code here and/or call default
    CMyContainerCntrItem* pItem = WhichObject(point);

    if(pItem == NULL || pItem != m_pSelection)
    {
        COleClientItem* pActiveItem =
            GetDocument()->GetInPlaceActiveItem(this);
        if(pActiveItem != NULL && pActiveItem != pItem)
        {
            pActiveItem->Close();
        }
    }
    Invalidate();
    m_pSelection = pItem;

    if (pItem == NULL)
        return;

    CRectTracker tracker;
    DoTracker(pItem, &tracker);
    UpdateWindow();
    if (tracker.Track(this,point))
    {
        Invalidate();
        pItem->m_ItemRect = tracker.m_rect;
        GetDocument()->SetModifiedFlag();
    }
}
```

When the left mouse button is clicked once on the document, this code will determine which object is selected and sets it as the active object. After an item is selected, the tracking rectangle is drawn around the selected object.

Drawing Multiple Objects

The MyContainer application is capable of using multiple objects, but you must now modify the `OnDraw()` function to handle drawing multiple objects. Go ahead and modify the `OnDraw()` function to match Listing 9.23.

LISTING 9.23 Drawing Multiple Objects

```
void CMyContainerView::OnDraw(CDC* pDC)
{
    CMyContainerDoc* pDoc = GetDocument();
    ASSERT_VALID(pDoc);

    // TODO: add draw code for native data here
    // TODO: also draw all OLE items in the document

    // Draw the selection at an arbitrary position.  This code should
    // be removed after your real drawing code is implemented.  This
    // position corresponds exactly to the rectangle returned by
    // CMyContainerCntrItem, to give the effect of in-place editing.

    // TODO: remove this code when final draw code is complete.

    if (m_pSelection == NULL)
    {
        POSITION pos = pDoc->GetStartPosition();
        m_pSelection = (CMyContainerCntrItem*)pDoc->
        ➥GetNextClientItem(pos);
    }

    POSITION pos = pDoc->GetStartPosition();
    while (pos)
    {
        CMyContainerCntrItem* pCurrItem =
            (CMyContainerCntrItem*) pDoc->GetNextClientItem(pos);
        pCurrItem->Draw(pDC, pCurrItem->m_ItemRect);

        if (pCurrItem == m_pSelection)
        {
            CRectTracker tracker;
            DoTracker(pCurrItem, &tracker);
            tracker.Draw(pDC);
        }
    }
}
```

Now, each item in the document is drawn to its proper location. You can go ahead and execute the MyContainer application now. You can now insert more than one object, as shown in Figure 9.45.

Double Clicks

The normal function of double-clicking an object is to open that object for edit. This is actually pretty easy to implement. Create a message handler for the WM_LBUTTONDBLCLK window message. You should create this message-handler function just like you did for the single click message handler. After you have the function created, modify the function so that the code matches Listing 9.24.

FIGURE 9.45

*MyContainer app with
multiple objects.*

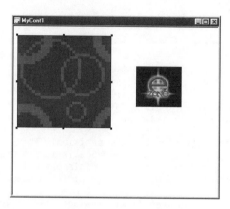

LISTING 9.24   The `OnLButtonDblClk()` Function

```
void CMyContainerView::OnLButtonDblClk(UINT nFlags, CPoint point)
{
    // TODO: Add your message handler code here and/or call default
    OnLButtonDown(nFlags, point);
    if(m_pSelection)
    {
        m_pSelection->DoVerb(OLEIVERB_PRIMARY, this);
    }

    CView::OnLButtonDblClk(nFlags, point);
}
```

Now, when an object is double-clicked, the `OnLButtonDown()` function is called, which
updates the current item and tracking rectangle. Then, the object is opened for editing in-
place.

Cursor Indications

You might not have noticed this, but you could actually move the objects when they were
active without going into edit mode. The only reason you didn't notice this was because
the mouse cursor shape didn't change when you moved across the objects. You can fix
this by capturing the `WM_SETCURSOR` message. After you create the function, modify it so
that it matches Listing 9.25.

LISTING 9.25   The `OnSetCursor()` Function

```
BOOL CMyContainerView::OnSetCursor(CWnd* pWnd, UINT nHitTest,
➥UINT message)
{
    // TODO: Add your message handler code here and/or call default
    if (pWnd == this && m_pSelection != NULL)
    {
```

```
        CRectTracker tracker;
        DoTracker(m_pSelection, &tracker);
        if (tracker.SetCursor(this, nHitTest))
        {
            return TRUE;
        }
    }

    return CView::OnSetCursor(pWnd, nHitTest, message);
}
```

Removing Objects

Now that you know how to add, resize, and move objects, you should know how to remove objects when they are no longer needed. You will need to add a menu option to the IDR_MYCONTTYPE menu. Go ahead and click the Link menu option and then press the Insert key to insert a menu option just before the Link menu option. Double-click the new blank menu option and enter an ID of ID_EDIT_CLEAR with a caption of Delete Object. Press the Enter key to save these changes.

After you have created the menu option, you need to create a message handler for the new menu option. Right-click the menu bar and select ClassWizard to bring up the ClassWizard dialog box. Click the IDR_EDIT_CLEAR object ID, then double-click the COMMAND message to create the handler function. Now do the same for the UPDATE_COMMAND_UI message.

With the two handlers created, modify them both so that they match Listing 9.26.

LISTING 9.26 The OnSetCursor() Function

```
void CMyContainerView::OnEditClear()
{
    // TODO: Add your command handler code here
    if (m_pSelection)
    {
        m_pSelection->Delete();
        m_pSelection = NULL;
        GetDocument()->SetModifiedFlag();
        GetDocument()->UpdateAllViews(NULL);
    }
}

void CMyContainerView::OnUpdateEditClear(CCmdUI* pCmdUI)
{
    // TODO: Add your command update UI handler code here
    pCmdUI->Enable(m_pSelection != NULL);
}
```

When there is an active object, it can be deleted by using the Edit, Delete Object menu option. This menu option will only be enabled if `m_pSelection` is not empty, which means it will only be enabled if an object is in the document.

Lesson Summary

Adding container capabilities can add a great deal of flexibility to your application. In this lesson, you learned how to use the MFC AppWizard to create an application that had basic container capabilities. By expanding on the framework created, you learned how to work with multiple objects within the same document, as well as resizing and moving the objects around the document.

You learned how to iterate through all of the objects that are in a document, and how to tell when a user has selected one of the objects to work with by capturing mouse clicks. You also learned how to invoke the editing capability of an object when a user double-clicks an object. And, when the user is done with an object, you learned how to remove an object from a document.

Quiz 3

1. When you generated the MyContainer application as an MDI application with container capabilities, which class was created that isn't created with normal MDI applications?

    a. `CMyContainerItem`

    b. `CMyContCntrItem`

    c. `CMyContainerCntr`

    d. `CMyContainerCntrItem`

2. To remove the active object from a container, which method of `m_pSelection` would you call?

    a. `Remove()`

    b. `Delete()`

    c. `DeleteObject()`

    d. `FreeObject()`

3. Which function is called when an item is moved during in-place editing?

    a. `OnChangeItemPosition()`

    b. `OnItemPositionChanged()`

    c. `OnItemMoved()`

    d. `OnItemResized()`

4. What is the standard name of the variable that is used throughout a container application to communicate with objects?

    a. `m_pSelection`

    b. `m_pSelectedItem`

    c. `m_pSelectedObject`

    d. `m_pSelected`

Exercise 3

Complexity: Easy

1. Create an MDI ActiveX container application named "Exercise 1." This application should include the capabilities to enable the user to reposition and resize an inserted object. You do not have to include a tracking rectangle.

Complexity: Advanced

2. Create an MDI ActiveX container application named "Exercise 2." This application should enable multiple objects to be inserted into the control. You should be able to move the objects simply by clicking on them and dragging them to a new location. If you double-click an object, the object should be edited in-place. Include a tracking rectangle.

LESSON 4

Developing an ActiveX Server Application

The main purpose of applications is to supply its documents to ActiveX container applications. By building your application with server capabilities, you are allowing other container applications to use the documents from your application. This capability will enable users to create special documents that can only be created with your application and then later added to an application such as Microsoft Word.

A server application functions just like a normal application, except for the fact that documents created with your application can be used by other applications. In this lesson, you will learn how to add server capabilities to an application.

Building the MyServer Application

To get started with this lesson, you will need to build an example application. Follow these steps to build the MyServer application:

1. Close any open projects.

2. Choose File, New from the menu to create a new project.

3. Name the project MyServer and select MFC AppWizard (exe).

4. Click OK to begin selecting options for the program.

5. Accept the default application type as MDI and click the Next button.

6. You don't need database support for this application, so just click the Next button.

7. On this next page, select Full-Server as the compound document support that you want to include, as shown in Figure 9.46.

FIGURE 9.46

Selecting to include server capabilities.

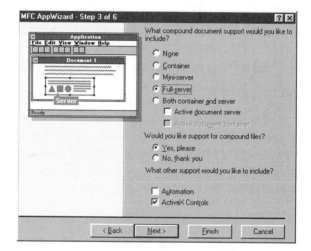

8. After selecting Container, click the Next button to move on to the next step.

9. On the MFC AppWizard—Step 4 of 6—click the Advanced button at the bottom of the dialog. This will bring up the Advanced Options for this application.

10. Change the File New Name (Short Name) to MyServer and change File Type Name (Long Name) to MyServer Document, as shown in Figure 9.47. You will see why you changed these names a little later on.

11. Click the Close button to close the Advanced Options dialog.

12. Click the Finish button to build the MyServer application.

FIGURE 9.47

Changing the short and long names for documents.

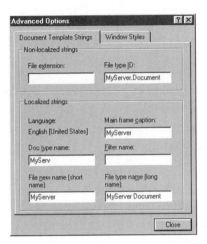

Inside the MyServer Application

The classes generated for a server application look pretty much like the classes generated for a container application, with the notable exception of the CMyServerSrvrItem class in place of the CMyContainerCntrItem class. The second new class that was added is the CInPlaceFrame class. The following sections outline the major differences for a server application compared to a normal MDI application.

CinPlaceFrame Class

This class handles the frame around the item and the control bars, such as the tool bar, the status bar, and the dialog box bars. This class has three member variables:

- m_wndToolBar of type CToolBar
- m_wndResizeBar of type COleResizeBar
- m_dropTarget of type COleDropTarget

The COleResizeBar looks like the CRectTracker, which you used in the last lesson. The COleDropTarget is used for implementing drag-and-drop capabilities, and you already learned about CToolBar in Chapter 6, "Customizing the User Interface."

The three major functions of this class are

- OnCreate()—This function creates the resize bar and registers a drop target.
- OnCreateControlBars()—This function is called when a server document is activated. It creates a docking bar and a resizable toolbar.
- PreCreateWindow()—This function is used to set up the style for the frame window.

CMyServerApp

Just like a container application, a member variable was added to this class. It is defined as

```
COleTemplateServer m_server;
```

Just before the `InitInstance()` function, a Class ID is defined for your application, which is shown in Listing 9.27.

LISTING 9.27 The Class ID for MyServer

```
// This identifier was generated to be statistically unique for your
// app. You may change it if you prefer to choose a specific
// identifier.

// {83DFD786-BF57-11D1-A94A-92D96E67A96B}
static const CLSID clsid =
{ 0x83dfd786, 0xbf57, 0x11d1, { 0xa9, 0x4a, 0x92, 0xd9, 0x6e,
➡0x67, 0xa9, 0x6b } };
```

This ID is unique to your application; therefore, the ID created here will be different from the one that you create.

The `OnInitialze()` function initializes the OLE libraries, just like a container application does. Before the `AddDocTemplate()` function is called in the `InitInstance()` function, more lines of code are added. These lines of code are used to register the menu used for editing objects:

```
pDocTemplate->SetServerInfo(
        IDR_MYSERVTYPE_SRVR_EMB, IDR_MYSERVTYPE_SRVR_IP,
        RUNTIME_CLASS(CInPlaceFrame));
```

The resources to which this function is referring are the menu resources that were generated by the AppWizard. If you were to look at your resources tab and expand the Menu branch, you will see that there are now four menu resources.

The `IDR_MYSERVTYPE_SRVR_EMB` menu is used when an embedded object is being edited in a separate window. The most noticeable difference for this menu is the File menu, as shown in Figure 9.48. The menu choices for this menu are different than the standard choices of the `IDR_MYSERVTYPE` menu. This menu is used when you are working on an object in a separate window that is embedded in your document.

The fourth menu, as shown in Figure 9.49, is the menu that will be used when an item is being edited in-place. This menu will be combined with a server in-place menu. The separators show where the menus will be combined.

FIGURE 9.48

The menu used for editing embedded objects.

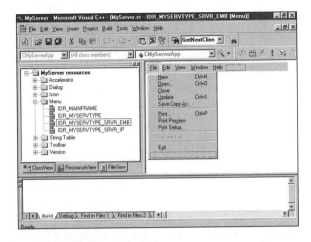

FIGURE 9.49

The menu used for editing objects in-place.

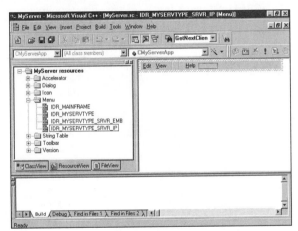

This next line of code, which is also in the InitInstance() function, connects the template for the document to the class ID.

```
m_server.ConnectTemplate(clsid, pDocTemplate, FALSE);
```

If the server application is already running, and if it is an MDI application, a new MDI window will be opened; otherwise the server application will be launched. This is handled by the next new line of code in InitInstance(), which is

```
COleTemplateServer::RegisterAll();
```

To finish off the InitInstance() function, after the command line is parsed, the code checks to see if the application is being launched as an embedded object. If not, the application is executed as a stand-alone application.

CMyServerDoc

The biggest difference for this class is the fact that it now inherits from the COleServerDoc class rather than the CDocument class. The first major difference is in the header file MyServerDoc.h. The public function GetEmbeddedItem() allows other functions to access the server item:

```
// Attributes
public:
    CMyServerSrvrItem* GetEmbeddedItem()
        { return (CMyServerSrvrItem*)
        ➥COleServerDoc::GetEmbeddedItem(); }
```

Inside the constructor for this class, CMyServerDoc(), a new line has been added:

```
EnableCompoundFile();
```

This line of code allows the use of compound files. A new function has been added as well. The OnGetEmbeddedItem() function. This function creates a new server item for the document and returns the pointer, as shown in Listing 9.28.

LISTING 9.28   The OnGetEmbeddedItem() Function

```
COleServerItem* CMyServerDoc::OnGetEmbeddedItem()
{
    // OnGetEmbeddedItem is called by the framework to get the
    // COleServerItem that is associated with the document.
    // It is only called when necessary.

    CMyServerSrvrItem* pItem = new CMyServerSrvrItem(this);
    ASSERT_VALID(pItem);
    return pItem;
}
```

CMyServerSrvrItem

This class provides an interface between the container application and a document. The constructor for this class passes the document pointer back to the base class. The AssertValid() and Debug() functions are used for debugging. Other than these normal functions, this class has four override functions for you to use.

- GetDocument()—This function simply calls the base class function and casts the results.

- Serialize()—This function checks to see if the item is embedded and if it is, the Serialize() function for that item is called.

- OnDraw()—This function is used to draw the item when it is inactive.

- OnGetExtent()—This function is used to return the extent of the item, measured in HIMETRIC units.

CMyServerView

There are very few changes in this class. A message handler to handle the `ID_CANCEL_EDIT_SRVR` message has been added to the message map, which can be seen about half way-down Listing 9.29.

LISTING 9.29 A Message Handler Was Added to Handle the `ID_CANCLE_EDIT_SRVR` Message

```
BEGIN_MESSAGE_MAP(CMyServerView, CView)
    //{{AFX_MSG_MAP(CMyServerView)
        // NOTE - the ClassWizard will add and remove mapping macros
        // here.   DO NOT EDIT what you see in these blocks
        // of generated code!
    ON_COMMAND(ID_CANCEL_EDIT_SRVR, OnCancelEditSrvr)
    //}}AFX_MSG_MAP
    // Standard printing commands
    ON_COMMAND(ID_FILE_PRINT, CView::OnFilePrint)
    ON_COMMAND(ID_FILE_PRINT_DIRECT, CView::OnFilePrint)
    ON_COMMAND(ID_FILE_PRINT_PREVIEW, CView::OnFilePrintPreview)
END_MESSAGE_MAP()
```

The function that catches this message was also created in the `CMyServerView` class, which is the `OnCancelEditSrvr()` function. This function is used to deactivate an item.

Working with the MyServer Server

At this time, you can go ahead and compile and execute the MyServer application. The very first time that you run a server application, it will register itself in the Registry. To see if your server application is functional, start a container application, such as Microsoft Word. Choose the Insert, Object menu option. You will be presented with a dialog box that will allow you to choose a registered object to insert. Scroll down the list until you see MyServer Document, as shown in Figure 9.50.

FIGURE 9.50

Inserting the MyServer document.

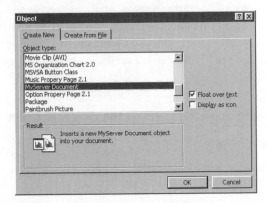

Note

When you were building the MyServer application, you were instructed to change the File New Name and the File Type Name. If you would have left the File Type Name as MyServ Document, that would be the name of the object in the Insert Object dialog box.

After you find the MyServer Document object, go ahead and click OK to insert it into the Word document. After the object is inserted, your screen should look something like Figure 9.51.

FIGURE 9.51

An empty server document.

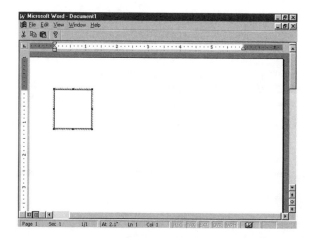

It might not look like much because you haven't added any code to draw the document, but you now have a fully functional server. Also, notice that most of the menus and toolbars are now gone. This is due to the fact that you have not developed any of these items in your server.

To draw something when the object is active, you will need to add some code to the CMyServerView::OnDraw() function. When the item is inactive, you will need to add code to the CMyServerSrvrItem::OnDraw() function. So, first you will add some code for the active drawing. Modify the CMyServerView::OnDraw() function to match Listing 9.30.

LISTING 9.30   Drawing Something When the Object Is Active

```
void CMyServerView::OnDraw(CDC* pDC)
{
    CMyServerDoc* pDoc = GetDocument();
    ASSERT_VALID(pDoc);
```

```
// TODO: add draw code for native data here

CRect rcBounds;
GetClientRect(&rcBounds);

CPen smile(PS_SOLID, 4, RGB(0,0,0));

CBrush white(RGB(255,255,255));
CBrush yellow(RGB(255,255,0));
CBrush black(RGB(0,0,0));

CBrush* oldbrush = pDC->SelectObject(&white);
pDC->Rectangle(rcBounds);

int xsize = rcBounds.Width() / 12;
int ysize = rcBounds.Height() / 12;
int top   = rcBounds.left;
int left  = rcBounds.top;

pDC->SelectObject(&yellow);
pDC->Ellipse(left,top,left+12*xsize,top+12*ysize);

CPen* oldpen = pDC->SelectObject(&smile);
pDC->SelectObject(&black);
pDC->Ellipse(left+ 2 * xsize,top+ 2 * ysize,
             left+ 5 * xsize,top+ 5 * ysize);
pDC->Ellipse(left+ 7 * xsize,top+ 2 * ysize,
             left+10 * xsize,top+ 5 * ysize);

pDC->Arc(left +2 * xsize,top+ 2 * ysize,
left+10 * xsize,top+10 * ysize,
left    * xsize,top+ 7 * ysize,
left+12 * xsize,top+ 7 * ysize);

pDC->SelectObject(oldpen);
pDC->SelectObject(oldbrush);

}
```

This block of code should look is active, you will very familiar. It draws Mr. Smiley. In order to get the bounding area to draw Mr. Smiley, a CRect variable, named rcBounds, was created. A call was made to the GetClientRect() function, which returns the rectangle area for the object. The rest of the code in this function should be self-explanatory by now. Go ahead and rebuild and execute the MyServer application. You should have a screen similar to Figure 9.52. This will show you that your document is actually drawing something.

FIGURE 9.52

Mr. Smiley in an MDI document.

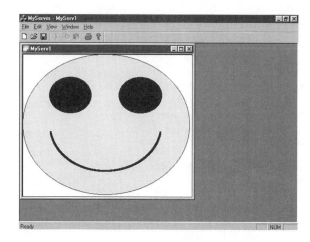

Open Word again and insert the MyServer Document object. This time you will have a little more than just an empty bounding box around the object, as shown in Figure 9.53.

FIGURE 9.53

Inserting the MyServer document object.

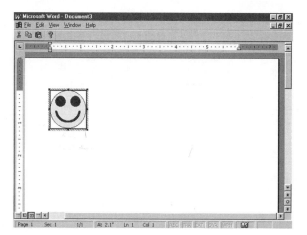

Lesson Summary

In this lesson, you learned about the differences between a container application and a server application. The code generated by the MFC AppWizard handles a great deal of the server capabilities for you. By adding server capabilities to your application, you enable users to create documents with your application and use them from within another application.

Quiz 4

1. Besides the standard classes that you would find in a normal MDI application, which two classes were created when you created the MyServer application, which has server capabilities?

    a. `CMyServerDoc` and `CMyServerView`

    b. `CMyServerSrveItem` and `AssertValid()`

    c. `CMyServerSrvrItem` and `CInPlaceFrame`

    d. `OnDraw()` and `OnDrawServer()`

2. Which function is used to draw the server document when it is inactive?

    a. `CMyServerView::OnDraw()`

    b. `CMyServerSrvrItem::OnDraw()`

    c. `CMyServerDoc::OnDraw()`

    d. `CMyServerView::OnDocumentDraw()`

3. Which function is called to create the docking bar and resizable bar when a server document is activated?

    a. `PreCreateWindow()`

    b. `OnCreateBars()`

    c. `OnCreate()`

    d. `OnCreateControlBars()`

4. Which class provides the interface between the container application and the document?

    a. `CMyServerDoc`

    b. `CMyServerSrvrItem`

    c. `CMyServerView`

    d. `OnDraw()`

Exercise 4

Complexity: Easy

1. Create an MDI ActiveX server application named "Exercise 1." In the `OnDraw()` function of the view, display the message `Hello Interactive World!`. Compile and execute the application to make sure it works as a stand-alone application. Now, start Microsoft Word, or any other application that will allow you to insert objects, and insert an Exercise 1 Document. The message should be displayed in the inserted document.

Complexity: Moderate

2. Create an MDI ActiveX server application named "Exercise 2." This exercise will function just like the previous exercise, however, except that the text is to be drawn in red. Also, when you click away from the object, rather than not having an inactive display for the document, draw a gray rectangle as the object.

Chapter Summary

In this chapter, you were introduced to the world of ActiveX programming. You started by learning about ActiveX and how to use ActiveX controls in your applications. After learning how to use someone else's controls, you learned how to build your very own controls.

After building your own controls, you went on to learn about container applications and how adding container capabilities to your application can give your application a great deal of flexibility for your users. You then moved on to developing an application with server capabilities. By adding server capabilities to your application, you give the user freedom to create a document in your application, and then use that document within another container application, such as Word or Excel.

CHAPTER 10

Enabling Your Applications for the Internet

Unless you've been away for quite a while, you probably know that the online computer industry is booming. As a programmer, it's quite evident that this boom has created a huge demand for applications that take advantage of this kind of technology.

The truth, however, is that the Internet has been around for a few years. It was originally created by parts of the U.S. government and expanded upon by colleges. Now it seems that everyone in the world is getting online. In fact, entire books have been written that cover the evolution of the Internet and speculate where it's headed.

One of the key benefits of the Internet is that it allows people from all over the world to communicate with each other without encountering too many boundaries. Because so many people are using the same technologies to communicate, it's important to follow standards when designing your applications, unless you are developing something that hasn't been standardized by the online industry.

This chapter focuses on how you can implement some of the key topics of Internet programming into your applications and what kind of programming models are involved. You will see some of the technologies involved such as SMTP, FTP, and HTTP. Don't worry if these terms scare you. You will see that VC++ 6 has made it quite easy to deal with these technologies.

LESSON 1

Working with Sockets

Would you believe that the Internet is no more than just a giant wide area network of computers? Well, it is. Even though most of the computers on the Internet have a specific purpose, they typically fall into one of two categories: *client* or *server*. Either way, each computer is called a *host*.

The Internet contains more than just PCs and servers. Devices such as routers and gateways help connect and control the Internet's traffic. Other technologies such as telephony are also taking advantage of the Internet. For example, specifically designed gateways have been developed that will allow you to place a call on your computer that will actually connect you to someone's phone, not their computer.

IP Addresses

Each house on the street where you live has an address. It's this address that distinguishes one house from the next.

So, too, does each host on the Internet have an address. This address allows you to communicate back and forth directly. The only real difference is that all the addresses on the Internet follow the same format. This addressing scheme is defined by the underlying network protocol on which the Internet communicates.

The base protocol that the Internet travels on is *TCP/IP* (*transmit control protocol/ internet protocol*). The history of this protocol and the underlying technologies that make it work are beyond the scope of this book, but you should understand the basics, such as IP addresses and ports, before moving on.

An IP address typically takes the form known as dotted-decimal format (`127.0.0.1`, for example). This address has four sections, also referred to as *octets*. They are called octets because each section can hold a value up to what 8 bits can represent. In this case, the range of numbers per octet is 0 through 255.

Even though there are so many combinations, you cannot use all of them. For example, 127.0.0.1 has a special meaning. This IP address is referred to as *localhost*. If IP is installed on your machine, this IP address points to your machine via a local loop back and can't be used on the Internet.

Your computer's actual IP address will depend entirely on your network. If you're connected to the Internet through an ISP, it will typically assign you an IP address when you connect. Windows 95 includes a utility to view your IP settings, WINIPCFG.EXE. Executing this program will display your IP settings, which should be similar to Figure 10.1.

FIGURE 10.1

Viewing IP settings with WINIPCFG.EXE.

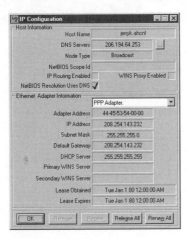

Looking at Figure 10.1, you can see that quite a few settings are involved with IP addresses. Depending upon the computer's operating system, more than one IP address may exist for a single host.

Remembering the IP address of a machine can be quite difficult, especially if you have to remember a lot of them. For that reason, a common service for IP addressing is Domain Name Service (DNS). A DNS will convert a host name to an IP address.

Looking at Figure 10.2, you can see that an MS-DOS session was used to find the address of the machine named "localhost" by issuing the command PING LOCALHOST. You can see that the name "localhost" resolved to an IP address of 127.0.0.1. A reverse lookup found that the name of the machine used in Figure 10.2 was named "jerryk" in the "ahcnt" domain.

FIGURE 10.2

Using PING *to see host names and IP addresses.*

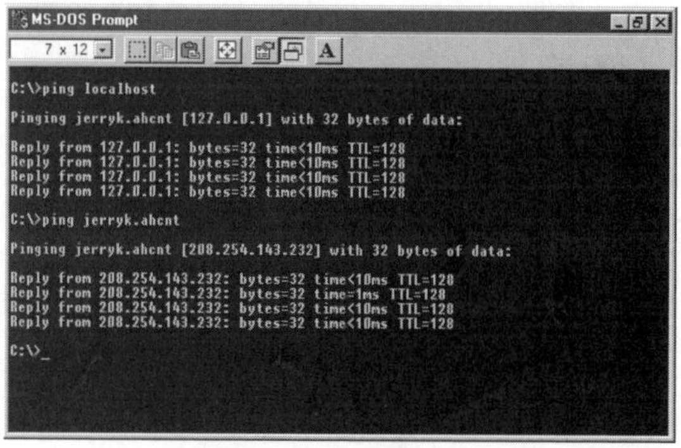

When that combination (jerryk.ahcnt) was issued as a parameter for PING, the current IP address of the machine was resolved.

In this example, "ahcnt" is the domain for the machine named "jerryk." Domains are used to organize names, which in turn organize IP addresses.

Ports

Now that you can see how each host on the Internet is separated from the next, you need to understand how ports work.

It's quite possible (and probable) that a single machine manages several services at once. For example, a machine could be used to manage Web connections (HTTP), email (SMTP), and files (FTP).

To expand on the analogy used earlier: imagine that each house had two (or more) phones. Two separate people in that house could talk to separate people at different houses without interfering with each other.

In this case, the people in the analogy are programs running on the computer and the phones are the ports. Each program uses a port to make a specific request and communicate with another host.

When programming with sockets, some ports have a predefined function, whereas others are available for your use. Table 10.1 shows some of the most common ports and the service associated with them.

TABLE 10.1 Some Common Services and Their Ports

Port	Service
20/21	FTP
23	TELNET
25	SMTP

Port	Service
43	WHOIS
79	FINGER
80	HTTP
110	POP3
119	NNTP

Table 10.1 is by no means exhaustive. For a more thorough and up-to-date list, you can check out http://www.internic.net with a Web browser. Colleges and other companies also maintain searchable archives for these and other related documents.

When programming with sockets (which are Internet addresses that combine the IP with a port number), your application will make use of addresses and ports to complete specific tasks.

The MFC and Sockets

You should not be surprised to know that the MFC has included special classes that encompass the functionality of sockets. These classes define the interface the MFC uses to access the Winsock DLLs.

Two of these classes that directly relate to sockets are CAsyncSocket and CSocket. Other classes are used in conjunction with these classes to simplify the sending and retrieving of data across the socket connection, but these two classes do the hard work.

CAsyncSocket

CAsyncSocket is the base class for programming with sockets in MFC. This class encapsulates the Windows Socket Application Programming Interface (API) and is typically used by programmers who want to program closer to the Sockets API directly and want the benefits of having callback functions.

The main purpose of this class is simply to use an object-oriented approach in C++ for sockets. One key benefit of doing this is allowing some Windows messages to be converted to callbacks.

CSocket

CSocket directly derives from CAsyncSocket, giving it all the functionality of CAsyncSocket. This class also manages most of the aspects of communications that you would have to handle manually when using CAsyncSocket.

One major advantage to this class is that it provides blocking. This allows synchronous operation, which is required when working with the CArchive class. CArchive resembles using MFC's serialization protocol to store and retrieve files, and comes with limitations of its own.

Other Socket-Related Classes

There are two kinds of sockets: streams and datagrams. *Stream* sockets provide data flow without record boundaries. They are guaranteed to be delivered and in proper sequence. *Datagrams* are typically record-oriented sockets. Their delivery is not guaranteed and may be delivered out of sequence or more than once.

Several classes are also available that manage sending data back and forth when using streams. CArchive and CSocketFile classes can manage file I/O and sending data across the socket connection.

Writing a Socket Application

Now that you know the basics of sockets and some of the classes that the MFC provides for working with sockets, it's time to learn how to implement them in code.

For this lesson, you will be creating a small application that will send an email message through SMTP. *SMTP* stands for *simple mail transfer protocol* and is defined in the Internet Engineering Task Force's RFC 821. For detailed information on this protocol, you can point your Web browser to http://www.isi.edu/in-notes/rfc821.txt.

 Note

> It's important to note that there are several other RFCs that define the current specification for SMTP. These include RFCs that define how to add attachments and perform other functions. You should do a thorough search of the RFCs to make sure you are using the latest information.

In order for this application to work, you will need to have a connection to an SMTP server. If you have an Internet email account somewhere, you should have this kind of service. Some installations, however, require special control codes that instruct their email server to send email using SMTP.

With that said, it's time to let AppWizard build the application framework. This time, a special step tells the AppWizard that you want to have socket support in your application. Create the application framework by completing the following steps:

1. Use AppWizard to create a new MFC EXE Application named SMTPMAIL.
2. Select a dialog-based application and click the Next button.

3. On Step 2 of the AppWizard, select the Windows Sockets option. This will add the necessary code to your program to add basic support for sockets. Figure 10.3 shows this step.

FIGURE 10.3

AppWizard Step 2 with Windows Sockets option checked.

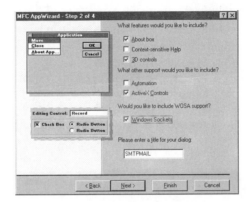

4. Click the Finish button, and complete the creation process.

With the basic application framework created, you need to design the input screen. Using Figure 10.4 as a guide, modify your main dialog resource to resemble the one seen in the figure.

FIGURE 10.4

SMTPMAIL's modified main dialog resource.

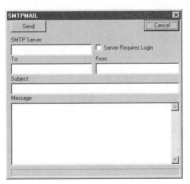

Use the following settings for the controls on this dialog box:

- SMTP Server edit box—Resource ID of IDC_SERVER
- Check box control—Resource ID of IDC_LOGIN and caption of Server Requires Login
- To edit box—Resource ID of IDC_TO

- From edit box—Resource ID of IDC_FROM
- Subject edit box—Resource ID of IDC_SUBJECT
- Message edit box—Resource ID of IDC_MESSAGE; turn on the Multiline, Vertical scroll, and Want Return options on the Styles page of the edit control's properties.
- Status static control—Resource ID of IDC_STATUS and no caption; set the Align Text property to Center and turn on the Center vertically and Sunken options on the Styles page of the static text control.

With the dialog resource created, use ClassWizard to create member variables for each dialog box. Because this is the main dialog box for the program, the member variables will need to be created to access the controls. Use Figure 10.5 as a guideline to create the member variables.

FIGURE 10.5

Member variables in ClassWizard.

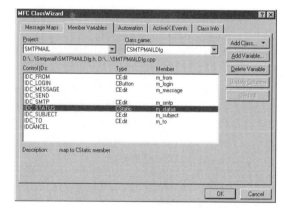

With the member variables created, you need to add the necessary code that will send the message when the Send message is clicked. Create the empty function handler for the Send button by double-clicking it and accepting the default name given for the function.

With the function handler created, edit the function handler to match the following listing by simply adding the lines of code after the //TODO comment, as shown in Listing 10.1.

LISTING 10.1 OnSend Function Handler

```
void CSMTPMAILDlg::OnSend()
{
    // TODO: Add your control notification handler code here
    // declare variables
    CString s_smtp;
    CString s_to;
    CString s_from;
    CString s_subject;
```

```
CString s_message;

CString buffer;
char in_buffer[1024];
CSocket mailsocket;

// populate variables with window control values
m_smtp.GetWindowText(s_smtp);
m_to.GetWindowText(s_to);
m_from.GetWindowText(s_from);
m_subject.GetWindowText(s_subject);
m_message.GetWindowText(s_message);

// create and connect socket
m_status.SetWindowText("Connecting to server");
mailsocket.Create();
mailsocket.Connect(s_smtp,25);

// Login to server
// Some SMTP servers require you to identify yourself
// and/or check the IP address that is trying to send
// the mail against a table of valid IP addresses defined
// by someone such as your ISP

m_status.SetWindowText("Logging into SMTP server");
if (m_login.GetCheck())
    buffer = "HELO " + s_from + "\r\n";
else
    buffer = "HELO \r\n";
mailsocket.Send(buffer,buffer.GetLength());
mailsocket.Receive(in_buffer,1024);

// send smtp envelope
m_status.SetWindowText("Sending message envelope");

buffer = "MAIL FROM:  <" + s_from + ">\r\n";
mailsocket.Send(buffer,buffer.GetLength());
mailsocket.Receive(in_buffer,1024);

buffer = "RCPT TO:  <" + s_to + ">\r\n";
mailsocket.Send(buffer,buffer.GetLength());
mailsocket.Send("DATA ",5);
mailsocket.Receive(in_buffer,1024);

// Send smtp headers
m_status.SetWindowText("Sending message headers");

buffer = "From:  " + s_from + "<" + s_from + ">\r\n";
```

10

continues

LISTING 10.1 continued

```
    mailsocket.Send(buffer,buffer.GetLength());

    buffer = "To:   " + s_to + "<" + s_to + ">\r\n";
    mailsocket.Send(buffer,buffer.GetLength());

    buffer = "Subject: " + s_subject + "\r\n";
    mailsocket.Send(buffer,buffer.GetLength());

    // Send Message Data
    m_status.SetWindowText("Sending Message");

    mailsocket.Send("\r\n",2);
    buffer = s_message + "\r\n";
    mailsocket.Send(buffer,buffer.GetLength());

    mailsocket.Send("\r\n",2);
    mailsocket.Send(".\r\n",3);
    mailsocket.Receive(in_buffer,1024);

    //Disconnect from the server
    m_status.SetWindowText("Disconnecting from the server");

    mailsocket.Send("QUIT ",5);
    m_status.SetWindowText("Message Sent");
    mailsocket.Close();
}
```

At first, this may seem like a lot of code just to send a message, but, in all fairness to VC++ 6 and the MFC, you are shielded from quite a bit of code because the CSocket class hides most of the implementation details from you.

Because this function contains a good bit of code, each logical section will be discussed in turn. The first such section is as follows:

```
// declare variables
CString s_smtp;
CString s_to;
CString s_from;
CString s_subject;
CString s_message;

CString buffer;
char in_buffer[1024];
CSocket mailsocket;
```

The purpose of this section is to declare the variables needed to hold the necessary data to make this function work.

The first set of CString variables contains the values of the edit controls on the dialog box. Because the dialog box doesn't get the chance to close and perform the data exchange features of the MFC, you need to obtain the values of the controls manually.

The buffer variable is used throughout the function to hold the text that will be passed through the socket.

The next variable, in_buffer, holds the data passed back from the server. In this case, the buffer's size was set to 1,024. This is fine in this instance, because the SMTP server typically doesn't send back long messages.

The last variable declared is mailsocket. This object is of type CSocket, one of MFC's special classes for working with sockets. This object will do most of the work in this application.

The next section of code is responsible for obtaining the values of the edit controls and placing them into the function's variables:

```
// populate variables with window control values
m_smtp.GetWindowText(s_smtp);
m_to.GetWindowText(s_to);
m_from.GetWindowText(s_from);
m_subject.GetWindowText(s_subject);
m_message.GetWindowText(s_message);
```

Each of these lines uses the CEdit class' GetWindowText function to obtain the current value of the edit control.

The next section of code is responsible for creating the socket and establishing a connection:

```
// create and connect socket
m_status.SetWindowText("Connecting to server");
mailsocket.Create();
mailsocket.Connect(s_smtp,25);
```

The first line of this section updates the pseudo-status bar at the bottom of the screen that the application is trying to use for establishing a connection to the SMTP server.

The CSocket class provides several member functions. The first one used here is the Create() function. This function's signature is as follows:

```
BOOL Create( UINT nSocketPort = 0, int nSocketType = SOCK_STREAM,
➥LPCTSTR lpszSocketAddress = _NULL );
```

This function could create the socket and make the connection in one call, but for the purposes of this lesson, the Connect function establishes the connection.

CSocket's Connect function is derived from CAsyncSocket. This function has two signatures, both of which take two parameters. In this case, the first parameter is an address and the second is a port. Those two values create the connection. In this case, the address is the name of the SMTP server and the port is SMTP's standard port, 25.

With the socket created and connected, you are ready to start sending data. In this case, because you are using SMTP, you need to login to the server. The following code accomplishes this task:

```
m_status.SetWindowText("Logging into SMTP server");
if (m_login.GetCheck())
    buffer = "HELO " + s_from + "\r\n";
else
    buffer = "HELO \r\n";
mailsocket.Send(buffer,buffer.GetLength());
mailsocket.Receive(in_buffer,1024);
```

First, the pseudo-status bar is updated to reflect the program's stage of operation. Next, the value of the check box on the dialog box is checked to determine whether the server requires an account to use when connecting.

If a user account is required, the entry in the From edit box must be entered in a format that is understood by the server. This code could be modified to strip anything after the @ character in an email address, but for the simplicity of this lesson, it simply concatenates the value of the From field. You could also provide another mechanism for obtaining this kind of information from the user.

After the buffer line is built, it is sent to the server using CSocket's Send function. This function takes two parameters: a string buffer and the length of the string. MFC's CString class works well here. The variable name (in_buffer) is passed for the first parameter, and then CString's GetLength function is called to get the length of the string. That value is passed for the second parameter.

An important thing to note about the buffer lines in this application: The carriage-return and new-line control characters are added at the end. Without those characters, the SMTP server doesn't know that the command is complete.

Because this application uses SMTP, it's good practice to obtain the reply from the server when necessary. For this, CSocket's Receive function obtains the data from the socket. This function takes two parameters: a buffer to hold the data and the length of the buffer.

Even though this program doesn't do anything with the response from the server, a thorough SMTP client would interrogate the server's response to make sure everything is in order. Again, for the simplicity of this lesson, those steps are not taken. If you wanted to delve deeper into SMTP, however, exploring the RFCs for this protocol should give you the needed information.

The next step with SMTP is to send an envelope:

```
// send smtp envelope
m_status.SetWindowText("Sending message envelope");

buffer = "MAIL FROM:  <" + s_from + ">\r\n";
mailsocket.Send(buffer,buffer.GetLength());
mailsocket.Receive(in_buffer,1024);

buffer = "RCPT TO:  <" + s_to + ">\r\n";
mailsocket.Send(buffer,buffer.GetLength());
mailsocket.Send("DATA ",5);
mailsocket.Receive(in_buffer,1024);
```

The envelope for SMTP is similar to an envelope that you would use to send a paper letter. You need to tell the SMTP server who the mail is from, and then, to whom the message goes.

You do this by simply building the appropriate lines in the buffer variable and sending them to the server.

In this case, a MAIL FROM: command tells the SMTP server who is sending the mail; RCPT TO: tells who will receive the message. To specify more than one recipient, just send another line after the RCPT TO: without the RCPT TO: text in the buffer.

Once you have sent the addresses, you need to signify this to the server. This is accomplished by sending it the command DATA. This tells the server that the next command should be the message headers. The following code sends the headers:

```
// Send smtp headers
m_status.SetWindowText("Sending message headers");

buffer = "From:  " + s_from + "<" + s_from + ">\r\n";
mailsocket.Send(buffer,buffer.GetLength());

buffer = "To:  " + s_to + "<" + s_to + ">\r\n";
mailsocket.Send(buffer,buffer.GetLength());

buffer = "Subject: " + s_subject + "\r\n";
mailsocket.Send(buffer,buffer.GetLength());
```

Several commands can be passed in the headers. You should refer to the RFC for valid commands.

The first header command sent is From: name <email>. This command takes the display name and email address of the sender. In this application, they are the same, but they could be different values.

10

The second header command sent is To: name <email>, again taking a display name and an email address. This time, it's the recipient's information.

Next, the subject of the message is sent with the Subject: command. After the subject is sent, the SMTP server starts looking for the body. If you want to send other commands, you should do them before you send the body.

After the headers are sent, you can send the body of the message. The next section accomplishes this task:

```
// Send Message Data
m_status.SetWindowText("Sending Message");

mailsocket.Send("\r\n",2);
buffer = s_message + "\r\n";
mailsocket.Send(buffer,buffer.GetLength());

mailsocket.Send("\r\n",2);
mailsocket.Send(".\r\n",3);
mailsocket.Receive(in_buffer,1024);
```

The only thing of significance in this section is the command "." on a line by itself (second line from the bottom). This tells the SMTP server that the message is over.

After the body is sent, you just need to quit the session and close the socket. The following section of code accomplishes this task:

```
//Disconnect from the server
m_status.SetWindowText("Disconnecting from the server");

mailsocket.Send("QUIT ",5);
m_status.SetWindowText("Message Sent");
mailsocket.Close();
```

To quit the session with the SMTP server, send it the QUIT command.

With the connection to the server terminated and the socket closed, the process is complete.

Now that you understand what the application is supposed to do, it's time to test it. Go ahead and build and execute the application. Remember, you will need valid email account information in the fields to send an email successfully.

Figure 10.6 shows the SMTPMAIL application running. The values entered into the application in Figure 10.6 are only examples. They are provided so that you can see what kind of information needs to be entered.

Figure 10.6

*SMTPMAIL applica-
tion running.*

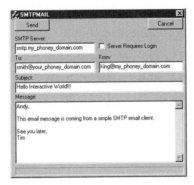

Lesson Summary

In this lesson, you learned the basics of how sockets operate. The key items needed for sockets are the host address and the port in which the two hosts communicate.

You saw that programming with sockets works well in a client server environment such as an SMTP client connecting to an SMTP server.

The MFC has nicely encapsulated socket programming into simple-to-use classes, `CAsyncSocket` and `CSocket`. Using these classes within your application makes it a snap to implement sockets. You learned how to do this by writing a simple SMTP email client application.

Quiz 1

1. From which class does `CSocket` derive?

    a. `CWinSock`

    b. `AsyncSocket`

    c. `CBaseSocket`

    d. None of the above

2. From which class does `CAsyncSocket` derive?

    a. `CObject`

    b. `CWinSock`

    c. `CSocket`

    d. None of the above

3. Which `CSocket` and/or `CAsyncSocket` functions create a socket connection?

    a. `Create` and `Connect`

    b. `SConnect`

    c. `SCreate`

    d. `CreateConnection` and `SocketConnect`

4. Which `CSocket` function transmits data over the socket?

    a. `Send` and `Receive`

    b. `Put` and `Get`

    c. `Out` and `In`

    d. `SendData` and `GetData`

Exercise 1

Complexity: Easy

1. Create a generic WHOIS application that prompts the user for an address. Send this address to rs.internic.net on port 43 and dump the response into an edit control large enough to hold several lines of data.

   The response that comes back will need to be cleaned up a bit for Windows-based machines. A new-line control character only separates the lines returned. You will need to replace this character with carriage-return and new-line control characters (\n for \r\n).

Complexity: Moderate

2. Create a generic FINGER application that asks the user to enter a user name to search for and a server to execute against. The Finger protocol operates on port 79.

   Sending a blank line (when the user name is left blank) typically results in a default report, but specifying all (or even sometimes just part) of a name will yield detailed information about that user.

   When running your example, you may want to try educational servers (such as `osu.edu` and `mit.edu`). A lot of commercial establishments turn this service off as it's an easy way to find out user names on a server.

   For a sample result, try looking for John at `mit.edu`.

LESSON 2

Querying HTTP Servers

In the last lesson, you learned about sockets and how to use the `CSocket` class to make an application that communicates directly with sockets.

You can easily communicate with a server using the HTTP protocol via the CSocket class, but the MFC has defined more classes that encapsulate the normal operations for using the HTTP protocol.

Typically, Web browsers use the HTTP protocol to retrieve documents from Web servers using sockets on port 80. As with any socket protocol, you can change this port, but you typically want to use standard ports. Microsoft titles their Web browser Internet Explorer. VC++ 6 includes classes that will let you take advantage of Internet Explorer's WebBrowser control in your own projects. Clients that fit this scenario typically interpret and display pages that are written in HTML.

What follows is a list of the most common classes when dealing with HTTP and HTML:

- CHtmlView—This class encapsulates Internet Explorer's WebBrowser control. Using this class in place of a CView class will enable your application to display HTML-rendered pages without having to parse the HTML code yourself.
- CHttpConnection—This class manages a connection to an HTTP server.
- CHttpFile—This class can retrieve a file from an HTTP server.
- CHttpFilter—This is a base class for writing Internet Server Application Programming Interface (ISAPI) DLL filters.
- CHttpFilterContext—This class is used in conjunction with CHttpFilter to process data passed through the ISAPI DLL filter.
- CHttpServer—This class extends the functionality of an ISAPI-compliant HTTP server.
- CHttpServerContext—This class is used in conjunction with CHttpServer to process data sent by the client.

Using the CHtmlView class requires that Internet Explorer version 4 or later be installed on the machine running your program.

Connecting to an HTTP Server

Typically, when connecting to an HTTP server, you are going to ask for an HTML document. You can, however, make a request to an HTTP server asking for virtually any kind of file, such as images and programs.

The purpose of the program built in this section is to connect to an HTTP server and display the source HTML that is returned to the client.

As seen in the previous lesson, you can see that AppWizard can build the application framework for you that will include socket support. Go ahead and build a new dialog-based application named HTMLVIEW. Make sure to check the box for Windows Sockets in Step 2 of the AppWizard.

With the application framework created, edit the IDD_HTMLVIEW_DIALOG resource so that it appears as shown in Figure 10.7.

FIGURE 10.7

Modified HTMLVIEW dialog resource.

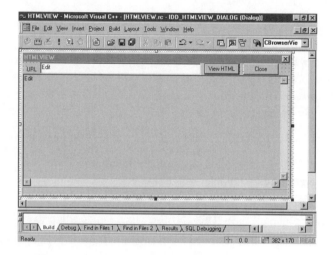

Use the following settings for the controls on this dialog box:

- URL edit box—Resource ID of IDC_URL
- View HTML button—Resource ID of ID_VIEW_HTML and a caption of View HTML; make sure that this is set as the default button
- Close button—Use the resource ID of IDCANCEL; this button will close the dialog box (and exit the program) when clicked
- HTML View edit box—Resource ID of IDC_HTML; use Multiline, Want Returns, Read Only, Horizontal scroll, and Vertical scroll.
- Status static text control—Resource ID of IDC_STATUS; align text to center, sunken, and center vertically

With the dialog resource created, you need to create member variables that will let you reach the necessary controls' value. In this example, you need to be able to access the URL Edit box, the HTML edit box, and the status static text control. Create the following member variables:

- m_url using IDC_URL returning the control
- m_html using IDC_HTML returning the control
- m_status using IDC_STATUS returning the control

Use Figure 10.8 as a guide to add the preceding member variables.

FIGURE 10.8

ClassWizard showing member variables for HTMLVIEW.

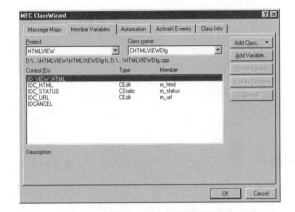

10

When connecting to an HTTP server, you only connect long enough to send a request and obtain a response. Once that transaction is over, the connection is over as well. Because this is the case, the entire process of connecting to the server and retrieving the HTML page can be done within one function. In this case, you need to make this happen when the View HTML button is clicked.

Go ahead and add a function handler for the View HTML button, accepting the default name given by VC++ 6. Once this stub is created, edit the function to match Listing 10.2.

LISTING 10.2   Function Handler for `OnViewHtml`

```
void CHTMLVIEWDlg::OnViewHtml()
{
    // TODO: Add your control notification handler code here
    CString s_url;
    CString line;
    CString buff;

    m_url.GetWindowText(s_url);

    CInternetSession session;
    try
    {
        m_html.SetWindowText("");
        m_status.SetWindowText("Finding File");

        CHttpFile* source = (CHttpFile*)session.OpenURL(s_url);

        m_status.SetWindowText("Retrieving File");
        buff = "";

        while (int x = source->ReadString(line) == 1)
        {
            buff = buff + line + "\r\n";
```

continues

LISTING 10.2   continued

```
            m_html.SetWindowText(buff);
        }

        source->Close();
        m_status.SetWindowText("File Retrieved");
    }
    catch (CInternetException* E)
    {
        m_status.SetWindowText("Error retrieving file");
        E->ReportError();
    }
    session.Close();
}
```

Don't build the application yet; you still need one line of code to make it work! You need to add the following line of code after the other includes in this file (HTMLVIEWDlg.cpp):

```
#include "afxinet.h"
```

Once this line has been added after the other includes, the program should compile.

Looking at the first logical section of OnViewHtml, you can see that the only thing that takes place is the declaration of variables needed in the function:

```
CString s_url;
CString line;
CString buff;

m_url.GetWindowText(s_url);
```

After the variables are declared, the variable s_url is populated with the value from the m_url edit control.

The next logical section actually spans most of the function. The first line creates an Internet session by using the MFC's CInternetSession class. Next, the entire procedure of opening a connection and retrieving a file is processed within a try..catch exception block. The exception block is specifically looking for a CInternetException error. If one occurs, the status bar is updated and the error is reported:

```
CInternetSession session;
try
{
  —· code removed —·
}
catch (CInternetException* E)
{
    m_status.SetWindowText("Error retrieving file");
    E->ReportError();
}
```

CInternetSession is typically used when you need to make an Internet connection, and you aren't coding for sockets directly (as used in Lesson 1 with the SMTP protocol).

The Internet session can last as long as the program operates, but, for this example, the session is created only when needed. Table 10.2 lists some of CInternetSession's most common class members.

TABLE 10.2 Common CInternetSession Class Members

Class Member	Description
OpenURL	Opens the given URL. If successful, a file handle is returned. The file handle type returned depends on the service used. Valid services are http://, ftp://, file://, and gopher://.
GetFtpConnection	Creates a connection to an FTP server and returns a pointer to a CFtpConnection object.
GetHttpConnection	Creates a connection to an HTTP server and returns a pointer to a CHttpConnection object. This function is needed if you plan on querying the HTTP headers. This object can also be used to pass a user name and password without manipulating the headers directly.
GetGopherConnection	Creates a connection to a Gopher server and returns a pointer to a CGopherConnection object.
EnableStatusCallback	Enables or disables status callbacks. This tracks the progress of an asynchronous operation. To use this operation, the session must include INTERNET_FLAG_ASYNC in its dwFlags parameter when created. The dwContext parameter must also be set to 1 in the constructor, which is already done by default. You also need to override the OnStatusCallback function.
ServiceTypeFromHandle	Returns the service type of the connection. Valid return values are INTERNET_SERVICE_FTP, INTERNET_SERVICE_HTTP, INTERNET_SERVICE_FILE, INTERNET_SERVICE_GOPHER.
Close	Closes the connection.
SetCookie	Sets a cookie for a URL.
GetCookie	Gets a cookie for a URL.
OnStatusCallback	Function to override when using EnableStatusCallback to track progress of a process.
HINTERNET	Handle to the current Internet session. Can be used with ServiceTypeFromHandle to determine session type.

10

Looking at the next section of code from Listing 10.2, you can see that the HTML edit box is cleared and the status bar is updated to represent its current process:

```
m_html.SetWindowText("");
m_status.SetWindowText("Finding File");

CHttpFile* source = (CHttpFile*)session.OpenURL(s_url);
```

The last line in this section creates an object-named source. This object is declared as a CHttpFile. Because you know at this point that you are looking for an HTTP file, you can safely cast the file handle to CHttpFile when the session opens the URL.

After the file has been opened, it's time to retrieve it from the server. The following section does just that:

```
m_status.SetWindowText("Retrieving File");
buff = "";

while (int x = source->ReadString(line) == 1)
{
    buff = buff + line + "\r\n";
    m_html.SetWindowText(buff);
}

source->Close();
m_status.SetWindowText("File Retrieved");
```

First, the status bar is updated to indicate that the program is retrieving the file. Next, the file is retrieved in a while loop until the file is completed.

You accomplish this by using CHttpFile's ReadString function. This function reads text from the server a line at a time. Carriage return and line feed control characters indicate the end of each line. If the ReadString function was successful, the value returned is 1; otherwise, 0 is returned.

While the file is being read, a string buffer is continually concatenated with the new line. Using m_html.SetWindowText() at this point is purely cosmetic. This gives visual indication in the edit box that something is happening. This step could have been done after the file was retrieved.

When the file is complete, it's closed and the status bar is updated. With the entire operation complete, the session is then closed by calling Close() for the session.

Table 10.3 lists some common class members for CHttpFile.

TABLE 10.3 Common `CHttpFile` Class Members

Class Member	Description
AddRequestHeaders	This function adds headers that were sent to the HTTP server. This is typically used when a client needs to send specific headers.
SendRequest	This function sends the request to the HTTP server.
QueryInfo	This function returns the response or request headers from the HTTP server. This function should only be used after a successful call to `SendRequest` or `OpenURL` (from the session).
QueryInfoStatus	This function obtains the status code associated with an HTTP request. The result is placed in the supplied `dwStatusCode` parameter.
GetVerb	This function returns a string that contains the verb used for a request.
GetObject	This function returns a string that contains the name of the object associated with a `CHttpFile`.
GetFileUrl	This function returns a string that contains the URL of the `CHttpFile` object.
Close	Closes the file.

Now that you know what the program does and how it does it, go ahead and build and execute the program. You need to have an Internet connection for this program to work. If you have an HTTP server running on your local machine, you can use the URL `http://127.0.0.1` to connect to your own machine.

Using Internet Explorer to Display HTML Pages

It would be an understatement to say that displaying an HTML page takes quite a bit of work. You would have to parse the HTML page to display images, links, and other resources properly. As the popularity of the Internet grows, so does its complexity.

Most likely, if you want to code an HTML viewer from scratch, you're beyond the scope of this book. If you want to use browser technology in your applications and want to leave the hard work up to the people at Microsoft, however, you're in luck.

VC++ 6 includes classes that will allow you to encapsulate Internet Explorer's WebBrowser control in your own applications. This does come at a price, however: Internet Explorer 4 (IE4) or later must be installed on the computer on which your application is running. In order to complete the second example in this lesson, you need to have IE4 installed.

For this example, you need to create a new project named BROWSER. Each of the following steps coordinates with a step in the AppWizard. Make sure to follow them exactly:

1. Select Single Document and click the Next button.

2. No database support is needed; click the Next button.

3. The default settings are okay; click the Next button.

4. In the section that asks, "How Do You Want Your Toolbars to Look?," select Internet Explorer ReBars. You do *not* need to check Windows Sockets at this point because this application won't be using them directly. If you wanted to perform other socket-related functions, however, you would need to check this box. Click the Next button.

5. The default settings are okay here, so click the Next button.

6. Select CHtmlView as the base class for this project. Figure 10.9 shows this selection in the AppWizard. Click the Finish button and complete the creation process.

FIGURE 10.9

AppWizard with the CHtmlView *base class selected.*

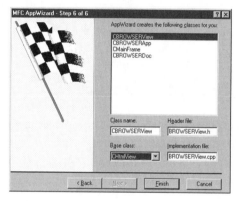

The most important step in this process is Step 6. This process changes the default view for the application from CView to CHtmlView, which encapsulates the WebBrowser control and allows your applications to use it.

To see how this immediately affects the program, go ahead and build and execute the program. Figure 10.10 shows the results of running this program.

Note

You will need an Internet connection for this lesson.

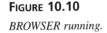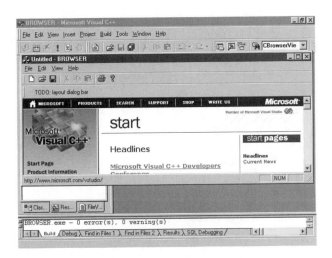

FIGURE 10.10

BROWSER running.

10

You should notice a couple of things with this application. First, it's quite evident that the document being displayed is an HTML page from Microsoft. The second is the toolbar. You can see a comment stating that you need to design a layout for the dialog bar.

Also, while the page was being loaded from Microsoft, the status bar was being continually updated to reflect the current status.

Even though the application does not have any navigation capabilities, it is an actual Web browser. You can click the links in the pages and download files.

Because the CHtmlView class wraps the functionality of the WebBrowser control, you can control its navigation by using its member functions to navigate to a specific URL. Any valid URL can be used. This includes http://, ftp://, file://, and Gopher://. You can also use the WebBrowser control as an active document container. This means that Excel spreadsheets, Word documents, and other files can be activated in place and edited.

Customizing the Toolbar with a Dialog Bar

In Chapter 6, "Customizing the User Interface," you learned the basics of dealing with toolbars. When AppWizard built this application, it created a special kind of toolbar: a Dialog Bar. Dialog bars are unique in that they allow you to create toolbars that contain common controls.

Another toolbar topic introduced is the use of rebars. The primary function of a rebar is to have resizable toolbars, such as those found in Internet Explorer.

With that said, it's time to modify the dialog bar. Bring up the IDR_MAINFRAME dialog resource in VC++ 6 dialog editor. As you can see from Figure 10.11, this is a normal dialog resource.

FIGURE 10.11

IDR_MAINFRAME *dialog resource.*

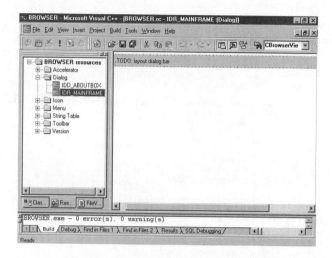

For this example, you need to edit the IDR_MAINFRAME dialog bar so that it resembles the one in Figure 10.12.

FIGURE 10.12

Modified IDR_MAIN-FRAME *dialog resource.*

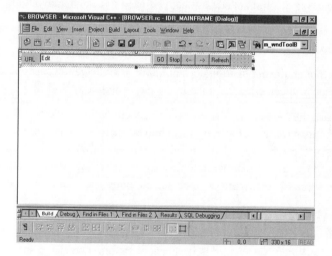

Make sure that the controls have the following properties:

- Static text—Caption of URL

- Edit box—Resource ID of m_url

- GO button—Resource ID of IDC_GO and a caption of GO; also set this as the default button

- Stop button—Resource ID of IDC_STOP and a caption of Stop

- Back button—Resource ID of IDC_BACK and a caption of <--

- Forward button—Resource ID of `IDC_FORWARD` and a caption of `-->`
- Refresh button—Resource ID of `IDC_REFRESH` and a caption of `Refresh`

With the dialog resource modified, you need to create a member variable for the URL edit box. Before you can create the needed member variable, you need to associate this dialog box with a class. Do this by displaying ClassWizard and instruct it to create a new class named `CNavBar`.

Once you have the dialog box's class created, go ahead and create a member variable for the URL edit box (`IDC_URL`) named `m_url` that returns the control.

Before adding code to control the navigation, it would be a good idea to do some clean up work to this application. For example, the default toolbar and rebar can both be removed from this application. Also, when this application starts, it automatically jumps to Microsoft's Web site. You'll probably want to prevent that.

To clean up the toolbars, you will want to remove the creation of the standard toolbar and the rebar, but leave in the dialog bar. This can easily be accomplished in the `CMainFrame`'s `OnCreate` function. This is where the toolbars and status bars are created. Simply commenting out the code that creates the toolbars will accomplish this task. Modify the `OnCreate` function so that it looks like the following:

```
int CMainFrame::OnCreate(LPCREATESTRUCT lpCreateStruct)
{
    if (CFrameWnd::OnCreate(lpCreateStruct) == -1)
        return -1;

//  if (!m_wndToolBar.CreateEx(this) ||
//      !m_wndToolBar.LoadToolBar(IDR_MAINFRAME))
//  {
//      TRACE0("Failed to create toolbar\n");
//      return -1;      // fail to create
//  }
    if (!m_wndDlgBar.Create(this, IDR_MAINFRAME,
        CBRS_ALIGN_TOP, AFX_IDW_DIALOGBAR))
    {
        TRACE0("Failed to create dialogbar\n");
        return -1;      // fail to create
    }

//  if (!m_wndReBar.Create(this) ||
//      !m_wndReBar.AddBar(&m_wndToolBar) ||
//      !m_wndReBar.AddBar(&m_wndDlgBar))
//  {
//      TRACE0("Failed to create rebar\n");
//      return -1;      // fail to create
//  }
```

10

```
        if (!m_wndStatusBar.Create(this) ||
            !m_wndStatusBar.SetIndicators(indicators,
              sizeof(indicators)/sizeof(UINT)))
        {
            TRACE0("Failed to create status bar\n");
            return -1;      // fail to create
        }

        // TODO: Remove this if you don't want tool tips
    //  m_wndToolBar.SetBarStyle(m_wndToolBar.GetBarStyle() |
    //      CBRS_TOOLTIPS | CBRS_FLYBY);

        return 0;
    }
```

Notice that the only lines not commented out where those that created the dialog bar and the status bar. Now when this program runs, the old toolbar and the resizing capabilities will be gone. The only thing left is the dialog bar.

To prevent the program from going to Microsoft's Web site when the application starts, you need to remove (or change a line of code that AppWizard added. This is found in the view's OnInitialUpdate function. In this case, it's CBROWSERView:: OnInitialUpdate.

Modify this function to look like the following by commenting out the line of code that instructs the WebBrowser control to go to Microsoft's Web site:

```
void CBROWSERView::OnInitialUpdate()
{
    CHtmlView::OnInitialUpdate();

    // TODO: This code navigates to a popular spot on the Web.
    //  change the code to go where you'd like.
    //Navigate2(_T("http://www.microsoft.com/visualc/"),NULL,NULL);
}
```

With that taken out, you are finally ready to add the code that will enable the navigation controls added to the dialog bar.

Special consideration needs to be addressed when using buttons (and other controls) when they are on a dialog bar. You need to determine where the code goes when the button is clicked. In this case, you need to add the code for the buttons in CMainFrame. To do this, display the ClassWizard while the IDR_MAINFRAME dialog resource is selected in the editor and select CMainFrame from the list of classes.

Next, select IDC_GO from the list of Object IDs and create the message handler for the BN_CLICKED message using the default function name. Figure 10.13 shows ClassWizard with the BN_CLICKED message handler defined for the IDC_GO Object ID.

FIGURE 10.13

ClassWizard showing message handler for the GO button.

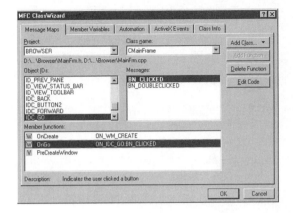

Modify the OnGO function to look like the following:

```
void CMainFrame::OnGo()
{
    // TODO: Add your control notification handler code here
    CString new_url;

    CWnd* pURL = m_wndDlgBar.GetDlgItem(IDC_URL);

    pURL->GetWindowText(new_url);

    ((CHtmlView*)GetActiveView())->Navigate2(new_url,0,NULL);
}
```

The first three lines get the URL typed into the edit control. The last line uses CHtmlView's Navigate2 member function to go to the specified URL.

Following the same process to create the functions as you did with the GO button, create the function handlers for the remaining buttons. Modify each function's contents to match the respective functions from the following section of code:

```
void CMainFrame::OnStop()
{
    // TODO: Add your control notification handler code here
    ((CHtmlView*)GetActiveView())->Stop();
}

void CMainFrame::OnBack()
{
    // TODO: Add your control notification handler code here
    ((CHtmlView*)GetActiveView())->GoBack();
}

void CMainFrame::OnForward()
```

```
{
    // TODO: Add your control notification handler code here
    ((CHtmlView*)GetActiveView())->GoForward();
}

void CMainFrame::OnRefresh()
{
    // TODO: Add your control notification handler code here
    ((CHtmlView*)GetActiveView())->Refresh();
}
```

Each of these function handlers simply calls their respective function for CHtmlView to control the navigation of the WebBrowser control.

Once you have all of these functions coded, you need to add the following line at the end of the includes to the MainFrm.cpp file (the one you just added all the functions to):

```
#include "NavBar.h"
```

All the code is in place to make this application operable. Go ahead and build and execute the application. Figure 10.14 shows the application running with the URL pointing to www.mcp.com/catalog.

FIGURE 10.14

BROWSER application pointing to www.mcp.com/catalog.

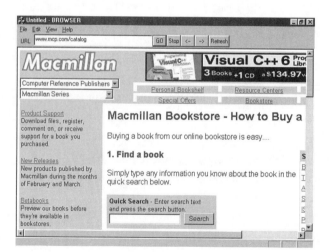

The functionality of this browser is simple at best, but it would be quite easy to add extra functionality to this program to make your own custom browser. The whole purpose of the CHtmlView class is to save you the time and effort of developing your own browser from scratch, or adding HTML rendering to your application.

Lesson Summary

This lesson introduced you to several MFC classes that make programming client applications that request documents and files from an HTTP server quite simple.

You learned that you typically make an Internet session and then use one of the other MFC Internet classes (also referred to as WinInet classes) to work with a specific kind of file. In this lesson, you used the CHttpFile class to retrieve a file from an HTTP server.

You also saw that the MFC harnesses the power of Internet Explorer's WebBrowser control. Using the CHtmlView class allows you to easily add HTML-rendered pages to your application.

Quiz 2

1. Which class member of CInternetSession opens a resource on the Internet?

   a. OpenURL()

   b. GetURL()

   c. GetInternetFile()

   d. GetResource()

2. Which CHttpFile member function reads a line of text from the HTTP server?

   a. ReadLine()

   b. ReadHTTP()

   c. ReadString()

   d. GetString()

3. When reading a file from an HTTP server a line at a time, what can you check to see if the file is complete?

   a. CHttpFile::EOF() returns TRUE

   b. Check the return value of GetString()

   c. Check the return value of ReadString()

   d. The entire file is retrieved by default.

4. Which class member of CHtmlView can instruct the WebBrowser control to change its location (URL)?

   a. Navigate2()

   b. GoBack()

   c. GoForward

   d. Refresh()

Exercise 2

Complexity: Moderate

1. Create an application based on the CHtmlView class as shown in this lesson.
   Modify the standard dialog bar to have a place where you can enter a URL with a
   GO button.

   Also, add a button to the dialog bar that will display a dialog box showing the current page's source.

Complexity: Moderate

2. Create an application based on the CHtmlView class as done in exercise 1. This
   time, replace the standard toolbar with the toolbar located in this lesson's directory
   (LESS02\TOOLBAR.BMP).

   This toolbar has 6 buttons on it. Back, Forward, Stop, Refresh, Home, and Search.
   Utilize these buttons to navigate the WebControl.

LESSON 3

Querying FTP Servers

In the previous lesson, you saw how to use the CInternetSession class to create an
Internet session and how to use CHttpFile to retrieve a file from an HTTP server. This
lesson uses some of the same concepts as far as creating a CInternetSession and using
CInternetFile to retrieve and send files, but you will also see that you need to create a
connection to the server as well. When working with the FTP service, the
CFtpConnection class is used.

When writing an application that uses CFtpConnection, you need to determine if the
connection should remain open to let the user perform multiple actions, or to open the
connection each time it's needed. In this example, you will create an application that
keeps the connection open as long as it's needed.

To begin this example, create a new dialog-based application that has Windows Sockets
support. Name this application FTPAPP. After you have the framework created, go ahead
and modify the IDD_FTPAPP_DIALOG so that it resembles the one in Figure 10.15.

FIGURE 10.15

The modified FTPAPP main dialog resource.

Use the following properties for the controls on this dialog resource:

- URL edit box—Resource ID of IDC_URL. This control specifies the FTP server name.

- User edit box—Resource ID of IDC_USERNAME. This control specifies a user name. If left blank, Anonymous is assumed.

- Password edit box—Resource ID of IDC_PASSWORD and select the Password property. This edit box is used as a hidden entry field to enter a password.

- Path static text—Resource ID of IDC_CURRENT_DIR and select sunken property. This control shows the current path on the FTP server.

- Directory list box—Resource ID of IDC_DIRLIST. This list box displays directories found on the server.

- Files list box—Resource ID of IDC_FTPLIST. This list box displays files found on the server.

- Connect button—Resource ID of IDC_CONNECT and a caption of Connect. Select the Default button property. This button is used to attempt a connection to the FTP server specified.

- Disconnect button—Resource ID of IDC_DISCONNECT and a caption of Disconnect. Select the Disabled property. This button is used to close the FTP connection to the server.

- Exit button—Resource ID of IDOK and a caption of E&xit. This button uses the standard resource ID of IDOK to close the dialog resource.

- Change Dir button—Resource ID of IDC_CHANGE_DIR and a caption of Change Dir. Select the Disabled property. This button displays another dialog box that prompts the user for a path.

- Get button—Resource ID of IDC_GET and a caption of &Get. Select the Disabled property. This button is used to retrieve a file using CFtpConnection's GetFile function.

10

- Put button—Resource ID of IDC_PUT and a caption of &Put. Select the Disabled property. This button is used to send a file to and FTP server using CFtpConnection's PutFile function.

- Get (manual) button—Resource ID of IDC_GETFILE and a caption of Get (manual). Select the Disabled property. This button obtains a file from an FTP server by opening the file and using CInternetFile's Read function to obtain the data.

- Put (manual) button—Resource ID of IDC_PUTFILE and a caption of Put (manual). Select the Disabled property. This button sends a file to an FTP server by opening the file and using CInternetFile's Write function to send the data.

- Status static control—Resource ID of IDC_STATUS with no caption. This control shows the status of the FTP client.

Before writing the code to implement the features of this program, read the next two sections to see what functions are available to CFtpConnection and CInternetFile.

CFtpConnection

CFtpConnection establishes and manages a connection with an FTP server. This class also has several commands that make transferring files to and from and FTP server simple with very few lines of code. Table 10.4 lists some of CFtpConnection's class members.

TABLE 10.4 CFtpConnection Class Members

Class Member	Description
SetCurrentDirectory	Changes directory on the FTP server.
GetCurrentDirectory	Returns a string containing the current directory on the FTP server for this connection.
GetCurrentDirectoryAsURL	Returns a string containing the current directory as a URL for the current connection.
RemoveDirectory	Deletes a directory on the FTP server.
CreateDirectory	Creates a directory on the FTP server.
Rename	Renames a file on the FTP server.
Remove	Deletes a file from the FTP server.
PutFile	Sends a file to the FTP server.
GetFile	Retrieves a file from the FTP server.
OpenFile	Returns a pointer to a file on the FTP server.
Close	Closes the file.

Looking at the list of available functions, you can see that the MFC has made light work of writing complex tasks when dealing with FTP connections.

CInternetFile

Unlike HTTP, FTP does not have its own type of file. HTTP has CHttpFile whereas FTP uses CInternetFile.

Because CInternetFile is derived from CStdioFile (which is derived from CFil), you can read and write files on FTP servers as if they were local. MFC handles the details of implementation, but there are some limitations. You can't use CInternetFile's Open, LockRange, UnlockRange, or Duplicate functions. Using them will result in a CNotSupportedException exception.

Table 10.5 lists CInternetFile's class members.

TABLE 10.5 Common CInternetFile Class Members

Class Member	Description
SetWriteBufferSize	Sets the size of the buffer where the data will be written.
SetReadBufferSize	Sets the size of the buffer from where the data will be read.
Seek	Sets the pointer in an open file to a specific location.
Read	Reads data from the file.
Write	Writes data to the file.
ReadString	Reads a line of text from the file.
WriteString	Writes a line of text to the file.
Abort	Closes the file and ignores all warning and errors.
Flush	Flushes the data in memory and makes sure that the data in buffer is written to the file.
Close	Closes the file.

Building the FTP Client

With the dialog box built and a basic understanding of the classes involved, you are ready to start building the FTP client application.

By looking at the user interface to the program, you can see that users are expected to enter a URL and click the Connect button to create the connection. When they are done, they are supposed to click the Disconnect button to close the connection. To help enforce how the user interacts with the program, only certain buttons are enabled at specific times.

Your first step is to create the necessary member variables for the controls that are need-ed in this application. Create the member variables for the controls as follows:

- IDC_URL—Name the variable m_url and have it return a CEdit object.
- IDC_USERNAME—Name the variable m_username and have it return a CEdit object.
- IDC_PASSWORD—Name the variable m_password and have it return a CEdit object.
- IDC_CURRENT_DIR—Name the variable m_currentdir and have it return a CStatic object.
- IDC_DIRLIST—Name the variable m_dirlist and have it return a CListBox object.
- IDC_FTPLIST—Name the variable m_ftplist and have it return a CListBox object.
- IDC_CONNECT—Name the variable m_connect and have it return a CButton object.
- IDC_DISCONNECT—Name the variable m_disconnect and have it return a CButton object.
- IDC_CHANGE_DIR—Name the variable m_change_dir and have it return a CButton object.
- IDC_GET—Name the variable m_get and have it return a CButton object.
- IDC_PUT—Name the variable m_put and have it return a CButton object.
- IDC_GETFILE—Name the variable m_getfile and have it return a CButton object.
- IDC_PUTFILE—Name the variable m_putfile and have it return a CButton object.
- IDC_STATUS—Name the variable m_status and have it return a CStatic object.

After you have the member variables created for the dialog controls, you need to create a couple of variables that will manage the Internet session, the FTP connection, and the current ftp directory. You need to add the following member variables to the CFTPAPPDlg class. You can do this manually or through the ClassView of the project workspace:

- CFtpConnection* m_ftpConn
- CInternetSession m_inetSession
- CString m_curdir
- CString m_ftp

Connection and Navigation

Once you have these member variables created in the CFTPAPPDlg class, you are ready to begin coding the function handlers. Starting with the top button and working down, the first button is the Connect button. Add a function handler for this button and modify it to match the function as shown in Listing 10.3.

LISTING 10.3   CFTPAPPDlg's OnConnect Function

```
void CFTPAPPDlg::OnConnect()
{
    // TODO: Add your control notification handler code here
    try
    {
        CString username;
        CString password;

        m_username.GetWindowText(username);
        m_password.GetWindowText(password);

        m_url.GetWindowText(m_ftp);

        m_status.SetWindowText("Establishing FTP Connection");
        m_ftpConn = m_inetSession.GetFtpConnection
        ➥(m_ftp, username, password);

        m_status.SetWindowText("Getting Default Directory");
        m_ftpConn->GetCurrentDirectory(m_curdir);

        GetFTPFileList();    // own function to save space!

        m_currentdir.SetWindowText(m_curdir);
        m_status.SetWindowText("List Completed");
        m_connect.EnableWindow(FALSE);
        m_disconnect.EnableWindow(TRUE);
        m_change_dir.EnableWindow(TRUE);
        m_get.EnableWindow(TRUE);
        m_put.EnableWindow(TRUE);
        m_getfile.EnableWindow(TRUE);
        m_putfile.EnableWindow(TRUE);
    }
    catch (CInternetException* E)
    {
        m_status.SetWindowText("Error establishing connection");
        E->ReportError();
    }
}
```

10

When clicked, this function establishes a connection to the specified FTP server using the supplied user credentials. The following line of code from Listing 10.3 accomplishes this task:

```
m_ftpConn = m_inetSession.GetFtpConnection(m_ftp, username, password);
```

The member variable m_ftpConn is a pointer to a CFtpConnection object. This value gets assigned by CInternetSession's GetFtpConnection function. The three parameters being used in this function are the URL for the server, the user's name, and the password. If the username and password are left blank, MFC will try to establish an anonymous FTP connection.

Once the connection is established, the current directory is retrieved from the server by the following line of code:

```
m_ftpConn->GetCurrentDirectory(m_curdir);
```

Once the current directory has been retrieved, you can obtain the list of files in that directory. In this program, a utility function was created that retrieves the list of files to conserve program space. The name of the function is GetFTPFileList and will be discussed in just a few moments.

Once the list of files is retrieved, you can update the user interface to enable and disable controls. In this case, you want to disable the Connect button, because you don't want to try to connect to another server without first disconnecting from the current one. Because most of the buttons were predisabled, you need to enable them so that they can be used.

This whole block of code resides within a try..catch block just in case an error occurs. If so, the status bar is updated and the error is reported.

The utility function, GetFTPFileList, mentioned a moment ago builds the list of directories and files on the FTP server. Listing 10.4 shows this function.

LISTING 10.4   GetFTPFileList Function

```
void CFTPAPPDlg::GetFTPFileList()
{
    m_ftplist.ResetContent();
    m_dirlist.ResetContent();

    m_status.SetWindowText("Listing Files");

    CFtpFileFind ftpFileFind(m_ftpConn);
    try
    {
        ftpFileFind.FindFile();

        BOOLEAN getting_list;
        do
        {
            getting_list = ftpFileFind.FindNextFile();
            if (ftpFileFind.IsDirectory())
                m_dirlist.AddString(ftpFileFind.GetFileName());
            else
                m_ftplist.AddString(ftpFileFind.GetFileName());
        }
        while(getting_list);
        m_ftpConn->GetCurrentDirectory(m_curdir);

    }
    catch (CInternetException* E)
```

```
    {
          E->ReportError();
    }
    m_status.SetWindowText("Listing Complete");

    if ( (m_dirlist.FindStringExact(0,"..") == LB_ERR) &&
  ➥(m_curdir != "/") )
          m_dirlist.InsertString(0,"..");
    ftpFileFind.Close();


}
```

You can use the ClassView pane in the project workspace to create the function header or code it manually. If you code it manually, you will need to add the function declaration in the FTPAPPDlg.h file.

Looking at Listing 10.4, you can see that the first thing it does is clear the list box controls to remove any entries that may exist. Next, a CFtpFindFile object named ftpFindFile is created using the current CFtpConnection. The CFtpFindFile class locates files on the FTP server. The following code segment is from Listing 10.4 and is responsible for building the list of files on the server:

```
ftpFileFind.FindFile();

BOOLEAN getting_list;
do
{
    getting_list = ftpFileFind.FindNextFile();
    if (ftpFileFind.IsDirectory())
        m_dirlist.AddString(ftpFileFind.GetFileName());
    else
        m_ftplist.AddString(ftpFileFind.GetFileName());
}
while(getting_list);
```

The first line uses CFtpFileFind's FindFile function to locate the first file. If desired, a specific file name can be passed to get a handle on a specific file. Next, a do..while loop is used to iterate through the files until no more are found.

The FindNextFile function is used to find files. If no more files are found, a result of FALSE will be returned.

Next, the IsDirectory function interrogates the current file to determine whether it is a directory. If it is a directory, the name is added to the list of directories; otherwise, the name is added to the list of files. The GetFileName function retrieves the name of the file. The following list shows some other functions that could be used to obtain additional information about a file:

- `GetLength`—Gets the length of the file in bytes
- `GetFilePath`—Gets the whole path of the file
- `GetFileURL`—Gets the URL of the file including its path
- `GetRoot`—Gets the root directory for the file
- `GetCreationTime`—Gets the time the file was created
- `GetLastWriteTime`—Gets the time the file was last saved
- `IsDots`—Tells whether the file is a directory named . or . .
- `IsDirectory`—Tells whether the file is a directory

After the list of files is retrieved, the member variable holding the current directory, `m_curdir`, is updated. Lastly, the list of directories is loosely interrogated to see if there is an entry for the parent directory. If the directory isn't shown as an absolute root (/) and there isn't a . . entry, then a . . entry is added.

The next button to work on is the Disconnect button. When this button is selected, the FTP connection needs to be closed and the screen elements updated. Listing 10.5 is the function handler for the disconnect button. Add the `OnDisconnect` function handler to your application.

LISTING 10.5   `CFTPAPPDlg`'s `OnDisconnect` Function Handler

```
void CFTPAPPDlg::OnDisconnect()
{
    // TODO: Add your control notification handler code here
    m_status.SetWindowText("Disconnecting From Server");

    m_ftplist.ResetContent();
    m_dirlist.ResetContent();
    m_currentdir.SetWindowText("");

    m_ftpConn->Close();
    m_ftpConn = NULL;

    m_status.SetWindowText("Connection Closed");
    m_connect.EnableWindow(TRUE);
    m_disconnect.EnableWindow(FALSE);
    m_change_dir.EnableWindow(FALSE);
    m_get.EnableWindow(FALSE);
    m_put.EnableWindow(FALSE);
    m_getfile.EnableWindow(FALSE);
    m_putfile.EnableWindow(FALSE);
}
```

The operation of the Disconnect button is quite basic. First, it updates the status of the screen and removes the contents from the list boxes. Next, it closes the FTP connection by calling CFtpConnection's Close function. Lastly, the button controls are updated to indicate user interface operation.

The next button, Change Dir, prompts a user for a new directory. In order to ask the user for a new directory, you need to add another dialog resource. Figure 10.16 shows the new dialog resource.

FIGURE 10.16

IDD_NEWPATH *dialog resource*

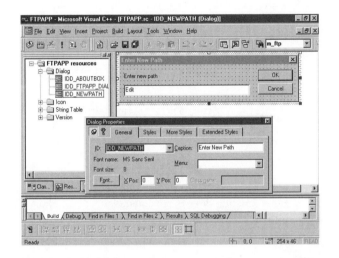

Create the IDD_NEWPATH dialog resource with the following control and property:

- New Path edit box: Resource ID of IDC_PATH

Once you have the controls aligned on the form, you need to add a member variable for the edit box. When you go into ClassWizard, it will recognize that this is a new dialog resource. Go ahead and create a new class and name it CDlgPath.

Once the dialog box's class has been created, add a member variable for the IDC_PATH control. Name this member variable m_path and have it return the control's value.

With the dialog resource and the member variable created, you are now ready to add the code that will be executed when the Change Dir button is clicked. Go ahead and create the function handler for the Change Dir button. Modify your function handler so that it looks like the function in Listing 10.6.

LISTING 10.6 CFTPAPPDlg's OnChangeDir Function Handler

```
void CFTPAPPDlg::OnChangeDir()
{
    // TODO: Add your control notification handler code here
    CDlgPath newdir;
```

continues

LISTING 10.6   continued

```
m_currentdir.GetWindowText(newdir.m_path);
if (newdir.DoModal() == IDOK)
{
    CString dir = newdir.m_path;
    m_status.SetWindowText("Checking directory");
    BOOLEAN validdir = m_ftpConn->SetCurrentDirectory(dir);
    if (validdir)
    {
        GetFTPFileList();   // own function to save space!

        m_currentdir.SetWindowText(m_curdir);
    }
    else
        m_status.SetWindowText("Invalid Directory");

}

}
```

The first thing this function does is create an object for the new dialog box and set the value of the edit box on the dialog box. Next, the dialog box is displayed modally.

If the user clicks the OK button, the new path is passed to the CFtpConnection's SetCurrentDirectory function. The return value is checked to see if the path entered by the user was valid, and if so, the list of files are retrieved and the current directory member variable is updated. If the directory was invalid, the status bar's text is set to reflect so.

When navigating directories, this method may be OK if the user needs to move to an entirely new location on the FTP server and knows what to type. For casual browsing, this method is a bit cumbersome. To address this issue, you need to devise a better mechanism for changing directories. In this example program, you can accomplish this by letting the user double-click the directory names.

To do this, you need to use ClassWizard to process the LBN_DBLCLK message for the IDC_DIRLIST Object ID. Go ahead and use ClassWizard to create the stub for this function. Once you have created the stub, modify the code so that it matches Listing 10.7.

LISTING 10.7   CFTPAPPDlg's OnDblclkDirlist Function Handler

```
void CFTPAPPDlg::OnDblclkDirlist()
{
    // TODO: Add your control notification handler code here
    CString newdir;
    int selected = m_dirlist.GetCurSel();

    m_dirlist.GetText(selected,newdir);
    CString dir;
```

```
if (m_curdir[m_curdir.GetLength()-1] != '/')
    dir = m_curdir + '/' + newdir;
else
    dir = m_curdir + newdir;

m_status.SetWindowText("Checking directory");
BOOLEAN validdir = m_ftpConn->SetCurrentDirectory(dir);
if (validdir)
{
    GetFTPFileList();    // own function to save space!

    m_currentdir.SetWindowText(m_curdir);
}
else
    m_status.SetWindowText("Invalid Directory");
}
```

10

The first thing of substance that this function does is obtain the name of the directory that the user double-clicked. This is done with the GetCurSel and GetText functions of the CListBox class. GetCurSel returns an index to the selected item in the list. GetText returns the text of an item in the list. Used together, they return the name of the directory to which the user wants to switch.

After the name has been fetched, it's appended to the current path. After the path name is built, the function attempts to change the current directory for the connection by calling the SetCurrentDirectory function. If this function succeeds, the GetFTPFileList utility function is called to populate the list of files with the new directory. Once that is done, some housekeeping is needed to update the display.

Sending and Retrieving Files

Now that all of the connection and navigation functions are out of the way, you can concentrate on the tasks of retrieving and sending files. Depending upon your needs, there are a couple of ways to complete these tasks.

CFtpConnection provides mechanisms for opening, reading, and writing files, whereas CInternetFile provides more low-level functions for accomplishing the same tasks. The result of either scenario is virtually the same: It's just the code needed for implementation that's different.

First, you will see how CFtpConnection retrieves and sends files with the Get and Put buttons, and then you will see how CInternetFile is used via the Get (manual) and Put (manual) buttons.

Transferring with `CFtpConnection`

To begin with, you need to create the function handler for the Get button because it's the next in the list. Go ahead and create the function handler and modify its source code to look like Listing 10.8.

LISTING 10.8   CFTPAPPDlg's OnGet Function Handler

```
void CFTPAPPDlg::OnGet()
{
    // TODO: Add your control notification handler code here
    CString filename;
    CString newfilename;

    int selected = m_ftplist.GetCurSel();
    m_ftplist.GetText(selected,filename);


    CFileDialog savefile(FALSE,NULL,filename);

    if (savefile.DoModal() == IDOK)
    {
        newfilename = savefile.GetPathName();
        CWnd* pWnd = AfxGetMainWnd();
        pWnd->UpdateWindow();
        m_status.SetWindowText("Downloading File");
        m_ftpConn->GetFile(filename,newfilename);
        m_status.SetWindowText("Download Complete");
    }
    else
        m_status.SetWindowText("File Download Stopped");

}
```

The first few lines of this function obtain the name of the file that needs to be retrieved from the FTP server from the list of available files. Once the name of the remote file is determined, the user is asked to specify a name for the local file via a save dialog box. If the user selects the OK button, the transfer begins.

The name of the new local file is retrieved from the save dialog box and then the screen is updated via the `UpdateWindow` function. This ensures that the application has a fresh screen before starting the download process.

Now that the program knows the name of the remote file and the new local file, a call to `CFtpConnection`'s `GetFile` function is made and is passed the values of the two files. The MFC takes over at this point and completes the process, throwing an alert if anything goes awry. Once complete, the status bar is updated and the program resumes its normal operation.

This is quick and painless for applications that transfer small files, but when a large file is being transferred, no mechanism in this application exists to show the progress. The MFC does provide such a mechanism to track the progress of such tasks. The code needed to accomplish this task is beyond the scope of this book, though. If you are interested, you need to look into the CInternetSession's OnStatusCallback function.

Seeing how easy it is to retrieve a file from an FTP server, you can safely assume that it's virtually as easy to send a file to an FTP server. In this sample program, the Put button sends a file to the FTP server. Go ahead and create the OnPut function handler. Make sure it matches the function in Listing 10.9.

LISTING 10.9 CFTPAPPDlg's OnPut Function Handler

```
void CFTPAPPDlg::OnPut()
{
    // TODO: Add your control notification handler code here
    CFileDialog openfile(TRUE);

    if (openfile.DoModal() == IDOK)
    {
        CWnd* pWnd = AfxGetMainWnd();
        pWnd->UpdateWindow();
        m_status.SetWindowText("Sending File");
        m_ftpConn->PutFile(openfile.GetPathName(),
        ➥openfile.GetFileName());
        m_status.SetWindowText("File Sent.. Refreshing List");

        GetFTPFileList();
    }
    else
        m_status.SetWindowText("File Upload Stopped");

}
```

First, the OnPut function displays an open dialog box to obtain the name of the file the user wants to send to the FTP server. If the user selects a file and clicks the OK button, the file is sent to the FTP server using CFtpConnection's PutFile function. This function is passed the name of the file to send and the name to store the file as on the server.

Because a file is being sent to the server, the contents of the list boxes need to be updated when the process is complete. A call to the GetFTPFileList utility function refreshes the list.

As you can see, getting and sending files to an FTP server is quite a simple process when using the CFtpConnection class to do all the work.

10

Transferring with `CInternetFile`

Even though `CFtpConnection`'s `GetFile` and `PutFile` functions are easy to implement, they are sometimes not flexible enough to accommodate your application's needs. That's where `CInternetFile` comes into play.

`CInternetFile` is derived from `CStdioFile` and is ultimately derived from `CFile`. This gives this class some greater flexibility when dealing with files. Unfortunately, this comes at a price. The code needed to implement the file transfers is just a bit longer, but once you see how easy the MFC makes it to use, you'll agree that it's not really all that bad.

To begin with, you need to create the function handler for the Get (manual) button. Once you have created the function handler, modify its code to match Listing 10.10.

LISTING 10.10   CFTPAPPDlg's OnGetFile Function Handler

```
void CFTPAPPDlg::OnGetfile()
{
    // TODO: Add your control notification handler code here
    CString filename;
    CString newfilename;
    char* buffer[1024];
    CString msg;
    int counter;
    int count;

    int selected = m_ftplist.GetCurSel();
    m_ftplist.GetText(selected,filename);

    CFileDialog savefile(FALSE,NULL,filename);

    if (savefile.DoModal() == IDOK)
    {
        CWnd* pWnd = AfxGetMainWnd();
        pWnd->UpdateWindow();
        newfilename = savefile.GetPathName();
        m_status.SetWindowText("Downloading File");
        // m_ftpConn->GetFile(filename,newfilename);

        try
        {

            CInternetFile* in_file = m_ftpConn->OpenFile(filename);
            CFile out_file ( newfilename,  CFile::modeCreate |
            ➥CFile::modeWrite | CFile::typeBinary );

            counter = 0;
            do
            {
                count = in_file->Read(buffer,1024);
```

```
                    counter = counter + count;

                    if (count > 0)
                      out_file.Write(buffer,count);

                    msg.Format("Bytes downloaded :%d",counter);
                    m_status.SetWindowText(msg);

            }
            while (count != 0);

            out_file.Close();
            in_file->Close();

            m_status.SetWindowText("Download Complete");
            AfxMessageBox("Download Complete");

        }
        catch (CFileException*e)
        {
            e->ReportError();
        }
    }
    else
    {
        m_status.SetWindowText("File Download Stopped");
    }
}
```

Right from the start, you can see that the function is a tad bit longer than its OnGet equivalent. The nice thing is that this function provides visual feedback on the progress of the transfer.

The first section of the OnGetFile function is responsible for creating the needed variables and displaying the save dialog box:

```
CString filename;
CString newfilename;
char* buffer[1024];
CString msg;
int counter;
int count;

int selected = m_ftplist.GetCurSel();
m_ftplist.GetText(selected,filename);

CFileDialog savefile(FALSE,NULL,filename);
```

The new parts in this function as compared to the OnGet function are the addition of the buffer, msg, counter, and count variables. The following list describes each new variable's purpose:

- buffer—This variable works as the buffer that stores data retrieved from the server. Its length is set to 1,024 in this application but can be set to virtually any length you need. The size of this buffer can affect transfer performance.
- msg—This variable builds the message that is displayed in the status bar as the transfer progresses.
- counter—This variable holds the total number of bytes transferred.
- count—This variable holds the number of bytes that were transferred by the Read function. A count less than the buffer size indicates that the end of the file was reached.

The next section of code is responsible for creating the input and output files. This section of code is as follows:

```
CInternetFile* in_file = m_ftpConn->OpenFile(filename);
CFile out_file ( newfilename,  CFile::modeCreate ¦ CFile::modeWrite ¦
➥CFile::typeBinary );
```

The first line opens the file on the server using CFtpConnection's OpenFile function. The second line opens a local file for write access.

The next section of code is responsible for actually retrieving the file:

```
counter = 0;
do
{
    count = in_file->Read(buffer,1024);
    counter = counter + count;

    if (count > 0)
      out_file.Write(buffer,count);

    msg.Format("Bytes downloaded :%d",counter);
    m_status.SetWindowText(msg);

}
while (count != 0);

out_file.Close();
in_file->Close();
```

After the counter is initialized, a do..while loop continually reads the file until no more data is available. CInternetFile's Read function stores the retrieved bytes in the buffer. The number of bytes read is returned and placed in count.

After each read, the counter is increased. Next, the count is checked against 0 bytes to make sure the buffer has data. If the count is greater that 0 bytes, the buffer is written to the destination file.

Once the write is complete, the status bar is updated to indicate the progress. Once the entire download process is complete, both files are closed and the program returns to normal operation.

If you compare OnGet and OnGetFile, the only real difference is that you control the loop that reads the file in OnGetFile.

The last function to implement is for the Put (manual) button. Create your OnPutFile function handler and make it match Listing 10.11.

LISTING 10.11 CFTPAPPDlg's OnPutFile Function Handler

```
void CFTPAPPDlg::OnPutfile()
{
    // TODO: Add your control notification handler code here
    CFileDialog openfile(TRUE);
    char* buffer[1024];

    CString msg;
    int counter;
    int count;

    CString newfilename;

    if (openfile.DoModal() == IDOK)
    {
        CWnd* pWnd = AfxGetMainWnd();
        pWnd->UpdateWindow();
        m_status.SetWindowText("Sending File");

        // m_ftpConn->PutFile(openfile.GetPathName(),
        // openfile.GetFileName());

        try
        {
            CInternetFile* out_file = m_ftpConn>-openFile
            ➥(openfile.GetFileName(), GENERIC_WRITE);
            CFile in_file ( openfile.GetPathName(),
            ➥CFile::modeRead ¦ CFile::typeBinary );

            counter = 0;
            do
            {
                count = in_file.Read(buffer,1024);
```

continues

LISTING 10.11 continued

```
                        counter = counter + count;

                        if (count > 0)
                            out_file->Write(buffer,count);

                        msg.Format("Bytes sent :%d",counter);
                        m_status.SetWindowText(msg);

                    }
                    while (count != 0);

                    out_file->Close();
                    in_file.Close();

                    m_status.SetWindowText("Upload Complete");
                    AfxMessageBox("Upload Complete");

                }
                catch (CFileException*e)
                {
                    e->ReportError();
                }

                m_status.SetWindowText("File Sent.. Refresing List");

                GetFTPFileList();
            }
            else
                m_status.SetWindowText("File Upload Stopped");

    }
```

Because the OnPutFile procedure is essentially the same thing as the OnGetFile procedure, it will not be discussed in great detail. The only significant thing to note in this function is the use of CInternetFile's Write function, which sends the data in the buffer to the FTP server.

The last two lines of code you need to add before you can use this application are as follows:

```
#include "afxinet.h"
#include "DlgPath.h"
```

Add these to the top of the FTPAPPDlg.cpp file just below the other include statements.

Once you have all the code complete, you are ready to test the application. Go ahead and build and execute the program. Figure 10.17 shows the application running and pointed to ftp.mcp.com.

FIGURE 10.17

FTPAPP application running.

Lesson Summary

In this lesson, you learned about the CFtpConnection and CInternetFile classes, which encompass the functionality needed to write applications that use the popular FTP protocol.

In this lesson, you saw how to write a basic FTP client that allows you to navigate through directories and send and receive files while connected to an FTP server.

By utilizing the built-in MFC classes, you saw that writing such an application was quite easy, and with a little more thought and effort, a full-blown FTP client application could be written with ease.

Quiz 3

1. Which class is used when iterating through a list of files on an FTP server to find files?

    a. CFtpFileList

    b. CFtpFindFile

    c. CFtpFileFind

    d. CListFiles

2. Which member functions belong to the class that is the correct answer for question 1?

    a. GetFile

    b. FindFile

    c. FindNextFile

    d. FindFirst

10

3. Which member function of `CFtpConnection` would be used to remove a file from the FTP server?

    a. `DeleteFile`

    b. `KillFile`

    c. `RemoveFile`

    d. `Remove`

4. Which member function of `CInternetSession` would be used to open an FTP connection?

    a. `CreateFTPConnection`

    b. `GetFtpConnection`

    c. `FtpConnection`

    d. None of the above

Exercise 3

Complexity: Easy

1. The example you built in this lesson was actually a nearly complete FTP client. Using the example as a basis, create an FTP client that has all the same functionality of the sample program.

Complexity: Moderate

2. Modify the program you just built in part one of Exercise 3 by adding buttons that will Delete and Rename the currently selected FTP file.

LESSON 4

Web Programs Through Internet Server API

If you have any experience programming applications that work on the Web, you probably have heard of CGI. *CGI*, which stands for *common gateway interface*, is a mechanism for extending a Web server's functionality.

In one instance, ISAPI does just that; in another, it gives you finer control over each HTTP transaction. When referring to CGI-type applications, *ISAPI extensions* is the terminology used. When referring to applications that filter HTTP requests, *ISAPI filters* is the terminology.

ISAPI extensions and filters undoubtedly have some great benefits, ranging from flexibility and scalability to good performance and lower overhead.

A "normal" CGI application can be written in virtually any language the developer knows. If this takes the form of a batch file or an external .EXE, most likely that application needs to be loaded, executed, and freed each time an HTTP request is made for that application. Multiply that by just a couple of simultaneous requests, and you can see that resource usage adds up rather quickly.

On the other hand, a "normal" ISAPI application is typically written as a .DLL and is loaded by the server when needed the first time. From that point on, it's already in memory. Instead of loading and creating a new process for each request, a pool of threads is used. Threads, by definition, are more efficient. When a thread is needed, it's taken from this pool.

One key feature of ISAPI is the capability to create a filter. The ISAPI-compliant Internet server can give your ISAPI filter a high level of control over the HTTP request.

Going any further in depth about the differences between CGI and ISAPI at this point would be better left to a book that delves into the deepest realms of ISAPI—and those books are out there.

10

Note

In order to use the examples in this lesson, you will need access to an ISAPI-compliant Web server. If you are developing on an NT Server, IIS is more than adequate. If you are working on NT Workstation, you can use Peer Web Services. If you are working on a Windows 95 or 98 machine, you can use Personal Web Server. The good news is that Microsoft includes these servers in Visual Studio.

Writing an ISAPI Extension

As mentioned before, ISAPI extensions are applications that extend the functionality of an ISAPI-compliant Internet Server. Some common ISAPI applications are shopping carts and mailers. The only real limit to an ISAPI extension is your imagination (and of course, HTTP and HTML limitations).

One of your first questions might be why use ISAPI? Simple. If you want to add dynamic content to the Web, an ISAPI extension may be a good choice. Yes, other options are available, but having the flexibility that ISAPI extensions offer can heavily sway your decision to use them.

You must consider some things, however, when using ISAPI extensions. Unfortunately, several brands of Internet browsers are available on the market, and not all of them send requests to the server in the same manner. You need to consider the unknown when developing your extension.

On a good note, VC++ 6 has included an ISAPI Extension Wizard that makes creating the framework a one-step process. Select File, New as you would to create any other project, but this time select ISAPI Extension Wizard from the list of project types. Figure 10.18 shows the AppWizard with ISAPI Extension Wizard selected.

FIGURE 10.18

AppWizard with ISAPI Extension Wizard selected.

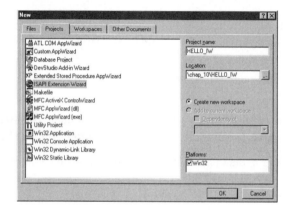

For this lesson, create a new ISAPI extension project named HELLO_IW. Creating the project will display the ISAPI Extension Wizard as shown in Figure 10.19.

FIGURE 10.19

The new ISAPI extension.

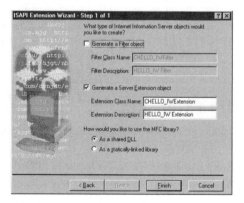

Looking at Figure 10.19, you can see that the choices are pretty simple. You tell the wizard what kind of objects to create. You can choose a filter, an application, or both. For the purpose of this lesson, the defaults are fine. Go ahead and click the Finish button and complete the creation process.

Now that the basic framework of the application is complete, you are ready to write the code to implement your project. As this project sits, it's a fully functioning ISAPI DLL. When it gets a blank request, it will display a default message. This is done by the code in the Default() function of the C<appname>Extension class. In this example, the <appname> is replaced with HELLO_IW, making it the CHELLO_IWExtension class (see Figure 10.20).

FIGURE 10.20

Class View with the CHELLO_IWExtension class expanded.

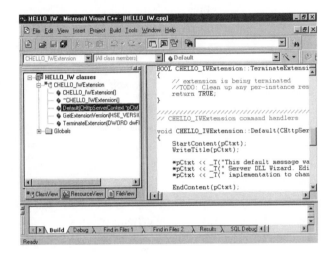

The following section of code is the CHELLO_IWExtension::Default function:

```
void CHELLO_IWExtension::Default(CHttpServerContext* pCtxt)
{
    StartContent(pCtxt);
    WriteTitle(pCtxt);

    *pCtxt << _T("This default message was produced by the Internet");
    *pCtxt << _T(" Server DLL Wizard. Edit your
    ➡CHELLO_IWExtension::Default()");
    *pCtxt << _T(" implementation to change it.\r\n");

    EndContent(pCtxt);
}
```

Looking at this code, you can see that the function is passed a CHttpServerContext object. This object links the request and your application together. Table 10.6 lists some of CHttpServerContext's class members.

TABLE 10.6 Common CHttpServerContext Class Members

Class member	Description
m_pECB	This member variable holds a pointer to an EXTENSION_CONTROL_BLOCK structure. This structure holds information such as content type and the query string.
GetServerVariable	This member variable copies the value of a server variable to a supplied buffer.
WriteClient	This member variable writes data directly back to the client.
ReadClient	This member variable reads data from the body of the HTTP request.
operator <<	This member variable writes data to an HTML stream.

Text is written directly to the HTML stream to create the page returned to the server. In this example, the text sent to the client is quite basic. If you were building a page on-the-fly, you would want to send normal HTML commands that would construct the page appropriately.

Typically, if the application you are writing is small, you can code your implementation in the Default() function. If your application performs more that one function, however, you will need to create separate functions dependent upon the commands issued in the URL.

For this lesson, you will leave the default function handler as it is. When you request the page with no parameters, you should get VC++ 6's default message.

To give this application some separate functionality, you are going to add a function that will process the command Hello. When this command is passed as the first parameter in the URL, the Hello() function will be called.

The first thing you need to do is create the function itself. When creating a function handler that processes an ISAPI command, the first parameter passed to the function *must* be CHttpServerContext* <variable name>.

When creating this function, you need to decide if any parameters are going to be passed from the URL to the function. If you must add appropriate code to the function's header to accommodate the passed parameters. For this example, a string value will be passed to the function.

Add the following line to the HELLO_IW.h file just after the public: statement:

```
void Hello(CHttpServerContext* pCtxt, LPCTSTR pstrMessage);
```

Next, add the following function to the `HELLOW_IW.h` file at the very end:

```
void CHELLO_IWExtension::Hello(CHttpServerContext* pCtxt,
►LPCTSTR pstrMessage)
{
    StartContent(pCtxt);
    WriteTitle(pCtxt);

    *pCtxt << _T("Hello Interactive World <br>");
    *pCtxt << _T("Your message was:");
    *pCtxt << pstrMessage;

    EndContent(pCtxt);

}
```

The sole purpose of this function is to process the `Hello` command and display the passed value. In order for this function to be called, you need to define a parse map.

Parse maps are used in ISAPI DLLs to link commands to messages. Their appearance is similar to a message map in that they have specific macros that define the parse map.

Parse maps begin with the statement `BEGIN_PARSE_MAP` and end with the statement `END_PARSE_MAP`. The parse map is usually located toward the top of the implementation file (`HELLO_IW.cpp`). The following is the default parse map created by ISAPI Extension Wizard:

```
BEGIN_PARSE_MAP(CHELLO_IWExtension, CHttpServer)
        // TODO: insert your ON_PARSE_COMMAND() and
        // ON_PARSE_COMMAND_PARAMS() here to hook up your commands.
        // For example:

    ON_PARSE_COMMAND(Default, CHELLO_IWExtension, ITS_EMPTY)
    DEFAULT_PARSE_COMMAND(Default, CHELLO_IWExtension)
END_PARSE_MAP(CHELLO_IWExtension)
```

Besides the `BEGIN_PARSE_MAP` and `END_PARSE_MAP` macros, three other macros are used to define the mappings and parameter requirements:

- `ON_PARSE_COMMAND`—This macro links a query command to a function.
- `DEFAULT_PARSE`—This macro links an empty query to a default function.
- `ON_PARSE_COMMAND_PARAMS`—Used to specify passed parameters. Parameters can be required or have default values.

The `ON_PARSE_COMMAND` links a command to a function. In the case of our example, this is the macro that is needed to link the `Hello` command to the `Hello` function. The link is made by the name of the command. The name of the command must match the name of the function in order to get processed.

10

Add the following line just before the END_PARSE_MAP macro in the HELLO_IW.cpp file:

```
ON_PARSE_COMMAND(Hello, CHELLO_IWExtension, ITS_PSTR)
```

This instructs the program to call the Hello function when it's the command in the URL. The last parameter instructs it to pass a string value. Valid values for this parameter are

- ITS_EMPTY—Specifies no value.
- ITS_PSTR—Specifies a string value.
- ITS_I2—Specifies a short integer value.
- ITS_I4—Specifies a long integer value.
- ITS_R4—Specifies a float value.
- ITS_R8—Specifies a double value.
- ITS_RAW—Specifies raw data as sent to the ISAPI extension. This value cannot be used with any other value.

You can specify combinations of these parameter types (except ITS_RAW) in the last parameter of an ON_PARSE_COMMAND macro by separating them with a space. For each parameter specified, a corresponding parameter must exist in the function.

Now that you have the macro defined that links the Hello command to the Hello() function, you can build the program. Go ahead and build the DLL. When the DLL is built, you will need to install it on your Web server according to that Web server's documentation.

Figures 10.21 and 10.22 show the HELLO_IW.DLL ISAPI extension DLL in action. In Figure 10.21, if no command is issued, the default screen is shown. If the hello command is issued, then the appropriate text is displayed.

FIGURE 10.21

Default screen when the DLL is called with no command.

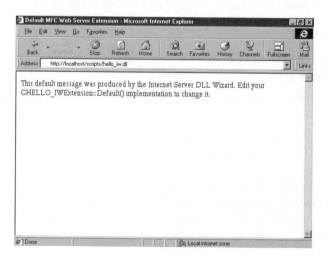

FIGURE 10.22

HELLO_IW.DLL when called with the `Hello` *command.*

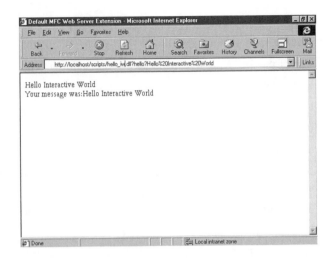

Typically, an ISAPI extension is used in the similar manner as a CGI program. An HTML form is created that gathers data from the users and when they submit the form, the ISAPI extension is called to process the form. Because coding HTML is not in the scope of this book, you can type a direct URL into your browser to call the DLL to see how it operates.

Lesson Summary

In this lesson, you learned about what role an ISAPI extension plays as compared to a CGI program. You saw that ISAPI DLLs typically come in two flavors: extensions and filters.

ISAPI extensions extend the capability of servers by giving them additional functionality by being able to pass the request onto an application designed for a specific task.

Even though you didn't code one in this chapter, it's important to know that ISAPI filters can play an important role when designing an interactive Web site. They can be used to help filter and process requests before the server does, hence enhancing the server's functionality.

Quiz 4

1. Which class must the first parameter be in that is passed to a function that handles an ISAPI command?

   a. `CHttpServer`

   b. `CHttpRequest`

    c. `CHttpConnection`

    d. `CHttpServerContext`

2. Which of the following macros links a command to a function?

    a. `ON_PARSE_MESSAGE`

    b. `ON_PARSE_COMMAND`

    c. `ON_ISAPI_COMMAND`

    d. `ON_HTTP_COMMAND`

3. Using the correct answer from question 2, the last parameter of that macro can take more than one value. Which of the following cannot be used with other values?

    a. `ITS_RAW`

    b. `ITS_PSTR`

    c. `ITS_PINT`

    d. `ITS_DATA`

4. If you wanted to obtain any additional data about a query, which class member of `CHttpServerContext` will hold this data?

    a. `m_pecb`

    b. `ITS_RAW`

    c. `RequestData`

    d. `m_pECB`

Exercise 4

Complexity: Easy

1. Create an ISAPI extension that displays the message `Hello Interactive World` as its default message. Use the HTML tags `<strong>` and `</strong>` to display the message in bold type.

Complexity: Moderate

2. Create an ISAPI extension that looks for the command `ezone`. This command should take one string parameter. If the command is not found, display an appropriate message stating the usage. If the command is found, display the passed string.

Chapter Summary

Without a doubt, the Internet has taken the online industry by storm. This evolution has propelled the need (or want) for information right into millions of homes and businesses.

As a developer, this means that there is untapped potential for work, and as the need increases, so does the demand for talented programmers.

In this chapter, you saw how to implement some of the most basic functionality of the Internet in your own applications. You learned how to do the following:

- How to add email to your applications
- How to connect to an HTTP server and request a file
- How to encapsulate the functionality of the WebBrowser control in your own applications
- How to connect to an FTP server to send and retrieve files
- How to write an ISAPI extension

If you want to develop applications for the Internet, it's imperative that you understand the basics of how these technologies work. Being able to implement these (and other emerging) technologies in your application will only increase their overall appeal.

10

CHAPTER 11

Using File I/O and Databases to Manage Information

Many programs you develop need to store information. In Chapter 7, "Saving, Loading, and Printing Your Documents," you were introduced to the concept of persistent objects.

This method of storing and retrieving data is fine if you are always working with objects that need to save and restore their states between program sessions. However, if you need to access files that are not object-oriented or that need to be accessed in a random type manner, you need to look at other mechanisms.

Typically, these other mechanisms are regular flat files where you use conventional methods to save and retrieve data to and from files. If these files become rather large or contain various elements of data, you may need to look at storing your information in a database.

Depending upon your need, the MFC has classes that get the job done. As you'll see in this chapter, implementing low-level file I/O calls and talking to databases has been made trivial when using the MFC.

LESSON 1

Storing and Retrieving Information in Files

There has always been a need to store information. Ever since the first computer, a mechanism to store and retrieve information has been in demand. Granted, in the very early days, information was stored on punched cards, providing a small amount of storage; today, we often take advantage of gigabytes (and possibly terabytes) of storage.

Going beyond the physical medium that the information is stored on, there are two ways to access flat files: sequentially and randomly. Sequential access goes from the beginning of the file to the end, stepping through each byte in the order in which they appear in the file. Random access lets you jump around in the file to any position desired.

The needs of your application will dictate the type of file access needed. Either way, the MFC has done an excellent job of giving you control over what needs to be done, yet makes it a simple process. The base class that makes this functionality possible is `CFile`. In fact, in the last chapter, this class was used when sending and receiving files from an FTP server. If you are strictly dealing with text files, you may want to consider the `CStdioFile` class, which is derived from the `CFile` class and has special handling for text files.

`CFile` and `CStdioFile` Classes

As just mentioned, the main classes used for direct file I/O are `CFile` and `CStdioFile`. `CFile` is the base class for file I/O from which `CStdioFile` derives.

When using `CFile` directly, you have access to all of its functions, but when using `CStdioFile`, you lose a couple of those functions. Those functions will be indicated in Table 11.1, but `CStdioFile` adds a couple of functions that make working with text files quite a bit simpler. Table 11.1 lists some of the available class members for `CFile` and `CStdioFile`.

TABLE 11.1   `CFile` and `CStdioFile` Class Members

Class Member	Description
`CFile::m_hFile`	Handle to the operating system file
`CFile::CFile`	Constructor that creates a `CFile` object from a path or file handle
`CFile::Abort`	Closes the file, ignoring all warnings and errors
`CFile::Duplicate`	Creates a duplicate object based on this file; this member is not implemented in `CStdioFile`

Class Member	Description
CFile::Open	Opens a file
CFile::Close	Closes a file
CFile::Read	Reads data from a file
CFile::Write	Writes data to a file
CFile::Flush	Flushes any unwritten data
CFile::Seek	Sets the position of the file pointer
CFile::SeekToBegin	Positions the file pointer at the beginning of the file
CFile::SeekToEnd	Positions the file pointer at the end of the file
CFile::GetLength	Returns the length of the file
CFile::SetLength	Sets the length of the file
CFile::LockRange	Locks a range of bytes in the file; this member is not implemented in CStdioFile
CFile::UnlockRange	Unlocks a range of bytes in the file; this member function is not implemented in CStdioFile
CFile::GetPosition	Returns the current file pointer
CFile::GetStatus	Returns the status of the open file
CFile::GetFileName	Returns just the name of a file, including its extension
CFile::GetFileTitle	Returns just the name of the file without its extension
CFile::GetFilePath	Returns the entire name of the file, including the path
CFile::SetFilePath	Sets the full path for the file
CFile::Rename	Renames the file
CFile::Remove	Deletes the file
CStdioFile::ReadString	Reads a line of text from a file
CStdioFile::WriteString	Writes a line of text to a file
CStdioFile::m_pStream	Pointer to a file stream

Implementing CFile and CStdioFile Classes

As you can see from CFile and CStdioFile's class members, writing a program to use these classes should be straightforward and should not involve too much code.

Reading and writing files is a fundamental task in any language, and the purpose of demonstrating how to do it in this lesson is just to show how easy VC++ 6 and the MFC make it.

11

With that said, it's time to create the application. For this lesson, you will be creating a program that reads a text file, allows you to edit it and then saves it back: sort of a rudimentary text editor. To begin with, create a new dialog-based project named file_io. Modify its dialog resource to resemble the one in Figure 11.1.

FIGURE 11.1

Dialog resource for the file_io *application.*

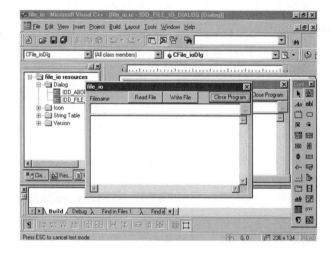

Modify the properties for the dialog box as follows:

- Read File button—Resource ID of IDC_READ and a caption of Read File.
- Write File button—Resource ID of IDC_WRITE and a caption of Write File.
- Close Program button—Resource ID of IDCANCEL and a caption of Close Program; this button uses the default IDCANCEL resource ID to close the program when clicked.
- Filename edit box—Resource ID of ID_FNAME.
- Button—Resource ID of IDC_BROWSE and a caption of . . . .
- Contents edit box—Resource ID of IDC_CONTENTS; set the Multiline, Horizontal scroll, and Vertical scroll properties.

With the dialog controls created, you need to create the member variables used to get access to the IDC_FNAME and IDC_CONTENTS controls. Both of these member variables categories should be the control pointing to the CEdit class. Use Figure 11.2 as a guide to create these member variables.

FIGURE 11.2

ClassWizard showing defined member variables.

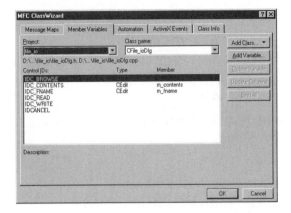

With the dialog resource created and the member variables defined, now you get to add the code that makes each button do its task. To start with, add a function handler for the ... button. The default name of OnBrowse should be fine. Once you have created the stub, modify the function so that it looks like the following:

```
void CFile_ioDlg::OnBrowse()
{
    // TODO: Add your control notification handler code here
    CFileDialog openfile(TRUE);

    if (openfile.DoModal() == IDOK)
    {
        m_fname.SetWindowText(openfile.GetPathName());
        m_contents.SetWindowText("");
    }
}
```

This function's purpose is quite basic. It creates an Open file dialog box to obtain a file name for reading and writing. If the user clicks the OK button, the selected file is stored in the IDC_FNAME edit control.

Reading a File

The next button to discuss is the Read File button. Create the function handler for this button and modify it to match the code in Listing 11.1.

LISTING 11.1 The OnRead Function

```
void CFile_ioDlg::OnRead()
{
    // TODO: Add your control notification handler code here
    CString contents;
```

continues

LISTING 11.1   continued

```
CString in_file_name;
CString buffer;

m_fname.GetWindowText(in_file_name);
m_contents.SetWindowText("");

CStdioFile in_file ( in_file_name,  CFile::modeRead |
➥CFile::typeBinary );

BOOL filestat;
do
{
    filestat = in_file.ReadString(buffer);

    if (filestat)
        contents=contents + buffer;

}
while (filestat);
contents.Replace("\r","\r\n");
in_file.Close();

m_contents.SetWindowText(contents);

}
```

The first five lines of code only declare needed variables and clear the results edit box. The next line is responsible for opening the file as shown here:

```
CStdioFile in_file ( in_file_name,  CFile::modeRead |
➥CFile::typeBinary );
```

In this example, CStdioFile is used in place of CFile. The reason to use it here is that CStdioFile has the capability to read and write a line of text at a time.

CStdioFile can be used one of two ways when opening a file. If you have a file handle, you can pass just that as a parameter; if not, you pass the name of the file and the flags that specify in which modes to open the file. Table 11.2 lists the available flags and their purposes.

TABLE 11.2   The CFile Open Flags

Flag	Description
CFile::modeCreate	Creates a new file. If it already exists, it's overwritten (truncated to 0 length).

Flag	Description
CFile::modeNoTruncate	Used in conjunction with CFile::modeCreate to create a file if it doesn't exist. If it does exist, the file will not be truncated. For example, CFile::modeCreate ¦ CFile::modeNoTruncate as parameters will open the file if it exists and will create it if it doesn't.
CFile::modeRead	Opens the file for read access only.
CFile::modeReadWrite	Opens the file for read and write access.
CFile::modeWrite	Opens the file for write access only.
CFile::modeNoInherit	Using this mode prevents the file from being inherited by child processes.
CFile::shareDenyNone	Opens the file and still allows other processes to read and write to the file.
CFile::shareDenyRead	Opens the file and denies read access to other processes.
CFile::shareDenyWrite	Opens the file and denies write access to other processes.
CFile::shareExclusive	Opens the file and denies any access to any other process.
CFile::typeText	Opens the file in text mode. This allows derived classes (such as CStdioFile) to have special processing features for the end-of-line characters.
CFile::typeBinary	Opens the file in binary mode. This mode is used in derived classes, such as CStdioFile.

The next section of code from Listing 11.1 is responsible for actually reading the file:

```
BOOL filestat;
do
{
    filestat = in_file.ReadString(buffer);

    if (filestat)
        contents=contents + buffer;

}
while (filestat);
```

First, a variable is declared as type BOOL. This variable is tested by the do...while loop to see if the end of the file has been reached. The first line of code within this loop assigns this variable.

CStdioFile's ReadString function obtains a line of text from the file. If you were working with a true binary file, you would not want to use ReadString; you would work with the Read function.

The line of text is read into the CString buffer variable. Inside the loop, the file status is checked again to make sure no extra data is added to the buffer. When the end of the file has been detected, the do...while loop ends.

The next section of code executes after the file has been read:

```
contents.Replace("\r","\r\n");
in_file.Close();

m_contents.SetWindowText(contents);
```

The first line is kind of important here. Because the program is reading the lines of text and placing them in a CString variable, the carriage-return only characters need to be replaced with the carriage-return and line-feed characters. If you use the LPCSTR operator of the CString class, this step isn't necessary.

Next, the file is closed and the edit control's content is updated.

Writing a File

The only operation (or button) to discuss is the Write File button. When this button is clicked, the text from the content's edit control is written back to the file.

Create the function handler for the Write File button and modify it to match Listing 11.2.

LISTING 11.2 The OnWrite Function

```
void CFile_ioDlg::OnWrite()
{
    // TODO: Add your control notification handler code here
    CString contents;
    CString out_file_name;

    m_contents.GetWindowText(contents);

    m_fname.GetWindowText(out_file_name);

    CFile out_file (out_file_name, CFile::modeWrite |
    ➥CFile::typeBinary);

    out_file.Write(contents,contents.GetLength());

    out_file.Close();

}
```

The first three lines are responsible for declaring variables needed and retrieving the text from the contents edit box and the file name.

This time, CFile is used in place of CStdioFile. You have no real reason to use it here other than CStdioFile's WriteString function doesn't give this application any real advantage.

Because the contents of the file are within a single edit control (and therefore in memory), the variable that holds that content can be used as the buffer to write from, and is.

A single call to CFile's Write function writes the entire contents back to the file. Because the contents variable is a CString class, its GetLength function specifies the size of the buffer when writing the file back to disk.

Once the write file is completed, the file is closed and the program's operation returns to normal.

Now that you know what the program should do, go ahead and build and execute the program. While it is running, click the ... button to point to an insignificant text file. After you point to a file, click the Read File button to read the contents of the file into the edit box. If you want, go ahead and make some changes to the text file and click the Write File button.

Figure 11.3 shows the file_io program running with a typical AUTOEXEC.BAT file retrieved.

FIGURE 11.3

The file_io *application running.*

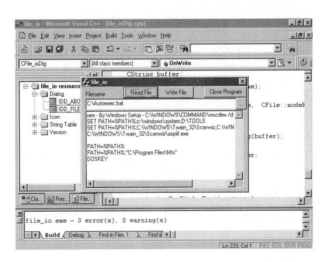

Lesson Summary

Saving data to a file is one of the most common tasks performed in most programs. Depending upon how the information needs to be stored dictates what mechanisms are used to complete the task.

The MFC does include some fantastic classes that go well above and beyond the basics of reading and writing directly to flat files, but sometimes, that basic functionality is needed the most.

In this lesson, you were introduced to two basic classes that deal with reading and writing files at the most basic level: `CFile` and `CStdioFile`.

These classes make working with basic flat files a snap. It's simple to call commands that do exactly what they sound like they should do. They are definitely up to par when it comes to dealing with these kinds of files.

Quiz 1

1. Which two extra functions does the `CStdioFile` class give that are not found in its base class?

    a. `GetText` and `PutText`

    b. `ReadString` and `WriteString`

    c. `ReadText` and `WriteText`

    d. `GetString` and `WriteString`

2. From which class does `CStdioFile` directly descend?

    a. `CIOFile`

    b. `CStdio`

    c. `CFile`

    d. `CObject`

3. Which of the following open flags are only available in `CStdioFile` and other classes derived from `CStdioFile`'s base class?

    a. `shareExclusive`

    b. `typeText`

    c. `typeBinary`

    d. `typeImage`

4. If you wanted to open a file and not let any other process have read or write access to the file, which flag would you use?

   a. `shareDenyNone`

   b. `shareDenyAll`

   c. `shareExclusive`

   d. `shareLock`

Exercise 1

Complexity: Easy

1. Create a dialog-based application that will read and display a text file. The dialog should have a button that browses for the file and opens it automatically. This program should not have any editing capabilities; therefore, a save feature is not needed.

Complexity: Moderate

2. Create a dialog-based application that will read, display, edit, and save a text file. No buttons should be on the dialog box. All commands to accomplish these tasks should be available from a menu. The File menu should contain the commands Open, Save, Save As, and Exit.

LESSON 2

Databases: Common Pieces and Parts

Most business applications have a purpose: they store and retrieve pertinent data that can affect the day-to-day operations of a business.

Considering that the sheer volume of data has the potential of scaling to a large degree, designing these types of applications may not function well when working with flat files. For that reason, databases have dominated the work environment.

Over the years, database tools and platforms have evolved just like any other technology has. These Database Management Systems (DBMS) have gotten faster, more efficient, and more complex. No matter what the database type, there is some common ground that makes them all seem alike.

11

Basic Theory of Design

Typically, databases fall into two categories: Flat and Relational.

Flat databases are typically a series of files that collect related data in one file. For example, a record in a database may contain a customer name, number, address, billing address, shipping address, and so on. After a while, this table would grow to an enormous size and have plenty of wasted space and duplicated data across tables.

A *relational database,* on the other hand, typically would have a customer master file that contained the customer name, number, and other unique data in one table. Another table would contain all the addresses for customers, linked by the customer number. This would allow one-to-many relationships. This means that if one customer had three separate addresses, he would have three address records. If he only had one address, only one address record would be in the table.

Relational databases are the newer of the two technologies, even though neither of them are new concepts. Relational databases also go through a process called *normalization* that reduces data redundancy to a minimum.

It would only be fair to say that there is no one real way to develop a database. There are many theories, each having its own merits and working well in scenarios where others fail, but who's to judge?

With that said, it's important to know what generic parts make up a database and how the parts relate to each other. Before jumping into that topic, you should know that each database vendor may (and often does) implement database behavior in its own manner. During this (and each successive) lesson, Microsoft's Access will be used to demonstrate techniques used.

Common pieces and parts are databases, tables, records, fields, and indexes. Each of these is discussed in turn.

Databases

The term *database* is used to encapsulate the individual pieces and parts. Typically, one application works with one database, but that is not always the case.

Take, for example, an accounting application: all of the pieces and parts used in the application would fit in this scenario rather well. All of the customers, vendors, inventory, and so on would be contained in this one large conglomerate of data.

Using that same accounting package as an example, if you managed more than one company, you may want to use the same application but would want to keep its data separate from the other; hence, a second database.

To draw a simple conclusion, a database is a collection of data that fits a specific application.

Tables

Databases consist of tables. *Tables* represent organized collections of similar data.

Using the accounting package as an example again, a table (or collection of related tables) would contain only information about your customers. Another table (or set of tables) would contain only information about your vendors. This cycle would continue for other areas such as Payroll, Inventory, and other possible functions.

As you can see, the database contains a series of tables. The tables are nothing more than a collection of related data. This helps organize the database into logical parts and eases the development process.

Records

Tables in databases consist of records. A *record* typically contains information about a single item.

Using the accounting example again, the employee master file (part of payroll) would contain a record specifying unique details about each employee.

This table would be linked to other tables based on some unique ID that would be in all of the related tables. This would allow for one table to contain all the employees and another to contain history about payments to this employee. This allows for a one-to-many relationship with very little data redundancy.

Fields

Records in tables are segmented into different parts. Often, these parts are called *columns*. Whatever the terminology is, the function remains the same.

Each column or field in a record should contain a specific piece of information. For example, some of the fields in an employee master file could consist of

- A unique ID
- The employee's last name (first name, full name, and so on)
- Employee's current salary
- Date of hire
- Emergency contact

The concept of the individual fields would be to store a piece of data that isn't somewhere else in the database and that is directly related to what the table needs to hold. For example, if you had the employee's full name in this table, you shouldn't need it in another.

11

Note

This rule has some exceptions, and depending upon your database design, you may want or need to have the same information stored more than once.

Indexes

Indexes are structures that allow fast retrieval of data. Often, an index is a database element that usually belongs to a table, but some database implementations make the index a part of the database itself: It depends upon the DBMS.

Indexes allow a query against a table to point right to a specific record without having to traverse the entire table from beginning to end to find the record it seeks.

Having good indexes is one of the most important key elements of database design, but what you as a developer may consider to be a good index may not be useful to end users. In fact, they may need an index on a field (or series of fields) that you may not have considered.

If you are writing an application that works against a database in which you have no control over the indexes, you may need to go out of your way to hit an index just to improve the efficiency of your program. This technique calls for extra work on the development end but can literally save hours of time on the user's end.

Suppose you had a simple database that had 200,000 records in it and was only indexed on a customer ID. If the user of your application needed to look up a customer by his name or phone number (or some other piece of information), the search would have to start from the beginning of the table and iterate through the records until a match was found.

In this same scenario, say that a user was looking up a company by its phone number and an index existed on that field. When the request was made, your program could take advantage of that index and immediately jump to the appropriate record, or be coded to jump to the nearest match.

There are several types of indexes, and going into too much detail would definitely be beyond the scope of this book, but you need to understand the basics.

One common type of index is commonly referred to as a *clustered index*. This type of index usually means that the data in the table is physically stored in sorted order based upon this index. You need to be careful when using this type of index because the more records that are inserted and updated, the longer it takes to update the table. This type of index typically results in the fastest data retrieval, though.

Another type of index (which is called almost anything and is one of the most common) is a sorted index of the field (or fields) in question that is stored in a separate area of the database. This collection would contain the data sorted on the respective field with a pointer back into the table pointing to a specific record.

Other Database Elements

Besides the basic database elements mentioned, other elements are worthy of mention but are simply not relevant to this book:

- Stored procedures—Not all databases implement this feature, but a stored procedure is usually found in a SQL database. These are statements that have been written and precompiled on the server. When called, they execute without having to be interpreted by the server again. These are useful for tasks such as housekeeping.

- Views—Views are like tables in that they are a collection of records. Views can be a combination of different tables. Typically a view is read-only because it has the potential of crossing tables. They are also used to hide columns of tables for people who are not supposed to see restricted data.

- Queries—These are similar to stored procedures but are usually just the query statements. They are typically not precompiled.

- Custom data types—Some databases give the luxury of combining the standard data types to create a custom type. For example, if the need arises where you must store an integer and a string in the same field, a custom data type would allow you to do that. This is useful if you have objects in your program and would like to store the data elements in a single structure in the database.

- Links—Some databases allow links to outside data sources, such as another database. If this is possible in your database, you are usually allowed to point to database servers of different brands.

- Primary key—A primary key is an index on a field in the database that usually must be unique in value. Often, an auto-incrementing field is used.

- Foreign key—A foreign key is a column that exists in a table that is an index (or primary key) in another table.

- Referential integrity—With the use of primary and foreign keys, a rule can be established that states that detail records must contain a master. With this kind of rule, the master record can't be removed until all of its detail records have been removed. This can also be referred to as a *constraint*.

11

Creating a Database

Hopefully, the last section wasn't too confusing, but if you are a little lost, don't feel bad. There are literally hundreds of books on the subject. In fact, some people have careers where all they do is manage a single database's elements.

To complete this lesson as shown, you will need Microsoft Access 97 or later installed on your machine. You may use another database tool, but there would be no guarantee that the example shown would not need any modifications to work on your specific DBMS.

Throughout the rest of this chapter, you will be using this database to complete the examples. The database will take the form of a "quick-and-dirty" contacts database.

It's usually a good practice to design the database layout on paper (or some other tool) before jumping right into the DBMS and creating it on-the-fly. For this example, you will be creating a database named Contacts that will have a single table in it named Contact. Table 11.3 lists the layout of the columns.

TABLE 11.3   Table Structure for the Contact Table

Column	Data Type	Length	Comments
IDENTITY	AutoNumber	*	Primary key
CONTACT_ID	TEXT	8	Unique ID
LAST_NAME	TEXT	30	
FIRST_NAME	TEXT	30	
MIDDLE_NAME	TEXT	30	
ADDRESS	TEXT	30	
CITY	TEXT	30	
HOME_STATE	TEXT	15	
POSTAL_CODE	TEXT	10	
COUNTRY	TEXT	10	
HOME_PHONE	TEXT	20	
WORK_PHONE	TEXT	20	
EMAIL	TEXT	30	

The first column, IDENTITY, is used strictly as a primary key. This column will be managed by Access. Each time a record is added, this column is automatically updated. A good reason to use such a field is that it guarantees a unique record, but this column is not actually necessary.

CONTACT_ID is used as a unique ID that distinguishes one contact from the next, independent of the IDENTITY column.

You may have noticed that the column name HOME_STATE was used in place of STATE. The word STATE is a reserved word in some DBMS systems and this could cause conflicts when working with the database. This is one reason to know the do's and don'ts of a DBMS before constructing tables.

The rest of the columns should be pretty much self-explanatory. Next, you actually create the Contacts database with the CONTACT table.

In Access, the steps are as follows:

1. Load Access. When it comes up, you will be prompted to create a new database or open an existing one. Select Blank Database and click the OK button.

2. Next, you will be prompted to give the database a path and a specific database. Navigate the dialog box to a path that you will remember, and create the database with the name CONTACTS.

3. Once you have the database created, you need to create the CONTACT table. This is done by clicking the New button.

4. The New Table dialog box will be displayed. Select Design View and click the OK button.

5. Next, you need to create each of the columns as indicated in Table 11.3.

6. Once you have entered all the columns, select the File, Save menu item. You will be asked for the name of the table. Enter CONTACT and click the OK button. Access will then ask you to create a primary key. Go ahead and click Yes. Figure 11.4 shows the CONTACT table definition in the design editor.

FIGURE 11.4

CONTACT *table design in Access.*

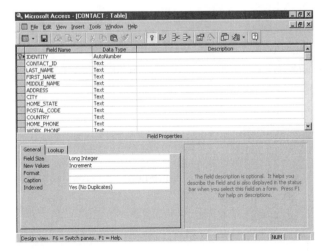

Go ahead and close the table in design editor to return to Access's main screen. You should now see CONTACT in the Tables tab. Go ahead and close Access as well.

 Note | If you don't have Access, you can obtain the CONTACTS.MDB file from this book's directory on the accompanying CD.

Lesson Summary

This lesson concentrated more on the theory of database design than actual database design.

In this lesson, you were introduced to key elements of database design such as Databases, Tables, Columns, and Indexes. Each of these elements plays an important role in database design.

You also saw that depending upon the DBMS system used, each may use different terminology and implement features that others don't have.

Quiz 2

1. Which of the following database elements can help the overall efficiency of the database?

   a. A Table

   b. A Record

   c. An Index

   d. None of the above

2. Which type of database model uses relationships between its tables for links?

   a. Hierarchical

   b. Relational

   c. Indexed Sequential

   d. None of the above

3. Which database element is housed on the server and is precompiled?

   a. Stored procedure

   b. Data Definition statement

   c. Custom Index

   d. Custom data type

4. Which of the following database elements would best represent a specific data item?

    a. Database

    b. Table

    c. Record

    d. Field

Exercise 2

Complexity: Easy

1. Create a single table database named "BASEBALL" with a table named "PLAY-ER." The player table should have the following structure:

Column	Data Type	Length
IDENTITY	AutoNumber	
PLAYER_ID	TEXT	8
PLAYER_NAME	TEXT	40
PLAYER_TEAM	TEXT	40
JERSEY_NUMBER	TEXT	3
AT_BATS	NUMBER	
HITS	NUMBER	
STRIKE_OUTS	NUMBER	
WALKS	NUMBER	
HOMERUNS	NUMBER	
TRIPLES	NUMBER	
DOUBLES	NUMBER	
SINGLES	NUMBER	

11

Complexity: Easy

2. Create a single table database named "RECIPES" with a table named "RECIPE." The recipe table should have the following structure:

Column	Data Type	Length
IDENTITY	AutoNumber	
RECIPE_ID	TEXT	8
TITLE	TEXT	50
INGREDIENTS	MEMO	
DIRECTIONS	MEMO	

LESSON 3

Creating a Connection to a Database

Writing a database application used to be a long and drawn-out process, but not anymore. Creating database applications with VC++ 6 is a snap, thanks to the MFC.

The MFC includes several classes that help you write database applications. The type of database access you want determines the classes you need to use.

Open Database Connectivity is a standard that allows applications to connect to a database by using a name registered with the system. This name is called a *data source name*, or *DSN*.

The DSN tells the system how to connect to the database by specifying DBMS-specific settings such as a server name, a database name, and a path. Once this DSN is created, your application can use this DSN to connect to the database.

Creating a DSN is quite simple. When setting up a DSN, you just need to know some DBMS-specific information, such as the server name, path, and database name. In Windows 95 and NT environments, this is handled through the ODBC Control Panel application.

Creating the DSN

To create a DSN, you need to locate the 32bit ODBC Manager located within the Control Panel. Figure 11.5 shows the Windows 95 Control Panel.

FIGURE **11.5**

*The Windows 95
Control Panel.*

In Figure 11.5, you can see that the 32bit ODBC Manager is in the top-left corner. This
may not be the case on your machine. To go into the ODBC Manager, double-click its
Control Panel icon. Figure 11.6 shows the ODBC Manager.

FIGURE **11.6**

*The 32bit ODBC
Manager.*

11

By looking at Figure 11.6, you can see that the System DSN page is selected. Where you
will put it depends upon the purpose of your DSN. If you are the only user on a system,
putting it in the Users section is fine. To make it available to all users on a workstation,
however, you will need to add them to the System DSN tab. Following is a brief description of each page in the 32bit system manager:

- User DSN—A data source only available to the user that created it. This data
  source can only be used on the machine that created it.

- System DSN—A data source available to everyone on this system. In Windows
  NT, this includes services.

- File DSN—This type of DSN allows you to connect to a data provider.

- ODBC Drivers—Lists the drivers installed on this machine.

- Tracing—Allows you to turn on ODBC tracing. This creates a log file of ODBC activity and can be useful when debugging an application.

- About—Lists version information about the installed ODBC system files.

For the sample application in this chapter, you need to create a System DSN named Contacts. To do this, complete the following steps:

1. With the 32bit ODBC Manager running, select the System DSN tab.

2. Click the Add button to display the Create New Data Source dialog box as shown in Figure 11.7.

FIGURE 11.7

The Create New Data Source dialog box.

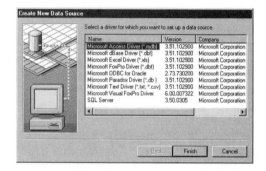

3. Select the Access driver and click the Finish button. This will display the driver-dependent setting screen.

4. Fill in the ODBC Microsoft Access 97 dialog box, as shown in Figure 11.8. Click the Select button to get an open dialog box to point to the drive and path of the CONTACTS.MDB file you created in Lesson 2 of this chapter.

FIGURE 11.8

ODBC Microsoft Access 97 Setup dialog box.

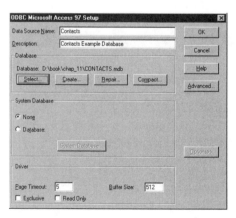

5. With the database selected, click the OK button to create the System DSN. The dialog box will close and return you to the ODBC Manager. Figure 11.9 shows the new entry for the Contacts data source.

FIGURE **11.9**

32bit ODBC Manager with new Contacts *data source.*

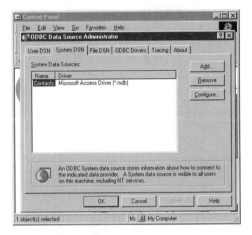

Creating a Database Application

With the Contacts system DSN created, you are ready to begin creating the application that will use this database.

Considering the flexibility of the AppWizard, you should not be surprised to learn that you can use it to build a basic database application simply by selecting a few options when creating the application.

Go ahead and use AppWizard to create a new MFC application named CONTACTS. Use the following steps to create the application. The numbers in the list correspond to the steps in the AppWizard.

1. Select Single document and click the Next button.

2. Click Database view without file support. Because most database applications don't need to store data in plain files, you can conserve program resources by not including those functions. If you need support for serializing, however, you can select the Database view with the file support option.

2a. Before you can move on to the next step, you must specify a data source and tables to use. In the dialog box shown in Figure 11.10, you need to select the Contacts data source that you just created. This links your application to that database.

FIGURE 11.10

Selecting a data source.

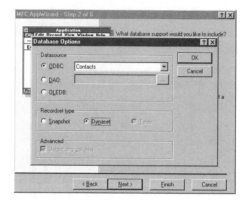

2b. After you select the data source, you must select the tables to use from that data source. Figure 11.11 shows the CONTACTS table. Because this is the only table, select it from the list and click the OK button. Click the Next button to go to Step 3.

FIGURE 11.11

Selecting tables from the data source.

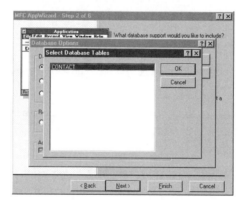

3. All the defaults on this page are OK; click the Next button to go to Step 4.

4. All the defaults on this page are OK; click the Next button to go to Step 5.

5. All the defaults on this page are OK; click the Next button to go to Step 6.

6. Looking at AppWizard Step 6, you can see that the base class for this application's view is CRecordView. This is a special view based upon a dialog resource that links controls to data elements. Click the Finish button to complete the creation process.

At this time, you have a functioning database application. Go ahead and build and execute the program. Figure 11.12 shows the bare application running.

FIGURE 11.12

CONTACTS *application running.*

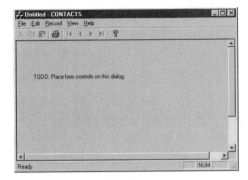

While this application has a database connection, it doesn't do much for you at this point.

Building the Form

When you built the application, you were introduced to the CRecordView class. This class replaces the CView class with a class that implements a dialog resource in the view.

Often, database applications use form-based user interfaces to manage the information in the database. This application is no exception.

To modify the dialog view, you edit it just like any other dialog resource. Go to the ResourceView in the project workspace and select the IDD_CONTACTS_FORM in the dialog editor.

The first thing you will want to do is remove the static text control that tells you to place controls on this form.

Using Figure 11.13 as a guide, modify the dialog resource using the following control properties:

FIGURE 11.13

Modified IDD_CON-TACTS_FORM *dialog resource.*

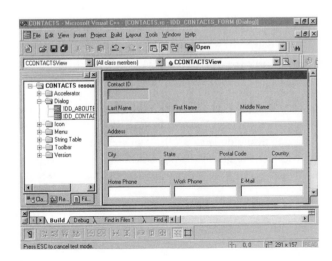

11

- Contact ID—Edit box control with the resource ID of `IDC_CONTACT_ID`. Set the read-only property.
- Last Name—Edit box control with the resource ID of `IDC_LAST_NAME`.
- First Name—Edit box control with the resource ID of `IDC_FIRST_NAME`.
- Middle Name—Edit box control with the resource ID of `IDC_MIDDLE_NAME`.
- Address—Edit box control with the resource ID of `IDC_ADDRESS`.
- City—Edit box control with the resource ID of `IDC_CITY`.
- State—Edit box control with the resource ID of `IDC_HOME_STATE`.
- Postal Code—Edit box control with the resource ID of `IDC_POSTAL_CODE`.
- Country—Edit box control with the resource ID of `IDC_COUNTRY`.
- Home Phone—Edit box control with the resource ID of `IDC_HOME_PHONE`.
- Work Phone—Edit box control with the resource ID of `IDC_WORK_PHONE`.
- E-Mail—Edit box control with the resource ID of `IDC_EMAIL`.

With the dialog resource created and the properties of all the edit controls set, you are now ready to link the edit controls to their respective data elements.

Linking Dialog Controls to Data

When users are working with your application, they need direct access to the data in the database in a format to which they can relate. This is accomplished with the form you just created.

To get the data to and from a user, you need to link the controls on the form to their respective data elements. VC++ 6 makes this a snap. This is accomplished through the use of member variables for the dialog resource.

Just like creating most other member variables, you use the ClassWizard. This time is no different except that you do it inside of the ClassWizard itself.

Go ahead and display the ClassWizard while the dialog resource is the currently selected item in the editor. When ClassWizard displays, switch to the Member Variables tab.

On this page, you should see the list of controls as expected. Select the `IDC_CONTACT_ID` Object ID and click the Add Variable button. When the Add Member Variable dialog appears, all you have to do is select the data element from the drop-down list of available predefined member variable names. In this case, you need to select `m_pSet->m_CONTACT_ID` from the list. Figure 11.14 shows this selection.

Figure 11.14

Add Member Variable for IDC_CONTACT_ID.

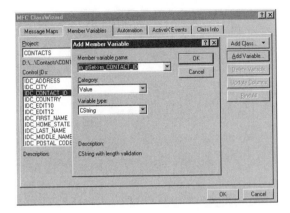

Click the OK button on the Add Member Variable dialog box to create the desired variable. Using Figure 11.15 as a guide, complete this process for the rest of the controls on the IDD_CONTACTS_FORM dialog resource.

Figure 11.15

ClassWizard showing member variables for data elements.

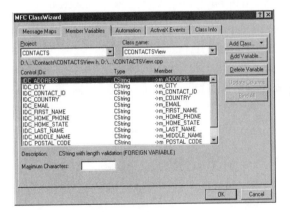

With all the dialog controls linked, you are ready to build and execute the application. Figure 11.16 shows the application running. This time, all the controls are shown on the form as designed.

Looking at this application, you can see that, at this point, it's quite useless. The reason nothing shows anything is that the database contains no data. The AppWizard did a nice job of creating the application framework that contains the CRecordView with a navigation bar for the database, but that's all. In order to get data into the application or delete records, you have to write that code yourself.

FIGURE 11.16

CONTACTS *application running with the modified dialog resource.*

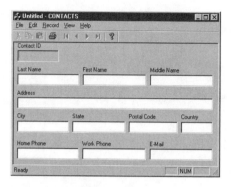

The next lesson, Manipulating Database Information, shows how to add functions that will allow the program to add and delete records.

Lesson Summary

In this lesson, you learned how to define data sources that are recognizable by any application on the system through the 32bit ODBC Manager in the Control Panel.

Most business applications require some kind of database connectivity. The AppWizard does a great job of creating the application framework that connects an application to the database with some navigation capabilities.

You were introduced to the CRecordView class, which is a special class derived from CView that uses a dialog resource to connect controls to database elements.

By linking controls on the main dialog resource to database elements, your application can browse the data in a database immediately. If your application needs modification capabilities, you will need to implement that yourself, but the MFC gives you classes that enable this functionality without much work.

Quiz 3

1. Which tool is used in the Control Panel to create a DSN?

   a. DSN Manager

   b. Database Connection Manager

   c. Access Manager

   d. 32bit ODBC Manager

2. Which statement best describes the difference between a User DSN and a System DSN?

    a. A User DSN is only accessible by the user that created it, whereas a System DSN can be accessed by any user on the system.

    b. User DSNs are DSNs that you create. System DSNs are DSNs that the operating system creates.

    c. A User DSN allows only one connection to a database resource, whereas a System DSN allows multiple connections to a database resource.

    d. A User DSN is created by installed applications, whereas a System DSN is created automatically by the system.

3. Which `View` class does AppWizard use when working with record sets?

    a. `CRecordView`

    b. `CRecordsetView`

    c. `CODBCRecordView`

    d. `CDBView`

4. Via what mechanism does the ClassWizard link a control on a dialog resource to a database column?

    a. By naming the resource ID the same name as the column name, the link is made automatically.

    b. ClassWizard creates a new class for each data element, and then a resource ID is linked to that class.

    c. It is linked through the use of member variables.

    d. ClassWizard does not make this connection.

Exercise 3

Complexity: Easy

1. Using the BASEBALL database created in Exercise 1 of Lesson 2, create a System DSN named BASEBALL that points to the BASEBALL.MDB file.

    Next, create an SDI application that connects to this data source. Modify the main dialog resource to contain the controls needed for working with the fields in that database.

Complexity: Easy

2. Using the RECIPE database created in Exercise 1 of Lesson 2, create a System DSN named RECIPE that points to the RECIPE.MDB file.

Next, create an SDI application that connects to this data source. Modify the main dialog resource to contain the controls needed for working with the fields in that database.

HINT: You will need to set certain properties on the Edit Box to allow more than one line of text to be entered in the INGREDIENTS and DIRECTIONS fields.

LESSON 4

Manipulating Database Information

In the last lesson, you saw how to create an ODBC data source and how to have AppWizard link your application to that data source.

After you modified the dialog resource to contain the necessary controls to represent the data in the database, you linked each control to a specific data element.

The AppWizard did a nice job of creating the application and linking it to the data source. What it didn't do was provide a mechanism for manipulating the information in the database. Unfortunately, database applications aren't that useful if you can't perform basic functions such as adding and deleting records.

Given this, the MFC has given you the means to make this happen; you just have to write the implementation code to complete the process.

Adding Menu Items for Special Functions

You've already learned how to modify menu resources in this book. Looking at the menu that AppWizard built for the CONTACTS application, you can see that it added a Record menu. This menu contains four items: First Record, Previous Record, Next Record, and Last Record.

These menu items are used for primary navigation of the database. Each has a toolbar button that operates analogous to a VCR. You can go to the very beginning, move in reverse, move forward, or go to the very end using the toolbar buttons as well.

This doesn't address the issue of needing menu items to add, delete, and save records. Modify the IDR_MAINFRAME menu resource's Record menu item by adding the following menu items:

- Add a separator menu item.
- Add a menu item with the caption &Add Record with a resource ID of ID_RECORD_ADD.

- Add a menu item with the caption &Delete Record with a resource ID of ID_RECORD_DELETE.

- Add another separator menu item.

- Add a menu item with the caption &Save Record with a resource ID of ID_RECORD_SAVE.

MFC Database Classes

As mentioned, the MFC allows your application to take advantage of databases. When working with ODBC databases, the most common classes are CDatabase and CRecordset. CDatabase controls the connection to the database, and CRecordset manages the records in the database.

CDatabase Class

The CDatabase class manages the connection to the database. When AppWizard built your application, it implemented the necessary code to make this connection work. Depending upon the needs of your application, you can change how the connection is made.

CDatabase makes available several class members that make working with this class a snap. Table 11.4 lists some common class members of the CDatabase class.

TABLE 11.4 Common CDatabase Class Members

Class Member	Description
m_hdbc	Links ODBC handle to a data source.
Open	Makes the connection to a data source.
Close	Closes the connection to a data source.
GetConnect	Returns a string containing the ODBC connect string used when connecting a CDatabase to a data source.
IsOpen	Checks to see if the database is currently open.
GetDatabaseName	Returns the name of the database.
CanUpdate	Tells whether the database can be updated.
BeginTrans	Begins a transaction on the server.
CommitTrans	Commits a transaction to the server.
Rollback	Rolls back changes made during the current transaction.
ExecuteSQL	Executes a SQL statement on the server. This function is not used to retrieve records from the server.

11

CRecordset Class

The CRecordset class works with the records in a database. Record sets usually come in one of two styles: Dynaset or Snapshot.

A Snapshot record set is a collection of read-only records, whereas Dynasets are record sets that allow updating. Dynasets also return to the server to get each record when navigating the record set. This gives Dynasets the capability to see changes made by other users in the database.

The CRecordset has quite a few class members that make this a rather versatile class. Table 11.5 lists some of the common class members for the CRecordset class.

TABLE 11.5 Some CRecordset Class Members

Class Member	Description
m_hstmt	ODBC statement handle for the record set.
m_nFields	Number of fields in the record set.
m_pDatabase	Pointer to the CDatabase object for this record set.
m_strFilter	CString that specifies a SQL WHERE clause. Used to link tables and restrict returned rows.
m_strSort	CString that specifies a SQL ORDER BY clause. Used to define how the records are sorted.
Open	Opens the record set.
Close	Closes the record set.
CanAppend	Specifies whether records can be added to the record set.
CanRestart	Specifies whether or not the Requery function can be called.
CanScroll	Specifies whether you can scroll through the record set.
CanTransact	Specifies whether transactions are supported.
CanUpdate	Specifies whether updates can be performed.
GetODBC.FieldCount	Returns the number of fields in the record set.
GetRecordCount	Returns the number of rows in the record set.
GetTableName	Obtains the name of the table.
GetSQL	Obtains the SQL statement used to get the record set.
IsOpen	Specifies whether the record set is open.
IsBOF	Determines whether the cursor is at the beginning of the record set.
IsEOF	Determines whether the cursor is at the end of the record set.
IsDeleted	Determines whether the current record has been deleted.

Class Member	Description
AddNew	Inserts a blank record.
CancelUpdate	Cancels any pending adds or edits.
Delete	Deletes the current record.
Edit	Puts the record in edit mode.
Updates	Saves changed data to the database.
Move	Repositions the cursor to a new location in the record set (bi-directional).
MoveFirst	Positions the cursor at the first record.
MoveLast	Positions the cursor at the last record.
MoveNext	Moves to the next record. You should test for IsEOF before using this function.
MovePrev	Moves back one record. You should test for IsBOF before using this function.
GetFieldValue	Obtains the value of a field in a record set.
Requery	Refreshes the record set by re-issuing the query.

As you can see from the list of available class members, the MFC gives a lot of functionality and a lot of flexibility when working with databases.

Adding the Necessary Function Handlers

Now that you've been bombarded with quite a few class members, it's time to put some of them to use.

When working with the CRecordset class, the controls on the form can edit a record if the record set isn't in a read-only state. One benefit of this is that the record set is automatically placed in edit mode when you start to change any of the data.

If the record set is in edit mode when you move to another record, the changes are saved for you automatically. If there are no records to maneuver to or you are adding a new record, the Update function needs to be called manually.

To keep track of when records are being added and to update the database properly, create a BOOL member variable that indicates whether the record being saved is new.

Because the CCONTACTSView class manages the form, create a member variable named m_UpdateMode to the CCONTACTSView class. You can do this manually by editing the CONTACTSView.h file, through the Class view of the project workspace.

After you add the member variable, you will want to initialize the value to FALSE. Do this in the OnInitialUpdate function inside of the CONTACTSView.cpp file.

Once you have the member variable created, you are ready to start coding the function handlers for the program. Start with adding a function handler for the Add Record menu item. When you go into ClassWizard, make sure you select the CCONTACTSView class. Figure 11.17 shows the ClassWizard with the ID_RECORD_ADD Object ID selected and the CCONTACTSView class selected.

FIGURE 11.17

ClassWizard with the ID_RECORD_ADD *Object ID selected.*

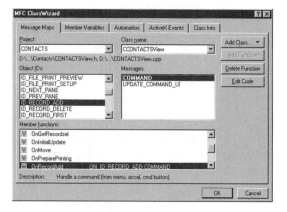

Go ahead and create the function handler for this menu item. Once you have created it, modify it so that it looks like the following section of code:

```
void CCONTACTSView::OnRecordAdd()
{
        // TODO: Add your command handler code here
    m_UpdateMode = TRUE;
    m_pSet->AddNew();

    CEdit* pContact = (CEdit*)GetDlgItem(IDC_CONTACT_ID);
    pContact->SetReadOnly(FALSE);

    UpdateData(FALSE);

}
```

Looking at this function, you can see that the member variable you created earlier gets set to TRUE first. This value will be used later to determine a course of action when the record set gets scrolled.

Next, the AddNew function is called to add a new record to the dataset. Because this is a new record, the Contact ID edit box's SetReadOnly function is called so that you can enter a value into this field.

Next, the UpdateData function for the dialog is called to initialize the controls on the form and ready them for input.

Once this function executes, it's up to the user to save his or her changes or move to another record. Moving to another record will implicitly update the information. If they select the Record, Save Record menu item, they are explicitly telling the program to save the data.

To update the data implicitly, you need to override CRecordSet's OnMove function. To do this, right-click the CCONTACTSView class in the Class view and select Add Virtual Function from the pop-up context menu as shown in Figure 11.18.

FIGURE 11.18

Selecting the Add Virtual Function menu item.

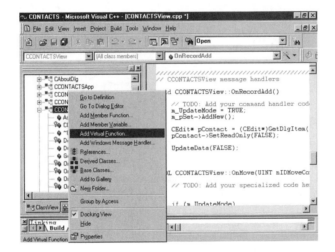

This action will display the New Virtual Override dialog box. Select the OnMove function from the list of New Virtual Functions on the left and double-click it. This will add it to the list of Existing Virtual Functions on the right. Figure 11.19 shows the New Virtual Override dialog box with the OnMove function added.

FIGURE 11.19

The OnMove virtual function selected.

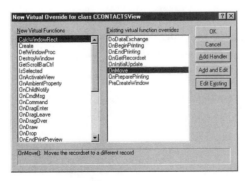

Once you have the new virtual function for OnMove selected, click the Add and Edit button so that you can immediately edit the code that belongs in this function. Modify the code to match the following section of code:

```
BOOL CCONTACTSView::OnMove(UINT nIDMoveCommand)
{
    // TODO: Add your specialized code here and/or call the base class

    if (m_UpdateMode)
    {
        m_UpdateMode = FALSE;

        UpdateData(TRUE);
        if (m_pSet->CanUpdate())
            m_pSet->Update();
        m_pSet->Requery();

        UpdateData(FALSE);
        CEdit* pContact = (CEdit*)GetDlgItem(IDC_CONTACT_ID);
        pContact->SetReadOnly(TRUE);

        return TRUE;
    }
    else

        return CRecordView::OnMove(nIDMoveCommand);
}
```

First, this function checks the value of the member variable created to manage updates. If it's false, the default behavior of the OnMove function is called. If it's true, meaning that a record was being added, the flag is set to false.

Next, the contents of the controls are copied to their member variables through the use of the dialog's UpdateData(TRUE) function.

After the member variables have been updated, a call to CRecordset's CanUpdate function is made to see if the record can be saved. If so, the Update command is issued to copy the contents of the member variable to the database.

Next, the Requery function is called to reset the record set. Because the record is now saved, the Contact ID edit box is set back to read-only.

The next menu item to be implemented is Delete Record. Bring the menu resource back up in the editor and go into ClassWizard. Select the CCONTACTSView class and the ID_RECORD_ADD Object ID. Create the function handler for the COMMAND message.

Once you have the function created, modify it to match the following code function:

```
void CCONTACTSView::OnRecordDelete()
{
    // TODO: Add your command handler code here
    m_pSet->Delete();
    m_pSet->MoveNext();

    if (m_pSet->IsEOF())
        m_pSet->MoveLast();

    if (m_pSet->IsBOF())
        m_pSet->SetFieldNull(NULL);

    UpdateData(FALSE);

}
```

Looking at this function, you can see that the first command called is the `Delete()` function. Typically, you would want to ask the user if he is sure he wants to delete the record, but in this case, it's not necessary.

After the record is deleted, the `MoveNext()` function is called to remove the cursor from the deleted record. After using this function, you should always test for the last record.

To check to see whether you are at the end of the record set, use the `IsEOF` function. If this returns `TRUE`, make a call to `MoveLast()`. This will update the cursor and screen elements properly. If `IsEOF` returns `FALSE`, don't worry about it.

Next, you should check to see if it's at the beginning of the file. If so, that means that the last record was deleted. To test for this condition, make a call to `IsBOF`. If this call returns `TRUE`, call the `SetFieldNull(NULL)` function to set all the fields to `NULL`.

Lastly, you need to update the dialog's controls. Initialize them by calling the `UpdateData(FALSE)` function.

That's all you need to do to delete a record from the database. Your next step is to add code for an explicit save.

An explicit save is really no different than an implicit save, other than the fact that the user asked to save the data without moving to another record.

Add a function handler for the `ID_RECORD_SAVE` Object ID as you did with the `ID_RECORD_ADD` and `ID_RECORD_DELETE` Object IDs in ClassWizard. Once you create the function handler, modify the function to match the following section of code:

```
void CCONTACTSView::OnRecordSave()
{
    // TODO: Add your command handler code here
    if (m_UpdateMode)
```

11

```
    {
        UpdateData(TRUE);
        if (m_pSet->CanUpdate())
            m_pSet->Update();
        m_pSet->Requery();

    }
    else
    {
        if (m_pSet->CanUpdate())
        {
            m_pSet->Edit();
            UpdateData(TRUE);
            m_pSet->Update();
        }
    }

    m_UpdateMode = FALSE;
    UpdateData(FALSE);
    CEdit* pContact = (CEdit*)GetDlgItem(IDC_CONTACT_ID);
    pContact->SetReadOnly(TRUE);
}
```

This function is a little more complex compared to the other functions used so far, because the program needs to check and see if it's adding a record or updating the current one.

The first thing it does is look at the m_UpdateMode variable. This variable is set to TRUE when a record is being added. If this is the case, the dialog box's values are updated via a call to UpdateData(TRUE). Next, the record set is checked to see if it is updateable. If so, the record is updated and the query is refreshed.

If this wasn't a save for a new record, it's a save for an existing record. In this section, the record set is tested to make sure it can be updated. If so, the record set is put into edit mode with a call to the Edit function. Next, the UpdateData(TRUE) function is called to update the values from the dialog controls. After the values are updated, the record set is updated with a call to Update.

After either type of processing is done, the member variable m_UpdateMode is set to FALSE and the data controls are initialized. After that, the Contact ID edit box is set back to read-only mode.

With those code changes complete, the program's new features are implemented. You now have a database application that can add, delete, and update records, making it useful.

Go ahead and build and execute the program. Figure 11.20 shows the application running.

FIGURE 11.20

The CONTACTS *application running.*

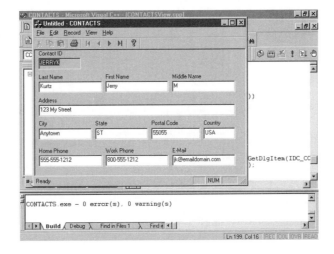

Because the database is blank, in order to save your first record, you will have to use the Record, Save menu item. Experiment a little bit with the application by adding, removing, and navigating through the records.

Lesson Summary

In this lesson, you learned that the MFC provides some very powerful classes that allow you to add database technologies into your applications.

When AppWizard built your application, most of the implementation details of CDatabase and CRecordset were hidden from you. To expand on that basic application, however, you needed to add the functionality that would allow your database to add, delete, and edit records.

Even though you had to implement these details yourself, you saw that the process was pretty much straightforward.

Quiz 4

1. Which function of the CRecordset class is overridden if you want to save a new record if the database is scrolled?

    a. OnMove

    b. OnScroll

    c. OnUpdate

    d. OnNewRecord

2. Which member function of the CRecordset class writes changes of either an add or an edit to the database?

   a. UpdateAll

   b. Update

   c. CommitAll

   d. Cancel

3. Which function of the dialog class copies the contents of the controls on the form to the member variables?

   a. UpdateData(FALSE)

   b. UpdateControls(FALSE)

   c. UpdateData(TRUE)

   d. UpdateControls(TRUE)

4. Which functions of the CRecordset class should be called when a record is deleted?

   a. MoveNext

   b. IsEOF with MoveLast

   c. IsBOF with SetFieldNull(NULL)

   d. None of the above

Exercise 4

Complexity: Easy

1. Expanding on the application you created in Exercise 1 of Lesson 3 in this chapter, add the functionality to add, delete, and edit the data in the database.

Complexity: Easy

2. Expanding on the application you created in Exercise 2 of Lesson 3 in this chapter, add the functionality to add, delete, and edit the data in the database.

Chapter Summary

Ever since the first application was written, there has been the need to store information.

For small applications, writing data directly to flat files may be a considerable approach. If this is the case, VC++ 6 and MFC offer several classes that make doing this work easy. CFile and CStdioFile are two of the more common classes that work with these kinds of files. CStdioFile descends from CFile and offers some extra flexibility when dealing with text files.

For applications that require just a bit more functionality when storing and retrieving data, a database is a popular choice.

If your application requires connections to a database, you need to create a data source and then build the application. AppWizard will take care of the details as far as connecting to the database and giving your application basic navigation capabilities.

If you need more functionality than what AppWizard gives you, which you probably will, you will need to write the code that implements your features.

Again, VC++ 6 and MFC has provided solid classes for dealing with databases. CDatabase and CRecordset are just two of the many classes at your disposal when working on these types of projects. By implementing their features, you can easily write a powerful database application.

11

CHAPTER 12

Advanced Topics

The term *advanced* can cover a very wide range of topics, but in general, most programmers would probably consider writing applications that deal with system-level topics, such as the Registry and threads, to be advanced topics. These are topics that beginning programmers should not play around with until they have a better understanding of how the Windows operating system functions.

People usually cringe when you tell them that you are going to write a multi-threaded application or that you need to create routines that maintain data in the Registry. Even though it may sound complicated, you will learn how simple these topics can be to add to your application.

In this chapter, you will explore the Registry by learning how to store and retrieve data. You will then move onto working with basic threads. Once you know how to create threads in general, you will then learn how to make threads communicate with each other. And, when working with threads, one of the things that you will have to take into consideration is synchronizing the threads to prevent the shared data or resources from becoming corrupt, which is how you will finish up this chapter.

LESSON 1

Programming the Registry

The Registry stores a wide variety of information about your computer, such as the software you have installed, hardware configurations, and user configurations. As a programmer, you will typically use the Registry to store information about your application. This information can range anywhere from tracking window coordinates to storing default values, or anything else that you need to track.

In this lesson, you will learn about the Registry hierarchy and how to store and retrieve information from it.

Examining the System Registry

In order to examine the Registry, you will have to use an application named *Registry Editor*. With this application, you can easily browse through the Registry and make any changes you wish. To start the Registry Editor application, simply click the Start button, select Run from the list and enter `regedit` as the program to open. Figure 12.1 shows you what the Registry Editor application looks like when you start it.

FIGURE 12.1

The Registry Editor application.

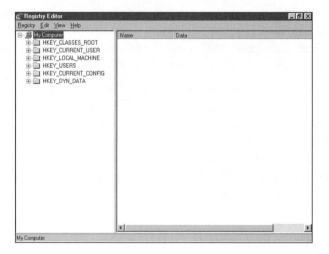

The Registry contains six predefined keys. Each one of these keys can be expanded to show their subkeys. Each subkey can have a value associated with it or even another subkey.

There are six predefined keys, only two of which are real keys. Three of the last four are aliases for a branch of one of the real keys, and the last key is a dynamic key, which isn't stored permanently. The two real keys, HKEY_LOCAL_MACHINE and HKEY_USERS, are listed first, followed by the tree aliases and then the dynamic key.

- The HKEY_LOCAL_MACHINE key contains configuration data that is specific to your computer. This includes all the hardware and software installed. The information stored under this key is specific to the computer and is the same for all users of the machine.

- The HKEY_USERS key contains configuration information for each user that uses the computer. This key would include the configuration of applications for each user.

- The HKEY_CLASSES_ROOT key is an alias for the HKEY_LOCAL_MACHINE\Software\Classes key. This class is used for file type associations.

- The HKEY_CURRENT_USER key is an alias for a branch of the HKEY_USERS key. This key contains configuration information for the current user. Usually, there is only one subkey for the typical home machine, so this key would map to HKEY_USERS\.Default. By examining Figure 12.2, you can see that the alias looks just like the real key.

FIGURE 12.2

The
HKEY_CURRENT_USER
alias key.

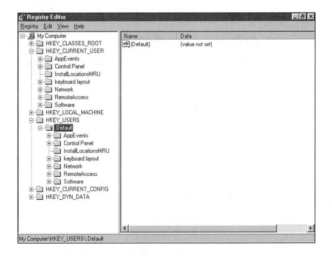

12

- The HKEY_CURRENT_CONFIG key is an alias for HKEY_LOCAL_MACHINE\Config\0001. The 0001 subkey represents hardware configuration 1. You can have multiple hardware configurations for the same machine, and if this is the case with your machine, you would see other configurations, such as 0002 under the Config subkey.

You can easily determine which hardware profile is in use by examining the HKEY_LOCAL_MACHINE\System\CurrentControlSet\Control\IDConfigDB key.

- The HKEY_DYN_DATA key contains information about the current status of the computer. This key is dynamically used and is not stored permanently to disk.

  The Windows NT 4 Registry does not contain the HKEY_DYN_DATA key.

If you want to have your application carry the Windows logo, you need to follow some standards, and one of them is where you store your information in the Registry. There are three primary pieces of information that you must store in the Registry:

- Company name
- Application name
- Version

As you might have guessed, a required key is already set up in the Registry for you. A complete key might look like HKEY_LOCAL_MACHINE\SOFTWARE\Company Name\Application Name\Version.

Of course, you can store whatever values you wish in the Registry, but for your application to pass the Windows logo specification, you should use this key layout. The sample applications for this lesson will use this layout.

Programming the Registry

Now you know just enough about the Registry to be dangerous. The next obvious step is to create a program that stores and retrieves data from the Registry.

The CWinApp class, which belongs to MFC, has several functions to make working with the Registry as easy as possible. Table 12.1 lists the functions of CWinApp that deal with the Registry.

TABLE 12.1   The Registry Functions of the CWinApp Class

Function	Description
GetProfileInt	Retrieves an integer value from a Registry entry.
GetProfileString	Retrieves a string value from a Registry entry.
LoadStdProfileSettings	Used to load the last preview state and a list of the most recently used (MRU) files.
SetProfileInt	Sets the integer value of a Registry entry. If the entry does not exist, it will be created.
SetProfileString	Sets the string value of a Registry entry. If the entry does not exist, it will be created.
SetRegistryKey	Sets the Registry key that your application will use.

These functions have a dual purpose. If you do not call the SetRegistryKey() function, your application will create or use a profile file (an .INI file).

Building the Registry Example Application

To show you how to use the Registry to store and retrieve information, you are going to build a sample application. This application will simply store and retrieve a string value and an integer value from the Registry.

Go ahead and create a dialog-based application, naming it Registry. Once the application is built, you will need to add a couple of controls to the dialog box. Using Figure 12.3 as a guide, create your dialog box.

FIGURE 12.3

The Registry example dialog box.

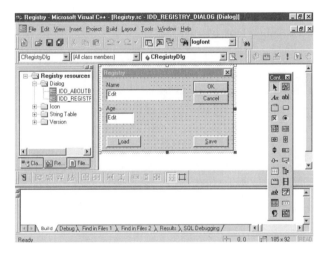

Looking at Figure 12.3, you can pretty much guess what properties need to be set. Most of the properties changed are the captions for the controls. The only property that needs to be set that is not a visual property is the Number check box on IDC_EDIT2. This edit box will be used to enter an integer value, so by selecting this property, the user will only be allowed to enter digits into the box.

Once you have all the controls in place, you will need to create the member variables for the two edit boxes. With Figure 12.4 as a guide, use the ClassWizard to create the variables.

Once you have created the two necessary member variables, you will need to add the necessary message handlers for both the Load and Save buttons. Go ahead and add these now. Use the default names for each of the message handlers.

12

FIGURE 12.4

*The member variables
for the edit boxes.*

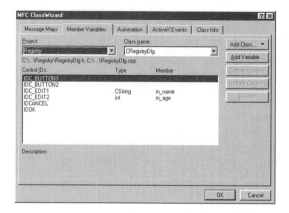

Before you add the necessary code to handle the loading and saving of the values to the Registry, you must first specify your Registry key for your application. You should do this in the `OnInitInstance()` function of your application. Listing 12.1 is a partial listing of this function to show you the needed code and its placement.

LISTING 12.1   Setting the Registry Key in `OnInitInstance()`

```
// Standard initialization
    // If you are not using these features and wish to reduce the size
    //  of your final executable, you should remove from the following
    //  the specific initialization routines you do not need.
    SetRegistryKey("Hello Interactive World");
    LoadStdProfileSettings(0);
```

When a new instance of your application is started, the `SetRegistryKey()` function is called using the name of this book. Typically, this would be the name of the company for the application you are writing or at least something meaningful that represents the application.

After the key is set, `LoadStdProfileSettings()` is called. This call is made to load in the list of MRU files. Because a value of 0 was passed as the parameter, no MRU list will be maintained.

Before you can load the settings in the sample application, you must first save something to the Registry. Therefore, you will add the necessary code to allow your application to save the Name and age entered to the Registry. Go ahead and bring the `OnButton2()` message handler function into the code editor and modify it so that it matches the code listed in Listing 12.2.

LISTING 12.2   Saving Information to the Registry

```
void CRegistryDlg::OnButton2()
{
    // TODO: Add your control notification handler code here
    CWinApp* pApp = AfxGetApp();
    UpdateData(TRUE);
    pApp->WriteProfileString("Settings","Name",m_name);
    pApp->WriteProfileInt("Settings","Age",m_age);

}
```

In order to call the Registry functions from within your application, you must first get a pointer to the CWinApp structure that is used for your application. You can easily accomplish this by using the AfxGetApp() function, which is precisely what the first line of code does.

Now, keep in mind that you are working with a dialog box and that the data in the controls are not updated until the dialog box is closed (by clicking the OK button). This would be too late for this example, because the dialog box is the main portion of the application. Fortunately, the UpdateData() function is called to update the values manually in the controls before you read them. By passing in the value of TRUE to this function, the member variables will be updated with the current values in the edit boxes.

The first bit of information that is saved is the m_name member variable, which is the name that is entered into the edit box. This edit box has a CString value; therefore, you will use the appropriate function for writing strings to the Registry. The WriteProfileString() function requires three parameters. The first parameter points to a null-terminated string, which specifies the section for the entry. The second parameter also requires a null-terminated string, which contains the entry for the specified section. The last parameter specifies the value to be written for the entry. If you were to pass a NULL value to this parameter, the entry would be removed from the Registry.

The second bit of information that is saved is the m_age member variable. Because this edit box has an integer value, you will use the appropriate function to store integer values. The WriteProfileInt() function requires three parameters, just like the WriteProfileString() function; only this time, the last parameter is an integer value rather than a string.

With the necessary code in place to save a Registry entry, go ahead and execute the sample application. Once you execute the application, your dialog box should look like the one shown in Figure 12.5.

12

FIGURE 12.5

Entering a name into the Registry example.

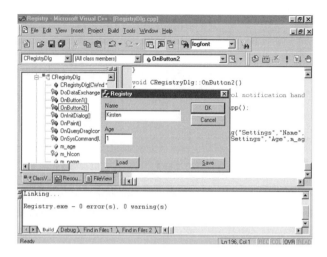

Once you enter a name and click the Save button, go ahead and start the regedit.exe application. Looking at the Registry entry created, you can see the information that was saved, as shown in Figure 12.6.

FIGURE 12.6

Looking at your key in the Registry.

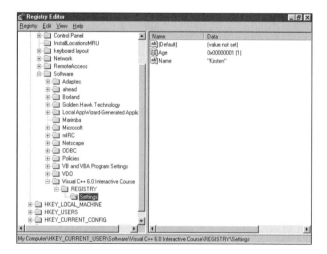

Now that you have information stored in the Registry, you will need to add the necessary code to read it from the Registry. Go ahead and bring up the OnButton1() message handler function and modify it so that it matches the code in Listing 12.3.

LISTING 12.3   Loading Information from the Registry

```
void CRegistryDlg::OnButton1()
{
    // TODO: Add your control notification handler code here
    CWinApp* pApp = AfxGetApp();
    m_name = pApp->GetProfileString("Settings","Name", "No Name");
    m_age  = pApp->GetProfileInt("Settings","Age", 0);
    UpdateData(FALSE);
}
```

The `GetProfileString()` and `GetProfileInt()` function act very similarly to their counterpart functions, except that they retrieve information rather than save it. The only other difference is in the last parameter. The third parameter is used as a default value to return if the section and entry are not found. After retrieving the name and age values, the dialog controls are updated by calling the `UpdateData()` function.

With this code added, the Registry example application can now load and save its information to and from the Registry.

Lesson Summary

The Registry stores a wide variety of details about your system. To make browsing and working with the Registry easier, a logical hierarchy of keys and subkeys are used.

By using the Registry functions provided by the `CWinApp` class of MFC, you can easily incorporate simple Registry management into your application.

Quiz 1

1. Which of the following is not one of the six predefined Registry keys?

    a. `HKEY_CLASSES_ROOT`

    b. `HKEY_USERS`

    c. `HKEY_USER_CONFIG`

    d. `HKEY_CURRENT_CONFIG`

2. Which Registry key is not stored permanently on disk?

    a. `HKEY_CURRENT_CONFIG`

    b. `HKEY_DYN_DATA`

    c. `HKEY_USERS`

    d. `HKEY_LOCAL_MACHINE`

12

3. What is the purpose of the `GetProfileInt()` function of the `CWinApp` class?

    a. To retrieve an integer value from an entry in the Registry

    b. To set a Registry entry value

    c. To set the key used for retrieving integers from the Registry

    d. To clear Registry entries

4. Three alias keys are used as predefined keys. Which ones are they?

    a. `HKEY_CLASSES_ROOT`, `HKEY_CURRENT_USER`, and `HKEY_LOCAL_MACHINE`.

    b. `HKEY_CLASSES_ROOT`, `HKEY_CURRENT_USER`, and `HKEY_CURRENT_CONFIG`.

    c. `HKEY_DYN_DATA`, `HKEY_CURRENT_CONFIG`, and `HKEY_USERS`.

    d. `HKEY_CLASSES_ROOT`, `HKEY_CURRENT_USER`, and `HKEY_USERS`.

Exercise 1

Complexity: Easy

1. Create a dialog-based application named "Exercise 1" that saves user information to the Registry. Using edit controls, let the user enter his name, address, city, state, zip code, and a phone number. You will need to add one button to the dialog box that will allow the user to save the information to the Registry. Verify that the data was saved to the Registry by using the Registry Editor.

Complexity: Moderate

2. Using the guidelines from the previous exercise, create another dialog-based application named "Exercise 2" that loads the name, address, city, state, zip code, and phone number from the Registry when the application first starts up. This application will have the same saving features as the previous exercise. Add a Load button to the dialog box so that the information in the Registry can be loaded in as well as saved.

LESSON 2

Working with Threads

One of the key advantages of the operating systems in use today, such as Windows 95, is the capability to run multiple applications at the same time. This is known as *multitasking*. The capability of a single application to execute more than one task concurrently is known as *threading*. A thread can operate individually from within the main application.

Every application always has at least one thread, which is the application itself. This is the primary thread of your application. By using MFC, you can easily create as many threads as you need.

How to Create a Thread

Creating a thread in MFC is very easy. In fact, it only takes one line of code to create the thread. The function that you will use to create a thread is AfxBeginThread(). The following is the declaration of the AfxBeginThread() function. Table 12.2 outlines the parameters for this function.

```
CWinThread* AfxBeginThread( AFX_THREADPROC pfnThreadProc,
➡LPVOID pParam, int nPriority = THREAD_PRIORITY_NORMAL,
➡UINT nStackSize = 0, DWORD dwCreateFlags = 0,
➡LPSECURITY_ATTRIBUTES lpSecurityAttrs = NULL );
```

TABLE 12.2 The AfxBeginThread Parameters

Parameter	Description
pfnThreadProc	The name of the function in your application to use as the thread.
pParam	A 32-bit value to pass into the function.
nPriority	The priority of the thread. A value of 0 indicates that the thread should have the same priority as the creating thread. Table 12.3 outlines the different constants that can be used for this parameter.
nStackSize	The size of the stack for the thread, measured in bytes. If this parameter is set to 0, the stack size of the creating thread will be used.
dwCreateFlags	Determines whether the thread should automatically execute after creating the thread. If you pass CREATE_SUSPENDED as the value for this parameter, the thread will be created, but it will not be executed until the ResumeThread() function is called. A value of 0 will execute the thread immediately after it is created.
lpSecurityAttrs	Points to a SECURITY_ATTRIBUTES structure. If set to NULL, the security attributes of the creating thread will be used. (This parameter is only valid under Windows NT.)

12

When creating a thread, you will need to determine the importance, or *priority*, of the thread. The priority level determines how much processor time a thread will be assigned. The higher the priority level, the more processing time the thread gets. You can choose from several settings. They are listed in Table 12.3.

TABLE 12.3   Priority Settings

Constant	Description
THREAD_PRIORITY_ABOVE_NORMAL	The priority level is set to one point higher than the normal priority level.
THREAD_PRIORITY_BELOW_NORMAL	The priority level is set to one point below the normal priority level.
THREAD_PRIORITY_HIGHEST	The priority level is set to two points higher than the normal priority level.
THREAD_PRIORITY_IDLE	The base priority level is set to 1.
THREAD_PRIORITY_LOWEST	The priority level is set to two points below the normal priority level.
THREAD_PRIORITY_NORMAL	The priority level is set to normal.
THREAD_PRIORITY_TIME_CRITICAL	The priority level is set to 15.

Threads in Action

Now that you know how to create a basic thread, your next step is to create an application that creates a thread. In order to do so, you will need to create a dialog-based application. Go ahead and use the MFC AppWizard to create this application, naming it Threads1.

Once you have the dialog-based application created, go ahead and add a button control to it. Change the caption of the control to Start Thread. Your dialog box should look like the one presented in Figure 12.7.

FIGURE 12.7

The Threads1 dialog box.

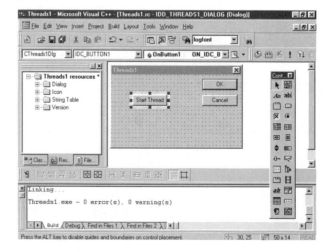

To create a message handler for the new button, simply double-click it. Accept OnButton1() as the name of the function. This will also bring the function into the code editor. Go ahead and modify the function so that it matches the code in Listing 12.4.

LISTING 12.4 Creating a Thread

```
void CThreads1Dlg::OnButton1()
{
    // TODO: Add your control notification handler code here
    HWND hWnd = GetSafeHwnd();
    AfxBeginThread(MyThread,hWnd,THREAD_PRIORITY_LOWEST);
}
```

The first line of code simply obtains the handle for the application window. This value will be passed as the parameter to the thread function, which you will see in a few minutes.

As discussed earlier, a call is made to the AfxBeginThread() function. You may notice that only three parameters are being passed in the function rather than all six. The last three parameters that were omitted have default values, which are acceptable for this example.

The first parameter is the name of the function that will be used as the thread. You haven't created this yet. The second parameter is the handle for the window that you retrieved in the previous statement. The last parameter specifies the priority level for the thread. Looking at these three parameters, the only thing you haven't specified is the MyThread() function. You are going to create it now.

To avoid compiler errors, you will need to add this function just before the OnButton1() function that you previously created. Go ahead and add the code in Listing 12.5. The OnButton1() function is shown in the listing as well so you can see where you need to add the necessary code.

LISTING 12.5 The MyThread() Function

```
UINT MyThread(LPVOID param)
{
    CTime time = CTime::GetCurrentTime();
    CString now = time.Format("%c");
    SetWindowText((HWND)param,now);
    return 0;
}

void CThreads1Dlg::OnButton1()
{
    // TODO: Add your control notification handler code here
    HWND hWnd = GetSafeHwnd();
    AfxBeginThread(MyThread,hWnd,THREAD_PRIORITY_LOWEST);
}
```

12

You added the `MyThread()` function right before the `OnButton1()` function because it is a global function rather than a member function.

Looking at the actual function, you can tell that it doesn't do very much. The first line obtains the current time, and the second line formats it. The third line of code is the key line of code for this example.

When you click the Start Thread button, the window handle for the application is retrieved and passed to the thread as the `param` parameter. This value is then used by the `SetWindowText()` function to change the caption of the dialog box. Therefore, when you run the application and click the Start Thread button, the caption of the dialog box will change to display the current date and time, as shown in Figure 12.8.

FIGURE 12.8

The thread was executed.

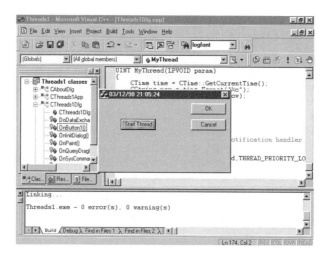

This is a very simple thread. After it changes the caption of the dialog box, it is complete. The thread is terminated with a result value of 0.

Lesson Summary

When using MFC, threads can be very easy to use. Only one call to the `AfxBeginThread()` function will create a new thread in your application. Once a thread is created, it can run concurrently along with the other threads in your application.

One of the key elements to threads is the capability to set its priority level. If you have a thread that needs to be completed as quickly as possible, you can easily set its priority above the priority level of other tasks running on the system. If the task is not as critical, you can set it to run below other tasks.

Quiz 2

1. Which statement is true about threads?

    a. You can only execute one thread at a time.

    b. You can execute multiple treads that run concurrently.

    c. Your main application is not considered a thread.

    d. You cannot change the priority of a thread.

2. When using MFC, which function creates a thread?

    a. `AfxCreateThread()`

    b. `AfxNewThread()`

    c. `AfxBegin()`

    d. `AfxBeginThread()`

3. Which thread priority constant sets the thread priority level to 15?

    a. `THREAD_PRIORITY_TIME_CRITICAL`

    b. `THREAD_PRIORITY_HIGHEST`

    c. `THREAD_PRIORITY_CRITICAL`

    d. `THREAD_PRIORITY_NORMAL`

4. If you wanted to create a thread but not execute it when you created it, what would you need to do?

    a. Pass `CREATE_NOEXECUTE` as the `dwCreateFlags` parameter of the `AfxBeginThread()` function.

    b. Set its priority level to 0.

    c. Pass `CREATE_SUSPENDED` as the `dwCreateFlags` parameter of the `AfxBeginThread()` function.

    d. You cannot keep a thread from executing when you create it.

12

Exercise 2

Complexity: Easy

1. Create a dialog-based application named "Exercise 1" that executes a thread when the Start button on the dialog box is clicked. This thread should simply pop up a simple dialog box to let you know that it executed.

Complexity: Advanced

2. Create a dialog-based application named "Exercise 2" that executes a thread when the Start button on the dialog box is clicked. When the thread is created, it should be created in suspend mode. When you click the second button, named Continue, the thread should continue and display a message stating the thread was finally executed.

LESSON 3

Thread Communications

In the last lesson, you learned how easy it was to create a thread in your application. For all practical purposes, though, it is more likely that your application will need to access data from the main thread of the application. When two threads access data of each other, this is known as *thread communication*.

There are several different ways of communicating between threads. The more common methods are to use global variables, messages, and events. In this lesson, you will learn how to use all three of these methods to communicate between threads.

Using Global Variables for Thread Communication

Using global variables to communicate between threads is the easiest method to use. To show you how easy it is to create threads that communicate with global variables, you will create a small dialog-based application that utilizes a global variable to stop a thread once it has started.

To begin, go ahead and create a dialog-based application named Threads2. Once created, place two buttons on the dialog box. Change the captions of the buttons to Start and Stop. When the start button is pressed, the global variable will be set to TRUE, and the thread will be started. The thread will monitor this variable, and when it is set to FALSE by clicking the Stop button, the thread will stop. Use Figure 12.9 as a guide for creating the dialog box. Once you have created the dialog box, go ahead and create the message handler functions for both buttons.

Once you create the message handlers, you will need to create the thread function, just like you did in the last lesson. Listing 12.6 shows you the thread function along with the two message handler functions. Go ahead and modify your project by adding this code.

FIGURE 12.9

The Threads2 dialog box.

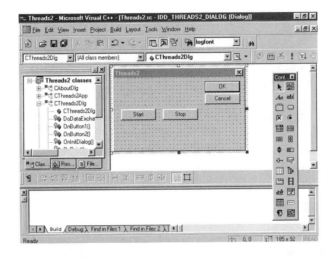

LISTING 12.6 The Code for the Threads and the Start and Stop Buttons

```cpp
volatile BOOL bRunThread;
UINT MyThread(LPVOID param)
{
    while (bRunThread)
    {
        CTime time = CTime::GetCurrentTime();
        CString now = time.Format("%c");
        SetWindowText((HWND)param,now);
    }

    return 0;
}

void CThreads2Dlg::OnButton1()
{
    // TODO: Add your control notification handler code here
    bRunThread = TRUE;
    HWND hWnd = GetSafeHwnd();
    AfxBeginThread(MyThread,hWnd,THREAD_PRIORITY_LOWEST);

}

void CThreads2Dlg::OnButton2()
{
    // TODO: Add your control notification handler code here
    bRunThread = FALSE;
}
```

The first thing that you will notice is the addition of the global variable bRunThread. The thread will determine whether it should continue or stop by checking this variable. This variable has a BOOL value, which means that it will either be set to TRUE or FALSE.

12

Note   The use of the `volatile` keyword tells the compiler that a variable can be changed asynchronously and that the compiler should not perform optimizations with it.

The next block of code is the `MyThread()` function, which is pretty much just like the example from the last lesson except for one minor change. The `while` loop continually checks the value of the `bRunThread` global variable. As long as the variable is set to `TRUE`, the code within the loop will continue to execute. The code inside the loop simply changes the caption of the dialog box with the current time and date.

The Start button is almost exactly the same as the code from the last lesson. In this lesson, you added a line of code to set the `bRunThread` global variable to `TRUE`.

The last function is the message handler for the Stop button. When you click the Stop button, the value of `bRunThread` will be changed to `FALSE`. Because the `MyThread` thread runs concurrent to the main thread, as soon as you click the Stop button, the `MyThread` thread will stop because the value of `bRunThread` is no longer set to `TRUE`, causing the while loop to exit. The thread is then terminated with a result of 0.

You can go ahead and execute the Threads2 application. You won't be able to see it here in Figure 12.10, but when you click the Start button, the caption will continually be updated with the current time and date. The caption will continue to update until you click the Stop button to cancel the `MyThread` thread.

FIGURE 12.10

The Thread2 application ticking away.

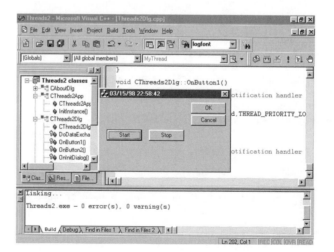

Using Messages for Thread Communication

Another way to manage thread communication is to use user-defined Windows messages. This is just as easy to accomplish as using global variables. For this reason, you will continue to modify the Threads2 application. For this portion of the lesson, if you are not comfortable working with user-defined messages, you should review Chapter 5, "Processing Windows Messages and Commands."

The first thing that you will need to do is define a constant for your user message. To do this, double-click the CThreads2Dlg class in the Workspace panel to bring up the Threads2Dlg.h file into the code editor. Place your cursor on the line for the class declaration for CThreads2Dlg. Move up one line and add the constant to use for your message, as shown here:

```
// CThreads2Dlg dialog
const WM_MYTHREADENDED = WM_USER + 100;
class CThreads2Dlg : public CDialog
```

Now you will need to add the message map function. Because you already have the necessary file open in the code editor, go ahead and scroll down and add the following line of code before the DECLARE_MESSAGE_MAP line:

```
//}}AFX_MSG
    afx_msg void OnMyThreadEnded();
    DECLARE_MESSAGE_MAP()
```

This defines your message handler, and now you will need to add your message to the message map. Go ahead and double-click the DoDataExchange() function in CThreads2Dlg to get close to the message map. Go to the bottom of the message map and modify it to look like the following:

```
//}}AFX_MSG_MAP
    ON_MESSAGE(WM_MYTHREADENDED, OnMyThreadEnded)
END_MESSAGE_MAP()
```

Your application will now process your custom message. You will now add the actual message handler function. Go to the bottom of the Threads2Dlg.cpp file, which you should currently have open anyway, and add the following function in Listing 12.7.

LISTING 12.7   The OnMyThreadEnded Function

```
void CThreads2Dlg::OnMyThreadEnded()
{
    AfxMessageBox("MyThread has ended!");
}
```

This function will be called when the MyThread function is terminated. In order to call this function, you will need to post a message to the window. You will need to modify the MyThread() function. Listing 12.8 shows you the modified function.

12

LISTING 12.8   The Modified `MyThread()` Function

```
UINT MyThread(LPVOID param)
{
    while (bRunThread)
    {
        CTime time = CTime::GetCurrentTime();
        CString now = time.Format("%c");
        SetWindowText((HWND)param,now);
    }

    PostMessage((HWND)param, WM_MYTHREADENDED,0,0);
    return 0;
}
```

You will notice that a `PostMessage()` call was added to the thread. When the thread is stopped by setting `bRunThread` to `FALSE`, a message will be posted to our application. The message handler for this message, which you just coded previously, will display a message box indicating that the thread was terminated.

Note

When working with threads, you should use the `PostMessage()` function because it places a message in the message queue and immediately returns control to your application. Using the `SendMessage()` function calls a procedure directly, and it will not return until that procedure has processed the message.

You can go ahead and execute the application now. When you start and then stop the thread, you will be presented with a message box, as shown in Figure 12.11.

FIGURE 12.11

The `OnMyThreadEnded`
function was called.

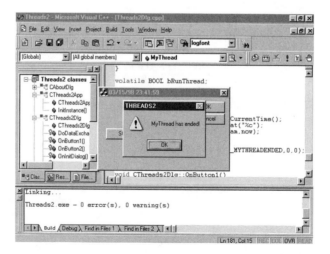

Using `CEvent` Objects for Thread Communication

The `CEvent` class, which MFC supplies, allows you to use event objects easily. Event objects are synchronization objects, which allow a thread to notify another thread that an event has occurred. An event object has two states: signaled and nonsignaled.

If you have any workspaces open in the Visual C++ editor, go ahead and close it so that you can create a new application. Now create a new dialog-based application and name it Threads3. Once you create the application, go ahead and add two buttons controls and change their captions to Start and Stop, just like you did in the first example for this lesson. Now, go ahead and create the two message handler functions for the two buttons.

To work with the `CEvent` object, you will need to add the necessary header file include to your application. Double-click the `CThreads3Dlg` class in the Work-space panel to open the Threads3Dlg.h file. The following excerpt shows you the necessary include statement that you need for the `CEvent` class:

```
// Threads3Dlg.h : header file
//
#include "afxmt.h"
```

Now that you have access to `CEvent`, you can declare a variable of this type. You are going to create a couple of global variables, so go ahead and double-click the `OnButton1()` message event function to bring it into the code editor. Now, just like you did in the previous example in this lesson, you will add the global variables just before this function. While you are at it, you might as well declare the `MyThread()` function too, as shown here:

```
CEvent StartMyThread;
CEvent StopMyThread;
UINT MyThread(LPVOID param)
{

}
```

You can now add the code that will execute when `MyThread()` is started. Go ahead and modify the `MyThread()` function, as shown in Listing 12.9.

LISTING 12.9 The `MyThread` Function

```
UINT MyThread(LPVOID param)
{
    WaitForSingleObject(StartMyThread.m_hObject, INFINITE);
    BOOL bRunning = TRUE;
    while (bRunning)
    {
        CTime time = CTime::GetCurrentTime();
```

continues

12

LISTING 12.9   continued

```
        CString now = time.Format("%c");
        SetWindowText((HWND)param,now);
        if (WaitForSingleObject(StopMyThread.m_hObject, 0) ==
        ➥WAIT_OBJECT_0)
            bRunning = FALSE;
    }

    AfxMessageBox("Thread has ended!");
    return 0;
}
```

By using CEvent objects, a thread can easily see whether an event has been signaled by using the WaitForSingleObject() function. This function takes two parameters. The first parameter is the handle of the event to check, and the second parameter indicates how long the function should wait. By indicating the INFINITE constant as the period of time to wait, WaitForSingleObject() will wait indefinitely, which in turn causes the thread to suspend execution until the function call returns.

Once the event has been triggered, the thread will continue on with its execution. For this sample application, you are going to use a second method of WaitForSingleObject() function known as *polling*. By specifying the time period of 0 for this function, it simply checks to see whether an event was triggered. If an event *has* been triggered, the function will return a constant value of WAIT_OBJECT_0.

Once the second event is triggered, the thread will terminate and a message will be displayed indicating so.

Now that you have the thread portion of the application coded, you will need to add the necessary code to the OnButton1() and OnButton2() functions. To start the thread, the StartMyThread event will be triggered. To stop the thread, the StopMyThread event will be triggered. Triggering an event object is very simple—you just call the SetEvent() function of the object. Listing 12.10 shows you the code you need for the OnButton1() and OnButton2() message handler functions.

LISTING 12.10   Starting and Stopping the Thread

```
void CThreads3Dlg::OnButton1()
{
    // TODO: Add your control notification handler code here
    StartMyThread.SetEvent();
}

void CThreads3Dlg::OnButton2()
{
    // TODO: Add your control notification handler code here
    StopMyThread.SetEvent();
}
```

As you can see, triggering an event is very simple. When the Start button is clicked, the StartMyThread.SetEvent() function is called and when the Stop button is clicked, the StopMyThread.SetEvent() function is called.

Before you can actually run the application, you still need to call the MyThread() function to put it into the wait state. To do this, you will need to add a message handler for the WM_CREATE message. When the Threads3 dialog box is created, this message is generated. By trapping this message, you can make a call to the MyThread() function when your application starts up. Go ahead and use the ClassWizard and create the message handler, as shown in Figure 12.12.

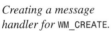

FIGURE 12.12

Creating a message handler for WM_CREATE.

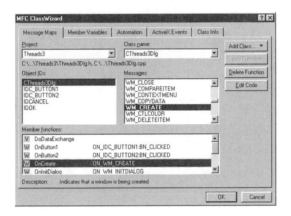

Once you have the handler function created, go ahead and modify it to match Listing 12.11.

12

LISTING 12.11   The OnCreate Function

```
int CThreads3Dlg::OnCreate(LPCREATESTRUCT lpCreateStruct)
{
    if (CDialog::OnCreate(lpCreateStruct) == -1)
        return -1;
    // TODO: Add your specialized creation code here
    HWND hWnd = GetSafeHwnd();
    AfxBeginThread(MyThread, hWnd);
    return 0;
}
```

This code should look very familiar. It's the same two lines of code that were used in previous examples in this lesson, just in a different place. When the Threads3 application starts, the handle for the window is captured and is passed along to MyThread().

Once you execute the application, MyThread() will execute and be placed into suspend mode while it waits for the StartMyThread object to be signaled. Once the thread has been started, it will continue to update the caption of the display until the stop button is clicked to signal StopMyThread. The thread will then end, and a message will be displayed on your screen, as shown in Figure 12.13.

FIGURE 12.13

The MyThread *thread for Threads3 has ended.*

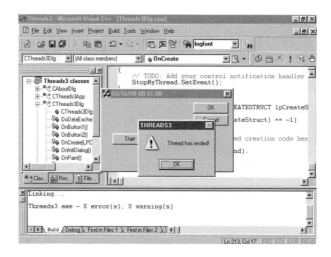

Lesson Summary

Communicating between threads is an essential part of multitasking applications. In this lesson, you learned about three different styles of thread communication.

The first method involved using global variables to determine when to stop a running thread. You then moved on to the second method, using custom Window messages. After implementing this style of communication, you moved on to using CEvent objects. These objects allow threads to notify other threads that an event has occurred.

By using these three methods of thread communication, you can easily create threads that are capable of communicating with other threads.

Quiz 3

1. Which form of thread communication allows a thread to notify another thread that an event has occurred?

    a. Global variables

    b. User messages

    c. Asynchronous threading

    d. Event objects

2. When using the `WaitForSingleObject()` function, which value would you pass as the amount of time to wait for the object to return if you want it to wait indefinitely?

    a. `INDEFINITE`

    b. A value of 0 (zero)

    c. `INFINITE`

    d. `CONTINUAL`

3. Which of the following methods of thread communication was not discussed in this lesson?

    a. Using global variables

    b. Using the `CreateThread()` API function

    c. Using event objects

    d. Using user-defined window messages

4. To use the `CEvent` class, which `include` file do you need to add to your project?

    a. afxthread.h

    b. afxtevents.h

    c. CEvent.h

    d. afxmt.h

Exercise 3

Complexity: Easy

1. Create a dialog-based application named "Exercise 1" that executes a thread when the Start button on the dialog box is clicked. The thread should terminate when the Stop button is clicked. This thread should use a global variable to determine when it should end. While the thread is running, update the caption of the dialog box with a counter that is updated by 1 each cycle.

Complexity: Moderate

2. Create a dialog-based application named "Exercise 2" that executes a thread when the Start button on the dialog box is clicked. The thread should terminate when the Stop button is clicked. The thread should be created automatically when the dialog box is created.

When the thread is created and first executed, it should immediately go into a wait-state, waiting for a trigger even to set it off. Once the thread has started, the thread should display a counter on the caption of the dialog box until a second event tells it to stop.

12

LESSON 4

Thread Synchronization

In the last lesson, you learned how simple it is to create and use threads in your application. Toward the end of the lesson, you actually used a very basic form of thread synchronization by using event objects. In this lesson, you will learn how to use objects that are designed for thread synchronization.

When using threads in your application, a potential problem exists. Imagine if you will, a thread is in the process of updating some very important data when the main thread accesses the same data. Did the main thread receive the updated data or the old data? This is the most common problem when dealing with multithreaded applications.

You can take some precautions to make your threads more reliable where data access is concerned. There are several different methods of thread synchronization, but the two most common thread synchronization methods that you will use are critical sections and mutexes. Using these methods of synchronization, you can better preserve the integrity of data, or other resources, in your multithreaded application.

A Multithreaded Application

To illustrate thread synchronization, you will need to build a small application. Go ahead and use the MFC AppWizard to create an SDI style application named Threads4. Once you create the application, you will need to modify the menu. Add a main menu named Thread, and add an option under that menu named Start. You will use this menu option to start the threads; therefore, after you create it, you will need to go into the ClassWizard and create a message handler for the COMMAND message for ID_THREAD_START. Make sure you have CThreads4View as the class name. This operation is shown in Figure 12.14.

FIGURE 12.14

Adding the message handler for the Thread, Start menu option.

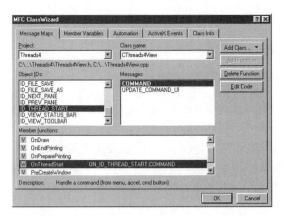

When the Thread, Start menu option is selected, two threads will execute. Each thread will modify the contents of an array to a certain value and then copy the new value into a secondary array for displaying. Thus, once you have the message handler created, go ahead and open it into the code editor and modify it so that it matches Listing 12.12.

LISTING 12.12 The `OnThreadStart()` Message Handler Function

```
void CThreads4View::OnThreadStart()
{
    // TODO: Add your command handler code here
    CDC* pDC = GetDC();
    ASSERT_VALID(pDC);
    CString value;
    AfxBeginThread(Thread50,0,0);
    AfxBeginThread(Thread75,0,0);
    Sleep(1000);
    for (int i=0; i < 20; ++i)
    {
        value.Format("%d      %d",all50[i], all75[i]);
        pDC->TextOut(10,i * 16, value);
    }
}
```

Looking at Listing 12.12, you will notice that two threads execute. Once the two threads begin, the main thread, which is the application itself, is suspended for 1,000 milliseconds, or 1 second. This wait gives the two threads time to complete their tasks. After waiting for one second, the arrays that hold the changed values are then displayed on the screen.

Because you have two threads that you want to execute, you will need to define the two functions to use as threads. Go ahead and move your cursor just above the `OnThreadStart()` function and enter the code presented in Listing 12.13.

LISTING 12.13 The Two Threads to Execute

```
int numbers[20];
int all50[20];
int all75[20];

UINT Thread50(LPVOID param)
{
    for (int i=0; i<20; ++i)
    {
        numbers[i] = 50;
        Sleep(10);
        all50[i] = numbers[i];
    }
```

continues

12

LISTING 12.13   continued

```
     return 0;
}

UINT Thread75(LPVOID param)
{
    for (int i=0; i<20; ++i)
    {
        numbers[i] = 75;
        Sleep(10);
        all75[i] = numbers[i];
    }
    return 0;
}
```

The first three lines that you entered are the arrays used in the threads. The first array is the main array that should hold 20 integers, all with the same value.

The next two blocks of code are the functions used for the threads. The first thread, which is named Thread50, will change all 20 values of the numbers[] array to 50. While the thread is changing each value to 50, and after a small waiting period, the value is copied back into another array, which will be used for displaying the changed values.

As a programmer, when you look at this function, it appears that the array value is set to 50 and then copied to another array, which would then have the same value of 50. This is exactly what would happen, that is, if no other threads were accessing the data at the same time. This is where the Thread75 function comes in. The Thread75() function accomplishes the same thing, except that it changes the value of the numbers[] array to 75.

To see how these threads interact with each other when using the same data, go ahead and execute the application. Your screen should look similar to Figure 12.15.

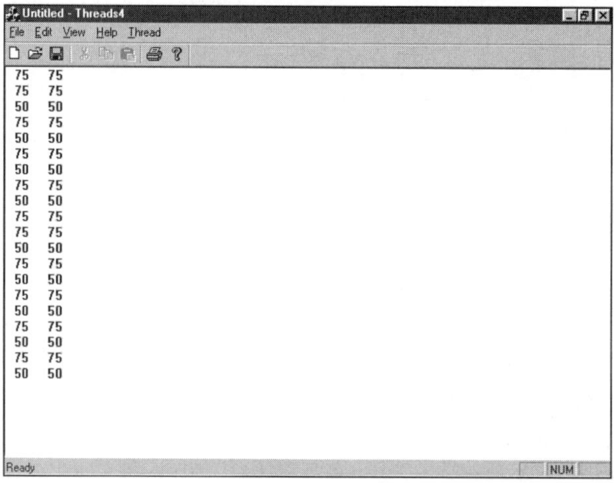

FIGURE 12.15

The Threads4 application without thread synchronization.

The result that you wanted was for the left column to have every value set to 50 and the right column with values of 75. Now that you know a problem exists, you need to correct it.

Implementing Critical Sections

One of the easiest ways to protect your data's integrity when working with threads is to use critical sections. Critical section synchronization is based on the CCriticalSection object. This object allows one thread at a time access to a resource or a section of code.

A critical section works by blocking another thread from using the protected data by not allowing it to have processing time, effectively stopping the other thread until the critical section is released.

To add a critical section object to the Threads4 example, simply create an instance of CCriticalSection in your application. Go ahead and add the following line of code just before the three array declarations:

```
CCriticalSection critical;
```

The CCriticalSection object provides a couple of functions that you will call when your application wants to access the data that you want protected. When your application is about to modify the protected data, you will make a call to the Lock() function. If no other threads are using the critical section, the calling thread will be granted access to the protected data. When the thread is done using the protected data, a call is made to the Unlock() function to release the object.

To implement the critical section, you will need to modify the two thread functions. Go ahead and modify the Thread50() function first, using Listing 12.14 as a guide.

LISTING 12.14 Adding the Critical Section

```
UINT Thread50(LPVOID param)
{
    critical.Lock();
    for (int i=0; i<20; ++i)
    {
        numbers[i] = 50;
        Sleep(10);
        all50[i] = numbers[i];
    }
    critical.Unlock();
    return 0;
}
```

Just before the thread modifies the numbers[] array with the for loop, the Lock() function is called. After the loop has completed, the Unlock() function is called. Go ahead

12

and modify the Thread75() function to resemble the change you just made to Thread50(). This time, when you run the Threads4 application and choose the Thread, Start option, the numbers in the two arrays will be correct, as shown in Figure 12.16.

FIGURE 12.16

The Threads4 application with thread synchronization.

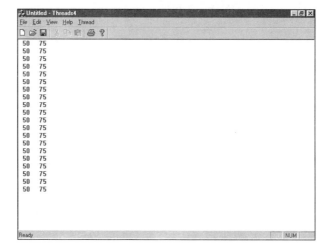

Implementing Mutexes

Mutexes are very much like critical sections, with one major difference. Not only do they allow threads of the same application to share data, but they also allow threads of different applications to share data. To a user, the behavior of your application is the same; it just handles synchronization a little differently internally.

Use Listing 12.15 to make the necessary changes to convert the Threads4 application to use a mutex rather than a critical section.

LISTING 12.15 Converting Threads4 to Use a Mutex

```
CMutex mutex;
int numbers[20];
int all50[20];
int all75[20];


UINT Thread50(LPVOID param)
{
    CSingleLock slock(&mutex);
    slock.Lock();
    for (int i=0; i<20; ++i)
    {
        numbers[i] = 50;
```

```
            Sleep(10);
            all50[i] = numbers[i];
        }
        slock.Unlock();
        return 0;
}

UINT Thread75(LPVOID param)
{
        CSingleLock slock(&mutex);
        slock.Lock();
        for (int i=0; i<20; ++i)
        {
            numbers[i] = 75;
            Sleep(10);
            all75[i] = numbers[i];
        }
        slock.Unlock();
        return 0;
}
```

The first thing you should have changed was the type of synchronization object to use. You changed the CCriticalSection object to a CMutex object.

Inside of the threads, you converted them to use the mutex object that you declared. In order for the thread to access data that is protected by a mutex, you must create a CSingleLock object. Before the loop executes, you construct the CSingleLock object, passing in a pointer to the mutex object.

If another thread owns the mutex, the calling thread will be suspended until the mutex is released. If the mutex is unowned, the calling thread is granted access to the protected data or resources.

Once you are done working with the data, you then call the Unlock() function to release the mutex.

When you run the application with the new changes, the output will be identical to the output of using critical sections, as shown previously in Figure 12.16.

Lesson Summary

One of the most important aspects of any program is its data integrity. If the data that your application uses is incorrect or corrupted, your application can return unpredictable results, especially if your application uses multiple threads that access the same data resources.

12

By using thread synchronization, you can easily keep threads in check when they try to access important data that is used throughout your application. In this lesson, you learned how to use the two most common types of thread synchronization to protect this data.

Quiz 4

1. Which thread synchronization object uses the `CSinglelock()` object to lock data or resources from other threads?

    a. `CMutexThreads`

    b. `CMutex`

    c. `CCriticalSection`

    d. `CriticalThreads`

2. Which statement is true about mutexes?

    a. Mutexes allow threads of different applications to synchronize.

    b. Mutexes can be used only on single-threaded applications.

    c. You must call the `Lock()` function of the `CMutex` object to lock resources from other threads.

    d. You release a mutex by calling the `Release()` function of the `CSingleLock` object.

3. Which statement will create a critical section object?

    a. `CriticalSection;`

    b. `new CCriticalSection criticalsection;`

    c. `CCriticalSection critical;`

    d. `CCriticalSect critical;`

4. Which function of `CCriticalSection` releases the ownership of critical section object?

    a. `Release()`

    b. `Unlock()`

    c. `Remove()`

    d. `Free()`

Exercise 4

Complexity: Moderate

1. Create an SDI-style application named "Exercise 1." When you click the Thread, Start menu option, two threads will execute. These threads will modify the same array of integers. The same thread function should be used for both threads. Pass the value that is used to fill the array in the `param` parameter of the `AfxBeginThread()` function.

   Use a critical section to preserve the data integrity of the array. The 20 values in the array should be displayed on the screen to verify that they were updated properly.

Complexity: Moderate

2. Create an SDI style application named "Exercise 2" that is based on the previous exercise. This exercise will have the same functionality, except that it will use a mutex-for-thread synchronization.

Chapter Summary

What may seem advanced to some users will seem like trivial tasks to others. Two topics that most programmers would consider advanced are working with the Registry and creating multithreaded applications.

In this chapter, you learned that programming the Registry and working with threads only sounds advanced. By using several of the MFC classes provided, you learned how to use the Registry to store and retrieve information for later use. You can use the Registry for a wide variety of reasons. In general, you would use it to store configuration information about your application. You may even track information about the person using your application as well.

After playing around with the Registry, you moved on to another advanced topic, working with threads. Threads are primarily used for two tasks:

- Scalability to multiple processor systems, such as Windows NT
- To keep the user interface responsive while a worker thread performs some processor intensive processing in the background

When working with multiple threads, you need to account for some considerations, such as data integrity. By using critical sections and mutexes, you learned how to keep threads in order so that they don't trample over each other's work.

12

APPENDIX A

Quiz Answers

This appendix provides the answers to the quizzes at the end of each lesson.

Chapter 1

Lesson 1

1. b
2. d
3. b
4. c

Lesson 2

1. b
2. b
3. d
4. c

Lesson 3

1. a
2. b, d
3. c, d
4. d

Lesson 4

1. b
2. c
3. b
4. a

Chapter 2

Lesson 1

1. b
2. c
3. d
4. d

Lesson 2

1. c
2. d
3. b
4. b

Lesson 3

1. c
2. d
3. c
4. a

Lesson 4

1. c
2. b
3. a
4. d

Lesson 5

1. a
2. a
3. d
4. b

A

Chapter 3

Lesson 1

1. b
2. c
3. d
4. a

Lesson 2

1. d
2. d
3. c
4. a

Lesson 3

1. b
2. d
3. c
4. b

Lesson 4

1. b
2. a
3. c
4. a, b, c, d

Lesson 5

1. b
2. d
3. d
4. a

Chapter 4

Lesson 1

1. c
2. b
3. a
4. b

Lesson 2

1. c
2. a
3. b
4. d

Lesson 3

1. c
2. a
3. d
4. b

A

Lesson 4

1. c
2. a
3. a
4. d

Lesson 5

1. c
2. b
3. d
4. c

Chapter 5

Lesson 1

1. b
2. d
3. c
4. b

Lesson 2

1. c
2. a, b, c
3. d
4. c

Lesson 3

1. a
2. a
3. b
4. c

Lesson 4

1. b
2. a, b
3. b, d
4. c

Lesson 5

1. a, b
2. c
3. c
4. b

Chapter 6

Lesson 1

1. c
2. d
3. d
4. a

A

Lesson 2

1. b
2. d
3. a
4. b

Lesson 3

1. d
2. b, c
3. b
4. a, b, c, d

Lesson 4

1. c
2. c
3. a, d
4. b

Lesson 5

1. c
2. c
3. b, c
4. a, b

Chapter 7

Lesson 1

1. d
2. b
3. a
4. b

Lesson 2

1. c
2. a
3. d
4. b

Lesson 3

1. b
2. a
3. d
4. a

Lesson 4

1. d
2. c
3. b
4. c

A

Lesson 5

1. d
2. a
3. c
4. a

Chapter 8

Lesson 1

1. c
2. d
3. a
4. b

Lesson 2

1. b
2. d
3. c
4. b

Lesson 3

1. c
2. b
3. a
4. c

Lesson 4

1. d
2. a
3. d
4. a

Lesson 5

1. b
2. c
3. d
4. c

Chapter 9

Lesson 1

1. d
2. c
3. b
4. c

Lesson 2

1. b
2. c
3. d
4. a

A

Lesson 3

1. d
2. b
3. a
4. a

Lesson 4

1. c
2. b
3. d
4. b

Chapter 10

Lesson 1

1. b
2. a
3. a
4. a

Lesson 2

1. a
2. c
3. c
4. a, b, c

Lesson 3

1. c
2. b, c
3. d
4. b

Lesson 4

1. d
2. b
3. a
4. d

Chapter 11

Lesson 1

1. b
2. c
3. b, c
4. c

Lesson 2

1. c
2. b
3. a
4. d

A

Lesson 3

1. d
2. a
3. a
4. c

Lesson 4

1. a
2. b
3. c
4. a, b, c

Chapter 12

Lesson 1

1. c
2. b
3. a
4. b

Lesson 2

1. b
2. d
3. a
4. c

Lesson 3

1. d
2. c
3. b
4. d

Lesson 4

1. b
2. a
3. c
4. b

A

INDEX

Symbols

0001 subkey, 585
3-D controls (dialog-based applications), 81
! NOT operator, 284
#include statement (GUIView.cpp file), 280
<<OLE VERBS GO HERE>> Option (Object menu), 450

A

Abort function (CInternetFile class), 514
About boxes, 199, 229

AboutBox() function (CSmileCtrl class), 434
accelerator collection, 40
Accelerator resources, 39
accelerators. *See* short-cuts
Access 97, 556-557
accessing
    data, thread synchronization, 611
    files, 541-542
    SDI Example.h file, 66
    toolbar resources, 312
accounts (user), 490
actions, 105, 109. *See also* events
Active Template Library (ATL), 85
ActiveX container applications, 447, 454
    bitmaps, 455
    classes, 448-453

creating menu options, 465
DoTracker() function, 458
double-clicking, 463
editing objects, 465
multiple objects, 460-462
Object menu options, 450
sizing/moving objects, 456-457
ActiveX Control Test Container application, 436
ActiveX controls, 420, 423-430
    ControlWizard, 86, 433
    creating, 438-441
        custom, 432-434
        default properties, 442-443

Get **FREE** books and more...when you register this book online for our Personal Bookshelf Program

http://register.samspublishing.com/

SAMS

 Register online and you can sign up for our *FREE Personal Bookshelf Program...*unlimited access to the electronic version of more than 200 complete computer books—immediately! That means you'll have 100,000 pages of valuable information onscreen, at your fingertips!

 Plus, you can access product support, including complimentary downloads, technical support files, book-focused links, companion Web sites, author sites, and more!

 And you'll be automatically registered to receive a *FREE subscription to a weekly email newsletter* to help you stay current with news, announcements, sample book chapters, and special events, including sweepstakes, contests, and various product giveaways!

 We value your comments! Best of all, the entire registration process takes only a few minutes to complete, so go online and get the greatest value going—absolutely FREE!

Don't Miss Out On This Great Opportunity!

Sams is a brand of Macmillan Computer Publishing USA.

For more information, please visit *www.mcp.com*

Read This Before Opening the Software

By opening this package, you are agreeing to be bound by the following agreement:

Some of the software included with this product may be copyrighted, in which case all rights are reserved by the respective copyright holder. You are licensed to use software copyrighted by the publisher and its licensors on a single computer. You may copy and/or modify the software as needed to facilitate your use of it on a single computer. Making copies of the software for any other purpose is a violation of the U.S. copyright laws.

This software is sold as is without warranty of any kind, either expressed or implied, including but not limited to the implied warranties of merchantability and fitness for a particular purpose. Neither the publisher nor its dealers or distributors assume any liability for any alleged or actual damages arising from the use of this program. (Some states do not allow for the exclusion of implied warranties, so the exclusion may not apply to you.)

CD-ROM Installation Instructions

If you have AutoPlay turned on, your computer will automatically run the CD-ROM interface. If AutoPlay is turned off, follow these directions:

1. Insert the CD-ROM into your CD-ROM drive.
2. From the Windows desktop, double-click the My Computer icon.
3. Double-click the icon representing your CD-ROM drive.
4. Double-click the icon titled START.EXE to run the interface.